FALL OF THE INCA EMPIRE

The tower of the Monastery of Santo Domingo, in Cuzco.
Courtesy of Mrs. Myra Brady.

Fall of the Inca Empire

AND THE SPANISH RULE
IN PERU: 1530-1780

BY

PHILIP AINSWORTH MEANS

AUTHOR OF "ANCIENT CIVILIZATIONS
OF THE ANDES," Etc.

NEW YORK

GORDIAN PRESS, INC.

1964

Originally Published 1931
Reprinted 1964

Copyright 1964
Published by Gordian Press, Inc. by
Arrangement with Mrs. Philip Ainsworth Means

Library of Congress Card Catalogue Number 64-8176

Lithographed in U.S.A. by
E D W A R D S   B R O T H E R S ,   I N C .
Ann Arbor, Michigan

TO
THE IMPERISHABLE MEMORIES OF
WILLIAM HICKLING PRESCOTT
1796–1859
AND

CLEMENTS ROBERT MARKHAM, K.C.B.
1830–1916
ALL THAT MAY BE GOOD IN THIS BOOK
IS GRATEFULLY DEDICATED

J'écris l'histoire, et je l'écris presque
toujours les yeux baignés de larmes.
—L'Abbé Guillaume-Thomas Raynal.

PREFACE

THE purpose of the present volume has been that of carrying onwards the story of the Andean area from the point where it was left in *Ancient Civilizations of the Andes*. As in the earlier book, the territory considered herein is that contained in the modern republics of Ecuador, Peru, and Bolivia, together with adjacent portions of Colombia, Argentina, and Chile. This territory, in colonial times, was divided between the Audiences of Quito, Lima, and Charcas. Chile, ruled by a captain-general, was practically independent of the Viceroyalty of Peru, which controlled the three Audiences just mentioned.

Originally, I had intended to go, in this volume, to the end of the viceregal period (1825). But as my work proceeded it became increasingly clear to me that I must stop at 1780, the year in which the great rebellion of Tupac Amaru II broke out. From that year onwards events and developments were quite definitely shaping themselves towards a final break with Spain, having relatively slight connection with what had gone before. Therefore, I decided to reserve discussion of events after 1780 to a future work, on *The Andean Republics in Modern Times*.

The reader will observe that Chapters I to V, inclusive, of the present volume emphasize events and that the remainder of the book emphasizes institutions. This shift of policy is not as arbitrary as might appear at first glance. The early part of Spain's career in the Andean area turned very largely on events; but, from the time of the great Viceroy Don Francisco de Toledo (ruled 1569–1581) onwards, events were vastly less important than institutions. The shift of policy mentioned is, therefore, a logical and necessary one in a book of this kind.

As was the case in *Ancient Civilizations of the Andes*, I

have received generous and valuable aid from personal friends in the matter of illustrations. It is a great pleasure, therefore, to express here my lively sense of gratitude to Mrs. Myra Brady, Mrs. Frank Barrows Freyer, Senator Hiram Bingham, Mr. W. V. Alford, and Mr. Robert Shippee for the excellent illustrations with which they have supplied me. Also, I am grateful to Mrs. Brady for assistance in connection with historical research and with index-making.

Many parts of this book are based upon research work done by me years ago in many libraries of Europe, Ecuador, Peru, Bolivia, and the United States. Everywhere, or perhaps I would better say nearly everywhere, I have received kindness and aid from library and museum officials and attendants, to all of whom I am most grateful. In its present form the book is chiefly the product of work done in Cambridge, Massachusetts, where the Harvard College Library has generously aided me during the process of whipping my materials into their present shape. I am especially indebted to my friend, Mr. Walter Briggs, Assistant Librarian, for his kindness in insisting that I acquaint myself with Sir Walter Raleigh's book on Guiana (Raleigh, 1928—see Bibliography). As usual, also, Mr. Andrew Keogh and his assistants at the Yale University Library and various officials of the New York Public Library have been most kind and helpful. To all who have striven to make my task easier I am deeply obliged.

PHILIP AINSWORTH MEANS.

June 7th, 1932.

CONTENTS

ix

ILLUSTRATIONS

The tower of the Monastery of Santo Domingo, in Cuzco *Frontispiece*

FALL OF THE INCA EMPIRE

CHAPTER I

THE EMPIRE OF THE INCAS IN ITS LAST YEARS

1. The Reign of the Inca Huayna Capac

IN 1528, more or less, the Inca Huayna Capac, then an ill and aging man who had a long and, on the whole, a distinguished reign behind him, was ruling Ttahua-ntin-suyu, the Land of the Four Sections, commonly called the Inca Empire. Behind him also lay a love-life of unusual complexity and productiveness, an amatorial career of majestic proportions which may or may not have been the cause of the very poor health which the monarch certainly suffered in his last days. Nor was ill-health the sole cause of the vague but profound disquiet which filled the mind of the Inca; for, while he was at his sumptuous palaces at Tumipampa—in what is now the southern highlands of Ecuador—he received news of the arrival at Tumbez of Francisco Pizarro and his small group of adventurous followers.

The strangers were described as being pale of face and bearded, clad in unheard-of shining apparel, bearing thunder and lightning in their hands, of ferocious mien, and wont to travel by sea in a floating wooden house, a sort of super-balsa, with sails. These tidings were all the more alarming to the Emperor because a prophecy had long been jealously guarded among the imperial caste to the effect that one day "there would come to that land a people never before seen, who would destroy the religion and the empire of the natives. This was briefly the substance of the prophecy, spoken in vague words, having double meanings, which were not understood."[1]

Now, apparently, the strangers whose advent had long ago been prognosticated were at hand, and the Inca Huayna Capac was greatly troubled, all the more so that a terrible plague was

3

sweeping through his realm and that unwonted disturbances among the stars were being noted. To make matters worse, there were serious rebellions in various parts of the huge empire, foci of weakness which menaced the safety of the whole fabric. Altogether, the last days of the Inca Huayna Capac were filled with gloom and forebodings indicative of the near presence of direful changes.[2]

In order fully to understand the situation of Ttahua-ntin-suyu as it was on the eve of the Spanish conquest we must examine matters in some detail. At this period, 1528 or thereabouts, the territory occupied by the Inca Empire was very great. It reached from the Ancas Mayu (Blue River, now known as the Patia River) in what is now southern Colombia down to the Maule River in Chile, and it ran eastwards from the Pacific Ocean over the coastal zone, into and across the lofty highlands of the Andes, and down their eastern slope until it faded away among the hot and humid shadows of the Amazonian jungles, the width of the empire varying from some 150 miles to more than 400 miles. The empire, therefore, contained some 380,000 square miles, or about as much territory as that now occupied by the Atlantic seaboard states of our country. In a sense, however, it was greater far than they because of the immense diversity of climates, topography, and environmental conditions within it, and also because of the wide divergence in culture, in language, and in customs on the part of the inhabitants, who probably numbered over 16,000,-000, or about twice the present-day population of the same territory.[3]

To the supreme office of this great realm came, in 1484, the Prince Titu Cusi Hualpa, aged then about twenty, who, on becoming Sapa Inca (Sole Inca, *i.e.*, Emperor), took the honorific name by which he is best known in history: Huayna Capac, The Young Chief Rich in Virtues. In its earlier years his reign was a glorious continuation of the imperial tradition which, during more than 350 years, had brought the empire to its highest development. In the quaint words of Father Acosta, one of the early Chroniclers of Peru, "Hee was very wise, planting good orders thorowout his whole realme, hee was a bold and resolute man, valiant and very happy in warre."[4]

Nevertheless, the reign of the Emperor Huayna Capac was a time of disturbance. While, after some ten years of prosperous reigning, he was in the southern part of the empire, news was brought to him, either through the system of chasquis (post-runners) or through the imperial system of beacon-fires,[5] that several parts of the Kingdom of Quito, in the far north, were in a state of revolt. The Emperor hastened to Cuzco, capital of the empire during nearly 400 years, and there, with all possible swiftness, he took the many measures necessary for the governance of the realm and for the assembling of an army of 200,000 warriors and of a great many yanaconas (hereditary servitors) and women, including a harem of 2,000 for his own pleasure.[6] With this immense force the Inca marched up through the highlands to Quitu where, not without difficulty, he re-established his authority. All this was but a part of the widespread unrest to which reference has already been made. In the last two-thirds of the Inca Huayna Capac's reign there were many outbursts of revolt, both along the frontiers and within the body of the empire.

It is impossible for me to accept the general opinion that the reign of Huayna Capac was the apogee of Inca greatness. Rather, it seems to me clearly to mark the beginning of a decline which would have been slow at first and then swifter and swifter if the natural disruptive forces had been left to operate unhindered. Had it not been for the coming of the Spaniards, the empire would have fallen into numerous self-sufficient fragments, each at war with all its neighbors, so that, in short, a condition such as that which had existed before the Incas spread abroad their imperial power would have been re-created. The Spaniards merely cut the process short by setting up a new order of things.

So far as the reign of the Emperor Huayna Capac is concerned the fundamental disruptive forces seem to have been latent in the following circumstances: Down to the time of the

Inca Pachacutec (about 1400–1448) the empire had been small enough—some 155,000 square miles in area when he became Sapa Inca—to permit the ruler personally to travel into all parts of it and to know, with some degree of intimacy, the conditions and problems of its divers regions and peoples. The imperial progresses of the Incas were something more than a prideful display of magnificence and might; they were a very important source of imperial strength and wisdom, and they were also the means of binding the allegiance of the chiefs and people to the person of the sovereign with an intensity arising from their having seen him and having paid their homage directly to him. Even in our own democracy, a man who succeeds in clasping the damp and pudgy paw of a President is thereby rendered a purblind admirer of that special Chief Executive.

Since the days of Pachacutec the empire had more than doubled in extent and probably tripled in population, becoming at the same time so heterogeneous as to be almost ungovernable in any case.

For an empire such as that of the Incas the prime necessity is efficient means of communication and transportation of a kind capable of counteracting the innumerable regionalistic tendencies, tendencies which could be overcome by the central authority only by artificial methods. The roads of the Incas, the Incaic system of post-runners and of beacon-fires, and the administrative hierarchy of the empire were all admirable creations tending to link every part of the empire to its paramount lord, the Inca.[7] Their efficacy was, however, overtaxed from the time of Pachacutec onwards; for, although they suited admirably the needs of an empire such as that left by the Inca Viracocha, father of Pachacutec, they served less and less perfectly the demands made upon them in the succeeding reigns. It came to pass, therefore, in the time of the Emperor Huayna Capac that cracks, not to say fissures, made their sinister appearance in the fabric of the empire. Of these, as after events prove, the Emperor himself was perfectly aware. True, he had the personal allegiance of most of the nobles and commoners of the realm, and to such an extent that he was remembered with respectful admiration long after his death;[8] but, nevertheless, the old universal homage to a sacrosanct sovereign was sadly corroded by distance from his person.

Whether this situation was partly due to certain personal qualities of the monarch is not clear. We know that Huayna Capac was prone to a superfluity of sensual pleasures—as witnesseth that huge harem of his—and we have good reason to suspect that the poor bodily, and perchance also mental, health of the Emperor in his last years was directly resultant from his mode of life. It is also well known that he seriously endangered the political equilibrium of the empire by residing almost wholly at Quitu and Tumipampa (in what is now Ecuador), leaving Cuzco, the traditional capital, to be governed by officials using delegated authority.

The marriages and concubinages of the Inca Huayna Capac constitute one of the most intricate subjects for study in the whole range of Andean history. The Inca had many children both legitimate—born of his sister-wife—and otherwise. For us the two most important of his sons were: the Prince Tupac Cusi Hualpa, better known as Huáscar, whose mother was the Coya (Empress) Mama Rahua Ocllo, sister-wife of the Inca; and Atahualpa, son of the Inca by a mother whose identity is variously stated by the Chroniclers but who, almost certainly, was a daughter of the last independent King of Quitu. Huáscar was brought up in Cuzco under the tutelage of his parents' kindred; but Atahualpa, although he may have been born in Cuzco, was reared in Quitu and Tumipampa his mother having died while he was still a lad.[9]

It is clear, at any rate, that the Inca very dearly loved his illegitimate son, Atahualpa, and that he planned to make over to him the Kingdom of Quitu as a separate dominion, leaving the southern four-fifths of the overgrown empire to the legitimate heir, Huáscar. The Inca reached this decision about 1524 while at his magnificent palace of Mulu Cancha, at Tumipampa. He summoned to him there his two sons and, after he had made known to them his commands, both the young princes promised to obey them.

In 1528 or 1529—albeit some authorities say as early as 1524 —the Emperor Huayna Capac succumbed to his infirmities and died full of fears for the future. The embalmed body of the Inca was solemnly borne in a superb litter to Cuzco for burial, the Empress Mama Rahua Ocllo devotedly accompanying her lord on his last earthly journey; but the heart of the Inca was laid to rest with equal pomp in that city of Quitu which he had loved too well.[10]   In this separation of the ruler's mortal remains we see a symbol of the impending disruption of his empire.

2. The Strife Between Huáscar and Atahualpa

According to Father Cabello de Balboa the will of the Inca Huayna Capac was set forth in legible form by means of a stick or rod around which lines of divers colors and meanings were made in order to indicate the intentions of the testator. We have, therefore, reason to believe that, just prior to the Spanish conquest, the Incas were on the point of inventing a new and perhaps better kind of quipu.[11]   Father Cabello goes on to tell us that this will replaced earlier testaments and that it appointed still another son, named Ninancayuchic, probably a child of the Emperor's later years, as inheritor of the entire realm. This little-known prince died, however, shortly after his father, with the result that the older arrangements retained their force.[12]

Although, fifty years later, the Viceroy Toledo tried to make it appear that Atahualpa was a mere usurper without a shadow of parental authority for his assumption of kingship, it is quite clear on other grounds that he had a very strong claim under his father's earlier will to the kingship of Quitu and that he became an usurper only when he tried to make himself Sapa Inca of the whole empire.[13]   Moreover, it is clear that Huáscar, the legitimate son of his father and by his father's will Inca of Cuzco and its widespread dominions, was far less

FIG. 1. Map of Trujillo and its environs in 1760. *After Feyjoo.*

popular with his subjects than Atahualpa was with the people of the Kingdom of Quitu. Pedro Pizarro says thus: "These Indians say that the reason why Huáscar was but little liked was that he was very grave, and he never let himself be seen by his people, nor did he ever come out to eat with them in the plaza, as it was the custom of former Lords to do sometimes."[14] Pedro Pizarro goes on to explain that another cause of Huáscar's unpopularity was his temerarious interference with the established customs relative to the honoring of dead Incas. Pizarro tells us that Cuzco was largely filled up with the palaces of deceased emperors in which were placed living relatives whose pleasurable task it was to obtain food, drink, and other good things, all in the name of the illustrious departed, wherewith they proceeded to hold prolonged and jovial orgies in which every sort of licentiousness prevailed. Huáscar, becoming disgusted with these practices, announced that he was going to have the dead decently buried and left to themselves. From that moment his followers fell away from him in great numbers, most of the prominent people of Cuzco having been participants in what we may style the honoring-the-dead racket.[15]

The task of tracing out the fratricidal strife between Huáscar and Atahualpa is fraught with difficulty because of the innumerable contradictions among our authorities. It is clear enough, at any rate, that both proceeded, after the death of their father, to make themselves strong in their respective realms, doing so amidst the universal and loud-voiced lamenting for the defunct emperor.[16] Not much time was lost by either of them in the insipidities of peace, however, for very soon each Inca began diplomatic manœuvres intended to ensure his supremacy. During this interval, about 1528 to 1530, the vague menace of the white and bearded strangers was in abeyance, albeit we are told that two Spaniards—Rodrigo Sanchez and Juan Martín—were brought to the presence of Atahualpa, in Tumipampa, and that, from their native captors and from themselves, he derived a deal of information concerning the outlanders.[17] Huáscar, too, we may suppose, had at least vague information regarding the presence of a strange people off the coast. Nevertheless, the two Incas went on with their internecine hostilities seemingly blind to the unheard-of perils which threatened their realms. Finally, probably in 1529 or 1530, Atahualpa's forces, amounting to some 30,000 warriors under the able leadership of his three generals, Chalcuchima, Quizquiz, and Rumi Ñahui, penetrated southwards to within six leagues of Cuzco, crossing the mighty Apurimac River by the famous suspension bridge flung across it and arriving on the plain of Xaquixahuana where, centuries earlier, the Chancas had been conquered by the Incas.[18]

For reasons that are far from clear Huáscar, although he had sent out a general call to arms, had mustered only 30,000 troops, and they, coming from the long peaceful provinces near to Cuzco, were lacking in that warlike frenzy which animated their adversaries. If Huáscar's hoped-for army of bellicose Collas from the region of Lake Titicaca had arrived in time he might have been victorious. Instead, he was defeated, his partisans and near kinsmen were decimated with greatest cruelty by triumphant Atahualpa, and he himself became the prisoner of his rival who, being thus the master of Cuzco and its realm, as well as of the Kingdom of Quitu, was now de facto Sapa Inca of Ttahua-ntin-suyu, in which position he was when Francisco Pizarro and his followers definitively entered Peru in 1530.[19]

3. The Character of the Inca Empire in Its Last Years

The condition and character of the Inca empire immediately before the dissolution of its last unmolested and absolute lord must now be briefly set forth. Enormous, variegated, and somewhat feebly held together, the empire spread itself over many kinds of country and over many types of society. Through the matchlessly logical administrative hierarchy which, since the days of the Inca Viracocha and of the still earlier Incas, had gradually grown to amazing efficacy, society was firmly welded vertically to the person of the supreme and absolute sovereign. The gravest lack in the Incaic system lay in the complete absence of horizontal bonds linking officials of equal rank together. The flow of authority was ever from the Inca at the top down through the orderly sequence of ranks to the officials in charge of ten families. Each official's jurisdiction was an entity answerable only to him, just as he was answerable only to the official immediately above him in the scale. All power, grace, and privilege proceeded from the Sapa Inca. Thus, to capture the person of the ruler was, as we shall see, to capture all the authority of the empire.[20]

The empire ruled by this most rational of systems was one whose people were as fortunate, in a material way at least, as any who have ever lived. If laws were severe, the people suffered but little from that severity because the laws were seldom flouted; if all, high and low, had to work in appropriate manners for the good of the state, all alike received recompense in the form of security against want of all kinds. Money was unknown, and so also were the myriad evils—avarice, corruption, cruelty, and oppression—which follow in its train; value alone was known, value in the form of flocks, utensils, apparel, food, drink, shelter, materials for handicrafts, and these came in abundance to all who would work for them diligently. Tribute was justly apportioned among the heads of families and was payable either in the form of work or in that of products of the soil. It is safe to say that a high proportion of the architectural and technological constructions built in the Incaic period—temples, storehouses, roads, tambos (inns), bridges, fortresses, reservoirs, irrigation ditches, agricultural terraces, etc.—was dedicated to the direct or indirect benefit of the people rather than to the selfish vanity of the rulers.[21]

As far as the mass of the people was concerned these admirable characteristics of the Incaic system persisted down to and even beyond the period of the Spanish invasion. At the same time, it is clear that the dynasty had begun to lose its impetus, to decline in intellectual strength—as, for instance, in the matter of extravagant attentions to the dead—and to give many signs of having lost the stark practicality of earlier times. Indeed, it is certain that, with the wars between Atahualpa and Huáscar, the Inca dynasty was beginning to crack up.

Nevertheless, there was still so much virtue left in the Incaic system of government, and so much felicity and well-being among the subjects of it, that all Spaniards who saw Peru in the first years of the Spanish occupation praised it unless some mean-spirited motive led them to do otherwise. All just men of those there and then present with the invading element united in saying that the Incaic system, as compared with that which came after it, was the better.

Such was the unique civilization which Spanish culture, bringing with it Christianity and money-worship, was destined to overwhelm and to change beyond recognition. As we shall see, the greatest, the fundamental and the universal source of evil brought into Peru by the Spaniards was the money-complex whence arose all the endless misery which has weighed down the Andean peoples ever since the money-less empire of the Incas was shattered.

NOTES TO CHAPTER I

[1] Garcilaso, Pt. I, Bk. V, Ch. xxviii. Means, 1931, pp. 273–277.

[2] In this connection, as in almost every part of Andean history, ancient and modern, there is great discrepancy between the sundry narratives upon which the historian must rely for information. Common sense is one's sole weapon for cleaving a way through the jungle of contradictory assertions. Authorities for this special period include: Garcilaso, Pt. I, Bk. IX, Ch. xiv; Cieza, Pt. II, Ch. lxviii; Sarmiento, Ch. lxviii; Cobo, Bk. XII, Ch. xvii; Cabello, Pt. III, Chs. xx–xxiv; Pedro Pizarro, 1921, I, pp. 196–199.

[3] Garcilaso, Pt. I, Bk. VIII, Ch. vii. Sarmiento, Chs. liv–lx. Oliva, Bk. I, Ch. i. Cieza, Pt. I, Ch. xl; Pt. II, Chs. lvi–lvii. Cobo, Bk. XII, Chs. xiv–xvii. Cabello, Pt. III, Chs. xvii and xx–xxiii.

Means, 1931, Ch. i, entire, and also pp. 266, 270, and 296. Markham, 1910, passim. Baudin, 1928, passim. Merriman, 1918–1925, III, pp. 548–553.

[4] Acosta, Bk. VI, Ch. xxii, 1880, p. 433.   [5] Means, 1931, pp. 333–334.

[6] A discussion of the yanaconas, an extra-tribal class of hereditary servitors or serfs, will be found in Means, 1931, p. 297. For Huayna Capac's military campaign in the north see: Cieza, Pt. II, Ch. lxiii.

[7] Baudin, 1928, Ch. v. Means, 1931, Ch. viii.   [8] Sancho, 1917, Ch. xix.

9 The late Sir Clements Markham held that the mother of Atahualpa was a cousin of the Inca Huayna Capac, that Atahualpa was born in Cuzco, and that he did not leave there until 1513, which is the date that Sir Clements mistakenly gave to the beginning of Huayna Capac's campaigns in the north. See Markham, 1910, pp. 240–241. On the other hand, Father Miguel Cabello de Balboa, a prime authority for the later phases of Incaic history, tells us, in Pt. III, Ch. xxi, that the northern campaigns began about the middle of the reign and that the Inca took Atahualpa with him to the north, the lad's mother, whom Cabello does not name, being already dead. If it be true that Atahualpa was born in Cuzco prior to Huayna Capac's departure thence (about 1500) that would not prove that his mother was not the heiress to the Kingdom of Quitu because it is probable that the Princess, whose people had been conquered by Huayna Capac's father, the Inca Tupac Yupanqui, was brought to Cuzco to be educated in the Incaic idea at the Acllahuasi, House of the Chosen Women. In that case, Huayna Capac might well have known her in the early part of his reign. The whole question is most interesting and merits careful study. Materials for it include: Garcilaso, Pt. I, Bk. IX, Chs. ii and xii; Cieza, Pt. II, Ch. lxix; Sarmiento, Ch. lxiii; Cobo, Bk. XII, Ch. xviii; Velasco, 1841–1844, II, pp. 62–66; Zárate, Bk. I, Ch. xv. Prescott, 1847, II, pp. 336–338; Means, 1931, pp. 273–277.

10 Garcilaso, Pt. I, Bk. IX, Ch. xv. Cieza, Pt. II, Ch. lxviii. Sarmiento, Chs. lxii and lxiii. Cabello, Pt. III, Ch. xxiv. Cobo, Bk. XII, Ch. xvii. Markham, 1910, p. 243. Means, 1931, pp. 276–277.

11 Cabello, Pt. III, Ch. xxiv, N. Y. P. L. MS., p. 633. Means, 1931, pp. 210, 305–306, 323–329.

12 Cabello, Pt. III, Ch. xxiv, p. 634. Sarmiento, Ch. lxii. Cobo, Bk. XII, Ch. xvii.

13 Compare: Garcilaso, Pt. I, Bk. IX, Ch. xii, and Toledo, 1882, p. 190.

14 P. Pizarro, 1921, I, p. 202.

15 P. Pizarro, 1921, I, pp. 202–206. 16 Cabello, Pt. III, Ch. xxiv, p. 635.

17 Cabello, Pt. III, Ch. xxvii, pp. 687–688. Prescott, 1847, I, pp. 287–288, tells us that Francisco Pizarro, when northbound along the Peruvian coast in 1527, left a number of his followers at Tumbez, by their own request. Perhaps two of them were taken up to Tumipampa and displayed before Atahualpa. Cieza, Pt. II, Ch. lxviii, speaks of a similar incident but puts it in the time of Huayna Capac. See also: Sarmiento, Ch. lxviii; Montesinos, 1906, Años 1527 and 1528.

18 Means, 1931, pp. 231, 243–245, 331.

19 Necessarily I have given a mere sketch of these events. The account of the war between Huáscar and Atahualpa set forth in great detail by Father Cabello in Part III, Chs. xxvi–xxxii, includes not only mention of the battles of Yanamarca, Tavaray, and Chontacaxa (this last at or near Xaquixahuana), but also the charming love-story of Quilacu Yupanqui, a young partisan of Atahualpa, and the adorable imperial maiden Curi Coyllur, daughter or near kinswoman of Huáscar. Other accounts of this period are to be found in: Garcilaso, Pt. I, Bk. IX, Chs. xxxii–xxxviii; Cieza, Pt. II, Chs. lxix–lxxiii; Sarmiento, Chs. lxiii–lxvii; Cobo, Bk. XII, Chs. xviii–xix. Prescott, 1847, I, pp. 340–351.

[20] In democratic societies the element of lateral cohesion is provided by the people themselves, from whom all officials derive their authority to rule. Under the Incas, or at any rate under the later Incas, the people had no authority at all. In earlier times, when Peru was a mosaic of independent tribes of varying degrees of size and power, there no doubt was a certain measure of strictly local self-government which enabled the heads of families in a tribe to elect the tribe's officials. But the Incas changed all that with the result that in the later reigns no man held office save by authority, direct or delegated, of the Inca. See: Baudin, 1928, Chs. vi–viii; Means, 1931, Ch. viii; Minnaert, 1925, pp. 5–18.

[21] Baudin, 1928, Chs. xiii–xiv. Means, 1931, Chs. viii–ix.

CHAPTER II

THE COMING OF THE CASTILIANS

1. Preliminary Explorations

WHEN, in 1513, the first real step towards the Spanish conquest of Peru was taken, Spain had been acquainted with America during some twenty years, each one of which had seen a considerable increase in the sum of geographical knowledge brought home by Columbus and other emissaries of the Crown of Castile. The incident destined to lead up to the first real step in question took place on the Atlantic side of the Isthmus of Panama. It befell thus: Vasco Nuñez de Balboa, a young gentleman-adventurer of respectable abilities and, on the whole, of good character, was supervising the weighing-out of some gold recently found among the Indians by his soldiers. A youthful Indian chief named Panciaco, who was looking on, was astonished by the, to him, abnormal interest of the strangers in everything relating to gold and, moved perhaps by some idea of ridding his own bailiwick of their presence, he told them of vague rumors which had reached him concerning a mysterious land far in the south where gold in huge quantities was to be found.[1]

This hint presently led Nuñez de Balboa to turn his steps southwards in company with about 190 Spanish soldiers—among whom was numbered one Francisco Pizarro—and with a number of Indian servitors and auxiliaries. The task of forcing a way through the trackless leagues of swampy and pestilential country must have been a formidable one; indeed, conditions in the country through which the adventurers passed were so hostile that sometimes they could cover no more than two miles in a day's march. At length, however, after sundry adventures with the natives, the weary explorers reached, on September 25th, 1513, a mountain-top whence they could see the southern ocean of which they had heard. Four days later they were on its shore, and Nuñez de Balboa was wading in its waters, brandishing a banner and a sword and taking possession of it for his King. Very soon thereafter confirmation of Panciaco's words was given by two chiefs on the southern shore of the Isthmus, one of whom, Tumaco by name, gave stirring accounts of the mysterious land of gold in the south, and he made a model of a llama to prove his knowledge of its many marvels. The wanderers were convinced that at last they were on the track of something really worthwhile. Gold-hunger, the besetting sin of the Spaniards in America, was thus early an active factor in their deeds.

Nuñez de Balboa was not destined to become the conqueror of Peru. His evil genius was Don Pedro Arias de Ávila—usually called Pedrarias—husband of a lady powerful at Court and, consequently, well able to act as he pleased towards his foes and rivals among whom was Nuñez de Balboa. Pedrarias, a thoroughly objectionable old man, arrived in Darien or Panama on June 30th, 1514, bringing with him some 1,500 young blades eager for wild adventure and for sudden wealth. The little colony, thus violently inflated in numbers, soon fell a prey to terrible famine so that, in less than a month, some 700 men died of hunger.[2]

These and other untoward developments led Pedrarias into outrageous courses which earned for him the epithet of Furor Domini. In spite of the unremitting hostility of this redoubtable old man, Nuñez de Balboa managed to conduct some preliminary explorations in the direction of Peru, doing so by virtue of a Royal appointment as Adelantado of the South Sea. At length, however, in 1517, Nuñez de Balboa was betrayed into the power of Pedrarias, who promptly beheaded him.[3]

The attitude of Pedrarias towards all who threatened to win renown that would eclipse his own checked explorations for several years so that it was 1522 before the next expedition purposing to trace to their source the rumors of the golden land set forth. It was led by Don Pascual de Andagoya, a worthy man, but one suffering at that time from poor health. He and his followers went as far south as they were able in view of the leader's physical condition, which was made worse by various misadventures suffered on the way. At the southernmost place reached by this abortive expedition, a river on the present Colombian coast, definite news about the Inca empire was received, albeit the explorers did not penetrate within its confines. Having gone so far, Andagoya was obliged to return, rather ignominiously, to Panama.[4]

At about this time a pair of men destined to become important in history appear upon the scene for the first time with some degree of importance. Francisco Pizarro was a bastard son of a gentleman by a woman of the people, Francisca Morales by name. The vicissitudes of his life began early. Although we need not take literally the ancient legend to the effect that he was suckled by a sow, we do know that his early life was such as to form him into an illiterate and selfish wastrel. He was well built, however, but of a gloomy countenance, and he had for his one outstanding virtue that of physical courage. He had been in America since about 1510, and by 1522, the year of Andagoya's unsuccessful voyage, he had risen to be a captain and the holder of a repartimiento (allotment) of Indians in Panama. He was about fifty years of age at that time.[5] The other member of the pair mentioned was Diego de Almagro. As he was a foundling his antecedents are even more obscure than those of Pizarro; but, although he, too, was illiterate, his long experience had made him a good soldier. He had qualities which endeared him to many of the rough men whom he was destined to lead and, in general, he seems to have been a more estimable character than his colleague, albeit not a man of high intelligence nor of lofty motives. He was somewhat older than Pizarro.

Associated with these two was Father Fernando de Luque who, in addition to being a priest, a schoolmaster, and an educated, worthy man of substance, was agent for a fourth and silent partner, the rich Judge Gaspar de Espinosa. Although not yet formally drawn up, the understanding between the three active partners was already tolerably clear as to the tasks to be performed by each one: Father Luque was to remain in Panama and look after the financial side of the affair; Pizarro was to lead the first exploring expedition southwards; and Almagro was to act as liaison and supply officer, going back and forth between the expedition and its base at Panama.[6]

Having purchased the necessary license for departure from Pedrarias at the price of a considerable share in the prospective profits of the enterprise, the partners despatched Pizarro in one ship from Panama in mid-November, 1524. With him went 112 men from Spain and some Indian servants, and somewhat fewer accompanied Almagro when, at last, he set off to join his partner, which he did after much difficulty caused by bad weather and inevitable geographical ignorance. The two ships went as far south as the River San Juan at about 4° north latitude. Their tribulations were appalling, and much of the time the explorers had to subsist on sea-weed and certain very bitter palm fruits. Some thirty of the men died of sickness and under-nourishment, so that, when the expedition returned to Panama in 1525, the company was sadly depleted. They had collected, however, a solacing quantity of gold during the voyage.[7]

On the return of the navigators to Panama they found Pedrarias in a more than usually truculent mood. Having given the explorers license to set out on their quest, he ought to have given them a decently cordial welcome on their return and to have commiserated with them on the trials through which they had passed. Instead, he raised a fearful pother about the men who had died of hunger, because he grudged them bitterly, being engaged on certain sinister enterprises of his own. Only Father Luque's skilful diplomacy prevented the testy old miscreant from revoking his license to the partners, of whose gains he, Pedrarias, was to receive a quarter part, although he had contributed nothing to their initial expenses.[8]

A half-hearted authorization having been extracted from Pedrarias, Father Luque proceeded to obtain from Judge Espinosa the then considerable sum of 20,000 pesos for further explorations. On March 10th, 1526, the understanding between the three active partners was formally embodied in a contract which Father Luque signed for himself and the two illiterate adventurers by proxies, all being done in good order before Hernando de Castillo, Notary Public of Panama.[9] The most singular aspect of the contract, aside from its practical arrangements whereby each signatory was to have a third of the proceeds, is the religiosity of tone, a religiosity prophetic of the vast amount of piety which was to be voiced during the conquest and colonial period of Peru.

In November, 1526, eight months after the signing of this momentous document, a second expedition set sail southwards. There were two ships, one for each of the leaders, about 160 men, and a few horses. An important member of this expedition was the Pilot Bartolomé Ruiz de Estrada who appears to have been the chief navigation officer of the little fleet. Stores were laid in with the idea of being gone a long time. Without touching at any of the intervening points of lugubrious memory, the partners sailed direct to the San Juan River. There the party was divided into three sections; one, under Pizarro, went ashore and long remained in the soggy and jungly country; another went back to Panama with Almagro in one of the ships in order to get new recruits and supplies; and the third, in the other ship, went southwards under the command of Pilot Ruiz.

It is this last group which now concerns us. Ruiz, using the favorable winds which were blowing, sailed rapidly towards the golden land. He sighted the Island of Gallo, whose inhabitants appeared to be in readiness to do battle with the newcomers, and then passed on to the bay of San Mateo, as it was then called, probably being that which is known today as Esmeraldas, just one degree north of the Equator. At about this time Ruiz encountered at sea a mysterious craft with cotton sails, a craft which appeared to have about thirty tons burthen. It was a balsa or sailing raft out of the Peruvian port of Tumbez, and the men and women upon it were the first subjects of the Inca whom the Spaniards had met. These voyaging Indians had with them a number of interesting things, including finely wrought ornaments of gold and silver and some excellent woollen cloths. Their vessel was a curiosity to the Spanish navigators, for it was a large raft made of a strangely buoyant wood and it was surmounted by a commodious hut-like deck-house in which there was a hearth and much equipment for comfortable living.[10]

Considerable satisfaction was derived from the evidence of the balsa and of its passengers, some of whom were captured by Ruiz with the intention of training them to act as interpreters. From the point where the encounter had taken place Ruiz proceeded onwards until he reached Cape Pasado, just south of the Line, which he was thus the first Castilian to cross southbound and in those waters. Having done so, Ruiz turned northwards again and in due course rejoined Pizarro.

When their ship came back to them with Ruiz and his men, Pizarro and those with him were in a dejected frame of mind owing to the unencouraging nature of the country through which, in the meanwhile, they had been making trips of exploration. Endless mangrove swamps, insects, starvation, disease, and the wounds inflicted by the poisoned arrows of the natives had reduced their number terribly and had worn down the strength of those who survived, bringing them to the verge of madness and despair. One can readily imagine, therefore, that a joyful intoxication warmed their breasts when Ruiz sailed into their detested haven with the delightful tidings of what he had seen and heard. Soon thereafter Almagro sailed in from the north with eighty new recruits and plentiful supplies, completing the relief felt by the men so long left upon that forlorn coast.[11]

By now the winds were blowing strongly from the south so that, after disheartening efforts to proceed southwards with both ships, the expedition withdrew to the Island of Gallo. There mutiny did not long delay to raise its ugly head and, though the leaders of the enterprise were still resolved to prosecute their venture, an alarming proportion of their men were so sick and dejected that neither eloquence nor promises could urge them to further efforts. It was now decided that Almagro should once more go back to Panama for additional men and new supplies and that the most discontented men should go back with him. Apparently Ruiz also went back, in the other ship, at this same time.

On arriving at Panama Almagro was dismayed to find that he had unwittingly brought with him a letter of complaint from some of the men left at Gallo to the wife of the new governor of Panama, Don Pedro de los Ríos, who had lately succeeded the detestable Pedrarias. This document, composed by a rebellious trooper named Juan de Saravia and signed by him and by other unhappy men, concluded with a quaint doggerel which is the earliest known Spanish-Peruvian "poem." It ran thus:

Pues señor Gobernador,	Look out Mister Governor
Mirelo bien por entero	For the drover when he's near;
que allá va el recogedor	Since he goes home to get the
y acá queda el carnicero.	sheep
	For the butcher who stays here.
	(Prescott's version.)

The letter was hidden in a ball of native South American cotton-wool which was sent to the Governor's lady as an example of the products of the country. On finding it, she, like a good wife, took it to her lord who, finding therein full corroboration of the complaints which he had received from the returned explorers, determined to rescue those unfortunate men who still remained with Pizarro on the Island of Gallo.[12]

This course was, indeed, the only one which an official in the Governor's position could rightly follow. Accordingly, he kept Almagro—and perhaps Ruiz, also—at Panama and sent off a man of his own, Pedro Tafur, with two ships and instructions to bring back from Gallo all the men left stranded there. Father Luque and Almagro managed, however, to send down a letter in which they urged Pizarro at all costs to stick to his purpose and to hold himself ready to go on with the great adventure.

Stimulated by this letter, Pizarro made a bold gesture which shows him at his best. Hearing the letter, and beholding his men, clad in rags and rheumatic from the incessant rains, preparing to leave him, he scratched a line with his sword from east to west upon the thin soil where he stood. Stepping across from the northern to the southern side of it, he curtly and hardily bade those of his men who were not fools and cowards to follow him and thus to dedicate themselves to further endeavors in the faith that rewards would come after. Thirteen brave spirits took the fateful step across the line as their leader commanded them to do. Only lately has their number and identity been determined.[13]

The fainter-hearted men went back to Panama with Tafur. Pizarro and the Thirteen of Fame presently built a raft and on it made their way to the Island of Gorgona, some seventy-five miles further north, where they would be less exposed to attack by hostile natives and to hunger and thirst. There, amid conditions that could not have been more trying, they remained during the last months of 1527. In the meantime Father Luque and Almagro were conducting themselves with real devotion to their cause at Panama. After Tafur's return Governor Ríos was furious with Pizarro and those who remained with him; but, little by little, Father Luque—a great wheedler, surely—smoothed him down and made him see that, although the "rebels" had flouted the Governor, they had also striven to serve the King. Finally, chiefly from fear of discipline at the hands of his superiors, Ríos so far abated his wrath against Pizarro as to permit a small and slenderly provisioned ship to go in search of the forsaken men. The vessel, with a few men only, was sent off and finally found the heroes at Gorgona.

Characteristically, Pizarro, instead of regarding the ship as

a means of ignoble retreat, seized upon it as a welcome vehicle
for further wanderings. In it the now slightly enlarged party
continued down the coast, passing Cape St. Helena, the Island
of Puná, and arriving, after some three weeks, at Tumbez. An
Inca noble, probably the chief official of the place, came out
to the little ship on a balsa and invited the voyagers to land.
For some reason which is not clear Pizarro neither went ashore
himself nor sent any considerable detachment of his men. Instead, Alonzo de Molina was appointed to go and look about.
In due course he came back to the ship with such a tale of
marvels and grandeurs that no one on board would believe
a word of it, so that, on the next day, the more serious-minded
Pedro de Candia went on shore. After sundry adventures in
the course of which he won the respect of the good folk of
Tumbez by means of a little musketry fire, and during which
he was attacked by a jaguar from the local menagerie whose
teeth made no impression on his suit of glittering armor,
Candia came back with the report that Molina had not lied
and that Tumbez possessed a massively built and heavily gar-
risoned fortress, a Sun-Temple adorned with gold objects of
beauty and worth, and various domiciliary edifices in which
the inhabitants dwelt urbanely. Had Pizarro taken the trouble
to go personally into the town he would probably have found
that it was a place of some importance, provided with a fane
of the official solar cult, and well fortified against attacks by
the fierce and hostile folk of Puná Island to the north, and
that, on this basis, had been reared the gorgeous reports of
Molina and Candia.[14]

From Tumbez Pizarro and his now delighted shipmates
went southwards, passing close along the shore, and so onwards at least as far as the Santa River and perhaps as far as
Chincha. In all the valleys which they passed they beheld
most cheering evidences of advanced culture and of intensive
occupation. The younger and lustier members of the expedition were greatly drawn to the Indian maidens whom they
saw, and Pizarro had some difficulty in inducing them to
desist from taking up their permanent abode upon that coast.

As it is, the whole party was often hospitably entertained, particularly by a capullana or chieftainess whose abode was near Amotape, in the Chira Valley.[15] South of Santa, by common consent, the boat was turned northwards. The explorers had had abundant proof that they had seen at last the long-dreamt-of golden empire. Stopping briefly at Tumbez, where Molina and two or three others were set ashore by their own wish and where several Indians, among them the afterwards notorious Felipillo, were taken on board so that they might learn to be interpreters on subsequent occasions, Pizarro sailed for Panama, arriving there early in 1528.[16]

2. *The Conquest of Peru Begins*

Naturally enough the returned explorers were greeted at Panama by a chorus of praise in which, however, Governor Ríos was far from joining. It soon became apparent to the three partners that, because of Ríos's stubborn and jealous hostility, one of them would have to go to Court in order to obtain the direct support of the King. After much discussion, and not without grave doubts on the part of Father Luque and Almagro, it was decided that Pizarro should go. The sum of 1,500 ducats (about $3,750) was provided somehow, and, in the spring of 1528, Pizarro, with various attendants among whom was the Indian boy, Felipillo, set out for Spain, arriving at Toledo, where the Court then was, late in the summer of the same year.[17]

Pizarro's stirring tale gained him the eager attention of King Charles. Matters moved very slowly at the Castilian Court, however, and on March 8th, 1529, the King had to depart from Toledo on his way to Barcelona and to Italy whither imperial affairs were calling him.[18] Before leaving he particularly urged the business of Pizarro upon his representatives. Consequently, on July 26th, 1529, the famous Capitulación or Agreement for the conquest of Peru was signed by the Queen and was duly delivered to Pizarro.[19]

The Capitulación, fated to be the origin of much turmoil,

made it clear that Father Luque's and Almagro's fears were only too well founded. True, Almagro was appointed commandant of the fortress of Tumbez with an annual salary of either 5,000 or 100,000[20] maravedis, with an additional 200,000 maravedis for expenses; true, also, Almagro was made an hijodalgo, or nobleman; true, once more, good Father Luque was appointed, subject to the Pope's approval, Bishop of Tumbez; true, again, all those of the Thirteen of Fame who were not already noble were made so; true, finally, Ruiz was made Grand Pilot of the Southern Sea with 75,000 maravedis annually. These guerdons, however, were but tinsel honors because the various salaries that went with them were to be derived from the revenues of Peru *when it should have been conquered;* in good hard cash the Queen gave away not a single penny.

The rewards meted out to Almagro and Luque and the rest seem all the more contemptible when compared with those which Pizarro won for himself. He was assigned, from the yet-to-be-acquired revenues of Peru, an annual stipend of 725,000 maravedis and annual expense-money of 1,000 ducats; he was made an hijodalgo and was allowed to use his father's coat of arms in spite of his illegitimacy; he was appointed Governor and Captain-General of Peru, Adelantado, and Alguacil Mayor (High Constable). But far more important than any high-sounding title or any gift of money not yet in hand was the territorial concession, with very ample administrative and patronal powers, which was made to him. It was a grant of 200 leagues (about 600 miles) to run down the coast from "the village which in the language of the Indians is called Zemuquella and which you afterwards called Santiago"[21] to "the village of Chincha, which will be the said two hundred leagues of coast, a little more or less."

The grant in question contained a serious ambiguity due to the then very imperfect knowledge of Peruvian geography. From Puná down to Chincha[22] is above 800 miles in a straight line (and much more along the coast) rather than the 600 miles set by the Queen. Thus, either the Chincha element[23] or the 200 league (600 miles) element must be disregarded in making calculations concerning Pizarro's jurisdiction. To all of this we shall have to revert later on.

The Capitulación and its pendant cédula gave to Pizarro the power to grant encomiendas (lands with Indians) in his territory, under various religious and legal provisos. The document further specified, with somewhat surprising common sense, the conditions under which the projected conquest was to be carried out. Pizarro was bound to provide at least 150 men from Spain and at least 100 more from Castilla del Oro and Panama; he was to sail from Spain not later than January 26th, 1530, and he was to depart with his followers from Panama for Peru within six months of his arrival at the former.[24]

Pizarro's chief difficulty after the signing of the Capitulación was the raising of the stipulated troops. He went to his native town of Trujillo, in Estremadura, and there endeavored to enlist the services of the town's young men. For some reason they omitted to rush to join him in his projected exploits, so that his only enthusiastic recruits were certain none too savory kinsmen of his own. These were: Hernando Pizarro, his half-brother, only legitimate son of their father; two full brothers, Juan and Gonzalo; and a half-brother on the mother's side, Francisco Martín de Alcántara. Young Pedro Pizarro, a cousin, also threw in his lot with Francisco Pizarro, becoming the latter's page. All of these men, and perhaps one or two less-known Pizarro kinsmen, were poor, proud, and avaricious, qualities which led them to do and dare anything for the sake of sudden wealth. At this period Francisco Pizarro received much help from Hernando Cortes, Marquis of the Valley of Oaxaca, conqueror of Mexico, to whom, indeed, he owed most of that moderate success which he had in recruiting. Meanwhile, time slid by. In January, 1530, when the period of six months within which he must sail was almost elapsed, his muster roll had not attained the required length. Nevertheless, Francisco Pizarro slipped away in one ship, with some of the men, from San Lucar de Barrameda, leaving his

FIG. 2. Air photograph of the town of Yanque in the Colca Valley, Peru.
By Aerial Explorations, Inc., Chrysler Bldg., New York.

brother Hernando to convince the suspicious officials that the men under him, together with those who had gone ahead with Francisco, were more than enough to make up the required number. That done, Hernando, in a second ship, set off to join his brother. When, early in February, the two contingents met at Gomera (in the Canaries) in accordance with the understanding between the brothers, it was found that there were 125 men out of the minimum of 150 demanded by the Capitulación. Nothing could have been more prophetic of certain phases of Andean colonial politics than the manner in which the Pizarros tricked their sovereign's officers and flouted their sovereign's commands.

Passing over the period of recriminations and ill-will which followed upon the arrival of Pizarro at Panama where his partners were awaiting him with high hopes—tinctured, however, with doubts—we come to January, 1531, when, quarrels about the terms of the Capitulación having been stilled for the nonce, and some ships having been obtained, Francisco Pizarro sailed for Peru. With him went all his kinsmen, a few ecclesiastics—of whom the most conspicuous in subsequent events was the Dominican, Friar Vicente de Valverde—and not more than 200 men, some of whom had horses.[25] As on previous occasions, Almagro was left behind to gather additional forces, supplies, and munitions, it being understood that he would follow after.

The presence in the army of a number of reverend representatives of the Prince of Peace did nothing to deter the leader or his men from displaying a martial pugnacity very different from the mild inquisitiveness which had been the policy on earlier trips. For about a year Pizarro and his men journeyed slowly down the coast to the Island of Puná, having many armed encounters with the natives and many horrible adventures with hunger, disease, and death in sundry forms.

At Puná the Spaniards had a terrific battle with the fierce natives of the place during which Tumpala or Tumbala, the curaca (chief) of Puná was captured together with some of his subjects. Then there came to the island a body of men from

Tumbez, whose people were traditional enemies of those of
Puná, and they besought Pizarro to aid them against the
islanders. The Spanish invaders thus became embroiled for a
time in the local strife of the natives, a highly uncomfortable
situation which was finally terminated by the opportune arrival from Panama of Hernando de Soto, in a good large ship
with one hundred new men and a number of excellent mounts
for the cavalry. The army was then transported over to the
mainland near Tumbez which place, however, they found to
have been sacked and burnt during a recent war with the
folk of Puná. This was early in 1532.[26]

Pizarro and his men remained at Tumbez for some months,
in which period they gathered from the chief of the town and
from its people—who gradually returned to their ruined homes
—a great deal of valuable information concerning the state of
the empire and its greatness. On May 16th, 1532, the main
body of the army moved southwards, reaching the broad,
fertile, and densely peopled Chira Valley about a week later.
Here again Pizarro mixed in local politics, committing a number of unnecessary cruelties among the chiefs who ruled various parts of that lovely valley. Having thus cowed the
inhabitants, Pizarro and Friar Vicente de Valverde set about
founding the first Spanish city in Peru, that of San Miguel
de Tangarará. To judge by the still visible remains it was a
town generously planned and built of adobe and algarroba-
wood. A church, a town hall, a storehouse, a fort, and a number of dwellings, as well as water-ditches, were laid out, and
a civic government on the Spanish plan was set up. Lands
and local Indians were allotted by Pizarro to those men who
chose to settle in San Miguel de Tangarará as citizens.[27]

Leaving Sebastián de Benalcazar in command at San Miguel with a suitable number of men, most of them being the
older and more worn-out members of the expedition, Pizarro
and the main body of the army left that place on September
24th, 1532, and began the epochal march towards Cajamarca.
By this time the Spanish leader was in communication with
Atahualpa, whose camp was near the mountain city men-

tioned, and various messages were exchanged through native ambassadors as the army progressed towards the Inca's quarters. However much one may deprecate the purposes and methods of the Spanish invaders he cannot but admire the sublime audacity which enabled them thus to penetrate, with less than 200 men,[28] the heart of such a mighty realm as Ttahua-ntin-suyu still was.

The route taken by the invaders lay through the upper part of the Piura Valley and along the western base of the mountains to the Saña or to the Leche River in one or the other of which the perilous ascent into the highlands was made. Every step of the way was full of danger which quite failed to daunt the Castilians and full also of occasions upon which Atahualpa might have, but did not, hurl his warriors upon them to crush them. Instead of doing so, he sent them handsome gifts and generally beckoned them on. The Spaniards, on their part, behaved circumspectly on the whole, committing only a few atrocities, and returning gift for gift. We may reasonably suppose that Atahualpa's forbearance was due to an overwhelming curiosity to behold these daring strangers.

At last, on November 15th, 1532, the little army of Pizarro came out upon the margin of the oval plain, some five leagues by nine, whose focal point was the city of Cajamarca. Noting with satisfaction the broad expanses of cultivated fields and all the other evidences of intensive and civilized occupation, the Spaniards marched along the well-made road and, at the hour of vespers, entered the city itself. As they had been led to expect, they found the city deserted save for a few of the lower classes and a small number of soldiers who were there as guards or spies. A few miles away, however, and well within sight, were thousands of gleaming white tents, well made and well arranged, in which Atahualpa's army of some 40,000 men was sheltered, the whole encampment being so large that it occupied some miles of valley land. Naturally enough the sight of this impressive camp filled the invaders with mixed feelings, fear and a wish to retreat being conjoined with a knowledge that to show any signs of dread would be enough to bring a terrible death upon them. So, with that hardy courage which was their best characteristic, the Castilians smiled grimly at one another and went on with the game.[29]

It is difficult to reconstruct the course of events at Cajamarca with exactitude because our various informants differ from one another in regard to every detail. The general trend of the matter seems, however, to run as I shall now set forth.

Entering the plaza of Cajamarca, Governor Pizarro (as I shall henceforth call him) scarcely gave his men time to relax before he despatched thirty horsemen, under the command of either Hernando Pizarro or Hernando de Soto (or both), to interview the Inca. The emissaries found Atahualpa in a small house of only a few rooms which was kept for his use when he went thither to take the bath, and for that purpose he had a finely made tub hewn out of sightly stone into which hot and cold waters were led in pipes from certain springs nearby. This very modern-seeming bath was reserved, under pain of death, to the Inca and his wives.

Atahualpa, then in early middle life, pleasantly plump in person, with a handsome, grave countenance, a charming smile, but with fierce and somewhat bloodshot eyes, received the envoys of the Governor in his house. He was seated on his *tiana* or throne behind a thin cotton gauze curtain held by two native ladies. It was, apparently, his custom thus to shroud himself from the direct gaze of his subjects, but, when the Spaniards arrived, he ordered that the curtain be dropped. Whether this was done out of courtesy to the visitors or from a wish to see them more clearly one cannot know. Details concerning the interview which followed are most unsatisfactorily reported, some writers representing the Inca as maintaining an attitude of imperial reticence and another (Pedro Pizarro) declaring that the Emperor took a strong tone with the envoys, complaining of their behavior along the road and of their having meddled with certain mats which were in a house formerly used by Huayna Capac, at Tumbez. At any rate, there was an exhibition of equestrianism for the benefit of the Inca who had shown a lively curiosity regarding the horses and particularly a fiery and small but well-trained horse ridden by Soto. Nothing loath to display his skill, that cavalier put his steed through its paces, making it gallop, prance, and curvet, and, in so doing, he terrified some of the courtiers, who fell back in fright before these unheard-of antics, their terror being paid for with their lives that very night, by the Inca's orders. Atahualpa, however, preserved his imperial calm even when the little horse's head was brought so close over his own that flecks of foam fell upon his raiment. After this little incident the Inca dismissed his visitors, assuring them that, when his fast should have ended on the morrow, he would go to visit them in their quarters in Cajamarca.[30]

That Friday night of November 15th, 1532, found the little band of Spaniards in the blackest despondency. From their bivouac in the plaza, where the sinister shadows of deserted buildings crowded upon them and the massive shapes of two great fortresses hung over them, they could see the countless fires of the Inca's camp, so numerous that they looked like "nothing else than a very starry sky."[31] During the night the Governor first cheered on his dejected men with all the manly eloquence which distinguished him at his best, and later he held a council of his officers in which the plans for the next day's action were drawn up.

The hour of sundown was approaching when, on the next day, to the pulsing rhythm of drums and the plaintive wail of trumpets and flutes, the Inca with only a few thousand troops drew nigh the city. First came bands of servitors bearing brooms with which they carefully swept the highway over which their lord was to be borne. Afterwards, arranged in companies, came contingents of soldiery bearing massive clubs with star-like heads of copper, silver, or gold, and singing wild, triumphant war-songs which sounded to the Spaniards like the yells of hellish demons. Last of all came the Cañari guard, arrayed in richly ornamented azure, who surrounded the imperial litter as it was carried by trained bearers. Seated on a golden throne under a canopy blazing with gorgeous feathers

and plates of gold and silver, Atahualpa, with the Lord of
Chincha at his feet, rode onwards in silence. His dress was of
becoming brilliance, for around his neck were enormous emeralds and to the imperial fillet on his head had been added
many embellishments of gold.

In complete silence and with perfect decorum some six thousand Indians filed into the plaza, leaving a pathway clear for
the imperial palanquin. Arrived at the centre of the square
without seeing a single Spaniard (for, upon order, they were
all lurking within the houses), the Inca at last broke that in-
effably majestic silence of his, asking: "Where, then, are the
strangers?"

As if in answer Friar Valverde now scuffled forward to the
imperial litter, a Breviary in one hand and an upraised Cru-
cifix in the other. Being completely ignorant of practical
psychology, the Friar plunged at once into a long-winded
theological discourse in which he set forth the more absurd
sacerdotal dogmas of his day, linking the Apostle St. Peter to
Pizarro through that sordid fellow, Pope Alexander VI, and
relating how he, Alexander, had given Peru to King Charles,
whose vassal Atahualpa was now blandly invited to become.
Not only was the Friar's address supremely ridiculous from the
standpoint of common sense, but also its general obscurity
was enhanced by the translation given to it by the mischief-
making interpreter, Felipillo. To Atahualpa, rigidly maintaining an imperturbable mien upon his lofty litter, the whole
thing must have sounded like the ravings of madmen, the
only clear points in it being that an individual styling himself
the Pope had given his, Atahualpa's, realms to some king or
other and that he, the Inca, was being bidden to become that
other king's vassal.

Naturally enough Atahualpa was furious. But he held his
peace until the verbose Valverde was quite done. Then he ex-
ploded. In spicy language he voiced his scorn for the God
"who was three persons and one more, which makes four"—
such being Felipillo's version of the Trinity—for the silly Pope
who gave away things that did not belong to him, and for

that distant king who had the colossal impudence to put himself above the Inca. Pausing in his raging tirade only to catch his breath, he went on to say that he would make the scoundrelly outlanders pay dearly for all the damage they had done since coming into his empire, and he wound up by asking Valverde what authority he had for all the arrant nonsense with which the imperial ears had been insulted. The Friar indicated the Breviary and handed it up to the monarch. The volume was closed with clasps, and the Inca, being inexpert in bookish matters, could make nothing of the lumpish object which he found in his hands. Becoming bored he nonchalantly dropped the holy tome upon the pavement.

This "sacrilege" served as an excuse for the attack upon the Inca's person which Pizarro and his officers had planned to make. In the short, sharp scuffle which ensued, with guns barking, horses prancing, and steel armor, swords, and trappings flashing in the sundown light, Spain, represented by her handful of adventurers, rolled a proud empire in the golden dust of the plaza of Cajamarca. Mere numbers, though great, were of no avail to Atahualpa's cause in the presence of firearms and horses and of the raucous shouts of "Santiago and at them" which the Christians constantly uttered. Valverde, who had paused only long enough to snatch up his book, rushed hither and yon yelling out absolution to the attackers. In the scrimmage the bewildered Inca was tumbled out of his splendid litter, his sacred imperial llautu was snatched from his head by the soldier-chronicler, Estete, and he was almost stripped of his glittering apparel before Governor Pizarro himself, at the cost of a wound from one of his own frenzied men, rescued him—from policy, not mercy—and led him into captivity. Even then the carnage did not cease; for hundreds of unarmed or lightly armed native warriors were hacked to pieces with swords or trampled into slime by the horses without being able to deliver one effective blow for their lord. Thus did Christianity prove its superiority to the pagan faith which Atahualpa had scorned to betray.[32]

3. *The Ransom of an Emperor*

The Inca's first idea seems to have been that Pizarro and his men were partisans of Huáscar and that they would kill him and place his brother, then held in captivity at Antamarca, upon the seat of power. He soon learned his mistake, however, and rightly gauged his adversaries' overwhelming lust for gold and silver. Accordingly he made an offer of ransom, promising to fill with gold a certain good-sized chamber in his palace and another large space with silver. On November 18th or 20th, 1532, the terms were formally set down in a notarial document wherein it was agreed that all the Spaniards then in Cajamarca should partake of the resultant treasure and that, if he refrained from "treasonable" actions, the Inca would be set free.[33]

Thereafter the Inca sent forth many couriers into the southerly regions of his realm with orders to bring to Cajamarca gold and silver taken from temples and palaces. In the meantime, the captive monarch was treated reasonably well, being allowed to see his women in private, to receive great numbers of his vassals, and to learn chess, for which complicated game he displayed great aptitude. True, he had also to submit to prolonged harangues from that sacerdotal chatterbox, Valverde, but on the whole his situation was not too uncomfortable.

On December 20th the gold and silver for the ransom began to arrive and afterwards it flowed in steadily. The promptness with which the Inca's orders were obeyed and the great deference which his vassals paid him even in captivity were eloquent of the extremely efficient organization of the empire. A more subtle mind than that of Governor Pizarro would have perceived therein an indication that the surest and most commendable path to power in Peru would have been to rule the land through Atahualpa as a mouthpiece. For months after the capture of the Inca the Governor continued at Cajamarca without ever having the wit to understand this. It was in this period that the Inca, using a clever stratagem, tricked the

Governor into forgiving him for the secretly ordered murder of Huáscar.[34]

Between January 5th and April 25th, 1533, the Governor's brother, Hernando, led a very important reconnoitring party to the celebrated holy city of Pachacamac and thence back to Cajamarca. Arriving at the great oracular creator-god's special seat on February 5th, the little party were not at first disappointed in what they saw. The city was large, the buildings handsome and imposing, and a considerable population crowded the streets. But when they succeeded in penetrating to the fane of the god they found that it was nothing more than a stinking and maculate cubicle besmeared with the blood of sacrifices and containing a hideously carved wooden idol to which there remained of the great treasure already hidden by the priests only a few fragments of gold and some emeralds. The folk of the city, to assuage the wrath of their visitors, afterwards collected for them gold and silver to the value of 80,000 pesos (about $160,000).[35]

During the absence of Hernando Pizarro from Cajamarca various interesting incidents took place. The chief of them was the arrival of Almagro at Cajamarca, with new soldiers, horses, and munitions of war. The recruiting done by Almagro for the Peruvian venture after the Governor had departed from Panama had not met with conspicuous success. When, in November, 1532, he sailed from Panama in three ships he had with him only about 150 men, most of whom seem to have been the dregs of the Isthmian grog-shops. Later he was joined by some 50 more men of better class, many of them having mounts. Thus reinforced, Almagro's contingent arrived at San Miguel de Tangarará late in December, 1532, and at Cajamarca in mid-February, 1533. Although the two partners embraced one another with superficial cordiality, there was soon much hidden friction between them and their respective followers. As for the Inca, he was thrown into a deep gloom by the arrival of these reinforcements, and his chief real friend among the conquerors, Hernando de Soto, strove in vain to cheer him up.[36]

By May 3rd, 1533, the promised ransom of Atahualpa was completed to the satisfaction of his captors. Between that date and June 17th the bulk of the treasure, both gold and silver, was melted, refined, and made into bars or ingots. Thus was lost forever an immense array of exquisite, intricate, and lovely objects wrought in those choicest of materials but with no thought of money, their sole purpose being to do honor and to give pleasure to the gods and rulers of the now shattered empire. Never, perhaps, before or since, has there been a more wondrous assemblage of beautiful handicraft productions. It is, therefore, something of a comfort to know that, before the barbarous, but no doubt necessary, process of melting was carried out, gold to the value of 100,000 pesos (about $200,000) and 5,000 marks' worth of silver were taken out for the purpose of sending them in their original and fascinating forms to King Charles. The deduction was a part of the Royal fifth. The total value of the gold and silver in bars was 1,326,-539 pesos of gold and 51,610 marks of silver. The Royal fifths of the two metals came, respectively, to about 270,000 pesos and 10,000 marks.[37]

In short, we are left in no doubt whatever as to the exceeding splendor and sightliness of the golden objects assembled by Atahualpa's orders. We have several descriptive lists of the golden articles, the said lists constituting incontrovertible proof that the outward magnificence of the Incaic civilization was fully as dazzling as even the most romantic reader could desire.[38]

Immediately after the distribution of the ransom, Governor Pizarro caused a notarial document to be prepared and publicly proclaimed both in Spanish and in Quechua to the effect that Atahualpa had fulfilled his promise with respect to the ransom.[39] Just what this proclamation was worth will be told in the next chapter.

Soon after that the Governor, annoyed by the constant bickering between that big bully, Hernando Pizarro, and the small but pugnacious Almagro, availed himself of his brother's services in order to send him on business to the King. The emis-

sary took with him the specimens of gold and silver selected
for the edification of His Majesty, and with him went twenty-
five of the older and more homesick soldiers who wished to
enjoy their newly received riches in their native land.[40]

NOTES TO CHAPTER II

[1] Benzoni, 1857, pp. 69–71. Herrera, Dec. I, Bk. X, Ch. ii. Prescott, I, pp.
193–195. Merriman, II, pp. 215–216. Helps, I, pp. 337–352. Fiske, II, pp. 374–
376. Anderson, 1911, p. 162.

[2] Fernández de Oviedo, Bk. XXIX, Chs. vi, vii, and ix.

[3] Benzoni, 1857, pp. 71–75. Casas, Bk. III, Chs. lxxiii–lxxv. Fernández de
Oviedo, Bk. XXIX, Ch. xii. Helps, I, pp. 392–438. Fiske, II, pp. 378–384.
Merriman, II, pp. 216–217.

[4] Andagoya, 1865. Montesinos, 1906, Año 1524, tells us that Andagoya went
as far south as the land of the cacique (chief) Pirú. This name is sometimes
written Birú. In any case, it is probably the original form of the name Peru
which was later applied to Ttahua-ntin-suyu, although various other explana-
tions of the name Peru are not lacking.

[5] Nearly one hundred years after Francisco Pizarro's death a descendant of
his strove to supply his ancestor with legitimate birth and sixteen quarterings.
See: Pizarro y Orellana, 1639, pp. 127–196 and pp. 4–5 of the Discurso legal
y político which should—but often does not—follow the main work, separately
paged but all in one binding. See also: Prescott, I, pp. 202–206; Helps, III,
pp. 419–427; Fiske, II, pp. 384–391.

[6] P. Pizarro, 1921, I, pp. 133–135. Garcilaso, Pt. II, Bk. I, Chs. i and ii.
Prescott, I, pp. 206–209. Helps, III, pp. 427–441. Fiske, II, pp. 390–392. Merriman, III, p. 543.

[7] Xerez, 1872, pp. 3–6. Herrera, Dec. III, Bk. VIII, Chs. xi–xiii. López de
Gómara, Ch. cviii. Prescott, I, pp. 207–229. Helps, III, pp. 427–445. Fiske,
II, pp. 390–391.

[8] Fernández de Oviedo, apud Prescott, II, pp. 484–485, gives a lively account of how, in February, 1527, Pedrarias finally sold out his interest in the
enterprise for 1,000 pesos.

[9] This document is copied in full by Montesinos, 1906, Año 1526, and by
Prescott, II, pp. 487–490.

[10] Samanos, 1844, pp. 195–197. Xerez, 1872, pp. 6–7. For notes on the
balsas of the Peruvians see: Means, 1931, pp. 341–342, and notes thereto. Also,
Figure 160.

[11] Prescott, I, pp. 241–250.

[12] Zárate, Bk. I, Ch. ii. Montesinos, 1906, Año 1527. Garcilaso, Pt. II, Bk.
I, Ch. viii. Herrera, Dec. III, Bk. X, Ch. iii. Cabello, Pt. III, Ch. xxv. P.
Pizarro, 1921, I, pp. 136–138. Prescott, I, pp. 256–259. Helps, III, pp. 403–406.

[13] Helps, III, pp. 444–448, rather doubts this version and makes a somewhat similar incident take place on board one of Tafur's ships, his authority
therefor being a passage in Herrera, Dec. III, Bk. X, Ch. iii. But Prescott, I,
pp. 262–264, Fiske, II, pp. 393–394, and Merriman, III, pp. 545–546, all accept

it. The prime authority on this point, however, is Romero, 1919. Dr. Romero examines all the available source materials and finds that, in all likelihood, the following list is the correct one:

Pedro Alcón
Alonzo Briceño
Pedro de Candia
Antonio de Carrión
Francisco de Cuéllar
García de Jarén

Alonzo de Molina
Martín de Paz
Cristóbal de Peralta
Nicolás de Rivera el viejo
Domingo de Soraluce
Juan de la Torre

Francisco de Villafuerte

All these men are vouched for in one or more of certain contemporary documents cited by Dr. Romero which are: An Información of August 8th, 1528, another of August 25th, 1528, and the Capitulación of July 26th, 1529, between the Queen and Pizarro (of which more, presently). The Pilot Ruiz de Estrada was not one of the thirteen heroes, but his object in returning to Panama was the worthy one of getting aid for those who remained behind and of returning to them with it. This is a point often overlooked by historians, but it is settled by Romero, 1919, pp. 118, 133–135. See also Romero, 1906. Shay, 1932, pp. 102–103, gives sixteen as the number of the faithful men; but it is likely that he has not seen Romero's work on the subject.

[14] Descriptions of Tumbez are numerous, the most important being those in: Cieza, Pt. I, Chs. iv, liv, lix; Pt. II, Chs. lviii and lxv; Estete, 1918, pp. 15–16. See also: Prescott, I, pp. 272–281; Velasco, II, p. 13.

[15] Casas, 1892, p. 111. Legends still abound in the Chira Valley concerning the hospitable capullana in the vicinity of the modern village of Amotape.

[16] Estete, 1918, p. 16. Garcilaso, Pt. II, Bk. I, Chs. xi–xiii. Montesinos, 1906, Año 1527 and 1528. P. Pizarro, 1921, I, pp. 138–140. Prescott, I, pp. 281–289. Merriman, III, pp. 547–548.

[17] Fernández de Oviedo, Pt. III, Bk. VIII, Ch. i. Herrera, Dec. IV, Bk. III, Ch. i. Zárate, Bk. I, Ch. iii. Montesinos, 1906, Años 1528 and 1529. Garcilaso, Pt. II, Bk. I, Ch. xiv. Prescott, I, pp. 289–293. Merriman, III, pp. 553–554.

[18] Foronda y Aguilera, 1914, p. 318.

[19] The question of which Queen signed the document is obscure because, in accordance with Spanish custom, it is signed merely "Yo la Reyna," without any name. Many writers have assumed that the signer was Charles's mother, Juana. (Cf. Markham, 1892, p. 75, for instance.) But Merriman, III, p. 554, says that it was the Empress Isabella, Charles's wife, who was also Queen of Castile. Strong support is given to this assertion by two letters signed by Charles at Barcelona on July 25th, 1529, in which he states that Isabella is left in charge of affairs. (Foronda, 1914, pp. 326–327.) On the other hand, those of the printings of the Capitulación listed below which are marked * have elaborate headings in which Queen Juana is mentioned by name. The printings are:

1. That of Prescott in Appendix VII, Vol. II, pp. 490–497.
2. That of Fuentes, 1866, pp. 5–11.*

3. That of Colección de documentos inéditos del archivo de Indias, Vol. XXII, pp. 271–285, Madrid, 1874.
4. That of Raimondi, 1874–1911, in Vol. II (1876), pp. 11–18.*
5. That of Torres Saldamando in Libro Primero de Cabildos de Lima (hereinafter cited as Cabildos), III, pp. 136–142, Paris, 1900.

Although Raimondi states that he copied his version from Fuentes (first edition, not second here used) and that Fuentes got his version out of the Libro de Cabildos, Fuentes himself does not indicate where he got his material. In the headings of the Fuentes and Raimondi printings here cited Pizarro is called "El Marques Pizarro," which he did not become until eight years later than 1529. One cannot, I think, trust the headings of the Fuentes and Raimondi printings. My own belief is that Queen Isabella signed, acting for King Charles, but with due recognition of the peculiar sovereign position of Queen Juana, called la Loca, the Mad.

20 Printings 3 and 5 on the list in the preceding note say "cinco mil"; the three others say "cien mil." It is altogether probable that the larger sum is the correct one. Only the original document—said to be in the Archives of the Indies—can settle this and other points.

21 Prescott, Fuentes, and Raimondi have "Tenumpuela" instead of "Zemuquella" as in the two other versions. There is a pendant to the Capitulación in the form of a Cédula (decree) of the same date which is printed in Cabildos, III, pp. 142–145 and in Traversari, 1919, pp. 10–14. In that Cédula the name is given as "Tempula" (Cabildos) or "Temumpalla" (Traversari). Although Traversari, and after him Merriman (III, p. 554) tries to make out that the Santiago in question was the town of Riobamba, up in the highlands of Ecuador—then, of course, totally unknown to the Spaniards—we may be quite sure that Zemuquella, Tenumpuela, Tempula, or Temumpalla, otherwise Santiago, was the Island of Puná, whose chief was named Tumbala or Tumbalá (according to Cieza, Pt. I, Ch. liv, p. 195 of Markham's edition, and Pt. II, Ch. lxv, p. 211 of Markham's edition), or Tumpalla (according to Garcilaso, Pt. I, Bk. IX, Ch. iv), or Tomalá (according to Salazar de Villasante, in Relaciones Geográficas de Indias, I, p. 9). This point about the identity of the Santiago mentioned in the Capitulación and in the Cédula of July 26th, 1529, with the Island of Puná is highly important. I have in preparation a very ample study of the matter, but, in the meantime, I can say that the maps of the period bear out the identity and that it is clinched by a sentence in Xerez which says: "an island called Puna, to which the Spaniards gave the name of Santiago." (Xerez, 1872, pp. 13–14.) Two of the maps on which the Island of Puná is plainly marked "y: de s. tiago" are the Wolfenbüttel-Spanish, 1525–1530, and the Ribero, 1529. I am much indebted to my friends, Dr. Edward Luther Stevenson and Mr. Walter Briggs, for aid in studies of the maps which concern this matter. Shay, 1932, p. 122, assumes, correctly and without question, that Santiago is Puná Island.

22 The "puerto y prouincia de la cibdad de chinchax" figures on both the maps just cited.

23 How the Spaniards who, in 1527–1528, went no further south than Santa found out about Chincha is a great puzzle. The probable explanation is that

they went, not merely as far south as Santa (as most authorities aver) but considerably farther, in fact as far as Chincha. Only thus can the appearance of "chinchax" on the maps cited be explained.

[24] Prescott, I, pp. 302–308. Moses, 1898, pp. 112–114; 1914, I, pp. 96–98. Merriman, III, pp. 554–555.

[25] The Capitulación called for 250 men. Xerez, who was secretary to Pizarro at this time, says that there were 180 men and 27 horses (1872, p. 12). Pedro Pizarro, who was also present, says that there were some 200 men but does not say how many horses (1921, I, p. 147). The document hereinafter cited as the Anonymous Conquest of 1534 and thus listed in the bibliography says (fol. 1) "250 men, of whom 80 were cavalrymen." But, perchance, this figure was contrived to agree with the terms of the then recent Capitulación. Prescott, I, pp. 318–319, dates the sailing on St. John the Evangelist's Day, December 27th, 1530, which he gets from Ruiz Naharro's work.

[26] P. Pizarro, 1921, I, pp. 136–159. Estete, 1918, pp. 16–20. Anonymous Conquest of 1534, fol. 1. Xerez, 1872, pp. 12–19. Zárate, Bk. II, Chs. i–iii. Montesinos, 1906, Años 1529–1532. Garcilaso, Pt. II, Bk. I, Chs. xiv–xvi. Prescott, I, pp. 319–331. Merriman, III, pp. 556–558. Schurig, 1922, pp. 55–66. Baudin, 1930, pp. 27–65.

[27] The present city of San Miguel de Piura is a direct descendant of this foundation, having been established in its present locality in 1587, after various vicissitudes. See Eguiguren, 1895, and Note 62 to P. Pizarro, 1921. Authorities for the founding of San Miguel de Tangarará include: P. Pizarro, 1921, I, pp. 165–167; Estete, 1918, p. 20; Xerez, 1872, pp. 22–24; Cieza, Pt. I, Ch. lv. Prescott, I, pp. 357–359.

[28] The figures vary from 150 to 190 men according to the different authorities. All are agreed that there was a high proportion of horsemen and that there were some arquebusiers and crossbowmen. See: P. Pizarro, 1921, I, p. 171; Anonymous Conquest of 1534, fol. 1; Estete, 1918, pp. 20–21; Xerez, 1872, p. 26.

[29] Xerez, 1872, pp. 25–44. Estete, 1918, pp. 21–22. P. Pizarro, 1921, I, pp. 173–174. Anonymous Conquest of 1534, fols. 1–3. Prescott, I, pp. 366–390. Merriman, III, pp. 558–559.

[30] Estete, 1918, p. 23. P. Pizarro, I, pp. 174–177. Zárate, Bk. II, Ch. iv. Anonymous Conquest of 1534, fols. 3 recto and verso. Enríquez, 1862, p. 92. Xerez, 1872, pp. 47–50. Prescott, I, pp. 389–400.

[31] Estete, 1918, p. 23.

[32] P. Pizarro, I, pp. 177–185. Xerez, 1872, pp. 51–62. Estete, 1918, pp. 23–25. Zárate, Bk. II, Chs. iii–v. Anonymous Conquest of 1534, fols. 3 verso to 4 recto. Cabello, Pt. III, Ch. xxxii. Garcilaso, Pt. II, Bk. I, Chs. xviii–xxvii. Montesinos, 1906, Año 1532. H. Pizarro, 1872, pp. 113–119. Prescott, I, pp. 400–424. Merriman, III, pp. 560–561.

[33] Xerez, 1872, pp. 65–69. Anonymous Conquest of 1534, fols. 4 recto to 4 verso. Estete, 1918, pp. 25–26. P. Pizarro, I, pp. 185–187. Zárate, Bk. II, Ch. vi. Prescott, I, pp. 424–436.

[34] P. Pizarro, I, pp. 189–191. Anonymous Conquest of 1534, fols. 4 verso to 5 recto. Estete, 1918, p. 26. Zárate, Bk. II, Ch. vi. Garcilaso, Pt. II, Bk. I, Ch. xxxiii. Prescott, I, pp. 436–439. Merriman, III, pp. 562–563.

[35] P. Pizarro, I, pp. 208–211. Estete, 1918, pp. 26–28. Estete, in Xerez, 1872,

pp. 74–93. Cieza, Pt. I, Ch. lxxii. Prescott, I, pp. 444–451. Merriman, III, p. 563. For data on the significance of Pachacamac, see: Means, 1931, pp. 184–186, 259, 422–429.

[36] P. Pizarro, I, pp. 212–213. Estete, 1918, pp. 28–29. Xerez, 1872, pp. 69–72. Anonymous Conquest of 1534, fol. 6 verso. Garcilaso, Pt. II, Bk. I, Ch. xxxiv. Zárate, Bk. II, Chs. v–vii. Prescott, I, pp. 459–462.

[37] Prescott, I, pp. 466–468, arrived at the conclusion that the modern money-equivalent for the value of the ransom would come to something over $15,000,000, the Royal fifth being in the neighborhood of $3,000,000. Merriman, however, on p. 565 of Vol. III, cites modern authorities for reducing the figure by more than two-thirds. We are told by Prescott, in the place cited, that ancient and modern authorities are agreed that the *peso de oro* and the *castellano* were identical, and we are told in Xerez, 1872, note 13, that they are worth 8 shillings, or about $2.00. Therefore, the value of the ransom would be, for the gold alone, about $2,650,000. It is difficult to judge how much greater the purchasing power of money was in those days than now. The ransom was distributed among the soldiers and officers, as set forth in the Acta de Repartición signed by Pedro Sancho and printed on pp. 131–143 of the same volume as Xerez, 1872; it is also to be found in Cabildos, III, pp. 121–126. Shay, 1932, p. 222, asserts that the ransom was worth, at present values, a little less than $50,000,000. This figure is certainly far too high, even if due allowance be made for difference in purchasing power as between that day and ours.

[38] See: Fernández de Oviedo, Pt. III, Bk. VIII, Ch. xvi (who saw some of the objects at Santo Domingo when they were en route for Spain); Medina, 1904–1907, I, pp. 160–174; the Anonymous work entitled *Nouvelles certaines des Isles du Peru,* published at Lyons by Françoys Juste in 1534; Sancho, 1917, pp. 9–11. Also: Estete, 1918, p. 29; Xerez, 1872, pp. 94–102; Anonymous Conquest of 1534, fol. 6 verso.

[39] Sancho, 1917, pp. 12–13.

[40] P. Pizarro, I, pp. 214–215. Estete, 1918, p. 29. Anonymous Conquest of 1534, fol. 6 verso. Xerez, 1872, pp. 108–109. Cieza, Pt. I, Ch. lxv. Garcilaso, Pt. II, Bk. I, Ch. xxxv. Zárate, Bk. II, Ch. vii. Montesinos, 1906, Años 1532 and 1533. Prescott, I, pp. 463–475. Merriman, III, pp. 562–563.

CHAPTER III

THE CONQUEST OF PERU BY CASTILE

1. *The Last Days of Atahualpa*

IN the same proclamation—mentioned near the close of the preceding chapter—in which Governor Pizarro announced that Atahualpa had fully discharged his obligations respecting the ransom, he, Pizarro, also announced that the Inca was not to be released from durance. The sole justification alleged for this breach of faith was a bare assertion that it suited the service of the King that the Inca be held a prisoner until the arrival of Spanish reënforcements. Very soon, however, it became clear to all that this anomalous condition could not long endure. Atahualpa had kept his promise honorably and acknowledgment thereof had been made by his captors. Therefore it was now incumbent upon Pizarro either to set the Inca free or else to show good reason for not doing so.[1]

The doing to death of Atahualpa, usurper and fratricide, may seem to some to have been a condign punishment for his crimes. It is one, however, which reflects little credit on Pizarro, Almagro, and all the other Spaniards who connived at it. The diabolus ex machina in this matter was one of the Indian lads whom Pizarro had taken into his service at Tumbez in 1528. This youth, known as Felipillo, had accompanied his master to Spain and so had acquired a knowledge of Castilian sufficient to lead to his appointment as chief interpreter. During the long sojourn of the Spaniards at Cajamarca Felipillo had had the unparalleled audacity to fall in love with one of Atahualpa's minor concubines; but, to judge by the young miscreant's efforts to ruin his imperial rival, the lady did not respond favorably to the advances of the low-born coast Indian. Atahualpa's pride was deeply wounded by this affair, and he did everything in his power to induce Pizarro to oblit-

42

erate the offender and all his kin. Although he failed in this, he confirmed Felipillo in an implacable hatred nurtured by amatorial ambition and by fear for his life. Unfortunately, Felipillo was rich in low cunning, and by dint of circulating false reports of Atahualpa's military plans, as well as by means of systematic mistranslations of Atahualpa's sayings, he quickly created a situation which could have but one outcome for his imperial enemy. With consummate skill the interpreter fomented an increasing terror among the Spanish soldiery who came to imagine themselves to be hemmed in on every side by armies of fierce warriors from Quito and elsewhere, eager to drink wildly jubilant potations from Spanish skulls converted into drinking-cups.[2]

At last, in August, 1533, a crisis was reached. The Governor was still feebly opposed to killing Atahualpa, and Don Hernando de Soto, together with perhaps a score of honorable men, was stoutly opposed to all hasty and faithless action. But all the rest, and especially Almagro and his followers, and also Valverde, were loud in their demands for a violent death for Atahualpa. Late in August Soto was sent off with a small following to hunt for the supposed hidden armies of warriors, and during his absence a formal legal process was hastily instituted against the Inca in which the Indian witnesses were examined through the unscrupulous interpreter, Felipillo. The only sane charges made in the indictment were: that Atahualpa had first usurped Huáscar's rightful sovereignty of Cuzco and had later killed him; and, that he, Atahualpa, had plotted against the Spaniards. All the other charges were based upon Catholic morality, touching upon such questions as polygamy, incestuous marriage, idolatry, and other practices licit under Incaic law by which alone Atahualpa could be properly judged. These farcical and fatal accusations were set forth in what the historian Fernández de Oviedo indignantly describes as "a badly contrived and worse written document, devised by a factious and unprincipled priest, a clumsy notary without conscience, and others of like stamp, who were all concerned in this villany."[3]

The men who opposed the murder of Atahualpa were: Soto; Francisco and Diego de Chaves, brothers from Trujillo, Spain; Francisco de Fuentes; Pedro de Ayala; Diego de Mora; Francisco Moscoso; Hernando de Haro; Pedro de Mendoza; Juan de Herrada; Alonzo de Ávila; Blas de Atienzo; "y otros muchos." Among the pleas advanced by these righteous men was the argument that Atahualpa, as a sovereign Prince, could be adjudged rightly only by King Charles, theoretically his direct liege. This point was well taken, and for a time it threatened to produce a serious rift in the Spanish forces. But at length the small minority of the righteous were obliged to content themselves with writing, for the King's information, a formal protest.[4] Father Valverde, be it noted, approved of the slaying of Atahualpa and signed the documents pertinent thereto. He had found the Inca an obdurate pagan who resisted the cleric's every effort to convert him to the Faith of his destroyers.[5]

Friar Valverde, who, after all, was only performing what he and his contemporaries held to be his duty, kept up his spiritual solicitations to the end, and with outward success at the last; for Atahualpa, in order to win the comfortless privilege of being garrotted rather than burned at the stake, made the gesture of accepting baptism. Ironically enough he received the name of Francisco. On the night of August 29th, 1533, amid the smoky flare of torches and the disconsolate wailing of his women and vassals, Atahualpa was garrotted. As Estete puts it, "he died a Christian, and it is to be believed that he went to Heaven."[6] There is some doubt, however, as to the moral profundity of the Inca's conversion; for, although he was interred the next day, with Christian rites, in the church of San Francisco, at Cajamarca, he was soon dug up again, presumably on his own instructions, and his body was borne away to its final and pagan resting-place, somewhere in Quito.[7] Huáscar, murdered by the secret orders of his rival, was thus terribly avenged.

Some days after the murder of Atahualpa, Hernando de Soto, his staunchest friend among the Spaniards, returned to

Fig. 3. Air photograph of a pre-Spanish village in the Colca Valley, Peru.
By Aerial Explorations, Inc., Chrysler Bldg., New York.

Cajamarca from his detective work in the adjacent districts. Great and just was his indignation when he learned of the regicidal activities of his companions; for, during his journey, he had found no trace whatever of those formidable hosts which Atahualpa had been accused of gathering. Soto could do no more than to berate fiercely the murderers, pointing out how much simpler and better it would have been to have allowed him to accompany the Inca to Spain, where King Charles could have judged him. These sane remarks merely led Pizarro to blame Valverde and others and to cause bitter recriminations to fly between the culprits most concerned.[8]

2. The Castilians Conquer Cuzco

From that time the Conquest proper moved swiftly. In September, 1533, Pizarro and his forces left Cajamarca and moved eagerly southwards along the inter-Andean plateau. Unfortunately lack of space forbids the narration here of many picturesque and stirring events which marked the march on Cuzco, along the backbone of the doomed empire whose greatness made itself apparent to the invaders more and more as they advanced. On November 15th, 1533, Pizarro led the Castilian army triumphantly into Cuzco, having successfully passed through numerous skirmishes with Indian hosts which vainly endeavored to stay his progress.

Very soon after their arrival in Cuzco the Spaniards perceived that they had acquired a city which would disappoint them neither as regarded its wealth nor as regarded its general importance. We are told that, in the city itself, they found "very sightly things wrought with plumes and wool," as well as many magnificent buildings, some with handsome towers, and a vast quantity of gold and silver objects of the greatest variety. In one province near Cuzco were found 150 slabs of silver from 15 to 20 feet long and about 8 inches wide. Countless other wonders of equal magnitude were encountered wherever the adventurers, in their eager curiosity, penetrated.[9]

Naturally enough, perhaps, the first months of the Spanish occupation of Cuzco were occupied by the exhilarating task of seeking treasure and of distributing it among the invaders according to each man's rank and merits in the conquest. Not until March 24th, 1534, therefore, was Pizarro able to attend to two important matters. The first of these was the formal establishment of a Spanish municipality in Cuzco. The manner in which the act of foundation was performed was significant and picturesque. Drawing a poniard, Pizarro cut lines with it on the gibbet which, some days earlier, he had caused to be erected in the plaza, and he cut out a knot in one of the beams, declaring that the name of the place was The Great City of Cuzco. Thus did he make himself master of the gibbet, symbol of his power in Cuzco. Two alcaldes were inducted into office, and eight regidores, including Juan and Gonzalo Pizarro, were appointed. At the same time the Spaniards present were invited to become vecinos, or citizen-householders receiving grants of lands and Indians, in the new municipality, and to all who became such were allotted town houses, and rural possessions with Indian dependents. Nor were the interests of the Holy Catholic Faith neglected; for a cathedral church was planned to occupy the northerly side of the plaza (where the fane of the Creator-God, Viracocha, and the palace of the Inca Viracocha had stood), and also other religious houses were established, most of them resting upon pagan foundations.[10]

The second important matter attended to by Pizarro in March, 1534, was the raising up of the young Prince Manco to be the new Inca. This youth was a legitimate half-brother of the late Atahualpa, and as such he was highly valued by Governor Pizarro, who met him for the first time at Xaquixahuana (now Anta or Zúrite) while on his way to Cuzco. After that meeting, according to Pedro Pizarro, there was a deal of dastardly plotting between Don Diego de Almagro and Manco, which resulted in the violent death of various brothers and close kinsmen of the new Inca. It is not clear whether these alleged adventures in manslaughter befell before or after the formal crowning of Manco; nor is it even certain that they befell at all. If they did, the motive on Almagro's part was a wish to hear about hidden treasure, and that on Manco's was a desire to strengthen his claim to the Inca-ship by obliterating all rivals.[11]

It is certain that, when Governor Pizarro decided to make Manco a puppet Inca, he, Pizarro, was acting far more wisely than he had hitherto done with regard to the native imperial dynasty. He was quite aware that this young Prince was of the legitimate line of Peru's rulers and that, as such, the new Inca would be far more likely to control and direct the populace of Cuzco and its dependent regions than any member of the Quito or bastard branch of the dynasty could do. This consideration became all the more important when, at last, Pizarro came to understand that much of the strife with the natives through which he had passed was due to the enmity between the legitimists and the Quiteños. It now became Pizarro's plan to crown Manco and thereafter to rule the native population through him. In short, he was doing with the Inca Manco what he ought to have done with Atahualpa while the latter was still supreme in the land.

The ceremonial of Manco's coronation with the llautu or imperial fillet was carried out with ironical pomp. A great concourse of native notables partook in the gaudy festivities during which oceans of chicha (maize-beer) were drunk whilst the Inca and his greatest vassals, not to mention numerous mummies of illustrious dead persons, were carried about on gorgeous litters among the adoring multitude. Although the rites were largely in accordance with the bibulous etiquette of the Incas' court, there was a thin veneer of Christian ritual overlaid upon them, including, as a conspicuous feature, a Mass performed by Friar Vicente de Valverde, in those days the chief link between Peru and Heaven. Conspicuous also was the homage which the Inca Manco and his vassals were compelled to render unto Cæsar, that is, their new, unseen, and distant overlord, King Charles, and to the Governor Don Francisco Pizarro as his all-too-present and visible representative.[12]

3. The Coming of Don Pedro de Alvarado—and His Going

While Governor Pizarro was thus establishing his power at Cuzco, events were preparing in the Kingdom of Quito which were profoundly inimical to his interests there. Don Pedro de Alvarado y Contreras, whose renown in the conquest of Mexico is second only to that of Cortes, had established himself in Guatemala as Governor thereof and had acquired great personal wealth. Using his private resources he built up a fleet of 12 or more ships and a splendidly equipped force of 450 Spanish soldiers most of whom were of far higher social standing and much better general character than the majority of those who were then in Peru with Pizarro and Almagro. Thus prepared, Alvarado proceeded, in the early part of 1534, to what is now the coast of Ecuador, intending to take for his own the Quito region of whose riches he had received very glowing accounts.[13]

Historians, including Prescott—whose error is excusable—and Merriman—who should have known better—have assumed that Alvarado was wrongly invading Pizarro's territory.[14] The truth was quite otherwise. I have shown, on pages 25 and 39, that Pizarro's northern boundary as set forth in the Capitulación of July 26th, 1529, was an east-west line drawn through the Island of Puná. The territory which Alvarado purposed to invade and acquire lay well to the north thereof. Moreover, there was important legal justification for Alvarado's going thither. It consists of a Capitulación signed by the Queen at Medina del Campo on August 5th, 1532, the King being then in Germany,[15] in favor of Don Pedro de Alvarado, and incorporating an earlier document signed (according to the printed version of this Capitulación) by King Charles at Granada on November 17th, 1527, in which the regulations regarding conquests are laid down, with ample provisions for the spiritual and temporal welfare of the natives.[16] In this Capitulación the Queen empowers Alvarado to explore and conquer islands and mainland of the South Sea

with the idea of later acquiring primary jurisdiction over them
for himself after he shall have reported on them to the Crown.
We are told that, in preparation for this enterprise, Alvarado
had prepared a fleet of 12 ships and an army of 400 Christians,
horse and foot, all at his own cost and at an outlay of 40,000
castellanos ($80,000). The work was all to be done in accord-
ance with the incorporated document of King Charles.

Alvarado's going to what is now Ecuador was therefore
legally justified and was not, so far as he could tell, a trespass
on the territory previously assigned by the Queen to Pizarro.
At the same time, one must admit that Pizarro's attitude in
the matter was not unreasonable, as I shall now set forth.
Alvarado and his excellent following left Guatemala on January 23rd, 1534, and landed at or near Caraque in March. He
promptly put himself in touch with the garrison which Pizarro
had left at San Miguel, and, finding that there were many
gentlemen there and at Tumbez who would gladly come away
if only a ship could be found, he sent one of his own ships to
fetch as many as wished to come to him at his expense, together with their servants and horses.[17] This, as far as I can
see, is the sole approach to a trespass on Pizarro's rights attributable to Alvarado.

As a result of the contact between the newcomers and the
garrison at San Miguel news of Alvarado's arrival reached
Pizarro in mid-March, probably by chasqui-service (the superb system of relay-runners set up by the Incas). Dates are
here somewhat puzzling because we are told that, on Easter
Day (which was April 5th) Almagro was already at Saña, on
his way from Cuzco to treat with Alvarado at Quito. It is
clear, at any rate, that, in response to the tidings of Alvarado's
coming, Pizarro sent his partner, Almagro, northwards to deal
with their rival. Pursuant to a vague apprehension of some
such event as this—but not, of course, with any special reference to Alvarado—Pizarro, some months previously, had
ordered Sebastián de Benalcazar, his commandant at San Miguel, to go up to Quito and take possession of it. A possibility
that Pizarro was aware of the weakness of his claim to Quito

is indicated by Pedro Pizarro, who says that the Governor "was suspicious lest some captain come and occupy this province of Quito on the ground that it was not settled by Spaniards."[18] It was on precisely this supposition that Alvarado was proceeding.

Benalcazar, therefore, set out with a following for Quito. In some quarters there were doubts as to the loyalty of his plans. Thus, towards the middle or end of April, 1534, the situation was a triangular one. Benalcazar, who, notwithstanding the unkind suspicions of his motives, was acting in good faith, had gone up into the highlands of Quito; Almagro, urged on by his worry about Benalcazar's purposes, was pursuing him "in order to detain him until together they could arrange the necessary provisions for this war";[19] Alvarado was marching eastwardly from Puerto Viejo towards Quito.

That march of Alvarado and his brilliant company was one of the most stirring events in Andean history. First they had to flounder as best they could through the jungly, fluvial region of western Ecuador, where poisonous insects and other noxious animals fairly jostled one another in the endless thickets and swamps; then, after prolonged and agonizingly arduous progress, they arrived at the western foothills of the Andes and, by dead reckoning (their native guides having deserted), they made their ever more and more painful way onwards and upwards. The heat and dense airs of the lowlands gave way to the icy winds, deep snows, and thin air of the highlands, to which by chance was added a volcanic eruption that sounded ominously like hostile artillery and sprinkled the unhappy expeditionaries with gobs of hot mud. In these varied torments many weeks were spent and hundreds of Indian auxiliaries, scores of Spaniards, and numerous fine horses were lost through hunger, freezing, and exhaustion. At length the drooping band of adventurers, now reduced by at least a quarter of its original number, struggled out upon the inter-cordilleran plateau, probably not far from Riobamba. For sole reward of their incredibly heroic perseverance they found, not the imagined golden treasures of Atahualpa, but the imprints of horses' hoofs. Almagro and Benalcazar had arrived there ahead of them![20]

Diplomatic negotiations between Alvarado on the one side and Almagro, with Benalcazar, on the other. The situation was delicate; for each party believed itself to be in the right. Alvarado behaved with chivalrous generosity towards some horsemen of Almagro captured by him, and otherwise displayed a spirit of forbearance. Almagro, in turn, preserved the peace and aided the conversations which were being carried on between the two armies through the mediation of a Sevillian lawyer named Calderón. The result was that, on August 6th, 1534, an agreement was reached whereby, in return for 100,000 pesos of gold ($200,000), Alvarado resigned from all pretension to the rôle of conquistador in those parts. As nearly as one can judge the price was a fair one—albeit Almagro afterwards whimpered about it—and it gave Alvarado a substantial return for this trouble. The great chronicler of Mexico, Bernal Diaz del Castillo, states that Alvarado "returned from Peru a very rich man,"[21] an assertion which can be explained only on the assumption that the price paid for his withdrawal yielded Alvarado a handsome profit.

For Peru the chief result of Alvarado's going thither was the influx of a goodly number of men of superior rank, quality, and training. Nearly all of Alvarado's followers, on being given the choice of returning with him to the north or of remaining in Peru, elected to remain in the latter country. The popular conception of the character of the Spanish conquerors in Mexico and Peru fails, as a rule, to take into account the social origins of the men involved. The majority of those whom the Pizarros had recruited in Spain and at Panama (in imperfect fulfilment of the terms of the Capitulación) were a scratch lot of desperate fellows, wastrels of low caste, with a few men of good family scattered among them. Those whom Alvarado brought into Peru were, for the most part, very different. They may have been as avaricious, as ribald, and as tumultuous as the earlier conquerors, but many of them were gentlemen of superior education, endowed with intelligence too great to permit them to be lacking in praiseworthy qualities in addition to physical courage.[22]

In November and December, 1534, Alvarado, now in the rôle of a highly respected guest, went down to Pachacamac. Some time previously the Governor Don Francisco Pizarro had gone thither from Jauja with the intention of defending his interests, if need were, against the "intrusive" Adelantado of Guatemala. In the meanwhile, Cuzco was left in charge of Juan Pizarro at the head of a garrison of only ninety Spaniards, his instructions being to make himself as solid as possible with the native population. At Pachacamac there was an urbane and jovial meeting between Alvarado and Pizarro, marked by games and other diversions, after which Alvarado left Peru and returned to Guatemala.[23]

4. The Question of Cuzco

During the year 1534, also, the never-appeased rivalry between Pizarro and Almagro took a new turn. It will be remembered that the Capitulación had conferred upon Pizarro the governorship of 200 leagues of country, from the Island of Puná down to Chincha (a definition containing an ambiguity already noted and to be discussed later). The boundaries set were all west-east lines extending inland indefinitely from the coastal points designated. The question which now arose was: To whom did Cuzco belong, Pizarro or Almagro? To understand the matter we must go back a little.

It was told, in the preceding Chapter, that Hernando Pizarro left Cajamarca for Spain at some time prior to August 29th, 1533. He carried with him a part of the Royal fifth of Atahualpa's ransom, mostly in gold and silver bars, but partly in its original artistic shapes. These objects were intended to fascinate the King and to raise his enthusiasm regarding Peru to a high pitch. In the day of his arrival at San Lucar de Barrameda, January 14th, 1534, Hernando Pizarro wrote to the King, at Calatayud,[24] to report his arrival and to inform His Majesty that he was bringing to him 100,000 castellanos of gold and 5,000 marks of silver. "They come in pitchers and jars and other rare shapes which are worth seeing," says Hernando in his letter. He goes on to assure the King that nothing like the array of beauty and interest which he has prepared to show to His Majesty had ever before been possessed by any prince, and he beseeches the King to instruct the Casa de Contratación to speed him on his way to the Royal presence with the exquisite and marvellous objects which he bears.[25]

The King was not interested in archæology to any great extent. His reaction to the letter from Hernando was no more than a curt order to the Casa, from Calatayud, January 21st, 1534, to the effect that the collection might be inspected by the curious for a short while, but that, to save time, he wanted all the gold and silver objects to be made into coin except a few small, light things which Hernando Pizarro might bring to show him. A few days later, however, His Majesty reversed this order about coining.[26] Hernando Pizarro went to the Court, then at Toledo, towards the end of February, 1534, taking with him the exhibition-pieces selected by the Casa. These pieces were: Two vases of gold, one of silver, a group of two images, a stalk of maize made of gold, and a small drum garnished with gold. These objects were turned over to the Royal jewel-keeper. The King mentions no pleasure at the sight of them.[27]

Hernando Pizarro was received by the King and his Court in a manner befitting one who brought such news as he did—and so much hard cash, as well. The King was graciously pleased to grant certain favors and privileges to Pizarro and Almagro, out of which grew all the troubles soon to be related.

The most important of these Royal benefactions must now be set forth. First, there was a grant of 70 additional leagues to Pizarro to run southwards from Chincha (which is here, again, said to be 200 leagues from "Tempula" or Santiago). The territory now granted is said to belong to two Caciques (Chiefs) named Coli and Chipi. Thus, this grant did nothing to clear up the old confusion as between the 200-league element and the Chincha element. Second, there was a grant made by the King at Toledo, May 21st, 1534, in which, at the direct intercession of Hernando Pizarro, His Majesty conceded to Don Diego de Almagro a territory and government to be named New Toledo. The vagueness of definition in this grant rises to ludicrous heights because, while the northern limit of New Toledo was to be the new southern limit of Pizarro's New Castile, the former was to run "along the coast of the South Sea in an Eastwardly direction, for two hundred leagues towards the Strait of Magellan."[28] Of the territory thus crazily defined Almagro was made Governor, Captain-General, and Adelantado, under terms of privilege, recompense, and obligation similar to those set forth in the Capitulación of 1529 for Pizarro. Moreover, it was specially enjoined that Almagro and Pizarro should aid and succor one another in every possible way, each being the other's partner.

Laden with these Royal provisions, Hernando Pizarro sailed from San Lucar de Barrameda, with numerous new forces, some time after September 25th, 1534.[29]

As a result of the King's generosity with territories to which he had no title, other than Pope Alexander VI's Bull of Donation (1493), which no modern-minded person, Catholic or otherwise, takes very seriously, Pizarro's jurisdiction now ran 70 additional leagues southwards from his old southern boundary, and Almagro's territory ran 200 leagues southwards—or, according to the King, eastwards—from that. Whether Pizarro's original frontier was to be considered to run through Chincha, or whether through a point 200 leagues south from Puná, depends entirely on individual interpretation. The trouble has been, hitherto, that writers have assumed that the Santiago mentioned in the Capitulación of 1529 and in the King's documents of 1534 was the Santiago River which flows into the Pacific on the present Ecuadorian coast at about 1° 40' north. This error was corrected above on pages 25 and 39.

Because of the uncertainty regarding the exact position of the royally appointed boundary lines there was no certainty as to whether Cuzco, with all its riches and its great prestige, fell within New Castile or within New Toledo. In any case, during the last two months of 1534 Governor Pizarro had come to the conclusion that Cuzco, far from the sea and predominantly an Indian city, would not make a good capital for Spanish colonial Peru. A number of places were considered as possible capitals, and discarded. On December 6th, 1534, "the town of Trujillo was founded by the Adelantado Don Diego de Almagro, while on his way to Pachacamac."[30] There were eighty original settlers, many of them men of distinction, such as Don Diego de Agüero, Captain Don Diego de Mora y Escobar, and Don Miguel de Estete, the Chronicler, who, on December 26th, 1534, made a careful plan of the new town.[31] This distinguished foundation, in the midst of fertile country, near to mines, close to a seaport, situated so that both highland and coastland Indians could go there readily to labor,[32] grew to be of great importance as a walled city surrounded by large and rich encomiendas allotted to its vecinos or citizen-householders holding lands and Indians.[33] It appears, however, that in spite of its obvious advantages Trujillo never really stood a chance of becoming the capital of colonial Peru.

On the contrary, Jauja, which had been settled by Pizarro in 1533 while on his way from Cajamarca to Cuzco, was a very strong candidate for that honor, notwithstanding its retired highland situation. But within a year of its foundation, on November 29th, 1534, Jauja's vecinos met in cabildo or town council and declared that they were all of the opinion that the town should be set up anew somewhere on the coast, and the resolution was passed to make such a move. Accordingly, a commission was appointed on December 4th to go down to the coast and study all the likeliest localities for the new city. Pachacamac seems to have been considered for a while, but on January 8th, 1535, Pizarro appointed three commissioners who, a few days later, reported that the best place would be on the margin of the Rimac River, a site counted upon as desirable because of the good air, plentiful wood, ample fields, and its proximity to the excellent harbor of Callao. Therefore, on January 18th, 1535, the City of the Kings, commonly called Lima, was founded in the place where it now stands.[34]

From the beginning it was intended that the new city should

be the seat of Royal power in Castile's Peru. A plan was made on paper with a breadth of vision commensurate with the significance of the foundation. The streets, 40 feet wide, were laid out on the left bank of the Rimac and were made to run in perfectly straight lines crossing one another at right angles. Originally there were 117 blocks 450 feet on a side, most of them divided into 4 rectangular solares or plots for residences and other buildings. Each vecino received 1 or 2 plots in the centre of the city and additional plots in the outskirts for gardens. Pizarro reserved for himself the entire square on the northerly side of the Plaza Mayor, where the Palace of Government now stands. To the church and its priest were allotted a plot at the southeastern corner of the Plaza and the plot immediately east thereof. The streets were not laid out exactly east-west and north-south because it was well understood that, by tilting them a little, either one side or the other would be given shade at all hours of the day.[35]

It is a tragic fact that, in spite of the belief of the founders that the air would be clear and bracing, Lima itself has an atmosphere which is "opaque, misty, and almost stagnant," whilst the country in the immediate vicinity has wholesome breezes and much sunlight. This is due to the hill of San Cristóbal, just north of the city, which creates a narrow zone of "dead" air in the middle of which Lima lies.[36]

The royal grants of 1534, already mentioned, contained ample materials for a grand explosion in Peru. Nor was it long delayed. Sometime between January and April, 1535, Governor Pizarro had become convinced that something handsome ought to be done for his partner in many trials and so, acting on his own authority, he had given him permission to reside in and govern Cuzco, and he had ordered his brothers, Juan and Gonzalo Pizarro, whom he had left in charge at Cuzco, to transmit the command of that city to Almagro. Before very long advance reports, probably incomplete or inaccurate, of the new Royal donations began to arrive in Peru. Almagro either did not know of or else paid no heed to the King's grant of 70 additional leagues to Pizarro; all that seemed to him to be important was the royal concession of 200 leagues to himself, and knowledge thereof seems to have gone to his head, putting him into a haughty mood in which he was only too willing to believe those of his partisans who assured him that Cuzco was now rightly his. Governor Pizarro, meanwhile, was still at Lima and was much disturbed by the tidings of the grant now said to be made to his rival and partner. To make the graceful gesture of allowing the old man to have Cuzco as a favor from himself was one thing; to let him keep it as properly his own was quite another. Accordingly, Pizarro ordered Juan and Gonzalo Pizarro to repossess themselves of the ancient city.[37] This sudden reversal of policy on the part of the Governor naturally engendered dissensions between the Pizarrist and the Almagrist factions in Cuzco and brought them to the verge of open warfare.[38]

Not long after this the Governor arrived in Cuzco from the coast. He and Almagro met with feigned friendliness, embraced one another publicly, and settled down to a period of armed vigilance. This phase of the hostilities lasted until after June 12th, 1535, on which day the partners had a solemn meeting, after Mass had been said, in the house of Almagro. They then drew up and signed a formal contract in which they swore by everything holy to maintain their ancient friendship, to keep good faith with one another, to desist from making any representations to the King without the full knowledge and consent of both parties, and to refrain from secretly calumniating each other to the King or to others. It is a curious document, redolent of piety and treachery. Nothing is said therein concerning Cuzco.[39]

The question of Cuzco having thus been set aside for a time, Almagro decided to go to and inspect his realm of New Toledo, which lay in the region now occupied by the northerly parts of Chile and Argentina. Accordingly, Almagro began, in June or July, 1535, to make ready for his march into his new jurisdiction. True, he had only the foggiest notion of its metes and bounds, but this did not temper his hopes and his avarice. Many of the more turbulent spirits who had come into the

country with Don Pedro de Alvarado were now staunch friends
of Almagro, feeling a dull resentment against the adventurer
who had "sold" them and a corresponding attachment to that
other adventurer who had esteemed them enough to "buy"
them.[40]

At this time—July, 1535—Cuzco was the scene of many
preparations for conquests in distant regions; for, by now, the
number of Spaniards in the country had increased considerably on account of the attractive fame of the land, and a large
proportion of them were eager for adventures and for sudden
wealth. So it came about that Captain Alonzo de Alvarado,
with 300 Spaniards, was making ready to invade the region of
Chachapuyas; Captain Garcilaso de la Vega (later to be father
of the historian) was setting forth to conquer Buenaventura (in what is now the coast of Ecuador) with 250 Spaniards; Captain Juan Poncel was planning to subject the
Pacamurus (Bracamoros, the modern Jaen in northern Peru)
with 250 Spaniards; and a re-enforcement of 150 men was
being sent to Benalcazar, at Quito. Of all these military dis-
persions the chief was that headed by Governor Almagro. By
dint of prodigal gifts from his private hoards of gold and silver
—said to amount to 20 mule-loads of the former and 120 of
the latter—he formed an army whose nucleus was 550 Spaniards and which came in time to include some hundreds more,
as well as thousands of Indian auxiliaries. Thus, upwards of
1,500 of the best Spanish troops were all leaving Cuzco at
about this time. It is to be doubted if more than half that
number remained in the city; for, of course, Governor Pizarro
had many Spaniards stationed at Lima. A feature of Almagro's forces was the large number of native notables, including
at one time or another, the Inca Manco, Prince Paullu (his
brother), and the Villac Umu, High Priest of the Sun. These
personages and the others of less note made an imposing native contingent which was intended to insure the friendly reception of the Spaniards by the Inca's subjects in the regions
to be visited. This formidable army was splendidly equipped
at the great expense of its deluded leader.[41]

Almagro's invasion of Chile was an epic of perils, hardships, and hopes; but, on the whole, it was also a crescendo of disillusionment. The route followed by the army of Almagro, with its Spanish soldiers travelling in hammocks borne by sweating Indian servitors called yanaconas, with chain-gangs of Indians bearing luggage, arms, and provender, with its valuable new-born colts likewise carried in litters whilst the Indians perished under their burdens, lay through the Collao (Titicaca basin) to Paria, and thence to Tupiza and from there, over snow-smothered Andean passes, to Copiapó. Thence, with greatest difficulty due largely to the plotting of the interpreter, Felipillo, and committing many atrocities on the hapless natives and yanaconas, the expedition penetrated as far south as the present city of Santiago. The absence of Almagro from the region of Cuzco lasted from July, 1535, to March, 1537. The results were pitifully small in comparison with the almost fantastic expectations entertained and the enormous efforts made, and, at last, Almagro turned back with his embittered men, his intention being now to take Cuzco for his own.[42]

In the meantime important events were taking place in and around Cuzco. The Inca Manco, after leaving Almagro's expedition, had returned thither, and had then entered in upon a period of growing discontent. He had been puppet-emperor for nearly two years and, albeit he was apparently content enough at first and found the alien tutelage to which he was subjected neither too onerous nor too humiliating, he gradually became profoundly dissatisfied with his position. If one reads carefully certain passages in Garcilaso, in which the bitter mockery of the Inca's crowning and the mortifications which he suffered subsequently are well shown forth, one will perceive that the young Inca had hoped, from the beginning of his pseudo-reign, that his ancestors' power would eventually be restored to him in full.[43]

Exactly why the Inca should have entertained a hope so groundless is not clear; it is probably to be explained by the flatteries of the Spanish leaders who desired to keep him and

his people tranquil. A process of disenchantment inevitably
set in, however, and the proud young Inca suffered the griev-
ous experience of seeing his greatest vassals reduced to serfdom
on the newly distributed encomiendas. Even worse than this
was the ill-treatment which the Spaniards gave to the thousands of high-caste native women in Cuzco—some in their
own homes and others in the House of the Chosen Women
—and to their female servitors, all of whom, whether high or
low, were obliged to become the toys of the Spaniards. Worst
of all was the desecration of temples and palaces, some of the
latter being taken as stables. In short, the Spaniards, by their
every act, made it clear that they felt only contempt for all
that the natives held most venerable.[44]

While the Indians' unrest was mounting in Cuzco, Francisco
and Hernando Pizarro were meeting in Lima, probably in
August, 1535.[45] Soon thereafter the Governor sent his brother
to Cuzco to hold and rule it on his behalf. Hernando's conduct in the ancient capital was such that the Inca Manco came
to detest the Pizarros more than ever, with the result that,
by playing with Hernando's lust for gold, he finally succeeded
in tricking that commandant into letting him escape to Yucay
on the plea of fetching thence "a man made of gold." Thus,
in February, 1536, the great revolt of the Inca Manco began.[46]

The question of Cuzco, which was the crux of the rivalry
between the Pizarros and the Almagrist faction, had thus
created a parlous situation: The Governor was in Lima with
a considerable body of soldiers and citizens; Almagro was in
distant Chile but was soon to re-assert his claim to Cuzco; the
Inca Manco was on the point of making a final and desperate
attempt to capture the traditional capital of his empire.

5. The Siege of Cuzco by the Inca Manco

The Inca Manco had chosen a good moment for his enterprise; for, as already shown, most of the few hundred Spaniards left in Cuzco were lame and halt. Moreover, in the
month between his escape and the beginning of the onslaught

on Cuzco, he had taken steps to besiege Lima, also, and to isolate there the Governor and his immediate followers. The siege of Cuzco, therefore, had to be sustained by a small number of men led by Hernando, Juan, and Gonzalo Pizarro.

The siege was a very terrible one. In the words of Don Alonzo Enríquez de Guzmán, an eye-witness, ". . . this was the most fearful and cruel war in the world; for between the Christians and Moors there is some fellow-feeling, and both sides follow their own interests in sparing those whom they take alive, for the sake of their ransoms; but in this Indian war there is no such feeling on one side or the other, and they give each other the most cruel deaths they can invent."[47]

From March, 1536, to April, 1537, the siege continued with fluctuating fierceness. The Indian forces may have amounted to as many as 100,000 warriors. The weapons used by them included axes, clubs, lances, arrows, slings, and a weapon called ayllu, consisting of three stones joined by long cords and used to entangle the legs of the horses. Moreover, the Indians employed a stratagem particularly dangerous for horsemen which was to dig deep holes in which sharp stakes were planted, the hole then being covered with wicker-work and earth. This device, or one very like it, had been used at the battle of Agincourt, and it is not certain whether the Indians invented it anew or whether the idea came to them through soldiers' tales of ancient warfare. It is astounding that the fury of the Indians' attack and the smallness of the defending force did not combine to give an overwhelming victory to the natives. Somehow or other—according to the Spaniards the Virgin and Saint James helped in the matter—the central portion of Cuzco was successfully defended, even though many of the thatched roofs were burnt by the flaming arrows and the red-hot stones wrapped in inflammable material which were directed into the city by the besiegers, as a result of which the Spaniards had to take up their abode in tents pitched in the plaza. It is probable that they were saved only by their armor and by the terrible destruction wrought by their firearms. Hernando Pizarro and all his men fought with sublime bravery. Juan Pizarro was killed while valiantly fighting to gain the fortress of Sacsahuamán, whence many of the fiery missiles came. Later the Spaniards captured the fortress after a terrific fight at the end of which the last defender gave his life by leaping from the topmost southern wall into the valley below.

On Lady Day, September 8th, 1536, Hernando Pizarro, made desperate by the non-arrival of expected help from his brother, the Governor, sallied forth with his squad to attack the enemy. To his dismay he found on the road the heads of five Spaniards murdered by the Indians and, with them, over a thousand letters which the unfortunate men had been carrying from Lima to Cuzco. From these it was learned that Lima, Trujillo, and other coast towns were as closely beset by vast Indian armies as was Cuzco, this being the reason why no help had come from that quarter.[48]

In September, 1536, also, the Indians found themselves to be threatened with starvation because no crops had been planted for a long time. Accordingly, the Inca Manco sent off thousands of his men to attend to this vital matter. This dispersion gave the beleaguered Spaniards greater liberty of movement, with the consequence that the war now became a series of raids and skirmishes. Manco, at this period, made his headquarters at Ollantaytampu and used the whole of the Urupampa Valley up to and even beyond Yucay as his granary, leaving, however, enough troops around Cuzco to keep the Spaniards in constant danger.[49]

6. The Last Days of Governor Almagro

Late in March, 1537, Almagro, in a mood of furious disgruntlement and of envious determination to possess Cuzco, entered the neighborhood of that city with his army. His coming brought the siege of Cuzco to a close. At that time, or not long afterwards, the Inca Manco withdrew into the wilderness of Vilcapampa and established himself at Vitcos, willing to be obscure, if free. From there he conducted a guerrilla warfare against the Spaniards, harassing them as often and as severely as he could in spite of various efforts to bring him into reconciliation.[50] In that situation we will leave him for a while.

The twelvemonth between April, 1537, and April, 1538, was filled with intricate martial adventures between the Pizarrists and the Almagrists as to which we need remember only that Cuzco was tossed about between the contending parties, being held now by the one, now by the other. To the last three months of 1537 belong the involved and fruitless negotiations with regard to the ownership of Cuzco. On May 31st, 1537, from Madrid, the King had given a cédula setting forth his decision regarding the matter, the gist of the decree being as follows: First, "Tempula" or Santiago was to be exactly located (every one by now having forgotten where it was); second, 270 leagues were to be laid off on its meridian of longitude and an east-west line drawn at the point so obtained was to be the southern boundary of Pizarro's New Castile; third, a similar line 200 leagues further south was to be the southern boundary of Almagro's New Toledo.[51] If the Royal will had been carried out, the boundary between the two would have run through or near Ica, Cotahuasi, and Vilcanota, and so would have passed to the south of Cuzco, with the result that that city would have fallen rightfully to the share of Pizarro. Naturally, however, no one in those days could be as sure of this as we of today can be and, amid all the prevailing ignorance of the facts, both sides were by now resolved to have Cuzco anyway. Various negotiations, legal and otherwise, having failed to bring about a friendly agreement between the partners, war became inevitable. On December 9th, 1537, Governor Pizarro signed a notarial document in which he announced that Hernando Pizarro—lately released from capture in Almagro's hands—was first to 'pacify' Peru by punishing Almagro for his 'many crimes,' and was later to go to Court with the Royal fifths which had been collected so far.[52] Thus cunningly did Governor Pizarro plan to allay the Royal ire.

Between December, 1537, and April, 1538, there was a period replete with frantic military activities whose convolutions it is fruitless to follow. At last, on April 6th, 1538, Almagro's fate overtook him. On that day, at the terrible battle of las Salinas (the Salt-Pits), not far from Cuzco, Hernando Pizarro, aided by Gonzalo Pizarro and a force of 880 men, inflicted an overwhelming defeat upon his old enemy, who had but 600 men. The battle of the Salt-Pits was a fratricidal carnage of the most ghastly description. Special havoc was caused by a new type of bullet lately imported by the Pizarrists from Flanders by way of Spain. It was made in two parts which were linked by a wire and it was used with great effect when directed against the enemy's pikes, each double bullet smashing several pikes and giving frightful wounds.[53] Throughout the raging tumult there were deeds of bravery and deeds of cowardice, all combining in a chaos of utterly deplorable destruction.[54]

Almagro, Enríquez de Guzmán, and other leaders of that party were captured in the battle or while fleeing towards Cuzco. There followed a period of plotting and confusion during which Hernando Pizarro was master of that city. He did all that he could to make himself strong, partly by diplomatic treatment of the conquered and partly by urging some of the more unruly spirits to undertake highly dangerous exploratory missions. Young Diego de Almagro, the vanquished Adelantado's natural son by an Indian lass of Panama, was taken from his father and eventually placed in the care of Governor Pizarro by whom he was decently treated, being considered harmless. At length, on July 8th, 1538, on a host of trumped-up charges, the Adelantado Don Diego de Almagro was unjustly put to death.[55]

7. The Marquis Pizarro

Modern geographical knowledge reveals the fact that Pizarro had a better claim to Cuzco than Almagro—provided one concedes the right of King Charles to make territorial awards in Peru. It is apparent, also, that Almagro was a shade less daring in his methods than Pizarro but that his undeniable personal charm made him at least as good a leader as his rival was, albeit a tendency to be swayed by the advice of the latest speaker made him appear at times to be weak and vacillating. There is not much to choose between them, however, for they were a pretty pair of avaricious old cut-throats.

King Charles clearly prized Pizarro the more highly of the two, perchance because His Majesty was aware that more hard cash was likely to come from New Castile than from New Toledo. At any rate, the King and Queen had long been showering heraldic and nobiliary honors on Francisco Pizarro while doing almost nothing of this sort for Don Diego de Almagro. First, in a cédula of July 26th, 1529, Francisco Pizarro was made a Knight of Santiago; later, by a cédula of November 14th, 1529, he was granted the right to use his father's coat of arms. Then there was a second grant of arms made to Francisco Pizarro by the King at Valladolid on January 19th, 1536. This document speaks of Pizarro as conquering "the cacique Atabalipa, Yngua, Lord of the Province of Peru, and the caciques Quizquiz, Ituqurebaliba, Ynitatupanqui, Enminani (Rumi Ñahui), Villachuelo (Villac Umu?), Urcogaragua, and Chaliquichana (Chalcuchima)," some of whom it is impossible to identify but all of whom must have been generals of Atahualpa. It also speaks of the conquest of Cuzco, Xauxa (Jauja), Caxamalca (Cajamarca), and other cities, "all of which you have done and are doing at your own expense."[56]

All this was nothing, however, to the final honor conferred on the onetime swineherd whose activities had produced so much greatly needed wealth for the King. On October 10th, 1537, His Majesty granted to Pizarro the title of Marquis, but without territorial designation. The reason for this was that the King wished, not unreasonably, to have more complete knowledge of Peru before assigning any special lands to the marquisate. But the King, in this grant, authorizes Pizarro to call himself "the Marquis Pizarro" as he himself now does. It is to be noted that, in the second grant of arms (January 19th, 1536) there is no mention of the title of Marquis; but, in a third and final grant of arms, made at Valladolid on December 22nd, 1537, the beneficiary is styled "El Marqués D. Francisco Pizarro," and the arms then given have the coronet of a marquis as a part of the crest.

Incidentally, this document throws a blinding light on the King's attitude towards the conquest. Here, as in the earlier grant, there is a wish to celebrate the triumphs of Pizarro and to reward them at the expense of conquered chieftains. On the arms here granted seven chiefs are shown chained neck to neck with golden chains in such a way as to form an oval in the middle of which is "Atabalipa," also with a metal band around his neck, whose hands hang down into a treasure-chest on each side of him. Thus did the King heavily—if unconsciously—underscore the mercenary character of the Conquest.[57]

Thus it becomes plain that Pizarro never received a territorial designation for his marquisate, albeit the King, at different times, appointed Bishop Valverde and Governor Vaca de Castro to study the matter and assign lands for the marquisate. But Pizarro was too busy to attend to the affair and, by the time that Vaca arrived in Peru the Marquis Pizarro was already dead. His vast landed property called los Atabillos—up in the mountains northeast from Lima—had, in 1535, 20,000 vassals, or 100,000 inhabitants, but it was an encomienda, not a marquisate. It lapsed to the Crown on the grantee's death.[58]

8. The Last Years of the Marquis Pizarro

Not until after the news of the battle of the Salt-Pits reached him, causing him much joy, did the Marquis Pizarro depart from Lima, and even then he moved very slowly through the mountains towards Cuzco during the months prior to the death of his old comrade. Therefore, if he did not personally, participate in that crime, he was morally responsible for it, and also for the deceptions practised on Almagro's son and friends, because a word from him would have prevented the whole thing. The sole excuse for his offense against ordinary decency and, more especially, against the King's law, was that he believed, largely through the influence of Hernando Pizarro, that the safety of Spanish rule in Peru demanded the concentration of power in his own hands.[59]

When, at Abancay, the tidings of Almagro's execution came to him, the Marquis shed many tears.[60] They were the crocodile tears of a frightened old man aghast, too late, at the magnitude of his own temerity and at the fatal outcome of his implacable hatred. After a brief interval of natural trepidation the Marquis determined to brazen out the affair and, with a blare of trumpets and in gala raiment, he entered Cuzco, which he now regarded as belonging unconditionally to him. When it was pointed out to him by Diego de Alvarado, the Treasurer Espinar, and others, that he, Pizarro, ought now to obey not only the Royal documents with respect to Almagro's interests in New Toledo, and those of his son, but also the Will of Almagro himself, the Marquis, in a *folie de grandeur*, roared out that his government now "extended as far as Flanders, and that, therefore, he would not divide off the province of New Toledo." Thus did he flout the King's expressed will that the heritage of Almagro the Lad be guarded until his coming of age. Still worse, the Marquis permitted henchmen of his to lay violent hands upon Espinar and to hustle him out of his presence, using, at the same time, abusive language about the King and Queen.[61]

The period between Almagro's murder in July, 1538, and that of the Marquis, three years later, witnessed the perpetration by the paramount party of all the worst social and political crimes of that day. Favoritism, oppression of the Indians, and innumerable abuses prevailed. Terrible clashes between the Spaniards and the Inca Manco, as well as bitter strife between the Indians of the Collao and Charcas on one side and Gonzalo Pizarro's forces on the other, took place. In

1539 the Marquis appointed Gonzalo to be his Governor of Quito with the obligation to explore the unknown regions to the east of that city.[62] At about the same time, Hernando Pizarro was ordered to resume his old rôle of treasure-bearer. This had been planned in the latter part of 1537, as already stated. Five years had now gone by since King Charles had received a part of Atahualpa's ransom from the hands of Hernando and, in the meanwhile, the King's need of money had not grown less.

It is certain, however, that His Majesty was now receiving, little by little, definite information of the deplorable conditions in Peru. Diego de Alvarado, loyal friend of the Almagros, father and son, had at first endeavored vainly to induce the Marquis to make over to the son the rights and properties of the murdered father. That failing, he had gone to Court in order to relate the facts to the King. Furthermore, the circumstances of the elder Almagro's death had been fully reported at Court by Don Alonzo Enríquez de Guzmán and other highly connected gentlemen lately arrived from Peru.[63]

That proud nobleman, the Marquis Pizarro, who was now sole master of New Castile and of New Toledo—this last quite illegally—knew well that he had powerful enemies at Court, but he knew also that money would always abate the Royal anger, of which truth his own coat of arms, already mentioned, left him in no doubt whatever. The sum now gathered for the King was huge, and it was accompanied by a special little gratification for the Queen consisting of six fine emeralds, with a covering letter from the Marquis.[64] Hernando, after a solemn warning to his brother to beware of the discontented "men of Chile," left Lima in March, 1539, and, by a roundabout route—taken to avoid arrest at Panama—made his way to Spain, reaching the Court at Valladolid towards the middle of 1540.[65] His reception began by being a cold one, but the treasure which he bore mollified the King somewhat. The enemies of Hernando, and especially Don Diego de Alvarado, opposed him at every step. While friction was at its height Alvarado died, so opportunely that one wonders whether Her-

FIG. 4. The Anta or Zúrite or Sacsahuana or Xaquixaguana Valley.
Photograph by Isaiah Bowman, courtesy of Dr. Hiram Bingham.

FIG. 5. The Church of Santo Domingo, Cuzco, from the south.
Courtesy of W. V. Alford, Esq.

nando had become an adept at the Borgian art of court-chemistry.[66] Thereafter, the King, knowing well that Hernando had violated every decency, caused him to be imprisoned in the castle of la Mota, near Medina del Campo, although on lenient terms, where he remained for twenty years, dying some years after his release in 1560. His wealth was not taken from him, and he was allowed to marry his niece, Francisca, while in prison. Thus mildly did Charles I punish, in the person of Hernando, the Pizarro family who had so brazenly resisted his decrees.[67]

During this period, 1538–1541, two sociological processes characteristic of colonial Peru were being developed actively. The one was the founding of many Spanish towns and cities throughout the country, each one a focus of Castilian culture and power; the other was the injecting of a certain amount of Spanish blood into the population of Peru. To the first of these we shall revert in a future chapter. As for the second, it suffices to mention here that, although there were by now a few Spanish women in Peru, by far the greater number of Spanish men in that country had either married native women or taken them as concubines. Not only did the physical hardships and the inevitable perils incidental to going to Peru deter many Spanish women from accompanying their husbands, and lead them to quaint subterfuges to avoid it, but also the law tended to discourage the growth of a Spanish female population in Peru, not alone by prohibiting the going thither of unmarried women but also by authorizing marriage between Spanish men and Christianized native women.[68] Consequently, in these early days, an important class of mixed-bloods had begun to grow up, some of them being the children of marriages between Spanish men and native women, others being the children of mere concubinages. The mixture of blood was not necessarily a bad one; indeed, such men as Father Blas Valera and the Inca Garcilaso de la Vega prove that it could be a very good one. At all events, the mestizos of Peru came to form a large and important class in colonial society. Subsequently, as we shall see further on, greater numbers of Spanish women came into the country and helped in the formation of its small but powerful pure white uppermost class.

During 1540 and 1541 the Marquis and his party persisted in an increasingly harsh attitude towards the wretched and hopeless "men of Chile" whose unassuaged hatred and envy were notorious. In those days the son of the Adelantado, known as Don Diego de Almagro the Lad, was the titular head of the Almagrist faction. His character, although not lacking in courage, was such as to make him a difficult house-guest so that, after successively visiting the Marquis and Captain Francisco de Chavez, the Marquis's great friend, he set up in quarters of his own where he speedily gathered about him thirty or forty of his father's most desperate followers. They looked up to him, in spite of his being only nineteen or twenty, because the late Adelantado had intended him to inherit all his posts, possessions, and privileges, and in this intention the Crown had concurred. Bad though most of the members of this group were, they are to be pitied; for their poverty was so acute that there was only one cloak for ten or twelve of them, "and when one went out with it on," says Cieza, "the others remained indoors, so that the cloak was always in use."[69] To make matters still worse, the Marquis not only deprived the Lad of his chief estate but also allowed his own followers to browbeat and insult the unfortunate men of Chile in every way. Furthermore, he went out of his way to show his scorn of them by ostentatiously ignoring all the many warnings of his peril which he received.[70]

About the middle of 1540 the King, spurred on by a realization that he must do something drastic in order to re-establish his own authority in Peru, appointed the Licentiate Don Cristóbal Vaca de Castro, an Oidor (Judge) of the Audience (High Court) of Valladolid, to go to Peru and restore order. The appointment was engineered by friends of the Marquis in Spain, and it is impossible to regard it as a serious move against Pizarro for the reason that one of Vaca's duties was to be that of selecting lands and Indians wherewith to territorialize Pizarro's marquisate. Indeed, the Licentiate Vaca was empowered only to investigate and to report on what he found, with the added proviso that, on the Marquis's death, he was to become Governor of Peru. Almagro the Lad, Juan de Herrada, and other leaders of the Chile party were informed in private letters that they had little to hope for from Vaca.[71] The almost comical mildness of the measure taken by King Charles in sending Vaca to Peru with such limited powers shows clearly that His Majesty was not yet bitterly hostile to the Pizarros from whom he had derived such solid benefits.

The leader among the Marquis's enemies was Juan de Herrada and, undoubtedly, this man and his confidants were determined to kill the Conqueror. There is no real evidence that Almagro the Lad was personally implicated in the plot to an extent greater than that of sheltering the plotters in his house. There is, indeed, evidence that he thought that his friends intended merely to seize the Marquis in order to prevent his killing them.[72]

The death of the Marquis was sudden, terrible, and bloody. On Sunday, June 26th, 1541, at noon, Juan de Herrada led a band of twenty ruffians into the palace, having passed through the Plaza which was filled with people who looked on and heard their shouts for vengeance without moving a finger to halt them. In the palace a sharp scuffle took place between the assassins and twenty friends of Pizarro, of whom fifteen were fully as unsavory as their opponents. The Marquis was stabbed to death, along with his brother, Francisco Martín de Alcántara, his loyal and worthy adherent, Francisco de Chavez, and two noble and devoted young pages.[73]

Notes to Chapter III

1 Sancho, 1917, pp. 12–13. P. Pizarro, 1921, I, pp. 215–217. Anonymous Conquest of 1534, fols. 6 verso, 7 recto. Estete, 1918, p. 29.

2 P. Pizarro, 1921, I, p. 217, speaks of Felipillo as an instrument of the Devil. See also: Zárate, Bk. II, Ch. vii; Cabello, Pt. III, Ch. xxxiii, pp. 782–784; Garcilaso, Pt. II, Bk. I, Ch. xxxvi. Also: Markham's notes, Xerez, 1872, pp. 102–103. Prescott, 1847, I, pp. 476–482.

3 Fernández de Oviedo, Pt. III, Bk. VIII, Ch. xxii. The priest in question

was probably Valverde, the notary most likely Sancho. See also: Garcilaso, Pt. II, Bk. I, Ch. xxxvii; P. Pizarro, 1921, I, pp. 216–219; Sancho, 1917, pp. 13–17; Zárate, Bk. II, Ch. vii; Estete, 1918, p. 29; Anonymous Conquest of 1534, fols. 7 recto and verso. The notes given by Markham on pp. 102–105 of Xerez, 1872, are highly important. Prescott, I, pp. 474–483.

⁴ Markham, on p. 103 of Xerez, 1872, traces the subsequent careers of these men. He points out, moreover, that Soto, Francisco de Chaves, Fuentes, and Mendoza received portions of Atahualpa's ransom, but that their doing so was not due to hypocrisy—as some have supposed—but to the fact that the plan to murder Atahualpa had not then arisen. The other protestors do not appear on the list of spoil-receivers, probably because they were of Almagro's party. See: Garcilaso, Pt. II, Bk. I, Ch. xxxvii. Prescott, I, p. 284, cites Vattel (Bk. II, Ch. iv) as saying that the trial of Atahualpa by his inferiors was "a manifest outrage on the law of nations."

⁵ P. Pizarro, 1921, I, pp. 218–219. Sancho, 1917, pp. 16–17. Xerez, 1872, pp. 101–105. Herrera, Dec. V, Bk. III, Ch. iv. Garcilaso, Pt. II, Bk. I, Chs. xxxvi, xxxvii, and xxxviii. Prescott, I, pp. 484–487. So far as I know—and I have looked widely—Friar Valverde has found but one apologist among writers on Peruvian history. This is an obscure Franciscan, Friar Buenaventura de Salinas y Córdoba, a Limeñan aristocrat who wrote a ponderous tome entitled "Memorial de las Historias del Nuevo Mundo," published in Lima in 1631. Although I spent many hours making copious notes on this book, from the copy of it in the Biblioteca Nacional (Madrid)—the only copy of it ever seen by me— I find nothing in those notes touching upon Valverde. There is, however, a long quotation from Salinas on p. 78 of the Anonymous "Noticias Chronológicas de la Gran Ciudad del Cuzco" (MS. formerly in my library and now in The New York Public Library), under the year 1541. Translated, the passage runs thus: "He (Valverde) was the first man in Peru who erected temples to God, who dedicated Altars to Him, the first who consecrated unguents and chrism, who spoke against the death of Atahualpa King of Peru, who baptized him; the first who, for the propagation of the Gospel, passed through great trials until he lost his life on the occasion when barbarous Indians slew him with blows, in hatred against the Holy Catholic Faith which he was preaching to them." Elsewhere, on pp. 50–51, the author of the "Noticias Chronológicas" tries to make out that Atahualpa failed to complete the ransom. But this argument is vitiated by Pizarro's own proclamation on the subject.

⁶ Estete, 1918, p. 29. The baptismal name of Atahualpa is usually said to have been Juan, but Don Marcos Jiménez de la Espada, citing Santa Cruz Pachacuti-yamqui Salcamayhua and also a document of 1555, Lima, proves that the correct name was Francisco. See: Santa Cruz, 1873, pp. 118–119, and 1879, p. 326.

⁷ Xerez, 1872, pp. 102–106. Fernández de Oviedo, Pt. III, Bk. VIII, Ch. xxii. López de Gómara, Ch. cxviii. Sancho, 1917, pp. 15–19. P. Pizarro, 1921, I, pp. 218–220. Garcilaso, Pt. II, Bk. II, Ch. iii. Prescott, I, pp. 486–490, and Appendix X.

⁸ Fernández de Oviedo, Pt. III, Bk. VIII, Ch. xxii; also Appendix X of Prescott. P. Pizarro, 1921, I, pp. 219–220. López de Gómara, Ch. cxviii. (These writers deprecate the murder of Atahualpa.) Xerez, 1872, pp. 104–109. Sancho,

1917, pp. 16–19. Estete, 1918, p. 29. (These three tend to condone the outrage.)

9 Estete, 1918, pp. 31–32, 34. Sancho, 1917, pp. 99–105, 127–130. P. Pizarro, 1921, I, pp. 248–253, 264–277. López de Gómara, Ch. cxxv. Garcilaso, Pt. II, Bk. II, Ch. vii.

10 Sancho, 1917, pp. 130–132. P. Pizarro, 1921, I, pp. 250–251, 278–279. Ruiz Naharro, 1917, p. 208. Montesinos, Anales, Año 1534, 1906, I, p. 79. Garcilaso, Pt. I, Bk. VII, Chs. ix–xii, gives a full account of how Cuzco was allotted among the Spaniards; see also his Pt. I, Bk. III, Ch. xx, and Bk. VI, Ch. xxi.

11 P. Pizarro, 1921, I, pp. 268–271. Cobo, Bk. XII, Ch. xx, 1890–1893, III, pp. 203–204.

12 Sancho, 1917, pp. 104–113. P. Pizarro, 1921, I, pp. 275–278. Estete, 1918, pp. 34–35, gives a very lively, but in spots rather repulsive, account of the coronation carousings. It is to be noted that Sancho makes it appear that the crowning of Manco took place as early as Christmas, 1533, but the other authorities date it in March, 1534. Prescott, I, pp. 517–527 and II, pp. 3–5, covers this general period in great detail.

13 Diaz del Castillo, Bk. XVII, Ch. ccxiv, 1908–1916, V, pp. 320–323.

14 Prescott, II, p. 11. Merriman, III, p. 570. In January, 1932, I attempted to discuss this point, and others, with Professor Merriman, but I was greeted with the statement that this learned man had never heard of Pizarro! So I gave it up in despair of both his learning and his manners.

15 Foronda, 1914, p. 363.

16 This significant document seems to have been overlooked by modern writers, so much so that I do not recall having seen it cited. It is printed in CDI, Vol. XXII, pp. 307–324, Madrid, 1874. There is something wrong about the place and date of Charles's document as herein incorporated, because, according to Foronda, pp. 298–299, Charles was in Burgos throughout November, 1527. But Foronda, pp. 279–280, shows that Charles was in Granada on November 17th, 1526, and he cites what appears to be this very cédula as evidence for that day.

17 Alvarado, 1884. This is a letter sent to some very high official in Spain, probably Don Francisco de los Cobos, who was secretary to King Charles and a great friend and patron of Alvarado. It is dated from Puerto Viejo on March 10th, 1534.

18 P. Pizarro, 1921, II, p. 286.

19 Sancho, 1917, p. 139.

20 Herrera, Dec. V, Bk. VI, Chs. i–ii, vii–xii. Fernández de Oviedo, Pt. III, Bk. VIII, Ch. xx. López de Gómara, Ch. cxxviii. Garcilaso, Pt. II, Bk. II, Chs. i–ii, ix–x. P. Pizarro, 1921, II, pp. 286–287. Cieza, Pt. I, Ch. xlii, 1864, pp. 156–157. Ruiz Naharro, 1917, pp. 208–210. Prescott, II, pp. 10–18.

21 Diaz del Castillo, 1908–1916, V, p. 320. The date of the agreement is set down in a document now in the Library of Congress, being one of the documents in the great collection given by Mr. E. S. Harkness.

22 Cieza, Pt. I, Ch. xlii. Riva-Agüero, 1921, pp. 59–73.

23 P. Pizarro, 1921, II, pp. 286–289. Sancho, 1917, pp. 136–140. Cieza, Pt. I, Chs. xlii and lxxi. Garcilaso, Pt. II, Bk. II, Ch. xi, erroneously states that Alvarado and Almagro went to Cuzco. Prescott, II, pp. 19–22.

²⁴ Foronda, 1914, p. 383, makes Charles arrive there on January 20th, 1534, for one day only. Cabildos, III, p. 127.

²⁵ Hernando Pizarro to the King, 14th January, 1534, in Cabildos, III, p. 127.

²⁶ The two letters or decrees from the King to the Casa, one from Calatayud, January 21st, the other from Sigüenza, January 26th, 1534, appear in Cabildos, III, pp. 127–129.

²⁷ The King to the Casa, March 7th, 1534, from Toledo, in Cabildos, III, pp. 129–130.

²⁸ This grant is dated from Toledo on May 4th, 1534, and is said to be based on a relation by Sebastián Rodríguez, acting on behalf of Francisco Pizarro. (See Cabildos, III, pp. 147–148.) The identity of Coli and Chipi is problematical. They may have been minor chieftains in the region of Chincha, of whom there were several (see Means, 1931, p. 194); or Coli and Chipi may have been attempts at the names Cari and Chipana, who were great rival chiefs in the Collao or Titicaca basin in pre-Incaic times. (See: Cieza, Pt. I, Chs. c and cii; Garcilaso, Pt. I, Bk. III, Ch. xiv; Means, 1931, p. 200.) The grant to Almagro appears in Cabildos, III, pp. 148–154. A cédula, dated from Valladolid, July 19th, 1534, confirmed the grant. (See: Cabildos, III, pp. 154–157; Cieza, 1923, Ch. xxxix.)

²⁹ This is the date of the cédula bidding him to go to Peru and providing pilots for his ships. (Cabildos, III, p. 130.)

³⁰ Pizarro to the King, from Pachacamac, January 1st, 1535, in Cabero, 1906, pp. 367–371.

³¹ Cabero, 1906, pp. 343 and 345–349. In his masterly monograph Señor Cabero cites many source materials. On p. 344 he tells us that the King, by cédulas from Valladolid on November 23rd and December 7th, 1537, raised Trujillo to the rank of city and gave it a coat of arms.

³² Pizarro's letter, already cited, in Cabero, 1906, p. 370.

³³ Cabero, 1906, pp. 486–490.

³⁴ Important documents relative to all this will be found in Cabildos, I, pp. 1–13. See also: Cobo, 1882, Chs. i–v; Montesinos, *Anales,* Año 1535, 1906, I, p. 86; Garcilaso, Pt. II, Bk. II, Ch. xvii; Markham's notes and plan in Cieza, 1918, p. 104; Prescott, II, pp. 22–25.

³⁵ Cobo, 1882, Ch. viii. Unánue, 1815, p. 3. Mrs. Zelia Nuttall has published some documents interesting in this connection. They are dated from San Lorenzo del Escorial on July 3rd, 1573. In them Philip II laid down the rules for the planning of new towns, and it is clear that he must have been inspired to some extent by such cities as Lima and Trujillo, already founded. Consult: Nuttall, 1921–1922.

³⁶ Unánue, 1815, pp. 10–12.

³⁷ P. Pizarro, 1921, II, pp. 290–291. Garcilaso, Pt. II, Bk. II, Ch. xix. Prescott, II, pp. 30–33.

³⁸ P. Pizarro, 1921, II, pp. 291–295. Garcilaso, Pt. II, Bk. II, Ch. xix.

³⁹ This agreement or contract appears in Appendix XI of Prescott. See also: P. Pizarro, 1921, II, p. 295; Garcilaso, Pt. II, Bk. II, Ch. xix; Prescott, II, pp. 34–36; Amunátegui, 1862, pp. 81–82; Markham, on p. xvii of Cieza, 1923.

[40] Amunátegui, 1862, p. 80, where he cites: Fernández de Oviedo, Bk. XLVI, Ch. xx and Bk. XLVII, Ch. iv. See also: Zárate, Bk. III, Chs. i and ii; Garcilaso, Pt. II, Bk. II, Ch. xx.

[41] One cannot, of course, vouch for the accuracy of the figures given here for the various expeditions. As for the cost of that of Almagro, it is said that it amounted to the vast sum of 1,500,000 pesos gold and that the prices of necessary things were then enormous as, for instance: a horse from 7,000 to 8,000 pesos gold; a coat of mail, 1,000; a shirt, 300; a Negro slave, 2,000. See: Fernández de Oviedo, Bk. XLVII, Chs. i–vi. For the events related above see: P. Pizarro, 1921, II, pp. 295–296; Garcilaso, Pt. II, Bk. II, Chs. xix and xx; Herrera, Dec. V, Bk. VII, Ch. ix; J. I. Molina, Pt. II, Bk. I, Ch. v; Prescott, II, pp. 36–38; Amunátegui, 1862, pp. 82–84, 94–100.

[42] Herrera, Dec. V, Bk. X, Chs. i and ii; Fernández de Oviedo, Bk. XLVII, Chs. ii–iv and ix; Zárate, Bk. III, Ch. i; Garcilaso, Pt. II, Bk. II, Chs. xxi and xxii; Amunátegui, 1862, pp. 101–133. One of the few bright spots in the expedition of Almagro to Chile was the final discovery of all the crimes committed by the nefarious interpreter, Felipillo, who, after a full confession of his machinations against Atahualpa and all his other shameful acts, was slain and quartered.

[43] Read especially the last part of Ch. xii in Garcilaso, Pt. II, Bk. II, and the middle part of Ch. xxii of the same Book, where Garcilaso shows that the importunities of the Inca were a chief cause of Governor Pizarro's leaving Cuzco not long after Almagro did so.

[44] Prescott, II, pp. 40–41, cites and quotes an anonymous contemporary record, which I have been unable to identify, where the details of Spanish misconduct are set forth with indignation creditable to the narrator. See also: Enríquez de Guzmán, 1862, Ch. xliv.

[45] The date of Hernando's return to Peru is not, I think, exactly known. It must have taken place in early August, 1535, for Garcilaso, Pt. II, Bk. II, Ch. xxii, citing López de Gómara, Ch. cxxxiii, says that Francisco Pizarro was still at Cuzco when he heard of Hernando's arrival at Tumbez. Moreover, the same tidings reached Almagro, for the first time and in vague terms, shortly after his leaving Tupiza, in September of that year. See: Amunátegui, 1862, p. 104. Zárate, Bk. III, Ch. iii, confirms this date.

[46] P. Pizarro, 1921, II, pp. 298–300. Garcilaso, Pt. II, Bk. II, Ch. xxiii. Zárate, Bk. III, Ch. iii. Prescott, II, pp. 41–45.

[47] Enríquez, 1862, p. 101. See also: P. Pizarro, 1921, II, pp. 300–302; Garcilaso, Pt. II, Bk. II, Chs. xxiii and xxiv.

[48] Enríquez, 1862, pp. 98–104. P. Pizarro, 1921, II, pp. 302–315. Garcilaso, Pt. II, Bk. II, Chs. xxiv–xxviii. Valverde, 1539, MS., pp. 9–33. Prescott, II, pp. 51–72. Bingham, 1912; 1922, pp. 170–171.

[49] P. Pizarro, 1921, II, pp. 325–331.

[50] Valverde, 1539, MS. P. Pizarro, 1921, II, pp. 386–389 and 396–412. Garcilaso, Pt. II, Bk. III, Chs. i and ii. Cieza, 1923, pp. 232–237 and 246. Prescott, II, pp. 73, 91, 101, and 146–147. Bingham, 1912, pp. 6–13; 1922, pp. 170–178.

[51] This document is printed in Cabildos, III, pp. 167–168.

[52] Cieza, 1923, pp. 153–167. P. Pizarro, 1921, II, pp. 368–374. Enríquez, 1862, pp. 117–122. Maggs-Huntington, pp. 1–6.

[53] Garcilaso, Pt. II, Bk. II, Ch. xxxvii. See also Markham's note in Cieza, 1923, p. 199. Prescott, II, pp. 111–118.

[54] Enríquez, 1862, pp. 126–130. Cieza, 1923, pp. 196–202. P. Pizarro, 1921, II, pp. 378–383. Garcilaso, Pt. II, Bk. II, Chs. xxxvi and xxxvii. Zárate, Bk. III, Ch. xi.

[55] P. Pizarro, 1921, pp. 381–386. Enríquez, 1862, pp. 131–134. Cieza, 1923, pp. 202–223. Garcilaso, Pt. II, Bk. II, Chs. xxxviii–xxxix. Espinar, 1900, p. 210. Prescott, II, pp. 108–131.

[56] Nobiliario, 1892, pp. 40–43.

[57] Nobiliario, 1892, pp. 44–49. See also: Cabildos, II, pp. 159–188; Torres Saldamando, 1880; Moses, 1914, I, pp. 109–110, notes; Larrabure y Unánue, 1893, pp. 325–340; Pizarro y Orellana, 1639, Discurso legal, pp. 6, 10, 72, and *passim;* Llano y Zapata, 1759, p. 146. Older writers who provide data on this subject include: Zárate, Bk. III, Ch. v; Herrera, Dec. VI, Bk. VI, Chs. ix and xiii; Garcilaso, Pt. II, Bk. II, Ch. xxii, where he states, erroneously, that when Hernando Pizarro returned to Peru (about August, 1535), he brought to Francisco Pizarro the title of Marqués de los Atabillos, in saying which the Inca copies from and cites López de Gómara, Ch. cxxxiii; but later, in Pt. II, Bk. V, Ch. xxxvi, Garcilaso quotes Gonzalo Pizarro as saying to President Gasca (in 1548) that the Marquis had the title only, without territorial designation. Further citations are given by Torres Saldamando in the pages of Cabildos, already cited. Cieza, 1923, p. 245, tells us that the news of Pizarro's being made a marquis was brought to Peru by a messenger named Ceballos, who had taken to Spain the account of Pizarro's deeds in result of which the title was given. See also: Larrabure, 1893, p. 327; Cabildos, III, p. 220.

[58] Torres Saldamando, 1880. Cabildos, II, pp. 167–173, 179–180. All the children of the Marquis Pizarro were bastards, but two of them were legitimatized by the King. These were Gonzalo, who died young, and Francisca, children of Doña Inez Huaylas Ñusta, daughter of the Inca Huayna Capac. Doña Francisca later married her uncle, Hernando, and their great-grandson became, in 1622, the first Marquis of la Conquista, which title survives into our own day. See Cabildos, II, pp. 186–188.

[59] Espinar, 1900, pp. 210–211, shows very clearly the extent of Pizarro's moral responsibility. See also: Zárate, Bk. III, Ch. xii; Garcilaso, Pt. II, Bk. II, Chs. xxxvii–xxxix; P. Pizarro, 1921, II, pp. 379–383; Cieza, 1923, pp. 198–208, 214–223; Prescott, II, pp. 110–130; Moses, 1914, II, pp. 116–117.

[60] P. Pizarro, 1921, II, p. 386. Cieza, 1923, pp. 227–228.

[61] Espinar, 1900, pp. 212–213. Cieza, 1923, pp. 230–231.

[62] P. Pizarro, 1921, II, pp. 414–415. Cieza, 1923, pp. 250–269.

[63] Cieza, 1918, pp. 79–81. Enríquez, 1862, pp. 134–160. Espinar, 1900, pp. 212–214.

[64] From Cuzco, February 28th, 1539. Cabildos, III, p. 220.

[65] P. Pizarro, 1921, II, pp. 395–396. Garcilaso, Pt. II, Bk. II, Ch. xl. Zárate, Bk. III, Ch. xii.

[66] Herrera, Dec. VI, Bk. VIII, Ch. ix. Garcilaso, Pt. II, Bk. II, Ch. xl.

[67] López de Gómara, Ch. cxlii. Pizarro y Orellana, 1639, pp. 341–342. Prescott, II, pp. 138–143.

[68] See Teran, 1930, Ch. iii and Haring, 1918, p. 102, note.

[69] Cieza, 1918, pp. 52–53. Herrera, Dec. VI, Bk. VIII, Ch. vi. Prescott, II, p. 173, doubts this story, but to me it seems quite credible.

[70] Cieza, 1918, p. 53. Zárate, Bk. IV, Ch. vii.

[71] Cieza, 1918, pp. 79–82. P. Pizarro, 1921, II, pp. 413–414, makes it clear that the men of Chile meant to kill Vaca if he did not kill the Marquis. The long delay in his coming drove them to extreme measures. Prescott, II, pp. 143–144.

[72] See Markham's notes, Cieza, 1918, pp. xli–xlii, and the Lad's letter to the Audience of Panama, dated from Lima on July 14th, 1541, printed in Prescott's Appendix XII.

[73] Important details will be found in Cieza, 1918, pp. 94–110. See also: P. Pizarro, 1921, II, pp. 414–423; Zárate, Bk. IV, Chs. vii and viii. Prescott, II, pp. 179–184.

CHAPTER IV

THE CIVIL WARS AND OTHER TUMULTS, 1541–1569

1. *Governor Vaca de Castro and Diego de Almagro, the Lad*

THE coming of the Castilians and of their Christianity to
the Andean area had thus far resulted chiefly in turmoil, bloodshed, and every other kind of unrighteousness, all in the
strongest possible contrast to the settled polity and orderly
administration which had prevailed under the Incas. The Royal
authority had been flouted frequently, and a situation had
arisen which King Charles, quite naturally, found to be intolerable. In a somewhat feeble effort to end it he appointed,
as has been told, the Licentiate Don Cristóbal Vaca de Castro,
with orders to co-operate with the Marquis Pizarro—whom,
rather definitely, the King favored—in restoring peace to Peru.
Furthermore, Vaca bore authority to succeed Pizarro as Governor in case of Pizarro's death.

Vaca de Castro, after a terrible voyage from Panama in
March and April, 1541, entered his jurisdiction by way of Calí
and Popayán in what are now the highlands of Colombia. Illness and the necessity for dealing with various delicate political situations in those parts delayed him in his southward
progress so that he was still at Popayán when, one Sunday
morning, at Mass, he was told of the murder of the Marquis.
The news was brought by Lorenzo de Aldana, acting governor
of Quito (in the absence of Gonzalo Pizarro), who had made
a frantic journey thence northwards in order to inform Vaca
of the affair.[1]

In the meanwhile, at Lima, Diego de Almagro the Lad had
assumed titular leadership of the party opposed to Vaca, the
King's representative. The real direction of that party lay,

however, with Juan de Herrada and that unsavory clique
which had killed Pizarro. The campaign which followed between the two parties was extremely intricate in its details,
but the main facts are these: Vaca, in the north, and moving
southwards, was making it known that he was the representative of the King's law and that, as such, he was forming an
army wherewith to combat the Almagrists; at the same time,
in the south of Peru—at Cuzco, in the Charcas, and at Arequipa—other men, chief among them General Pedro Alvarez
Holguín, Captain Alonzo de Alvarado, and Captain Pedro
Anzures de Campo Redondo, were doing their utmost to aid
the Royal cause in those quarters. Gradually these forces
drew together, finally uniting, after amazing marches through
the mountains, at Eastertide, 1542, near Huaraz, in the beautiful valley now known as the Corridor of Huaylas.[2]

The Lad's party was far from prosperous during this period.
Strenuous but fruitless efforts were made to attack and defeat
one or another of the enemy's contingents; dissensions among
the Almagrist leaders were numerous, incessant, and fatal, so
much so that, after the leaders had all been murdered, the
Lad finally found himself alone in command, his former guides
having met violent ends. By now he had gained possession
of Cuzco, but it did him little good because Governor Vaca,
after ordering his now strongly united army to march to
Jauja, had gone down to Lima and had established His Majesty's authority there, an easy thing to do as the citizens were
profoundly weary of turmoil. The Royalist army, on arriving
at Jauja, laid in supplies of all kinds, especially of pikes ex-
cellently made of wood from the eastern forests, so that, when
Vaca rejoined them, they were well equipped.[3]

The Lad, finding Cuzco an uncomfortable abode on account
of the large body of public opinion contrary to his cause,
moved his quarters to the vicinity of the Apurimac bridge and
there he received word from the Inca Manco, at Vitcos, that
he, the Inca, would give aid against Vaca because of his, the
Inca's, hatred against the Pizarros and all who took their
part. Thus encouraged the Lad proceeded northwards as far

as Vilcas, where he and his army took up their quarters in the ancient buildings of that place.[4] From Vilcas, on September 4th, 1542, the Lad and his officers addressed two letters to Governor Vaca in which they eloquently protested their loyalty to God and the King and besought Vaca not to make war upon them for fear of dire consequences.[5] There is something rather touching about these letters because of the obvious belief of their writers that their cause was just; and yet they were in reality so very wrong. They had murdered the King's Governor (Pizarro), and they were even now, in spite of their protestations of loyalty, opposing the King's new representative. The letters did no good. On the contrary, they seem to have convinced Vaca that the other side was weakening and to have led him into negotiations with them, in the course of which he dishonorably sent spies among them while peace-terms were being discussed.[6]

This last act naturally infuriated the Almagrists and stiffened their resistance. Events now moved swiftly to September 16th, 1542, on the day of the terrible battle of Chupas. As Sir Clements Markham has shown, Chupas is a narrow spur jutting northwards into a valley some eight miles south of Huamanga (Ayacucho).[7] There Vaca de Castro and his able officers overwhelmed the Almagrist forces. In the strife Pedro de Candia, chief of artillery for the Lad, was treasonable and was slain by his young commander; there were, besides, some 240 deaths on the field. When the engagement was concluded, the Governor made a careful search among the many prisoners for murderers of the Marquis, and those whom he found were quartered forthwith. Over 30 Almagrists were killed after the battle, either at Huamanga or while fleeing towards Cuzco. The Lad was taken while trying to get away to the Inca Manco at Vitcos and was dragged back to prison at Cuzco under the orders of Captain Garcilaso de la Vega, father of the historian.[8] A few days later the Lad was publicly executed on the gibbet in the Plaza, where his father had died more than a year earlier.[9]

2. The Adventure of Gonzalo Pizarro

The rule of Vaca de Castro after the death of the Lad was, on the whole, good, except for a perhaps natural tendency towards too-great splendor combined with some degree of avarice and favoritism.[10] Nevertheless, he did make earnest and largely successful efforts to restore order. In addition, he sent many exploring and conquering expeditions into outlying regions to the south, southeast, and east, which had the result of carrying Spanish culture further and further in those directions. In short, Vaca's rule was so good as to impel Cuzco and other cities to write to the King begging that he be kept long in the office which he filled so well.[11] Unfortunately the King had planned otherwise.

We must now go back nearly three years in order to trace the career of Gonzalo Pizarro who presently becomes the central figure in Peru's historical tragi-comedy. It will be remembered that he had been appointed by the Marquis to be Governor of Quito and that he had been specially ordered to conduct an expedition into the "Land of Cinnamon," supposed to lie in the sylvan wildernesses east of the Quito highlands.

Departing from Quito on Christmas Day, 1539, with a well equipped army of eager adventurers, Gonzalo penetrated the eastern wilds as far as the confluence of the Coca and Napo Rivers. Great hardships were suffered and much heroism was displayed, as well as one piece of cowardly treachery. Of this last Francisco de Orellana was guilty. Deserting the main body of the expedition, and stealing a little ship into the building of which his companions had put their blood and sweat, he sailed away down the River Napo and thence by the Amazonian system of rivers, to the Atlantic coast. Thus, though unworthily, Orellana was the first Spaniard to cross South America by water. At last, after two and a half years of hideous tribulations, during which Gonzalo Pizarro amply demonstrated his many soldierly virtues, the battered remnant of the expedition crawled back to Quito, arriving there in June, 1542.[12]

On coming out of the wilds, Gonzalo learned that his brother, the Marquis, had been slain a year before, that Vaca de Castro was ruling Peru, and that Aldana and others of his own soldiers whom, as Governor, he had left in Quito, were upholding the new régime. He, Gonzalo, wrote at once to Vaca offering his support, but the Governor was then trying to treat with the Lad, and he politely snubbed Gonzalo, bidding him to stay where he was.[13] Gonzalo Pizarro's discontentment with Vaca was subsequently allayed by the Governor's tactful arguments, and finally Gonzalo retired to his estates near La Plata where he remained for some time, deriving great wealth from his mines and other properties there.[14]

As already hinted, important developments were taking place in Spain during these years. King Charles, long profoundly uneasy regarding many things in his American possessions, had lately come under the influence of Friar Bartolomé de las Casas, sometimes called "The Apostle of the Indians." Being incessantly worried and bothered by a too-great number of realms in Europe, King Charles could not devote any large proportion of his attention to the problems of his American kingdoms. Therefore, he became peculiarly accessible to any one who had a plausible scheme for rehabilitating the Royal authority therein, and for re-establishing the Royal benevolence, all the more so if the scheme included changes which promised solid monetary rewards to the chronically necessitous monarch.

It chanced that Casas was the man who seized upon the Royal mind and, for a time, concentrated it upon the American problems. His method was a simple one, consisting of moral indignation which expressed itself in highly sensational printed propaganda whose eloquence often bordered on the delirious. For instance, Casas, who had never been in Peru, described Francisco Pizarro as an abominable demon who laid waste whole cities and countries. Casas managed to create a legend, nurtured by that wrathfulness of his never wholly free from frenzy, to the effect that, because the Spaniards were hardly better than interlopers in America, it behooved them at least to treat the native peoples with justice and mercy. This view was shared by many, and even the King came to acknowledge the moral obligations implied by it. Altogether, it is not strange that Friar Bartolomé, a man who was known to be saintly and disinterested, who was believed to be learnéd, and who had travelled more widely in America than most men of his day, should have had sufficient influence with King Charles to induce him to promulgate the "New Laws" whereby the hitherto vague and theoretical benevolence of the Crown was given definition and specific application.[15]

Casas, we must remember, represented but one of two almost equally powerful parties at Court. He was the leader of the humanitarian group which always tended to emphasize the moral responsibilities of the Crown towards its American subjects and which, in its more extreme manifestations, even denied the right of the Spaniards to enter America.[16] Stoutly opposed to this group was the other which, largely on dogmatic grounds, sustained the legitimacy of Alexander VI's donation (1493) and the resultant absolute rights of the Crown of Castile in the Western Hemisphere. The most distinguished exponent of this school of thought was, years after the time now under discussion, the celebrated jurist, Dr. Juan Ginés de Sepúlveda, the gist of the school's belief being that the wide lands in America were given to the Crown as a recompense from God (through Alexander, his vicar upon earth) for all the devotion displayed during the centuries of the Reconquest in Spain.[17] It was against the background formed by this clash of diametrically opposed opinions that the New Laws were framed and sent forth for enforcement.

On November 20th, 1542, at Barcelona, King Charles and his mother, Queen Juana, issued the New Laws, the result of that Royal charitableness so assiduously cultivated by Friar Bartolomé. The New Laws were, moreover, supported by an extraordinary array of clergymen, lawyers, and officials, many of whom had been in America. Laws conceived in a spirit of princely benevolence though they were, this code was destined to produce, because of its sudden and drastic provisions, endless mischief. Information regarding the New Laws flew to the Americas with the speed which evil tidings always have, in scores of alarmed letters to and from persons vitally interested.[18]

Because the New Laws attacked the very roots of institutions already almost sacrosanct through use, which the Crown itself had set up in its American possessions for the exploitation of the native population, a few of their leading provisions must be mentioned specifically. The code begins with an explanation by the King that his innumerable duties outside of Spain have hitherto prevented his giving the affairs of America the attention which they merited. The duties and functions of the Council of the Indies were then outlined, apparently as a means of making them more widely known to the public. That Council, like the Council of Castile, attended the Court on all its wanderings, being the body through which the absolute King of Castile ruled his American realms. In like manner, the functions of the Royal Audiences in America were defined. The Royal Audience of Peru was to be presided over by a Viceroy and was to have four Judges called Oidores who, sitting in Lima, were to have criminal and civil jurisdiction. The Audiences were bidden to terminate all enslavement and abuse of the Indians, and their obligation to serve in dangerous employments. Furthermore, the Indians were declared to be free men on precisely the same footing as the subjects of the Crown in Spain itself.

All this was bad enough from the colonists' point of view, but there were much worse provisions besides. All officials, lay and clerical, who held encomiendas or repartimientos were ordered to give them up forthwith and turn them over to the Crown which, through its functionaries, would henceforth administer them. This law was followed by others still more radical. All persons who held Indians without authority were bidden to give them up and place them under the Crown. In case an individual held, even with authority, an excessive number of encomiendas or repartimientos, his holdings were to be reduced and the superfluity placed under the Crown.

Furthermore, grants were to be for but one life, instead of for two as formerly, which meant that the widows and children of the original grantees were not to enjoy the encomiendas which they had been led by the Crown to expect. Moreover, the encomenderos were commanded to insure the spiritual education of their Indians and to treat them well in every respect, and if the Indians were neglected or misused they were to be taken away and placed under the Crown. Finally, it was ruled that any encomendero who had been implicated as a leader in the factional strife between the Pizarros and the Almagros was to lose his encomienda to the Crown forthwith. Naturally enough, this law deprived practically every encomendero in Peru of his holdings; for the leaders in that strife had nearly all been of the vecino or encomendero class.

The threatened total effect of the New Laws upon the holders of the encomiendas set up in Peru, by virtue of the Crown's Capitulación of 1529 and which that same Crown now swept into its own possession, was nothing short of complete ruination. The significance of the situation was, however, more profound than this. The Crown, having called into being a nascent feudal aristocracy, now sought to replace it all at once by a system of Royal absolutism. This violent shift of policy entailed what the encomenderos of Peru could regard only as the blackest betrayal on the King's part.

Obviously, the King required men of exceptional ability and strength if the New Laws were to be enforced in Peru, both for the Viceroy and for the Judges of the new Audiencia. Unfortunately the man selected as Viceroy was Don Blasco Nuñez Vela, a highborn cavalier who presently revealed himself to be the possessor of a mentality like that of a lunatic hyena. As for the Judges, the Viceroy's description of them as "a boy, a madman, a booby, and a dunce"[19] shows clearly the relations which, almost from the moment of their leaving Spain, existed between the Viceroy and the Oidores.

Tidings of the New Laws had spread throughout Peru long before the Viceroy arrived there. Forced into a mood of rebellious desperation the holders of grants made an unmistakably authentic appeal to Gonzalo Pizarro to assume the leadership of their resistance.[20] There was ample time for the opposition to the New Laws to crystallize and to become general; for, although the Viceroy and the Judges were appointed early in 1543, it was not until November 3rd that they sailed from San Lucar de Barrameda. The four Oidores were the Licentiates Diego de Cepeda, Lisón de Tejada, Alvarez, and Pedro Ortiz de Zárate, all of whom had held high office in Spain or in the Canaries. The Chronicler, Augustín de Zárate, went out to Peru with them as Contador (Bursar). Stopping at the Canaries from November 15th to 29th, the Viceroy's fleet arrived at Nombre de Dios on January 10th, 1544. Nuñez Vela and the Judges travelled in a style commensurate with the magnitude of the task confided to them by the King. The Viceroy was attended by numerous gentlemen and 50 servants, and the splendid fleet of 49 vessels carried, besides the Judges, their families and suites, a notable company of 915 passengers, most of whom were gentlefolk going out to Peru to refurbish damaged fortunes. In this fleet came out the first considerable number of upper-class Spanish women, including 36 married women and 87 girls who accompanied their parents.[21]

Even during the voyage the unfitness of Nuñez Vela for his post began to appear, his egocentric pride and intolerance of advice making themselves painfully conspicuous. On the Isthmus serious trouble arose between him and the Judges because the latter, being detained by business at Nombre de Dios, resented the headstrong impetuosity which led Nuñez Vela to desert them and press on to Panama. There, finding that some 300 Peruvian Indians were employed as household servants by Spanish settlers, he arbitrarily applied one of the clauses in the New Laws in such a way as to take the Indians from their masters, whom he obliged to defray their expenses back to Peru. This order was distasteful not only to the masters but also to the servants, who, being devoted to those whom they served, were perfectly contented. Apparently Nuñez

Vela took this harsh course simply from a brutal desire to display his own authority.[22] Finally, the Viceroy, spurning every effort of the Oidores to induce him to wait for them, insisted upon leaving them at Panama and sailing south without them, his reason being that he had learned that Peru was already in an uproar on account of the New Laws. Accordingly, he took ship on February 10th, 1544, and arrived at Tumbez either late in February or early in March.[23]

Attended by his suite, Nuñez Vela proceeded southwards by land along the Peruvian coast, arriving at Lima in May, 1544. On the journey, and at Trujillo and other coast-country cities, his courses were such that, wherever he went, he left behind him increasingly indignant vecinos and Indians demoralized by his "benevolences."[24]

It was in this period that Gonzalo Pizarro, with a conspicuous degree of self-devotion, accepted the call to arms, came forth from his retirement near La Plata, and assumed the leadership of the now inevitable rebellion against the New Laws. Closely associated with him, almost from the beginning of the enterprise, was Francisco de Carvajal, a man of humble birth, but of long and honorable experience in arms, who had fought with great gallantry in Italy and later in Mexico. About 1536 he had gone from Mexico to Peru, with Catalina Leyton, his wife, and their family. Having served Pizarro against the Indians who were besieging Lima, he was rewarded by him with an encomienda somewhere in the south of Peru. At the battle of Chupas his personal bravery and his great skill as a leader of men had been very largely responsible for the victory won that day by Governor Vaca. Shortly before the time now in question Carvajal, being now about seventy-five years of age, had been eager to return to Spain with his wife in order to pass there his last days. But the ports were without northbound ships, and he had been unable to leave Peru. Not long after that Gonzalo Pizarro called upon him to throw in his lot with those who were opposing the New Laws. With that sententiousness for which he was famous old Carvajal had said, "I was very unwilling to put my hands into the warp of this cloth, but now that things are as they are, I promise to be the principal weaver."[25] Unflinching physical and moral courage was his most notable characteristic, and stinging wit, coupled with unfailing ribaldry, was a second prominent trait in his powerful and impressive personality. He was a devil, perchance a very "demon of the Andes," as his enemies called him, but with it all he was doughty, invincible, and splendid, capable, too, of mercy on occasion. His tall, obese, and vigorous person is one of the outstanding ones of this period. To him Gonzalo Pizarro owed much of the success that came his way.[26]

It appears that after the arrival of the Viceroy in Lima there was a flicker of hope that he would modify the stringency of the New Laws. This induced some of Gonzalo's more lukewarm adherents to fall away from him, and he himself toyed with the idea of withdrawing to Charcas again. Soon, however, news came from Lima that invigorated the spirit of resistance more than ever and stilled most of the dissentient voices in Cuzco. As Cieza puts it:

"Here the reader may see how fragile and slippery are the affairs of this world, and that there are many changes in every hour that we live in it. At one moment we find Gonzalo Pizarro about to retire into private life, and the people of Cuzco in no mind to make him their Procurator, nor to give him any other charge. In another, no sooner was it known that citizens of Lima were coming to arouse those of Cuzco, than Pizarro was accepted to take command over all others, march to Lima, and drive out the Viceroy. Afterwards, by virtue of a clause in the will of the Marquis his brother, Gonzalo Pizarro was to be received as Governor."[27]

The cause of this decided confirmation of Gonzalo as leader of the discontented was the fact that the Viceroy, having solemnly promised not to proclaim the New Laws prior to the advent of the Oidores, broke his word and ordered the common crier of Lima to proclaim them publicly.[28] The result of this breach of faith was the estrangement of many of the Viceroy's supporters in Lima. That dignitary now lost what little restraint he had ever had, and began issuing frenzied orders in vertiginous succession. Any one who spoke favorably of Gonzalo Pizarro was to be given a public flogging of one hundred lashes. Governor Vaca, who had come to Lima voluntarily after ridding himself of even the appearance of armed resistance to the Viceroy, was arrested and locked up in a room of the palace; but, through the mediation of Bishop Loaysa, he was released only to be rearrested a few days later and sent as a prisoner to a ship in Callao harbor.[29] A residencia (scrutiny of acts while in office) was declared by the Viceroy against Vaca. Much testimony of dubious worth was admitted against the man on trial, but friends of Vaca roundly stated his public services, showing how he had ended the war between the Pizarros and the Almagros and had saved the Indians from a general relapse into paganism. Nevertheless, Vaca was kept imprisoned.[30]

In June, 1544, the Oidores with their wives and attendants arrived at Paita. Their journey southwards by land was saddened by the constantly recurring proofs of the Viceroy's violence and ineptitude. The tambo service, highly efficient under the Incas, had been so completely wrecked by his "benevolence" to the Indians engaged in it that only with the greatest difficulty could they get bearers and provender along the road. In July, after much discomfort, the Oidores arrived in Lima where they were suitably lodged in citizens' houses. They found the city in a state of profound unrest because of the Viceroy's threats to hang his enemies by sixties and seventies.[31]

It is well to pause here in order to see exactly what was in Gonzalo Pizarro's mind at this time. Several documents, now in the Huntington Library at San Marino, California, are useful for this purpose. The first is a long letter written by Gonzalo to the King, probably from Cuzco or from his camp, in August, 1544. Written in behalf of the cities of Cuzco, La Plata, Arequipa, Huamanga, Huánuco, and Quito, and of all the encomenderos in Peru, it is phrased in the servile language then customary when addressing Royalty. Gonzalo beseeches the King to rescind the New Laws, particularly emphasizing those against appeal from Peruvian courts to the high courts in Spain and those taking repartimientos and encomiendas from the partisans of Pizarro and Almagro. On the subject of the Viceroy Gonzalo speaks with great sternness, but with truth and justice. Other letters of Gonzalo at this time, to Nuñez Vela, to the Cabildo of Lima and to the Oidores, show clearly what just charges he brought against the Viceroy and make plain the righteousness of his own cause. On August 23rd, 1544, three of the four Oïdores wrote to him approving his course.[32]

On Sunday, September 14th, 1544, the Viceroy, losing his few remaining wisps of common sense, murdered an upright and popular official, the Factor Illán Suárez de Carvajal.[33] This outrage brought matters to a head. The Oidores, on September 17th, first made fifty-nine grave charges against Nuñez Vela, and then captured his person, afterwards putting him on board a ship, in the custody of Judge Alvarez, with the idea of sending him to King Charles.[34] Unfortunately, Judge Alvarez was a very weak man, so that, soon after the ship sailed from Callao, the Viceroy managed to induce him to agree to their going ashore at Tumbez, and thence this tragi-comic couple went up to the highlands of Quito.[35]

The harassed Oidores, having seized the supreme command, were not destined long to enjoy the sweets of power. In October, Francisco de Carvajal, now Gonzalo's Master of the Camp, by dint of a few picturesquely executed murders among their adherents, terrorized the remaining Judges into appointing Gonzalo Pizarro as Governor and Captain-General of Peru, to hold office until the King should order otherwise.[36]

Towards the end of October, 1544, Gonzalo Pizarro made a triumphal entry into Lima. Although the Oidores were chagrined by the roughness with which recognition had been wrung from them, they received him with as good grace as could be expected. In the months that followed, the Royal Audience of Lima became practically defunct; for, as we know, Judge Alvarez was with the escaped Viceroy; and Lisón de Tejada and Ortiz de Zárate faded out of the picture; while Cepeda became a staunch supporter of Gonzalo, who appointed him to be Lieutenant-General and Chief Justice of Peru.[37]

Gonzalo Pizarro was now in a very strong position, so much so that his power even extended to Panama whither he sent a highly unscrupulous man named Hernando Bachicao to guard his interests. Committing various misdemeanors along the coast as he journeyed northwards, Bachicao not only tried in vain to come to grips with the Viceroy but also began the collection of a fleet which eventually included 15 vessels, most of them stolen, and of an army of 1,400 men, nearly all utter rascals. Bachicao's career on the Isthmus was lawless but efficacious, and for a time he was Gonzalo's chief man in Panama and on the sea.[38]

In March, 1545, having learned that his arch-enemy, the Viceroy, was in the vicinity of Quito, Gonzalo went northwards to attack him. After many months of intricate campaigning in the northern highlands, Gonzalo Pizarro finally brought his foe to bay, on January 18th, 1546, at Añaquito, not far from Quito. There a great victory was won by Gonzalo during or immediately after which the Viceroy Nuñez Vela met his death by the hand of the Licentiate Benito Suárez de Carvajal, who thus avenged his murdered brother.[39]

For some time it had been the cherished intention of Carvajal to make Gonzalo independent King of Peru. This startling idea is said to have come to the old fellow in Lima during a jollification which was held one night in his house with some jovial friends. At that pleasantly vinous party a plan was drawn up whereby, after making himself king, Gonzalo was to create dukes, marquises, counts, and great officials so that he might not lack supporters who would rally round his throne and enable him to rule forever. Suffused with the charming warmth of good wines and succulent food, the convivial company proceeded to burst into the French language, hailing Gonzalo as their true king and lord and crying out death to the Viceroy. A chill was thrown upon the heat of the proceedings, however, by Doña Catalina Leyton, wife of Carvajal. She, alarmed by her guests' sudden irruption into French, bade them to beware of crowning heads that ought not to be crowned.[40]

Although this audacious but alluring project was born in the expansive atmosphere of a tremendous binge, it became, none the less, a favorite and fixed idea in the mind of Carvajal, an idea which was enlarged upon and improved as time wore on and Gonzalo's cause prospered. In its final form it contemplated not only the erection of an independent Peruvian kingdom with a strong feudal nobility to support it, but also the marriage of King Gonzalo to an Inca princess, which union was to symbolize the dawn of a new and better day in Castilian-Indian relations.[41]

The plan, I am convinced, was intrinsically a good one. Properly carried out, it might have led to the renaissance, in bi-racial form, of the Inca empire. True, it is difficult to imagine ferocious old Carvajal as participating in the foundation of a monarchy so mild and beneficent as that would have been; indeed, it is clear from his letters that the old man, if not a trifle mad, was at any rate muddle-headed at times. For instance, we have a letter from him dated at Chuquisaca (La Plata, now Sucre) on October 13th, 1546, to Soria, Gonzalo's agent, in which he mentions a decree of King Charles making Gonzalo "permanent Governor of the country and Duke of Chile," and in which he suggests that they "buy from the King of Castile half of his possessions."[42] Needless to say, King Charles never issued any such decree, nor was such a purchase ever even remotely possible. Nevertheless, I persist in believing that the idea of an independent monarchy for Peru, albeit nearly 300 years ahead of its time, contained great potentialities for good.[43]

The moment upon which Gonzalo should have seized in order to make himself truly supreme was brief; it escaped him because he dallied for six months in Quito before taking his way slowly towards Lima by way of the coast towns, all of which greeted him rapturously. When, in September, 1546, he made his gorgeous triumphant entry into Lima, the moment was already past. We have an illuminating letter from Gonzalo to Alonzo de Alvarado, written from Lima on October 17th, 1546, in which he says as follows:

"What I have done is to save the country from ruin, and if you do not know of the services which I have rendered to the King at my expense and that of my friends, I will tell you. . . . I and my people want peace, . . . but if war is forced upon us, I cannot refrain from defending our persons and our property. . . . I cannot think of marriage at present: I am wedded to my lances and horses."[44]

These words indicate that Gonzalo's ideas were far less high-flown than Carvajal's.

By this time Nemesis was already journeying to Peru in the person of Father Don Pedro de la Gasca, a man poles apart from Nuñez Vela. If the Viceroy was a hyena, the new envoy was a wily spider. During a brilliant career in Spain in the fields of scholarship, theology, warfare, and administration, Gasca had displayed astuteness, bravery, and considerable histrionic ability. Possessed of a saintly and ingratiating exterior, he had an inner self of finely tempered steel.

This was the man upon whom, on February 16th, 1546, at Venlo in the Low Countries, King Charles conferred the simple title of President of the Royal Audience of Lima. That title carried with it—in Gasca's case—albeit concealed from view, powers judicial, administrative, and legislative hardly inferior to those which the King himself would have had.[45]

President Gasca sailed from Spain on May 26th, 1546, and, after touching at Santa Marta, where the news of the Battle of Añaquito was given to him, he reached Nombre de Dios on July 27th. Like his character, his mode of going to his post bore the greatest contrast to that of Nuñez Vela; for he had but a small fleet and a modest retinue. His powers, however, were infinitely more extensive than those which the Viceroy had had, so much so that he even carried a number of blank letters to be filled in as he deemed best over the Royal signature. Moreover, he was the bearer of a formal revocation of the New Laws, and he was authorized to grant an amnesty to all who had rebelled against them.[46]

Thus armed Gasca first proceeded to rob Gonzalo's cause of all real justification by announcing the repeal of the New Laws; second to beguile Hinojosa and Aldana (then in charge of Gonzalo's interests at Panama) into handing over the doomed rebel's fleet; and third to discharge on Peru a veritable bombardment of letters whose effect was that of bringing over to the royal side hundreds of waverers whose devotion to Gonzalo had sprung wholly from their hatred of the New Laws, now revoked. Likewise, he enlisted the support of Viceroy Mendoza, who gave him 600 men under the command of his son, Francisco de Mendoza.[47]

Having thus prepared the way, Gasca went to Peru in April–August, 1547, the worst season for a southward voyage in those waters.[48] Gonzalo was given several opportunities to yield to the King's law, but he would not. He must have known, too, that his cause was a lost one; for, early in October, 1547, he and Carvajal were trying to retreat into Charcas and Chile.

At that time Diego Centeno, one of the most formidable and skilful of the anti-Gonzalo leaders in Peru, a man whom even the redoubtable Master of the Camp had not been able permanently to crush, stood in the way of a southward retreat, being particularly strong in the regions of Cuzco and Arequipa and the Titicaca basin. Notwithstanding a grave admonition from Gasca against fighting Gonzalo Pizarro, Centeno did resort to arms because he could not help himself. He had some 1,000 men and Gonzalo but half as many, yet, in the tremendous Battle of Huarina, at the southeastern end of Lake Titicaca, on October 26th, 1547, Centeno suffered a decided defeat, losing 350 men and Gonzalo only 80. This unexpected victory was almost wholly due to the splendid leadership of stout Carvajal. Of the men of quality captured during and after the battle Gonzalo "justiced" all; but the common soldiers were enticed over to his side with the idea of using them as a nucleus for a new army.[49]

President Gasca, although naturally deeply chagrined by the reverse at Huarina, kept his head. Returning for a time

FIG. 6. Air photograph of the Colca Valley, Peru, showing the towns of Ichupampa (lower town) and Yanque (upper town).

By Aerial Explorations, Inc., Chrysler Bldg., New York.

to Lima, where he arranged a loan from 80 merchants to the sum of 300,000 pesos gold, he first assured himself that all of northern and most of southern Peru were at his back, and he then gathered a fresh army of 2,000 men, including 800 arquebusiers and 500 cavalry. Leaving Hinojosa in command of the capital, the President made Alonzo de Alvarado campmaster, and Aldana was given charge of the fleet. These preparations being completed, the President fixed his headquarters in Andahuaylas, northwest from Cuzco.[50]

To this period belong two important letters, the one written by President Gasca to Gonzalo Pizarro from Jauja on December 16th, 1547, in which he answers a letter written to the King by Gonzalo from Lima on July 20th, 1547, which letter had come into the President's hands. Gasca, mentioning specifically the protestations of loyalty inscribed by Gonzalo, rebuts them all in language at once dignified and convincing. In part he says:

"Insignificant as I am, your Excellency would have little to fear from me if I had not on my side God and the King, justice and fidelity, and all the good vassals who serve His Majesty; but fighting against all these things, your Excellency has good reason to quail; and if you do not repent and return to the service of both Majesties, Divine and human, you will lose both body and soul as you will shortly see."[51]

This letter, one must admit, puts President Gasca in a highly creditable light, not only because of its urbane language but also because, even at this late hour, he was offering Gonzalo a chance to return to his allegiance to the Crown. The spirit in which this generous gesture was received in the Pizarrist camp is revealed by the second letter to which I have referred, one from Carvajal to Gasca written from Cuzco on December 29th, 1547. It is scurrilous, blasphemous, and vulgar, but most amusing. The concluding sentence runs thus:

"May the Lord preserve your reverend personality by permitting, through His most holy clemency, that your sins should bring you into my hands, that you may once and for all cease to do so much harm in the world!"[52]

Matters were now tending towards the final and decisive contest. Gonzalo, holding Cuzco, made himself as strong as possible there, and, sheltered from immediate attack by his possession of the Apurimac bridge, he gathered an army of 900 men and a number of pieces of artillery. But, alas, when the President was ready, late in March, 1548, to proceed against his foes, the defense of the Apurimac bridge was so badly bungled by Gonzalo's men that the Royal army, after enormous difficulties with the river and the craggy nature of the country, succeeded in getting across and arriving at Abancay. On learning this, Gonzalo mustered all his men and led them to the Valley of Xaquixaguana (Sacsahuana, now called Anta or Zúrite) some fifteen miles from Cuzco. In that exquisite place, a flat plain enclosed by mountains and traversed by causeways and ancient aqueducts, the Incas had long ago defeated the Chancas and thus sealed themselves to an imperial career,[53] and there Gonzalo, who, if Viracocha had so willed it, might have revived the Incaic régime or something like it, met his fate. A good view of Xaquixaguana appears in Figure 4.

On April 8th, 1548, the Royal army moved into the Valley from Abancay. Vaingloriously Gonzalo tried to dismay his advancing enemies with cannon-shot and musketry-fire. That night there were skirmishes, and in the morning, after Mass and breakfast, four of the royalists' biggest cannons were placed and fired. The first round killed a squire of Gonzalo, who was arming him. From that moment his men lost all spirit; for he had lied to them, saying that the President had no cannon. The action which followed can hardly be called a battle because the Pizarrists deserted as fast as they could, with the result that, when Gonzalo and Carvajal were captured, they were almost alone. On the next day, April 10th, 1548, they were formally "justiced" and beheaded. Gonzalo made his peace with God, but Carvajal died as he had lived—daring, witty, blasphemous, and unrepentant to the end. There is no need to go into the horrid post-mortem vengeance which was wreaked upon their hapless bodies.[54]

3. Tumults, 1548–1569

After the downfall and death of Gonzalo Pizarro, President Gasca, acting in the closest conjunction with the Archbishop of Lima, Don Gerónimo de Loaysa, was occupied principally with a distribution of lands, Indians, honors, and privileges intended to be rewards to those who had helped to overcome Gonzalo. The pair of boodle-distributing ecclesiastics, accompanied by a secretary and a small suite of servants, withdrew from Cuzco—where most unpriestly venom had been displayed against the fallen foe—on July 11th, 1548, and took up their abode at Huayna Rimac, not far from the Apurimac bridge, about twelve leagues from Cuzco. There they went into what can justly be described as a "huddle" which lasted more than a month. Its inner spirit is well illustrated, albeit scurrilously, by a quaint contemporary caricature which shows Loaysa kneeling before Gasca, who says to him: "Bishop (sic) I give you this share of the kingdom, so that you may profit by it before the devil takes it all." To which Loaysa answers: "I kiss your Lordship's hands for your benefactions."[55] The methods of the pair were peculiar. As Dr. de la Riva-Agüero —Peru's greatest living historian—has shown, the mode of apportioning the guerdons was such that persons who had long been loyal to the Crown received the least, it being held that they were loyal anyway and needed not to be purchased, while those who had long served Gonzalo and had deserted him only in the last phases of his struggle were sealed to their renewed allegiance to the King by extravagant bonuses of lands, Indians, and money.[56] In other words, the New Laws being dead patronage bloomed anew in the land.

The administrative technique of President Gasca after he had won supremacy was not such as to reduce Peru to more than "a shadow of good order."[57] The country was boiling with every sort of indiscipline. Typical of the spirit of insensate pride and unlimited pretentiousness which prevailed among the great folk of Peru at this time were the following scandalous incidents:

Doña Ana Fernández de Velasco y Avendaño, wife of the Marshal Don Alonzo de Alvarado, was a lady of noble Spanish blood, though perchance not more noble than that of various others. She was a shrew of the worst description and, in spite of her good blood, made bad blood wherever she went because of the overweening pride which ruled her. So furious was she on the subjects of precedence and privilege that the sight of any woman less nobly born than she using a cushion in church, or occupying a better place at Mass, drove her quite mad. Her favorite battleground was the House of God. One day, in the cathedral of Cuzco, she caused her servants to knife an honorable widow who had taken a place which this haughty termagant wanted, and, not content with such shamelessly un-Christian conduct, she caused the mother of the widow to be shorn, the dress of the widow's sister to be slashed, and, worst of all, the bones of the dead husband to be disinterred and thrown out upon the ground. In these impious outrages the Marshal Alvarado complacently sided with his wife, so that the Chief Justice, Cianca, publicly and severely reprimanded him, whereupon the servants of Alvarado gravely insulted Cianca who, in turn, condemned Alvarado to death, from which he was saved only by the personal intervention of Gasca.[58] Incidents like this are innumerable in the annals of that time and, however trivial in themselves, they are a gloomy proof of the extreme lawlessness then rampant in Peru.

From September, 1548, to his departure from Peru in January, 1550, President Gasca had to struggle with the inappeasable discontent which was making Peru seethe. Nevertheless, he managed to put the chaotic finances of the colony into good order and to collect a vast sum of money for the King, so that, when he arrived in Spain in July, 1550, His Majesty and the Court gave him a welcome commensurate with his truly great services and with the great treasure which he brought. He was made Bishop of Palencia and later of Sigüenza, and was long consulted on Peruvian questions.[59]

The strong hand of Gasca having been removed, the general

disorder became worse than ever. From his going until September, 1551, the Judges of the Audience ruled the land, doing so abominably; for, in addition to brawling incessantly among themselves, they devoted far too much energy to annoying the Archbishop and to various nepotistical and corrupt activities of their own.

In 1551 there came to Peru the second of its long line of Viceroys, Don Antonio de Mendoza, a valiant, able, and honest administrator who had ruled New Spain since 1535.[60] Unhappily, when he and his son, Don Francisco de Mendoza y Vargas, sailed from Realejo for Peru, on March 7th, 1551, the Viceroy was a very sick man. Travelling in a small fleet with a modest retinue, they reached Tumbez on May 15th. Owing to the Viceroy's poor health they had to journey by land very slowly, reaching Trujillo on July 21st and Lima on September 12th, 1551. Instead of entering Lima with the bombastic pomp which Nuñez Vela and Gasca had loved so well, the Viceroy Mendoza entered his capital with sober dignity. Being so very ill, he could not inspect his new realm personally. So he sent his son, Don Francisco, on a tour of inspection throughout the central and southern highlands. When this studious journey was completed, Don Francisco went to Spain and made his report to the King.[61]

The Viceroy, who never knew an hour of good health in Peru, was weighed down by his knowledge that the benevolent frenzy of Bishop Bartolomé de las Casas was once more bearing fruit, in the form of a modified revival of the New Laws, this time abolishing, not the land-grants, but the mita or obligatory personal service of the Indians in mines, on estates, on the roads, and in private houses. This abolition was coupled with a new and disquietingly low tariff of tributes which the Indians would have to pay henceforth to encomenderos and other masters. The Viceroy knew that, once these regulations were published, tumults equal to those of 1544–1548 would burst forth. Gasca and the Judges, successfully, had postponed or tampered with them as a means of avoiding an explosion. Mendoza, too, was in favor of suppressing the new orders until such a time as the King could re-study the whole problem in the light of the formal protests against them. But, in June, 1552, there arrived Royal letters insisting upon the new regulations so strongly that the Oidores, now no longer restrained by the Viceroy because he was too ill to act, precipitately published them on June 23rd, 1552, with, however, certain quite illicit modifications designed to avert public wrath. Nevertheless, the results were similar to those of the publication of the New Laws, and, after the Viceroy died on July 21st, 1552,[62] new uprisings began which lasted for over a year, finally leading to the formidable rebellion of Francisco Hernández Girón.

That rebellion, the last of the Civil Wars of Peru, although interesting, demands no extended notice here. It was in the nature of a caricature of that of Gonzalo Pizarro, being equally without legal justification, but much more selfish in its motives, less intelligent in its aims, and supported by no such concourse of respectable citizens as had formerly upheld Gonzalo. The movement began at Cuzco on the evening of Sunday, November 12th, 1553, at a moment when the fashionable world was celebrating the marriage of Doña María de Castilla, niece of the Count of la Gomera, to Don Alonzo de Loaysa, nephew of the Archbishop. With exciting ups and downs, it lasted until crushed by the Oidores' general at the battle of Pucará on October 11th, 1554. Eventually, in December of that year, Hernández Girón was beheaded at Lima and his head was placed beside those of Gonzalo and Carvajal on the gibbet in the Plaza.[63]

After the death of Hernández Girón, during 1555 and most of 1556, Peru settled down to one of those periods of half-smothered unrest of which she has known so many. The ineptitude of the Oidores and the unsatisfied longing of numerous claimants kept the country constantly uneasy. On June 29th, 1556, the third Viceroy, Don Andrés Hurtado de Mendoza, Marquis of Cañete, entered Lima in state and assumed office. He came provided with powers somewhat resembling those of Gasca; for, when he left Spain, it was not yet known that Hernández Girón had been crushed. With him came the Marchioness of Cañete, their son, Don García Hurtado de Mendoza, and a suite of 120 poor relations and servants, not to mention a company of Gentlemen-Lancers of the Guard. Because of the presence, for the first time, of a Vicereine, Lima now assumed the courtly and etiquette-laden aspect, rendered gracious by urbanity and hospitality, which distinguished the society of that charming city until 1919. The Viceroy Marquis of Cañete ruled vigorously and well, albeit with a marked tendency to help his son and other kinsmen to the available good things of life. At Paita and Trujillo he had been beset by flocks of hungry claimants for rewards; but, on taking possession of his high office, he made it clear that he would stand no nonsense from any one. Overriding the pretentions of certain Oidores, he sent his son to pacify Chile, a task which the young man accomplished well. Likewise, Cañete stamped out the embers of Hernández Girón's rebellion so thoroughly that, in February, 1557, he wrote to his friend, the Duke of Alva, that he had caused the death of over 800 sympathizers with the late rebel. Some others of the less guilty he sent off on explorations into the east and southeast of the Viceroyalty, and various others were shipped out of the country to Panama and to Spain. If not always just and merciful, his methods were efficacious up to a certain point. But those whom he exiled made trouble for him at home, with the result that, in 1558, a successor was appointed by King Philip II, who had succeeded to his worn-out father on the latter's abdication; and, in Peru, he had grave difficulty with the Oidor Bravo de Saravia and also with Archbishop Loaysa. In spite of all this, Cañete succeeded in making a number of reforms in his kingdom, the chief being an arrangement with the Inca Sayri Tupac, of which more presently. On September 14th, 1560, the Marquis of Cañete died, after a sickness aggravated by rage on account of a discourteous letter which he received from his successor, written at Panama.[64]

This successor was Don Diego López de Zúñiga y Velasco,

Count of Nieva. With him came Don Diego de Carvajal Vargas, second Correo Mayor de las Indias (Postmaster General of the Indies), the Licentiate Briviesca de Muñatones, and the Contador (Bursar) Ortega de Melgosa, three commissioners specially appointed by King Philip to study the important question of whether or not the encomiendas of Peru should be converted from grants of one, two, or at most three, lives into perpetual feudal fiefs. To this vital matter we shall return in a later chapter.

Dishonest and lazy, Nieva's chief interest, besides gathering all the money he could, was love. He maintained a seraglio hard by the town of Chorrillos, near Lima, and there he had scandalous affairs with high-born ladies, chief among them his beautiful cousin, Doña Catalina López de Zúñiga, wife of Don Rodrigo Manrique de Lara. On February 18th, 1564, by night, the Viceroy was assassinated, probably with the connivance of Manrique. Complaints against Nieva had already been sent to King Philip, so that, on September 22nd, 1564, the Licentiate Lope García de Castro arrived in Lima, not as Viceroy, but merely as Governor-General and President of the Royal Audience of Lima. After a relatively quiet period in office, on November 26th, 1569, he handed over the command to the greatest of all Peru's rulers, the Viceroy Don Francisco de Toledo, the real establisher in Peru of the Spanish colonial system.[65]

NOTES TO CHAPTER IV

[1] Cieza, 1918, pp. 82–95, 137–141. P. Pizarro, 1921, II, pp. 413–414.

[2] Cieza, 1918, pp. 112–137, 151–154, 157–163, 178–179, 186–192, and 195–207.

[3] Cieza, 1918, pp. 124–125, 142–144, 169–178, 218–231. The astute reader will have guessed, from these long citations, that I am skimming along rather rapidly. This is the case. I do so in the belief that modern readers take only a moderate amount of interest in wars such as these and because the wars themselves, no matter how interesting their details may be, lack serious value for the student of colonial history in its larger aspects.

[4] Cieza, 1918, pp. 238–245.

[5] Cieza, 1918, pp. 250–253.

[6] Cieza, 1918, pp. 254–274.

[7] See Markham's careful description of Chupas at pp. 274–275 of Cieza, 1918.

8 Cieza, 1918, pp. 275–287, 292–293.

9 Cieza, 1918, pp. 297–299. It is to be observed that, although I have based my account of the events leading up to the Lad's death almost wholly on Cieza, doing so because his is the most completely trustworthy statement of the matter, there are other good accounts, including: P. Pizarro, 1921, II, pp. 423–439; Zárate, Bk. IV, Chs. x–xxi; Garcilaso, Pt. II, Bk. III, Chs. x–xviii. These three corroborate Cieza, on the whole, very well, but they are less complete and detailed than he is. Prescott, II, pp. 201–243, uses Garcilaso, Pedro Pizarro, and Zárate, but Cieza's "war of Chupas" (Cieza, 1918) was unknown to him; he cites, however, various passages in Herrera, Decs. VI and VII, none of which have I found as fresh and stimulating as Cieza. Merriman, III, pp. 594–595, covers this war in two pages, with some bad mistakes such as saying that Vaca came overland from the Isthmus and calling the site of the battle the "plains of Chupas," an error which Prescott, pardonably enough, had inaugurated, but which Markham corrected in Cieza, 1918, as a less superficial writer than Merriman would have known. A letter signed by Luís Roldán on September 25th, 1542, is now in the Harkness collection in the Library of Congress. It tells of the Lad's doings after the battle of Chupas.

10 Cieza, 1918, p. 295.

11 Cieza, 1918, pp. 314–337. Garcilaso, Pt. II, Bk. III, Ch. xix. Zárate, Bk. IV, Chs. xxi–xxii.

12 The authorities for this expedition include: Garcilaso, 1859; and Cieza, 1918, pp. 54–77.

13 Vaca's reply to Gonzalo Pizarro, dated from Huamanga, September 11th, 1542, is given in extract in Maggs-Huntington, pp. 9–10. Although he declines Gonzalo's offer of his services he speaks kindly of him and promises to safeguard the interests of the late Marquis's kinsfolk. See also: Garcilaso, Pt. II, Bk. III, Ch. xv.

14 Cieza, 1918, pp. 306–307, 311–314. P. Pizarro, 1921, II, pp. 439–440. Zárate, Bk. IV, Ch. xxii.

15 For the connection between Casas and the New Laws see: Gutiérrez de Santa Clara, 1904–1910, Bk. I, Ch. iii, I, pp. 45–51. (Hereinafter this work is cited as Gutiérrez.) Also, Garcilaso, Pt. II, Bk. III, Ch. xx; López de Gómara, Chs. cli–cliii; Cieza, 1918, pp. 338–340; Calvete, 1889, Bk. I, Ch. iii. As illustrations of Casas's methods of argumentation one may cite: Casas, 1552 and 1583. Authorities on his life are numerous, among them being: MacNutt, 1909, who says, erroneously, that Casas went to Peru (pp. 181–185); Means, 1928, pp. 334–342. Casas, 1892, pp. xvi–xvii, xxxiii–xxxv, and l–liv, contains proof by Don Marcos Jiménez de la Espada that Casas never went to Peru.

16 Falcón, 1918, p. 136.

17 A Peruvian version of these ideas appears in Anonymous Letter of 1571, pp. 429–433, where the writer shows how Casas's invectives—which were widely circulated throughout Europe—caused English, Dutch, French, and other foreigners to believe that the King of Castile was a mere tyrant and a despoiler of the helpless American peoples so that to despoil him, in turn, was a righteous act. This was an underlying element in the piratical activities of later times, as we shall see. For data on the conflict between Casas's mode of thought and that of Sepúlveda see: MacNutt, 1909, pp. 277–293.

[18] Gutiérrez, Bk. I, Chs. i and iii. Cieza, 1918, pp. 340–360, contains Markham's translation of the text of the New Laws. It is to be noted in passing that Queen Juana is specifically mentioned in the heading of the New Laws. Convenient summaries of the code will be found in: Fernández, 1913–1916, I, pp. 24–25, and Zárate, Bk. IV, Ch. xxiii. Prescott, II, pp. 251–256.

[19] Prescott, II, p. 316, citing López de Gómara, Ch. clxxii.

[20] P. Pizarro, 1921, II, p. 445. Cieza, 1913, pp. 25–44. Gutiérrez, Bk. I, Chs. xii and xiii. Fernández, Bk. I, Chs. xii and xiii. Albenino, 1549, pp. 12–13.

[21] Fernández, Bk. I, Ch. ii, 1913, pp. 25–27. Gutiérrez, Bk. I, Ch. iv. Cieza, 1913, pp. 1–5, and especially Sir Clements Markham's data on p. 1, derived from the official register of the Casa de Contratación where the passengers are listed.

[22] Cieza, 1913, p. 3. Fernández, Bk. I, Ch. vi. Gutiérrez, Bk. I, Ch. v. Prescott, II, pp. 259–261.

[23] Fernández, Bk. I, Ch. vi. Gutiérrez, Bk. I, Ch. v. Gutiérrez, Bk. I, Ch. vi, says that the voyage took forty days. Cieza, 1913, p. 10, gives February 19th, 1544, as the date of Nuñez Vela's arrival at Tumbez, adding that he reached there from Panama in nine days. Zárate, Bk. IV, Ch. xxiv, says that the voyage was a quick one. Fernández, Bk. I, Ch. vi, and López de Gómara, Ch. cliv, tell us that the Viceroy arrived at Tumbez on March 4th, and Albenino, 1549, p. 8, says that the journey from Panama to Tumbez occupied only eight days. In any case, we may be sure that the voyage was a short one.

[24] Cieza, 1913, pp. 14–16. Gutiérrez, Bk. I, Ch. vii.

[25] Cieza, 1913, p. 73.

[26] For the career and character of Carvajal see: Cieza, 1918, pp. 269–272; 1913, pp. 8–11 (text and Markham's note), 25, 30, 48–50, 73–82. Ricardo Palma's little book, *El Demonio de los Andes,* gives a vivid portrayal of Carvajal.

[27] Cieza, 1913, pp. 62–63.

[28] Cieza, 1913, pp. 83–85. López de Gómara, Chs. clvi and clviii. Zárate, Bk. IV, Ch. xxv, Bk. V, Chs. i–iii.

[29] This, at any rate, is what Cieza, 1913, pp. 85–86, says. We are told by Gutiérrez, Bk. I, Ch. x, that Vaca was first thrown into the common jail, later removed to a private house, and finally to a ship. Fernández, Bk. I, Ch. x, says that Vaca was first put in the jail and later, under bonds of 100,000 castellanos, in the palace. In any case he suffered great and unmerited indignity; for his conduct towards Nuñez Vela was altogether correct and the Viceroy's suspicion that he sympathized with the rebellion was unfounded.

[30] Gutiérrez, Bk. I, Ch. x. López de Gómara, Ch. clvi. As Sir Clements Markham says, on pp. 152–153 of the volume containing Cieza, 1913, Vaca finally made his way to Spain where he was first imprisoned for five years in the castle of Arévalo, after which he was tardily cleared of all the charges against him. He was then restored to the Royal favor and made a member of the Council of the Indies in which post he remained until his death, sometime after 1571 (in which year the Inca Garcilaso saw him in Madrid).

[31] Cieza, 1913, pp. 90–91. The new Bishop of Cuzco, Friar Juan Solano, wrote to the King from Lima on March 10th, 1545, giving a terrible account

of the state of Peru and of the mad courses of the Viceroy. See pp. 132–143 of the volume containing Cieza, 1913. Also, Gutiérrez, Bk. I, Ch. xi.

32 Maggs-Huntington, pp. 17–26.

33 Solano, 1913, p. 136; P. Pizarro, 1921, II, p. 447; López de Gómara, Ch. clix; Noticias Chronologicas, Ms., fol. 88; Albenino, 1549, pp. 22–23; Calvete, Bk. I, Ch. iii; and Garcilaso, Pt. II, Bk. IV, Ch. xiii; all say that the Viceroy committed the crime personally. Zárate, Bk. V, Ch. viii, of his printed work tries to put the onus on the Viceroy's guards or servants, but Prescott, II, p. 279, cites a Ms. of Zárate which says that the Viceroy did the deed himself. Only Montesinos, Anales, Año 1544; Pizarro y Orellana, 1639, pp. 368–370; and Fernández, Bk. I, Ch. xviii; say that the servants or guards did it. We may be sure that the Viceroy, personally, was the murderer. See also: Riva-Agüero, 1921, pp. 65–66.

34 The indictment, dated 19th–23rd of September, 1544, will be found on pp. 143–152 of the volume containing Cieza, 1913.

35 Gutiérrez, Bk. I, Chs. xliii and xlvi, Bk. II, Chs. iv–xiii, xviii–xxi. López de Gómara, Ch. clxvi. Fernández, Bk. I, Chs. xxii–xxiii. Albenino, 1549, pp. 29–32. Solano, 1913, p. 140.

36 Solano, 1913, p. 139. Albenino, 1549, pp. 28–29. Gutiérrez, Bk. I, Chs. li-liii. López de Gómara, Chs. clxi–clxiv. Garcilaso, Pt. II, Bk. IV, Ch. xix. Prescott, II, pp. 285–289.

37 Albenino, 1549, pp. 40–41. Gutiérrez, Bk. II, Ch. vi.

38 Gutiérrez, Bk. II, Chs. vii–xi. Albenino, 1549, pp. 41–48. López de Gómara, Ch. clxvii.

39 Zárate, Bk. V, Chs. xxxi–xxxii. Fernández, Bk. I, Chs. liii–liv. P. Pizarro, 1921, II, p. 450. López de Gómara, Ch. clxxi. Gutiérrez, Bk. II, Chs. xliii–xlv. Calvete, Bk. II, Ch. ii. Garcilaso, Pt. II, Bk. IV, Chs. xxiii–xxvi. Montesinos, Anales, Año 1546. Noticias Chronologicas, Ms., fol. 91 verso. Albenino, 1549, pp. 78–83. Important also are two letters from Gonzalo Pizarro, one to his agent, Pedro de Soria, from Quito, January 21st, 1546, describing the battle and referring to his need of money and to other matters (Maggs-Huntington, p. 80), the other to the Viceroy of New Spain, Don Antonio de Mendoza, from Tomebamba, June 26th, 1546, describing the Battle of Añaquito and the situation in general (Maggs-Huntington, pp. 109–110). This letter is curious because it implies that Mendoza, in a letter dated from Mexico on February 16th, 1546, had shown himself to be well disposed towards Gonzalo. Yet, as Dr. Aiton has shown, Viceroy Mendoza was very active only a year later in helping to crush the rebellion of Gonzalo. See: Aiton, 1927, pp. 175–176. This change of attitude on the part of a man who was as far as possible from being either frivolous or a turncoat merits close study. See also: Prescott, II, pp. 297–314.

40 Gutiérrez, Bk. II, Ch. xxxvii.

41 Gutiérrez, Bk. III, Chs. xlv–xlvi. Fernández, Bk. II, Ch. xiii. Garcilaso, Pt. II, Bk. IV, Chs. xl–xlii. López de Gómara, Ch. clxxiii. Calvete, Bk. III, Chs. iii and vi.

Prescott, II, pp. 322–225.

42 Maggs-Huntington, p. 141.

[43] Compare Moses, 1914, I, pp. 222–224.

[44] Maggs-Huntington, pp. 146–147. See also: Garcilaso, Pt. II, Bk. II, Ch. xli, where he describes Gonzalo's hesitation to throw off his allegiance to the King.

[45] Fernández, Bk. II, Chs. xvi–xvii. Gutiérrez, Bk. IV, Chs. i–iv. Garcilaso, Pt. II, Bk. V, Chs. i–ii. López de Gómara, Chs. clxxv–clxxvii. Albenino, 1549, pp. 86–89. Zárate, Bk. VI, Ch. vi. An idea of the amplitude of the powers confided to Gasca is given by an array of documents signed by Charles at Venlo on February 16th, 1546, in which officials from Guatemala down to La Plata are bidden to aid him in every way. (Maggs-Huntington, pp. 82–97.) See Prescott, II, pp. 341–346.

[46] Fernández, Bk. II, Chs. xvii–xviii. Gutiérrez, Bk. IV, Chs. iii–v. Albenino, 1549, pp. 87–88. Zárate, Bk. VI, Ch. vi. Prescott, II, pp. 344–347.

[47] Aiton, 1927, pp. 175–176. López de Gómara, Chs. clxxviii–clxxix.

[48] Dr. Robert Cushman Murphy tells me that the best season for going south along that coast is December to March, at which time the winds and the current called el Niño help. The worst period is August–September, with strong winds opposing so that this is the best period for a northward journey.

[49] Albenino, 1549, pp. 128–136. Fernández, Bk. II, Chs. lxxviii–lxxx. Gutiérrez, Bk. IV, Chs. xxxvii–xxxviii, liv–lix. López de Gómara, Ch. clxxxi. Garcilaso, Pt. II, Bk. V, Chs. xv, xviii–xxii. P. Pizarro, 1921, II, pp. 455–466. Zárate, Bk. VII, Ch. iii. Calvete, Bk. IV, Ch. iii. Prescott, II, pp. 383–398.

[50] Albenino, 1549, pp. 137–139. Fernández, Bk. II, Chs. lxxxii–lxxxv. Garcilaso, Pt. II, Bk. V, Chs. xxvi and xxix.

[51] Gonzalo's letter to the King is described in Maggs-Huntington, pp. 406–409; that of Gasca on pp. 439–443.

[52] Maggs-Huntington, pp. 453–454.

[53] Means, 1931, pp. 243–245.

[54] Albenino, 1549, pp. 140–156, who quotes from a letter written by Diego de Mora, Gonzalo's one-time lieutenant at Trujillo. Fernández, Bk. II, Chs. lxxxiii–xci. López de Gómara, Chs. clxxxiv–clxxxvi. P. Pizarro, 1921, II, pp. 456–466. Garcilaso, Pt. II, Bk. V, Chs. xxxiii–xliii. Zárate, Bk. VII, Chs. vi–viii. Calvete, Bk. IV, Chs. v–vii. The sentence pronounced against Gonzalo is given by Albenino, pp. 157–160. See also notes on a pathetically confident letter written by Gonzalo from Xaquixahuana on April 7th, 1548, to his friend and officer, Espinosa, in Maggs-Huntington, p. 472. Also, Gasca's letter to the Council of the Indies, from Cuzco, May 3rd, 1548, in which he gives a full account of the campaign ending at Xaquixahuana, and of his own doings after the battle, in Maggs-Huntington, pp. 474–482. Prescott, II, pp. 399–447. A stone was set up at the house of Gonzalo Pizarro relating how, after his death, the house was torn down and its site ploughed and salted. The stone was still in place about 1905. See: H. Fuentes, 1905, p. 182.

[55] Maggs-Huntington, Plate XX, and p. 497. See also: Calvete, Bk. IV, Chs. vii–viii; López de Gómara, Chs. clxxxvii–clxxxix.

[56] Riva-Agüero, 1922, pp. 12–13.

[57] So wrote the Prior of the Dominicans in Lima, Friar Domingo de Santo Tomás, in a letter to the Council of the Indies, from Lima, July 1st, 1550, quoted by Riva-Agüero, 1922, p. 16.

[58] Riva-Agüero, 1922, pp. 17-18, citing a letter to the King from Juan Barba de Vallecillo, dated at Nombre de Dios, September 29th, 1548.

[59] Calvete, Bks. VI and VII. Garcilaso, Pt. II, Bk. VI, Chs. x and xiii. P. Pizarro, 1921, II, pp. 461-462. Prescott, II, pp. 455-471. Riva-Agüero, 1922, pp. 19-21.

[60] Aiton, 1927, pp. 12-13.

[61] Riva-Agüero, 1922, p. 30. Aiton, 1927, pp. 190-191.

[62] Garcilaso, Pt. II, Bk. VI, Chs. xvii-xx. Aiton, 1927, pp. 191-192. Riva-Agüero, 1922, pp. 30-35.

[63] Early source materials for this rebellion include: Treslado de una carta, 1554 (?); Relación de lo acaecido, 1879; Levillier, 1922, pp. 102-123, where various contemporary documents will be found. See also: Markham, 1892, pp. 136-140; Riva-Agüero, 1922, pp. 35-49.

[64] Montesinos, Anales, Años 1558-1561, and especially, 1906, I, p. 273. Riva-Agüero, 1922, pp. 49-61.

[65] Markham, 1892, pp. 147-148. Riva-Agüero, 1921, pp. 60-61; 1922, pp. 61-70. Rich contemporary materials relative to these commissioners and to their task will be found in *Nueva colección de documentos inéditos para la historia de España*, Vol. VI, pp. 1-42 and 268-274. (Madrid, 1896.) In the same volume, at pp. 210-217, there will be found an interesting letter from García de Castro to the King, dated at Los Reyes, December 20th, 1567. Among other things, he says that a very serious Indian rebellion, involving all the natives from Quito to Chile, was stopped only by the capture of the leaders, who were betrayed by one of their own number. (P. 212.)

CHAPTER V

THE CONSOLIDATION OF THE COLONIAL GOVERNMENT

1. *Inca History from 1537 to 1570*

IT will be remembered that, after the sieges of Cuzco and of Lima, in 1537, the Inca Manco retreated down the Urupampa Valley into the region called Vilcapampa, in the heart of which, at Vitcos, he established the last capital of the Incas. From there, in his last years, the Inca Manco did all that he could to harry and harm the hated invaders. Some of his doings were, truth to tell, rather petty and would have elicited the scorn of his great ancestors. For instance, there was a diplomatic interlude between him and Pizarro in which the Inca fooled the Conqueror into thinking that he was ready to sue for peace. It was arranged that the two should meet at Yucay to discuss terms, and Pizarro, wishing to put the Inca in a receptive mood, sent ahead two Christian servants with a very handsome pony and other gifts. Manco himself with a few attendants came forth upon the road and without just cause slew the servants, returning with the pony to Vitcos. In revenge for this act Pizarro foully murdered the Inca's chief wife and caused her body to be floated down the Urupampa River in a basket so that her husband should find it. To Manco's credit be it said, however, that many of his other deeds against the Spaniards bear testimony to the general gallantry of his behavior.[1]

To Dr. Hiram Bingham we are indebted for our present detailed knowledge of Vilcapampa and of Vitcos. He has shown that that region contains a number of ruined villages or hamlets associated with the post-Conquest Incaic period. Vitcos itself was a small place, having two sizable buildings partly in the late Incaic coursed ashlar masonry, partly in the more quickly erected pirca or rubble style. In general, the doorways and niches of the buildings at Vitcos and the neighboring sites are finely made of granite ashlars, the walls being chiefly of rubble-work. Vitcos stands upon a small plain atop a high hill which commands one of the finest views on earth. Round about are other sites, notably that of an important Sun-Temple whose chief feature is a huge white boulder hewn to serve the purposes of the pagan cult.[2] Altogether, Vilcapampa constituted a survival in miniature of the once great Inca empire.

At Vitcos, then, the Inca Manco established his court. He had near him many hundreds of his kinsmen and subjects, and he seems to have lived, so far as he could, in accordance with the customs of his ancestors. His court became a refuge for various Spanish castaways, most of them low fellows who, after the defeat of Almagro the Lad, fled thither to escape the wrath of their foes. With Vitcos as a base, the Inca maintained a fitful resistance to Spanish authority, frequently raiding their provinces and especially the Cuzco-Lima highway, upon which he could swoop at will. In 1539 the city of Huamanga was founded to serve as a defense against the Inca's depredations, but they continued all the same.[3]

The Inca Manco also attempted, occasionally, to play politics with the Spaniards, sympathizing with the Lad, in 1542, and with the Viceroy, in 1544, his motive in each case being that they were enemies of the Pizarros, whom he abominated.[4] For the most part, however, he kept chiefly to himself, leading a life which was largely made up of various sports such as arquebus-shooting, chess, bowls, and quoits, taught him by his unsavory Castilian companions. These seemingly innocent diversions had a tragic outcome; for, during a game of quoits, a quarrel arose in which seven Spanish scalawags murdered the Inca to whom they owed so much. This took place in 1545, at a time when the Inca was planning to aid actively in Nuñez Vela's war against Gonzalo Pizarro.[5]

The Inca Manco having been slain, Sayri Tupac, his son by his murdered wife, succeeded to the Inca-ship; but, because of his tender age, he was placed under the regency of a near kinsman. The narrow realm ruled from Vitcos lay in the mountainous wilds between the Apurimac and Urupampa Rivers, and probably included also a strip of craggy country beyond the latter. Today it is easy enough to enter Vilcapampa by using the modern trail downstream along the right bank of the Urupampa,* but in the period which we are considering it was necessary to go downstream from Ollantaytampu a few miles, then to turn to the right, cross the lofty Pass of Panticalla, go down the steep descent called "Of the Eternal Father," and so arrive in the upper part of the Lucumayo Valley. The going therein was relatively easy, and at the junction of the Lucumayo with the Urupampa there was the bridge called Chuquichaca (Lance-bridge), some thirty miles below Ollantaytampu.[6]

In 1548 a part of the domain thus defined was granted by Gasca to the Inca Sayri Tupac's regent in the hope that the Inca would become a Christian and a vassal of the King. The concession did not have the expected result. Finally, however, in 1555, the Viceroy Marquis of Cañete made a determined effort to bring the Inca Sayri Tupac into submission to the Crown. The negotiations lasted some three years and various interesting personages took part in them, notably the Inca's aunt, Princess Beatriz, wife of Don Mancio Sierra de Leguízamo, and Don Juan de Betánzos, husband of Doña Angelina, sister of Atahualpa and onetime mistress of the Marquis Pizarro. Because of the exhortations of these kinsfolk and of other people the Inca Sayri Tupac was baptized with the name of Diego and, after a picturesquely splendid progress in a magnificent litter with a brave retinue to Lima, where he kissed the Viceroy's hand, the Inca Don Diego Sayri Tupac took up his residence in the gloriously beautiful Valley of Yucay. With his wife, Doña Coya María Cusi Huarcay, he lived there in peace until his early death in 1560.[7]

*The narrow-gauge railway to Santa Ana also follows the Urupampa.

On the death of the Inca Sayri Tupac—or possibly on his quitting paganism and Vilcapampa—the Inca-ship was seized by a natural son of the Inca Manco named Titu Cusi Yupanqui, who thus usurped the place belonging rightfully to Tupac Amaru, legitimate son of the Inca Manco by his wife.[8] So it befell that the usurper Titu Cusi Yupanqui was reigning at Vitcos when, in 1565, Don Diego Rodríguez de Figueroa was sent thither to "reduce" him to Christianity and the King's law. Rodríguez was acting under orders from the President of the Royal Audience of Charcas (La Plata), Judge Don Juan Matienzo de Peralta, who, in his turn, was obeying instructions from Lope García de Castro, Governor General of Peru.[9]

Setting out from Cuzco on April 8th (1565), Don Diego Rodríguez reached Chuquichaca, by way of Panticalla and the Lucumayo, on April 11th. The narrative of Rodríguez is most entertaining, and it shows clearly not only the precautions which the usurping Inca took to preserve himself from intrusion but also the terror which the Christian Indians accompanying Rodríguez felt for their pagan kinsmen of Vilcapampa. In addition to various letters and documents from Judge Matienzo, Rodríguez had with him several loads of presents for the Inca. He had great difficulty, however, about being received, and it was not until May 6th that he was allowed to cross the river in a basket travelling on a cable. At last, on May 13th, he found himself in the presence of Titu Cusi at a place called Pampaconas where "three hundred Indians . . . and others from the surrounding country, had made a great theatre for the Inca, of red clay."[10] The description given by Rodríguez of the Inca's arrival in the "theatre" (probably some sort of amphitheatre)[11] shows clearly that a great degree of pomp and etiquette was maintained, partly derived from the ancient usages, partly influenced by elements brought into the land by the Spaniards. Rodríguez so describes the whole affair that it stands out as a pageant replete with color and barbaric splendor. After the ceremonies of the envoy's reception were over, there was an interchange of gifts, the Inca sending to Rodríguez a cup of chicha, a macaw, and two baskets of mani nuts. Don Diego sent back four pieces of glass and a box of comfits (gifts from Judge Matienzo) and also a large amount of crystals and pearls, as well as seven silver bracelets. Suitable presents were made likewise to the various captains and notables of the Inca's suite.[12] Clearly the Indians got rather the better of the bargain!

Don Diego describes the Inca and his entourage thus:

"The Inca was a man of forty years of age, of middle height, and with some marks of small-pox on his face. His mien was rather severe and manly. He wore a shirt of blue damask, and a mantle of very fine cloth. He is served on silver, and there are also twenty or thirty fairly good-looking women, waiting behind him. He sent for me to dine where he was. . . . The food consisted of maize, potatoes, small beans, and other products of the country, except that there was very little meat, and what there was consisted of venison, fowls, macaws, and monkeys, both boiled and roasted."[13]

On the morning of May 14th (1565), the Inca sent for Don Diego to come to his house. On that occasion Titu Cusi was dressed in a shirt of crimson velvet and a mantle of the same. He was surrounded by a great concourse of his captains, and a large fire was burning in the middle of the audience chamber. Rodríguez gave a fine looking-glass, two coral necklaces and a paper book to the Inca, who was much pleased and invited him to a seat near him. It is evident that Titu Cusi was trying hard to be courteous to his guest, albeit he made it plain that he wished him to be brief and then depart. Then, with the Inca's permission, Don Diego delivered a discourse on Christianity which moved twenty or twenty-five Christian Indians among those present to tears. This softness on their part made the Inca very angry, and he scolded the speaker for his insolence in speaking, before him, of the Lord Jesus Christ, adding that he had a good mind to order the intruder killed. Rodríguez replied that he had but spoken with the Inca's permission and that, in any case, he had taken the Sacrament and was ready for death.[14]

Obviously Don Diego Rodríguez de Figueroa was a man of

rare courage and profound Catholic convictions. Throughout all his pleadings he comported himself with so much bravery, tact, and resoluteness that, by sheer strength of personality, he imposed his will to a large extent upon the recalcitrant Inca. Negotiations dragged on for hours, accompanied by much heavy drinking on the Indians' part, and by continued resoluteness on Don Diego's. The Inca's curiosity regarding Christianity was deeply engaged, in spite of his distaste for it, but most of his advisers were stoutly opposed to it. The proposal made to the Inca was that he should come forth from Vilcapampa and live as a Christian among Christians, in return for which he would be given an entailed estate for himself and his descendants in perpetuity, and all due honor.[15] Otherwise, war would be made upon him and his until they were overcome.

This threat naturally provoked manifestations of force on the part of the Inca and his followers. On May 15th there was a tremendous war-dance in Don Diego's presence, during which 600 wild Antis offered to eat "this little bearded one" raw. Don Diego laughed in their faces, commended himself to God, but asked for the Inca's protection, which was accorded. The next day Rodríguez was told that the whole thing had been in fun, and he asked them to cease from such sport and attend seriously to business. For a time matters went with comparative smoothness. On May 28th, Judge Matienzo himself arrived at Chuquichaca to conclude the peace-treaty. He was accompanied by 30 Spaniards, 10 Negroes, 20 arquebusiers, and 150 Christianized Cañari guards. An interview between the Inca and the Judge was arranged by Rodríguez in spite of the opposition of the Inca's captains. Nothing came of it, however, notwithstanding the professed eagerness on both sides. With uncharacteristic humility the Inca "threw himself at the feet of the Judge, weeping and relating the misfortunes of his father and himself." Suddenly the Inca was dismayed by an indiscreet move on the part of the arquebusiers, after which he hastily returned to his own territory in a mood upon which his advisers so worked that, after a brief statement that he would comply with his word to Rodríguez, he caused the bridge to be broken down and then retired into his own land. The Spanish envoys withdrew sadly to Cuzco.[16]

The usurping Inca, Titu Cusi Yupanqui,[17] continued to rule in Vilcapampa, but with a progressive diminution of that robust paganism which had distinguished his predecessors. In spite of the many difficulties surrounding the study of this part of Inca history it is clear that, from 1565 onwards, the Inca Titu Cusi and his subjects received unremitting missionary attention from the religious and civil authorities, all to the end that Christianity be planted among them and that the ancient pagan sovereign independence be abandoned. Inconveniently enough there is much conflict among our authorities so that one can only try to relate the main trend of events.

According to Titu Cusi himself, in documents dated on February 6th, 1570, he was indoctrinated in the new Faith by the Augustinian Friar Antonio de Vera, who, accompanied by two other Augustinians, Friar Marcos García and Friar Diego de Ortiz, made an intensive missionary campaign in Vilcapampa from some time in 1566 to August, 1568. Previously, in the first days of his being interested in Christianity, Titu Cusi had written letters of inquiry to the monks of St. Francis and to those of Our Lady of Mercy (La Merced), at Cuzco,[18] but, later, acting on advice from Rodríguez, he submitted himself to the instruction of the Augustinians whose Prior, so he was told, held a pre-eminent position among the religious of Cuzco. In a letter to the President Licentiate Don Lope García de Castro—whom he thought to be still ruling Peru—dated February 6th, 1570, the Inca says:

"Having heard this [about the Prior], I became more attached to the order of St. Augustine than to any other. I wrote letters to the Prior, requesting him to come in person to baptize me, because I would rather be baptized by him than by any one else. He took the trouble to come to my country to baptize me, bringing with him another monk and Atilano de Anaya, who arrived at Rayangalla[19] on the 12th of August, 1568, whither I came from Vilcapampa to receive baptism. There, in that village of Rayangalla, were the said Prior named Juan de Vivero and his companions. I was instructed in the things of the faith for a fortnight, at the end of which time, on the day of the glorious Dr. St. Augustine [August 28th], the Prior baptized me."[20]

The account of this period given by Father Calancha in his official history of the Augustinian order in Peru[21] differs from the purport of the contemporary documents. Because Calancha wrote more than sixty years after the events it seems safer to accept the evidence presented here.[22] Another writer, Captain Ocampo Conejeros, who wrote in 1610, would have us believe that the Inca was still a pagan in 1571, after the Viceroy Toledo's arrival in Cuzco.[23] To this point we shall return before long.

At all events it is clear that the rightful Inca, Tupac Amaru I, who was about twenty-one years old in 1568, was completely under his usurping half-brother's thumb, living among the Chosen Women of the Sun, possibly at Machu Picchu, or else in some other town of Vilcapampa. Dr. George F. Eaton has shown that the human skeletal material unearthed at Machu Picchu represents the female sex predominantly. Only a few of the male skeletons found were of the virile type, the rest being the remains of effeminate males of the type to which, so one gathers, the unfortunate Tupac Amaru I belonged. Dr. Eaton inclines to the belief that Machu Picchu sheltered a society of the so-called Virgins of the Sun.[24] Personally, I am convinced that Machu Picchu was the place in which Tupac Amaru spent his youth. Certainly no lad could ask for a more gorgeously beautiful environment in which to pass his days.

This leaves only the Prince Paullu Tupac Yupanqui to be accounted for. He was the fourth of the legitimate sons of the Inca Huayna Capac. Moreover, he was the only man of the imperial family of Peru who early accepted Christianity and Spanish civilization with anything resembling zest. Why he did so is not clear. We know only that, after his adventures at the time of Almagro's going to Chile and the siege of Cuzco by the Inca Manco, the Prince Paullu merged himself into the life of Hispanicized Cuzco and, in 1543, was baptized Cristóbal. He married his kinswoman, Princess Tocto Ussica, who was baptized Catalina, and with her he lived in the Colcampata Palace on the slope of Sacsahuamán, overlooking Cuzco. This couple, who received, for two lives, very rich encomiendas in various regions, never joined their pagan kinsfolk in Vilcapampa. Instead, they lived with considerable pomp in their lovely abode (now in ruins), whence they could gaze with brooding eyes upon the scene of their ancestors' greatness. Don Cristóbal and Doña Catalina had three sons, of whom one, Don Carlos Paullu Inca, married a Spanish lady of Cuzco, Doña María de Esquível. It was this pair who, after the death of Prince Don Cristóbal Paullu in May, 1549, became the heads of the Christianized and Hispanicized branch of the Inca family, in which position they were when the Viceroy Toledo arrived in Cuzco.[25]

2. The Reign of the Viceroy Toledo

King Philip II, ruling over fewer realms than his father, was able to concentrate upon his American possessions a greater proportion of his attention. As we have seen, matters had been going very ill in Peru with the natural result that the King resolved that turmoil should cease. He accordingly sought for a man capable of performing the miracle of reducing Peru to good order. Violence and guile had each been tried by emissaries of King Charles; neither was the panacea because neither was constructive. Whatever else it was, the reign which we are about to study was constructive, even in the midst of its destructiveness.

In July, 1568, King Philip chose as his new Viceroy and Captain-General of Peru Don Francisco de Toledo y Figueroa, third son of the Count and Countess of Oropesa, Knight Commander of the Order of Alcántara, and Majordomo of His Majesty the King. Not only had this lofty personage close kinship with some of the most noble houses of Spain, but also he had already served King Charles and King Philip with rare ability in Flanders, France, Germany, North Africa, and Spain itself. His appointment as Viceroy of Peru was hailed with delight by His Holiness Pope Pius V in a letter dated from Saint Peter's on August 18th, 1568, and by Buoncompagni, Archbishop of Rosano, afterwards Pope Gregory XIII, as well as by a great array of the chief men in Spain.[26]

The appointment carried with it a salary of 40,000 ducats annually and various special privileges which, however, amounted to much less than the sum of the powers formerly conferred upon Gasca. The dour and saturnine figure of this great Viceroy cast its shadow over Peruvian administration for two hundred years. As we shall see, the outstanding accomplishments of Toledo during his tenure of office were: First, the crushing of the native imperial family of Peru; and, second, the establishment of absolute royal Hapsburg power, an establishment which carried with it the nullification of the nascent colonial feudalism which had been the fundamental cause of so many grave disorders.

After many months of preparation for his heavy duties, and after farewell visits to highly placed kinsfolk and friends of his, Toledo and his immense retinue sailed on March 19th, 1569, from San Lucar de Barrameda in a specially prepared fleet, and, after a prosperous voyage, they reached Santo Domingo on April 28th. Touching at Cartagena on May 8th, they arrived at Nombre de Dios on June 1st. At that port Toledo, acting on his master's instructions, hastily collected 205,677 pesos which were sent back to Spain for the King. This done, the Viceroy and his retinue left Nombre de Dios on June 20th, arriving at Panama on the evening of June 23rd.

The progress of the Viceroy Toledo from his lordly Spanish environment to his still more lordly post in Peru is one which any lover of pageantry would wish to describe fully. Not only was the Viceroy attended by a numerous suite made up of secretaries, gentlemen in waiting, gentlemen of the guard, ecclesiastics, and various kinds of servants, but also he had with him a vast amount of fine Spanish furniture, paintings, tapestries, splendid hangings, linens, silver and china for the table, and every sort of elegant embellishment for his house, all of which is designated by the convenient little Spanish word, *recámara*. A very great lord himself and personal representative of the mightiest king in Christendom, Toledo always lived and moved in the grand style which, although decidedly cumbersome, was certainly impressive, constituting a background for his existence which can be appreciated fully only by those who have seen and studied the Spanish architecture and furniture and art of his time. Figure 18, albeit some 180 years later than Toledo's day, helps one to form an idea of the manner of his going across the Isthmus. Multiply the single craft there shown by fifty or more, and picture the fluvial fleet as gay with banners bearing heraldic devices, add the flash of armor and a riot of vivid hues in the finery of the Indian rowers and in that of the Spanish travellers, set the whole in a key of pomp and pride, and you will have a faint notion of the manner in which the Viceroy journeyed up the Chagres River and thence overland to Panama, a notion which will serve to indicate his mode of travel on other occasions.

From Panama the Viceroy, having sent ahead, in a fast ship, his Captain of the Guard, Knight of Calatrava Don Martín García Oñaz de Lóyola, with messages for the President García de Castro and for the Oidores, announcing his coming in terms of pride exemplified by the remark that "there was a Lord in Oropesa before there were Kings in Castile,"[27] took his own way southwards in a fleet of two ships which must have groaned with the load of blue-bloods and fine house-furnishings which they carried. Leaving Panama on August 12th, 1569, the Viceroy reached Manta on September 2nd, whither the Corregidor of Guayaquil and the chief vecinos of the region had come in order to greet him. Thence he pushed on to Paita, a seaport whose reconstruction he ordered, renaming it San Francisco de la Buena Esperanza de Paita, where he was towards the end of September. Having made a thorough study of conditions in that region of Peru, and having sent on the greater part of his retinue and all that pompous recámara of his, in the two ships with the idea that everything be made ready for his proper reception in Lima, Toledo, with comparatively few attendants, proceeded southwards by land, reaching Trujillo on October 15th. There the best houses in town were put at his disposal, and there he conducted further investigations into local conditions. Thus matters went on until, on November 30th, 1569, amid every possible circumstance of etiquette and solemnity, the Viceroy made his state entry into Lima, being duly welcomed there by President García de Castro, the Oidores, all the officials, ecclesiastics, members of the University of San Marcos, and the nobility.[28]

In Lima the Viceroy found himself loaded down with official duties. The Holy Tribunal of the Inquisition was installed and set upon its lugubrious path; the affairs of Chile, which country, up to that time, had been hardly more than a "sepulture for Spaniards," were ameliorated by the sending of a large new expedition, well equipped and led by General Don Miguel de Velasco; and the political administration and financial structure of the Viceroyalty were thoroughly overhauled. One of the most important acts of Toledo during his first sojourn in Lima was the founding of a special Indian town called Santiago del Cercado in the outskirts of Lima, hard by the Indian hospital of Santa Ana. This was a necessary and wise foundation because, hitherto, the Indians who had come to Lima to serve in various capacities had lived miserably in the city of Lima proper. Now they were provided with commodious quarters within walls whose gates were closed at night. This last sounds as though the new Indian town were no more than a ghetto, but it is plain enough that Santiago del Cercado was truly designed for the good and for the protection of its inmates, who were placed in the spiritual care of the Jesuits, and who were given their own local government. In their new town the Indians had gardens where they raised vegetables and fruits for sale in

Lima and produced poultry, pigeons, ducks, and eggs. Likewise, they were encouraged to cultivate music and their orchestras were much in demand for evening parties in the capital. In short, Santiago del Cercado was a paternalistic foundation of precisely the sort which Indians most require.[29] It is an eternal pity that the spirit displayed in this foundation was not universal in Viceregal Peru. On the whole, Toledo's first sojourn in Lima, full of hard work as it was, produced much good.

In that period, also, the Viceroy was preparing himself for his personal inspection of the country. Whether consciously or not, he was making ready to follow the example of the Incas whose wont it had been to know personally as much of their empire as possible, thereby increasing their strength and wisdom immeasurably.[30] In accordance with his habits, Toledo took with him his new secretary, Don Alvar Ruiz de Navamuel; his confessor, Father Gerónimo Ruiz Portillo, S.J.; and a suitable staff of servants.[31]

Having made arrangements whereby the Oidores would govern Lima and northern Peru during his absence, the Viceroy and his retinue left the capital on October 30th, 1570, and, travelling by way of Jauja, Huancavélica, and Huamanga, arrived at Cuzco in the first day or two of 1571. Along the road the Viceroy had been incessantly occupied, as usual, in arrangements concerning the Indians, the administration of mines, and other weighty matters.[32]

It will be remembered that, long prior to the arrival of Toledo in Peru, the Inca family had split into two parties, the one Christianized and Hispanicized, the other but lately baptized and in a mood of half-concealed resentment towards the new order of things. Both parties engaged the Viceroy's attention during his long stay in Cuzco and its region.

At the moment of Toledo's arrival in Cuzco Don Carlos Paullu Inca and his Spanish wife, Doña María de Esquível, had become the parents of a son. On a Sunday early in January, 1571, a gorgeous christening was held at the Colcampata Palace, and the Viceroy stood as a godfather for the little

Don Melchor Carlos Inca. All the leading Spaniards of Cuzco as well as all the Incas for miles round about were invited, and the affair was carried out with all possible pomp. Whether or not it was secretly attended by the usurper, Titu Cusi Yupanqui, and by the rightful Inca Tupac Amaru I, is not certain.[33]

Here we come up against one of those tangles which are the despair of historians of Peru. As already shown, the Inca Titu Cusi Yupanqui had been baptized in 1568; but Captain Ocampo Conejeros represents him as appealing to the Viceroy Toledo, in 1571, for missionaries to convert him and his people to Christianity.[34] I can only conclude that either Titu Cusi had turned apostate and now desired a new conversion to the Catholic Faith, or, as seems more likely, he was making sport of the Viceroy. It is clear, at any rate, that Toledo caused an embassy to be sent into Vilcapampa composed of Atilano de Anaya, who had been there before, and others. Apparently the usurper, Titu Cusi, had grown angry with Friar Marcos García and had had him chased away from Vilcapampa, permitting Friar Diego Ortiz to remain. At some time between January and October, 1571, Titu Cusi developed bronchial pneumonia. His people besought Father Ortiz to make use of the medical knowledge for which he was famous, and the Friar administered white of egg mixed with sulphur and pepper, a tonic which caused the Inca presently to vomit so severely that he soon passed to a better world. Thereupon the Indians, whose Christian convictions had never been more than skin deep, reverted to paganism, and they gave the most horrible torments to their Christian friend until he died, a martyr. The mestizo interpreter, Pando, was killed in the same manner.[35]

Immediately after the death of Titu Cusi, the Indian officials withdrew Tupac Amaru from his retirement among the Chosen Women, and raised him up to be their Sovereign. In doing so all the traditional ceremonies of the Incas were used by them, for the last time upon this earth. Amid an atmosphere of renewed resistance to Spanish rule, the young Inca was solemnly invested with the ancient insignia of his dynasty.[36]

These events befell before the final journey of Atilano de Anaya to Vilcapampa. Neither the Viceroy nor his ambassador was aware that the Inca-ship had passed to Tupac Amaru. From Yucay the Viceroy wrote a letter, dated October 16th, 1571, to Titu Cusi, reproving him for not having come forth to pay homage, and bidding him to come and live as a Christian vassal of the King. This letter Anaya carried with him. Accompanied only by a Negro servant—for the other envoys refused to go beyond Ollantaytampu—Anaya proceeded to the Chuquichaca bridge. He was fain to cross it alone, as the Indians would not allow the Negro to pass. They put the ambassador in a hut near the river, together with his camp bed and luggage, and there, by night, Anaya was done to death by certain Indian captains, probably without authority from the Inca Tupac Amaru. The Negro heard the noise made by the murderers at their work, and on the morrow he bravely made his way to the hut. Finding it empty, even the bed and luggage having been taken away, he understood that his master was dead, and with the sad news he hurried back to Cuzco without being caught.[37]

The Viceroy Toledo now had, we must admit, just cause for unlimited wrath. With characteristic vigor he caused a large army to be formed under General Don Martín Hurtado de Arbieto, with Captain Don Martín García Oñaz de Lóyola as second in command. There were ten other captains, as well, all men of good blood and position. Finally, in the Urupampa Valley, far downstream from Chuquichaca, Oñaz de Lóyola and fifty soldiers fought with and captured not only the Inca and many of his officers, women, and children, but also a vast booty made up of things held most holy by the Incas, including the great image of the Sun, formerly in Coricancha, in Cuzco.[38]

In the war thus ended against the Inca dynasty many Indians, both nobles and plebeians, were captured or slain. Most of those who were not killed were gathered into a large village called San Francisco de la Victoria de Vilcapampa where, under the rule of the Corregidor Hurtado de Arbieto, they were subjected to the process of Hispanization.[39]

The young Inca, Tupac Amaru I, was taken to Cuzco, and with him, as captives, went also his leading officials and kinsmen. It is pitiful to reflect that they, whose only crime was that of endeavoring to rid their country of tyrannical and oppressive invaders, were subjected to unspeakable humiliations and tortures. Efforts were made by priests, acting on the orders of Toledo, to baptize the Inca, just as Atahualpa had been similarly pestered forty years earlier in like circumstances. At the same time, charges which at most were only partly valid were made against the Inca while he was held in the fortress of Sacsahuamán, and Don Carlos Inca, recently so high in the Viceroy's favor, fell into deep disgrace and was obliged to submit to the sequestration of his Colcampata Palace, seized by Toledo's order.[40]

The important fact for us to remember in this connection is that all the testimony adduced for the so-called trial of Tupac Amaru was translated by the official interpreter, Gonzalo Jiménez. He was a mestizo, very well versed in Quechua, who surpassed in general depravity even that other sinister interpreter, Felipillo, who had been instrumental in Atahualpa's death. Some years after the events now in question Jiménez was found to be guilty of misconduct with the pages of the Viceroy's household. This abominable person was then secretly garrotted in prison by his master's order. Toledo feared that the scandalous immorality prevailing among his servants would become known, and he also dreaded, even more, that the public would learn that the evidence given against Tupac Amaru had been perverted in translation by Jiménez, who, in terror of his impending fate, had expressed a wish publicly to confess the mass of lies which constituted the chief basis of the legal process against the Inca and also of the versions of Incaic history put forth by Toledo and his henchman, Captain Pedro Sarmiento de Gamboa.[41]

The basis, then, upon which the Viceroy's order for the

death of Tupac Amaru rested was almost wholly false, as were also the grounds for the varying degrees of punishment meted out to his captains and kinsmen. Although the falsity of the charges and Jiménez's wicked part therein were not yet revealed, practically all the most distinguished Spaniards, lay and clerical, in Cuzco vigorously but vainly protested against the execution. It seems that, for some time, the Inca stoutly resisted the efforts to Christianize him but that, at the very end, moved by the words of one of his staunchest defenders, the Bishop of Popayán, he went through the motions of accepting a Faith which must have seemed to him anything but sweet and lofty. In the Plaza of Cuzco, thronged with a mourning multitude of Indians, he was beheaded. Later, the wrathful prohibition of Toledo notwithstanding, his body was given a splendid funeral, Mass being said by the compassionate Bishop of Popayán in the cathedral. After this the Inca's head was exposed on a pike in the Plaza, where thousands of Indians silently worshipped it until at last it was taken down and buried with the body in the cathedral.[42]

Thus ended one phase of Toledo's anti-Inca policy. The next phase was, if anything, even more nefarious than the first. It consisted of a systematic perversion of traditions relative to the Incas and their history all to the end that the Incas might be made to appear before the world as a set of ruffians, blackguards, bastards, and usurpers. In short, the Viceroy himself and certain associates of his among whom Sarmiento is the most important, made it their business to anathematize the Inca dynasty in such a way that their fair name would perish and that it would become clear to every one that the King of Castile is "legitimate Lord of these realms, whereas the Incas and curacas (chiefs) are tyrants and, as such, intruders in the government of these lands." When one recalls certain facts in Castilian dynastic history, the Toledo-Sarmiento objurgations against the Incas rise into the plane of high comedy. For instance: Sancho IV, second son of Alfonso X, called "the Learnéd," seized the somewhat feeble royal power in 1284, in direct contravention of his father's laws and last tes-

FIG. 7. Air photograph of a ruined Spanish town in the Colca Valley.
By Aerial Explorations, Inc., Chrysler Bldg., New York.

FIG. 8. An Indian town in the highlands behind Lima.
Courtesy of W. V. Alford, Esq.

tament; Peter "the Cruel," only legitimate son of Alfonso XI, was as tyrannical as any one could be and, after nineteen years of shameless misrule, was driven from the throne in 1369 by his bastard half-brother, Henry of Trastamara, who ruled as Henry II.[43] Moreover, a dynasty whose kings had conducted themselves in Italy, Germany, the Netherlands, Africa, and America, as had those of the House of Hapsburg, was most unwise to regard such a dynasty as that of the Incas as "intruders." The height of ridiculous pretentiousness is reached when we recall that the chief claim of the Hapsburgs to their American possessions was the donation of that saintly Pontiff, Alexander VI, born Borgia, the donation being a reward given by God for all the bravery and glory of the eight centuries of the Reconquest in Spain against the Moors![44] If we constantly bear in mind the fact that all the historical evidence submitted to Sarmiento and Toledo was interpreted by Jiménez, and if we remember that Toledo was determined at all costs to make his master believe that the Incas were tyrannical usurpers, we shall be in no danger of ascribing to the Toledan school of historical writings a greater weight than they deserve. At the same time, we may take satisfaction in the knowledge that neither Toledo's nor Sarmiento's work was published until modern times.

In spite of his anti-Inca literary and political activities, the Viceroy Toledo seems to have cherished a sneaking admiration for the native art of Peru. In this he had a certain pallid encouragement from his master, King Philip. The lukewarm interest of Charles I with regard to the archæological aspect of Atahualpa's ransom has already been noted. Philip II seems to have been a trifle more interested in the matter of native art than his father; for, in March, 1571, he wrote to Toledo, saying: ". . . in regard to objects that may be found and taken from the *huacas,* if there are any that seems to you to be of noteworthy quality, good enough to be seen here, you may send them." To this hint Toledo replied in two letters, the one dated from Cuzco, on March 1st, 1572, the other dated from Cuzco on October 9th, 1572. From these we gather that

Toledo had formed a collection of sightly Incaic objects which he sent to the King, probably at the same time that his own and Sarmiento's histories of the Incas were sent, so that they might be suitably housed in the Royal palace, and so constitute what we of today would call a Museum of the Peruvian Indian. The principal object thus sent was the great golden image of the Sun which had been one of the chief ornaments of Coricancha, the Temple of the Sun in Cuzco. This image had been taken from its place by Huáscar at the time of his war with Atahualpa, and later it had come into the possession of Huáscar's legitimate heir, Tupac Amaru. When that unfortunate young man was captured, the great image of the Sun was taken also, along with much other booty, and it was to this image that Toledo referred in the later of the two letters cited above. He made therein an acidly humorous suggestion that the King send the image to His Holiness the Pope as a token that Christianity was now triumphant in Peru over the ancient paganism.[45]

What was in reality done with regard to the objects mentioned by Toledo as being destined to the King and to the Pope is not known. Possibly some day they will come to light in one or another of the ex-royal palaces of Spain or even in some forgotten corner of the Vatican. A curious student might do worse than to seek for them.[46]

Toledo remained in Cuzco and its vicinity nearly two years all told. He was extremely busy with his nefarious literary campaign against the fair name of the Incas, with politico-sociological matters, and with administrative duties. During this period he gave very particular attention to the mines of Peru and to the discovery of the value of mercury or quicksilver as an element in the process of refining silver-ore. This discovery was made by Pedro Fernández Velasco, a metallurgical genius of that day, who had first studied the matter in Mexico and who, in 1573, brought it to the Viceroy's notice in Cuzco. With that personal devotion to duty which was one of his outstanding virtues, Toledo witnessed the working of Fernández Velasco's method and, assured of its practical value, introduced its use into the mines of Potosí, the mercury being derived from the royal mercury mines at Huancavélica. The result of this reform was a general abandonment of the ancient methods of refining which the Spaniards had inherited from the Incas.[47]

During the Viceroy's stay in Cuzco a letter was received by him from the King, dated December 26th, 1571, in which was related the victory won by Don John of Austria over the Turks at Lepanto, as well as the news of the King's remarriage and the birth of an heir. Such a letter as this naturally moved the good folk of Cuzco to hold sumptuous rejoicings in which the Viceroy took the leading part, and in which every one, Spaniards and Indians alike, participated.[48]

Not until October 5th, 1573, therefore, was the Viceroy able to set out from Cuzco for his tour of inspection in the Charcas, during which he visited La Plata, Potosí, and other important centres of Spanish civilization. It was in the course of that tour that he had a highly ridiculous and disastrous contact with the Chiriguanos, a fierce and intractable folk who inhabit that portion of the Gran Chaco which lies to the east of La Plata (Sucre) and Potosí. These savages, having heard of the sad end of Tupac Amaru, and being well aware that they had for centuries been in the habit of raiding and terrorizing the milder and more cultured folk west of them, came to the conclusion that they might be the next to feel the wrath of the Spaniards. Accordingly a number of them went up to La Plata or Chuquisaca, where the Viceroy then was, with an extraordinary tale of having received certain wooden crosses, which they bore, from angels who came down from Heaven and bade them go and ask for missionaries to convert their people to Christianity. The deluded Viceroy and the great ecclesiastics of La Plata showed the envoys and their miraculous crosses every sort of honor. But, alas, one stormy night the envoys ran away to their native wilds, thus making the Viceroy aware that he had been the victim of a jest. In his wrath he rashly determined to resort to punitive measures. The military expedition which he then prepared was one of

the most fully equipped and most sumptuously furnished ever
seen. The invasion of the Chiriguano country was, however,
a complete fiasco, and the great Viceroy had to flee in disorder. Because of the roughness of the country he had to give
up his litter and all the beautiful camp-equipment which he
had. Fine leather chairs were left behind, and the Indians,
we are told, ate the very leather with which they were covered. The Viceroy had to be carried in a sort of wicker-work
seat borne by his Spanish and Indian servants on their backs.
The Chiriguanos followed behind with derisive shouts, calling
out, "Throw that old woman out of the basket so that we may
eat her!" In short, the great Viceroy became a figure of fun
for once in his sombre life.[49]

On the legislative side of his career Toledo was powerfully
aided by such men as Judge Matienzo and the Licentiate Polo
de Ondegardo, both of whom realized to the full that the Indian and his civilization must inevitably form the basis of
Royal Spanish power in Peru, but neither of whom can justly
be blamed for the harshness of Toledo's administrative
measures.[50]

Toledo, in his ordering of Peruvian affairs, proceeded on the
major premise that the Royal authority *must* be made supreme. In this he was an even more thorough-going absolutist than were Richelieu and Mazarin in France in the next
century. To serve this fundamental purpose of his he adapted
to the needs of colonial government in Peru some of the social
and administrative machinery which had existed under the
Incas, but he did so in such a manner that what had been a
merciful and just system became one of great oppressiveness.
In short, Toledo set up a bi-partite government, one part of
which, the so-called minor government, was a perverted form
of the native administrative system, the other part of which,
the so-called major government, was wholly of Spanish origin.

The general result of Toledo's deliberate adaptation and
continuation, in perverted form, of the Incaic administrative
hierarchy was a great weighing-down of the native population under a tremendous load of tribute-obligations and other

impositions. It is to be noted, however, that conditions were already bad before Toledo came to Peru. Don Damián de la Bandera, writing in 1557, says as follows:

"The chief cause of the increase of tyranny by the caciques [correctly curacas or chiefs] over their subjects has been the fact that during Inca rule they had slight power over their Indians, but that, with the arrival of the Spaniards and the decline of the Inca's power, they have arrogated to themselves all that pre-eminence and authority which formerly belonged to the Inca, so that, now possessing civil and criminal jurisdiction hitherto not his, each cacique has made himself in his own dung-pile that which the Inca was in the whole realm."[51]

Obviously, Toledo cannot be blamed for the specific condition described by Bandera; but he can be blamed for adapting to his needs the same tyranny which existed before his day, doing so without any apparent effort to restore what was already a perverted system to its original excellent character. It is well to note, in passing, that Toledo so esteemed Bandera that he appointed him to be Corregidor of Potosí, the richest mining town in all Peru.[52] Toledo therefore made the perverted forms of native administration his own, creating a system which will be described further on. It should be remembered, in this connection, that the abusiveness of the Toledan bi-partite government, and specifically the oppressive rule of the curacas, otherwise styled caciques or mandones, dates, not from Incaic times, but from Spanish times. It was occasioned by the hunger for money, and that was wholly unknown under the Incas, as I have shown elsewhere.[53]

Toledo himself was well aware of the tyrannical behavior of the curacas since the coming of the Spaniards. In his account of it to the King, however, he implies that the Incas had been even more tyrannical than the curacas, in which we see the fell influence of Gonzalo Jiménez. He, Toledo, goes on to say that he provided the caciques with titles to their cacique-ships in the name of the King and that he arranged that the heir to each should be the most "Christian and virtuous," but not necessarily the eldest, son of each chief. He concludes this matter by urging the King to preserve the system which he had thus established "because, otherwise, there will arise among them [the Indians] much inconvenience, harm, and legal disputation."[54]

In short, Toledo made it clear enough to all that the object of the Crown was to get as much money as possible out of Peru and this chiefly through the incredibly hard work of the native people there. True, the tradition of Royal benevolence towards the American subjects of the Crown still had life in it, but it was rendered nugatory to a large extent by conditions to which reference will be made later. Besides, it concerned itself more with saving the souls of the people by "Christianizing" them than it did with making their sojourn on this planet reasonably comfortable and happy. Thus, amid a great deal of pious palaver, Toledo decided arbitrarily what tribute the Indians were to pay, and what was to be the nature of the mita or corvée system under which their work in mines, on farms, on public works, in factories and elsewhere was to be performed. These matters and all else pertinent to the administration of Peru were set forth in various documents such as the Libro de Tasas, the first part of which was dated at Checacupe, south of Cuzco, on October 18th, 1572, and such as the various Ordenanzas which Toledo gave on every conceivable subject at divers times.[55]

Toledo devoted much attention to the affairs of the Church, finding them in a very bad way. Many of the sees were either vacant or else held by sick and gouty old men unfit to perform the duties of their posts. Upwards of forty curacies were without priests. The regular clergy were far from showing the proper alacrity for missionary work. The administration of the Sacraments and the other services of the Church were too often neglected or else performed in a perfunctory manner. Some curacies, especially in the Bishopric of Quito, were so large that no priest could look after them properly. The schools for the children which the Church was supposed to maintain were too few. Most of the clergymen in remote places were given to trading, gambling, and misbehavior with their maidservants. In short, the state of the Church could not well be worse than Toledo found it. The reforms which he suggested were sane enough, but not particularly forceful.[56]

An ecclesiastical event characteristic of the Spanish régime in Peru from Toledo's day onwards is one with which the Viceroy was only indirectly connected. On Sunday, November 15th, 1573, Lima witnessed her Inquisition's first *auto de fé* (act of Faith). The victim was an elderly Frenchman who had lived a hermit's existence for some years atop one of the ancient mounds or *huacas* with which the Lima Valley is studded. This man, Mathieu Salade by name, was accused of being a heretic and was burned to death in the Plaza of Lima in the presence of an august audience composed of all the most distinguished Christian citizens of the place.[57] Thus did the Holy Inquisition begin its long career in Peru. A second auto de fé was held in the presence of Toledo and of the Oidores on April 13th, 1578, and it was an excellent example of practical Christianity as it was then understood and practiced. There were sixteen victims, including six priests, a merchant, and a lawyer, all of whom were marched in procession with ropes around their necks, some to be flogged with 200 lashes, some to be burned alive, and all to be bereft of their worldly possessions. Because of the virulent and sadistic fury of the Inquisitors no one in Peru felt safe to think freely for himself on any subject during the whole of the colonial period. The one good point about the Inquisition was that its jurisdiction did not extend to the Indians who, being regarded as catechumens, could not be guilty of heresy. To this lugubrious subject we shall have to return later on.

One of the chief virtues of Toledo was that he did not dread hard work. His visita or personal inspection of Peru occupied him during five years, and it has never been equalled in its way by any of the succeeding rulers of the country. To judge by the Viceroy's own words on the subject, it was productive of much good in the matter of improvements in town governments, public works, new and better buildings, stronger jails, and so on. In Lima, for instance, the Viceroy inaugurated the sytsem of waterworks, piping pure water from a place called La Atarjea (The Culvert), a few miles up the Rimac Valley, to the city. The spring which he used for this purpose is still an important part of the water-works of Lima.[58]

The Viceroy returned from the south by way of Arequipa, where he sojourned towards the end of 1575, and arrived in Lima early in 1576. There his life was filled with hard work, as usual, in connection with his multifarious official duties. Peru was by now brought to as great a degree of public and private peace as it was destined ever to know. True, unhappiness and misery of all kinds existed in the land, but at least it was freed from the incessant strife between factions which had so long disturbed it.

Suddenly, during the night of Friday, February 13th, 1579, a novel and dismaying excitement burst forth. Francis Drake in the *Golden Hind,* attended by a pinnace and a skiff, swooped into Callao Bay from the south. The corsairs were in quest of the ship of Miguel Angel which, so they had heard, was laden with silver bars. Learning that the cargo had not yet been put on board, they went about to all the ships in the harbor, cutting the cables of seven out of the nine vessels anchored there. They captured a merchant ship laden with a rich cargo of merchandise fresh from Spain and, taking her with them, they gaily skipped out of the harbor again and took a northerly course.

Rudely awakened from his slumber at one o'clock in the morning, the Viceroy Toledo combated this new danger with characteristic vigor. True, the corsairs managed to get clear away, but a naval expedition in which Captain Pedro Sarmiento de Gamboa took an important part was sent after the miscreants, sailing from Callao on February 27th, 1579, but, although they pursued their intended victims northwards, they never caught up with them and at length returned to Lima to report to the Viceroy.

Drake had left Plymouth on December 13th, 1577, with a regular commission from Queen Elizabeth for privateering under certain fixed provisos. On August 21st, 1578, he entered the Strait of Magellan and passed through it in sixteen days. He passed along the coasts of Chile and Peru between November, 1578, and March, 1579, intent on robbery rather than on murder, and he passed along the American shore to as far north as the 48th parallel of latitude. Finally he returned home by way of the Moluccas, Java, and the Cape of Good Hope, reaching Plymouth in September, 1580, soon after which he was knighted by Queen Elizabeth.

The news of Drake's doings was reported to King Philip in seven letters written by Don Antonio de Padilla, President of the Royal Council of the Indies. They are dated from Madrid between August 6th and September 5th, 1579, and one of them, that of August 11th, enclosed letters from Toledo dated at Lima on February 18th and March 21st, 1579. These Padilla letters bear marginal comments by the King showing that he took the terrible tidings with praiseworthy fortitude. He intended, through diplomatic channels, to seek redress from Queen Elizabeth, and also to prevent further incursions of this kind by fortifying the Strait of Magellan.[59]

At length, on September 23rd, 1581, Don Francisco de Toledo was relieved of his duties by his successor, Don Martín Enríquez de Almanza, who had been Viceroy of New Spain. Toledo went home to Spain, where, far from basking in the sunshine of the Royal favor, he was received by the King with a coldness so piercing that he presently died of a broken heart (September, 1584). Thus did Philip II reward a man who, however wrong his courses may have been, had served him with extraordinary devotion for many years amid the most difficult circumstances.[60]

Notes to Chapter V

[1] Cieza, 1918, pp. 2–3. P. Pizarro, 1921, II, pp. 405–408. Enríquez, 1862, pp. 98–115. Bingham, 1912, pp. 8–9; 1922, pp. 175–177.

[2] Bingham, 1910; 1912, pp. 40–60; 1913, pp. 453–461; 1922, pp. 170–178 and 198–265. For brief notes on Incaic architecture see: Means, 1931, pp. 529–535.

[3] Bingham, 1912, pp. 9–11; 1922, p. 178. Markham, 1892, p. 105.

⁴ Cieza, 1913, pp. 123–125; 1918, pp. 240–241, 292–293. Garcilaso, Pt. II, Bk. IV, Ch. vi.

⁵ Titu Cusi Yupanqui, 1913; 1916, pp. 92–97. Garcilaso, Pt. II, Bk. IV, Ch. vii. Bingham, 1912, pp. 15–18; 1922, pp. 179–183.

⁶ See: Wiener, 1880, Ch. xvii; Bingham, 1922, pp. 194–195, 201–202. In 1914 I followed this route and can testify to its great beauty and to the ease with which it could have been defended.

⁷ There were at least two Ñustas (Princesses) Beatriz, namely, the sister of Inca Manco who married Don Mancio Sierra, and another, almost certainly a sister of Atahualpa, who had two successive Spanish husbands, Don Martín de Mustincia and Diego Hernández, a one-time tailor who had won a good position in Peru, in spite of which the Princess, perhaps naturally, boggled at marrying a former *siri-camayoc,* but she was forced to do it. See: Markham's interesting notes on p. 272 of the first volume of his Garcilaso; also, Garcilaso, Pt. II, Bk. VI, Ch. iii; Pt. I, Bk. IX, Ch. xvii; Titu Cusi, 1916, p. 100. Modern authorities include: Cúneo-Vidal, 1925, pp. 197–210, where admirable data on Sayri Tupac and his travels are presented; Bingham, 1912, pp. 18–22; 1922, pp. 185–186; Means, 1919, pp. 1–7.

⁸ Sarmiento, 1907, pp. xvi–xvii, and 193 (where Sarmiento falsely accuses Tupac Amaru I of being a bastard and *uti,* impotent or incapable). See also: Garcilaso, Pt. I, Bk. VII, Ch. xvi. Don Rómulo Cúneo-Vidal points out that the Inca Sayri Tupac and his wife had but one child, the Princess Doña Beatriz Clara. After her father's death she, a great heiress with three estates on which were more than 1,600 tribute-payers and 9,000 ordinary Indians, was placed, with her mother, in the house of a vecino of Cuzco named Arias Maldonado so that the influence of his wife and daughters should Hispanicize her thoroughly. Maldonado permitted his brother, Cristóbal Maldonado, to rape the girl when she was less than ten in order that she might be forced to marry him. She did so, but the marriage was annulled later. When fifteen years old the Princess chose as her husband her first-cousin, Prince Felipe Quispi Titu, son of Titu Cusi Yupanqui, and for this match a Papal dispensation had to be obtained. After the death of Prince Felipe, Princess Beatriz Clara married, in 1572, the captor of Inca Tupac Amaru I, Don Martín García Oñaz de Lóyola, nephew of Saint Ignatius of Lóyola, founder of the Jesuits. Their daughter, Princess Doña Lorenza Ana María de Lóyola Coya, was taken to Spain by order of the King and there she married Don Juan Enríquez de Borja, son of Saint Francis of Borja, receiving, in 1616, the title of Marchioness of Oropesa. A son and a daughter of theirs married into the house of Idiáquez, Dukes of Granada, to which belonged San Francisco Javier. Thus did the blood of the Incas mingle with that of Saints. Let us hope that they are all cosy and happy in Heaven. See: Cúneo-Vidal, 1925, pp. 211–219, for valuable data. Also Mendiburu, 1874–1890, V, pp. 89–92.

⁹ See: Dr. Romero's remarks at p. xxiii of Titu Cusi, 1916; and Means, 1928, pp. 391–392. The year of Rodríguez's journey to Vitcos is not set down by him, but he mentions that Good Friday fell on April 20th. I find, on consulting the Trésor de Chronologie of Louis Count of Mas Latrie (Paris, 1889), that Easter fell on April 22nd in 1565. See: Rodríguez, 1913, p. 173.

¹⁰ Rodríguez, 1913, pp. 178–179. Dr. Bingham, 1922, pp. 268–277, describes

vividly this part of Inca-land and his adventures therein, but he opines that the modern village of Pampaconas is not the ancient one, and he makes no mention of the red clay theatre.

11 Mr. Robert Shippee describes and pictures some curious arrangements of terraces which he saw from the air fifteen miles northwest of Cuzco. There are four circular or oval depressions nicely lined with tiers of terraces. Although Mr. Shippee pronounces them to be amphitheatres, it seems to me more likely that they were primarily intended for agriculture, the depression being made for the sake of escaping from the winds. Arrangements similar to these, but smaller, are to be seen on the Istrian Peninsula, near Pola on the Adriatic, where, so I was told, their object is protection from the wind and the collection of warmth. Still, it may well be that, in Peru, these constructions were used in a secondary way as places in which ceremonies were performed. See: Shippee, 1932, Fig. 17 and p. 18.

12 Rodríguez, 1913, pp. 179–182.

13 Rodríguez, 1913, p. 182. The menu here given shows that at least some of the food was derived from the forest country downstream from Vilcapampa, over which the Inca exercised a degree of control.

14 Rodríguez, 1913, pp. 184–185.

15 Markham, in his translation of Rodríguez, pp. 185 and 190, says that the proffered income was upwards of $15,000; but Matienzo, 1910, p. 196, says 1,000 to 1,500 pesos, which was certainly not a lavish offer.

16 Rodríguez, 1913, pp. 185–199. Matienzo, 1910, pp. 193–198.

17 Titu Cusi admitted his illegitimacy to Rodríguez and excused his seizure of the Inca-ship on the ground of his being older than his half-brother. See: Rodríguez, 1913, pp. 188–189; Sarmiento, 1907, p. 193. One may remark in passing that Titu Cusi was, at this time, not so old as Rodríguez states; he was probably less than thirty. Indians age early.

18 Rodríguez, 1913, p. 193.

19 Dr. Bingham does not mention this place. But a late eighteenth-century map by Tadeo Haenke, in the British Museum, shows a place called Rayampata in the part of Vilcapampa nearest to Cuzco. This may be it.

20 Titu Cusi, 1913, pp. 167–168; 1916, pp. 104–106. Mackehenie, 1909–1913, pp. 379–385, reproduces important entries in the account-book of the King's Bursar, Miguel Sánchez, for 1569 which support the Inca's statement that Father Vera was the first Augustinian to come to Vilcapampa and that he came thither and remained for a year and a half (1566–1567) during which time he baptized Quispi Titu, the Inca's son, who took the name of Felipe. See Note 8, above. It seems that Father Vera left Vilcapampa soon after Prior Vivero and Friar Marcos García (not mentioned by name in the quotation just given) arrived there. Friar Marcos stayed longer than the Prior, and on February 15th, 1569, Friar Diego de Ortiz came to Vilcapampa to aid Father Marcos. The Augustinian order received payment for its missionary labors from the Crown at the rate of 600 pesos per annum for each missionary.

21 Calancha, 1639, Bk. IV, Chs. i–ix.

22 Bingham, 1912, pp. 51–55; 1922, pp. 186–191, relies chiefly on Calancha. His account of the missionary methods of Friars García and Ortiz is very

lively and well worth reading. Moreover, it is well supported by the archæology of Vilcapampa as revealed by Dr. Bingham.

23 Ocampo, 1907, pp. 210–211.

24 Eaton, 1916, pp. 93–95.

25 Ocampo, 1907, pp. 206–208. Sarmiento, 1907, pp. xvi–xviii, 160, 169, 185–186, 193. Garcilaso, Pt. I, Bk. IX, Chs. xxxviii and xl. Markham, 1910, pp. 260–261. Cúneo-Vidal, 1925, pp. 145–178.

26 These two Popes were among the most vigorous and worthy of the successors of St. Peter. See: Hayward, 1931, pp. 287–290; T. Sánchez, 1867, pp. 212–219.

27 T. Sánchez, 1867, p. 225.

28 T. Sánchez, 1867, pp. 221–232. Leguía y Martínez, 1921. Markham's Introduction to Sarmiento, 1907, pp. xiv–xvii. Markham, 1892, pp. 148–149.

29 Jesuit history in Peru began in 1568. See: Brucker, 1919, p. 401.

30 Means, 1931, p. 274, shows the significance of the Incas' tours.

31 T. Sánchez, 1867, pp. 241–245.

32 T. Sánchez, 1867, pp. 245–249. Sánchez mis-dates Toledo's arrival at Cuzco, saying that it took place in February instead of in the first days of January.

33 Ocampo, 1907, pp. 206–209, gives the date of this Christening as "Epiphany Sunday, January 6th, 1571." There is something wrong with that date as Sunday fell on the 8th, not the 6th, in 1571 (as I gather from Mas Latrie's tables). See also: T. Sánchez, 1867, pp. 281–282; Markham, 1892, pp. 149–150; 1910, pp. 289–290. Cúneo-Vidal, 1925, pp. 147–153, tells us that subsequently Don Melchor Carlos Inca went to Spain where he received a grant of arms from Philip III and the grant of an annual pension of 7,500 ducats payable at the Royal Treasury in Lima, and also a habit of the Order of Santiago. The pension turned out to be but a cheap gift; for, when the recipient sought for a royal licence to return to Peru in order to enjoy it, the permission was refused, and he died an exile at Alcalá de Henares in 1610. On this see also: Garcilaso, Pt. I, Bk. IX, Ch. xl; Ocampo, 1907, p. 225. Cúneo-Vidal, 1925, p. 153.

34 Ocampo, 1907, pp. 209–212.

35 Titu Cusi, 1916, pp. xxiii–xxiv, and Appendix E. T. Sánchez, 1867, p. 268. Ocampo, 1907, pp. 213–215. Mendiburu, VI, pp. 186–189. Markham, on p. 211 of Ocampo, 1907, cites a Life of Father Ortiz, in Italian, by Father Fulgencio Baldani, a book which I have been unable to learn more about, much less to see. Cúneo-Vidal, 1925, pp. 249–263.

36 Ocampo, 1907, pp. 215–217.

37 Ocampo, 1907, pp. 217–218. T. Sánchez, 1867, pp. 266–269.

38 Ocampo, 1907, pp. 218–224. T. Sánchez, 1867, pp. 265–267, gives in full a letter written by the Viceroy from Yucay on October 16th, 1571, to Titu Cusi, whom he addresses as "Very Magnificent Sir, my Son" (Muy magnífico señor hijo), and whom he chides for not coming forth to see him. On the other hand, we read in Ocampo, 1907, p. 222, that on the day of St. Francis, October 4th, 1571, Tupac Amaru was already captured; but this is surely a lapsus styli, 1571 for 1572. Oviedo, 1907, in speaking of these events, tells us that the Viceroy formally declared war on the Inca on Palm Sunday, 1572

(which was March 31st in that year, according to Count Louis de Mas Latrie's tables). His reason for doing so was the murder of his ambassador, Anaya, by the Indians. Oviedo adds that the prisoners were brought into Cuzco on St. Matthew's Day, September 21st, 1572. See: Oviedo, 1907, pp. 69–71. But the "proofs of services" drawn up by Oñaz de Lóyola himself, as printed on pp. 22–23 of Volume VII of the Juicio de Límites entre el Perú y Bolivia (edited by Dr. Victor M. Maúrtua in 12 volumes, Barcelona, 1906), bear the dates October 2nd and 3rd, 1572, from Cuzco. From all this one gathers that the capture was made in September rather than in October, 1572. See also: Cúneo-Vidal, 1925, pp. 277–281.

[39] Ocampo, 1907, pp. 222–223.

[40] Ocampo, 1907, pp. 224–225. T. Sánchez, 1867, p. 282.

[41] See the letter from Don Lope Diez de Armendáriz, an Oidor of the Audiencia of Charcas or La Plata, written from that city to the King on September 25th, 1576, and printed in Levillier, 1918, pp. 331–385, especially p. 337. Riva-Agüero, 1922, pp. 7–9, has made valuable comments on this matter. See also: Means, 1928, pp. 487–497.

[42] Ocampo, 1907, pp. 225–229. Oviedo, 1907, pp. 69–73. T. Sánchez, 1867, pp. 279–282. Markham, 1892, pp. 153–155. Cúneo-Vidal, 1925, pp. 298–301. Zimmerman, 1929, pp. 9–10. Riva-Agüero, 1921, pp. 55–56.

[43] Chapman, 1918, pp. 118–121. Altamira, 1913–1914, I, pp. 589–591. H. J. Chaytor, in Peers, 1929, p. 50.

[44] The Toledan attitude towards the Incas will be found in Toledo, 1882, and in Sarmiento, 1907. In Means, 1928, pp. 462–497, will be found a full treatment of the significance of these two men as historians, and on pp. 298–299 of the same work will be found a description of the Anonymous Letter of 1571 wherein the extreme of Toledo's anti-Inca attitude is expressed.

[45] Very interesting data on this subject will be found on pp. xviii–xxi of Don Marcos Jiménez de la Espada's letter to the Count of Toreno, in the front of the volume containing editions of Santillán, Santa Cruz Pachacuti, and the Anonymous Jesuit (i. e., Blas Valera), Madrid, 1879. Further data are given by Jiménez on pp. 926–928 of the magazine Inca whose sole volume appeared in Lima in 1923. Dr. Robert Lehmann-Nitsche, in his magnificent work, "Coricancha," has traced the history of the great image of the Sun and has shown that the figure of the Sun which Don Mancio Sierra de Leguízamo once had and played away at cards was a minor object, probably the cover of the great monolithic basin which stood in the cloister of the temple. See: J. R. Gutiérrez, 1879; Cúneo-Vidal, 1925, pp. 283–289; Lehmann-Nitsche, 1928, pp. 35–43; Means, 1928, pp. 491–493.

[46] Jiménez de la Espada, on p. 928 of Inca, quotes a letter written from Madrid on January 10th, 1667, by a Father Muret in which American antiquities existing then in the Palace of the Buen Retiro, in Madrid, are described. This letter was published in Morel-Fatio, 1879, pp. 53–54.

[47] T. Sánchez, 1867, pp. 282–289. Moses, 1914, I, p. 327, and II, p. 23.

[48] T. Sánchez, 1867, pp. 288–289.

[49] Valuable data on the Chiriguanos and their culture will be found in: Nordenskiöld, 1920; Métraux, 1930. Accounts of Toledo's contact with the Chiriguanos will be found in: Garcilaso, Pt. I, Bk. VII, Ch. xvii; Lizárraga,

1908, Pt. II, Chs. xxvii–xxxvii. See also: Cieza, Pt. II, Chs. xxii and lxii; Acosta, Bk. VII, Ch. xxviii; Corrado, 1884, pp. 37–72, and especially pp. 57–58; Lozano, 1733, pp. 56–59; Church, 1912, pp. 213–215.

[50] For accounts of these two men see: Means, 1928, pp. 391–395 and 428–433.

[51] Bandera, 1881, p. 99. See also: Ramos Gavilán, 1621, Ch. ii, pp. 5–9.

[52] T. Sánchez, 1867, pp. 289–290. See also Jiménez de la Espada's notes accompanying Bandera, 1881.

[53] Means, 1931, pp. 287–288.

[54] Toledo, 1921, pp. 86–88.

[55] The legislation of Toledo has never yet, that I know of, been presented in really satisfactory form. Not until one hundred years after Toledo's time in Peru were his laws codified and printed under the direction of the Licentiate Thomás or Tomás de Ballesteros acting on orders from the Viceroy Duke of La Palata, who, in his preface to the volume, specifically mentions Don Francisco de Toledo as having been the originator of most of the laws appearing therein. See: Ballesteros, 1685, and Ballesteros, 1752. Other very important sources for the study of Toledo's enormous legislation are: Toledo, 1867; 1867b; 1889; 1896; 1896b; 1896c; 1896d; and 1921; Leguía y Martínez, 1921; Levillier, 1929.

[56] Toledo, 1889, pp. 255–264.

[57] Markham, 1892, pp. 171–172. Moses, 1914, I, pp. 368–371. Lea, 1908, pp. 328–329. Leguía y Martínez, 1921, pp. 89–90. Palma, 1863, pp. 1–14. Verrill, 1931, pp. 293–294. Medina, 1887, I, pp. 1–56.

[58] Compare Toledo's own account of the results of his visita, Toledo, 1921, pp. 84–86, with the adverse comments in Levillier, 1918, pp. 386–395.

[59] Rich materials on this episode of Drake in Peru will be found in Nuttall, 1914, especially pp. 57–99, and 400–405. See also: Sarmiento, 1895, especially pp. 8–17, where Toledo's orders for exploring the Strait of Magellan are set forth under the date of October 9th, 1579. Eloquent testimony by a Spaniard of how much Drake was dreaded appears in an intercepted letter whose writer says, concerning the Peruvian fleet for 1585: "God grant that Drake have not met with them, for upon advice of his going to sea all foreign ships were stayed in all the ports of Spain and Portugal." See: Corbett, 1898, p. 51.

[60] Montesinos, Anales, Años 1569 to 1581.

CHAPTER VI

THE THEORY OF SPANISH COLONIAL GOVERNMENT IN PERU

1. *Institutions of Spanish Origin*

DON FRANCISCO DE TOLEDO gave to the colonial government of Peru its final shape, which it preserved, in the main, for over two hundred years. Institutions of Spanish origin in the Viceroyalty of Peru were based upon the significant major premise that the King of Castile was the sole owner and absolute arbiter of his ultramarine possessions, being so by grace of the Apostolic donation made on May 4th, 1493, by Pope Alexander VI, in favor of the Kings of Castile.[1]

The result of this premise was that the Crown, when desirous of creating an administrative mechanism in its American possessions, simply had to delegate to sundry functionaries appropriate portions of its all-inclusive authority. When powers were thus delegated by the King it was always done with the assumption that he could reassume the powers whenever he wished. Authorities thus created fell into two groups: Those resident in Spain and those resident in America.

Of the former the most important was the Council of the Indies. This august body followed the King wherever he went and, to all intents and purposes, it was merely an extension of the Royal person designed to conduct the routine of colonial administration. The King frequently presided over it in person. Second in importance only to the Council was the Casa de Contratación, sometimes styled "India House" in English. The Casa had general supervision and direction of the economic life, the trade, and the enterprises of the colonies, whether of the State or of private persons.[2]

The Casa, through its control of trade, more intimately affected the daily lives of the colonists than any other body in Spain. Although subjected to the control of the Council, as the Council was to the Crown, it preserved a great degree of administrative freedom which, however, gradually diminished. Its seat was long at Seville, where much of its many-sided business was conducted in conjunction with the Consulado (gild of merchants) and with the Consulados at Burgos, Valencia, Mexico, Lima.[3] The work of the Casa was largely analogous to that of the Department of Commerce in the United States. Like the colonial government itself, however, it rested upon major premises: 1, Trade with the colonies was to be wholly monopolistic; 2, Seville, with its dependency, Cadiz, was to be the sole port for colonial trade. Modifications came into being but this was the original idea.[4]

It will gradually appear in this and later chapters that the governmental polity of Spain in Peru was, *in intention*, as enlightened as any then known in Europe. But the machinery set up was so cumbersome and so intricate that it permitted every sort of abuse arising from human stupidity or human avarice to creep in to hamper its workings. Moreover, the time-space complex intervened like an invisible but impenetrable wall between the Crown's functionaries in Spain and its subjects in America. The Casa, however, by selecting the persons who should go to the colonies, made itself a powerful agent in shaping the Spanish element which grew up in Peru and other American countries. Neither at the time when the Western Hemisphere was discovered nor afterwards was Spain overpopulated. It contained, however, vast numbers of poverty-stricken people, some of them plebeians, others of gentle or even of noble blood. Consequently, emigration which resulted from the discoveries across the Atlantic had for its principal motives a desire for adventure and, still stronger, a wish to acquire much wealth quickly. The Crown of Castile, therefore, had not to contend with any overwhelming outward flow of its subjects, and it could, consequently, make a deliberate choice of those who might go and of those who must go. As far as Peru is concerned it may be said, in general, that the emigration seems to have been limited to subjects of the Crown of Castile and of certain others of the kingdoms of the Spains. As matters stood from 1540 onwards the classes of people excluded from migration to Peru (and other parts of America) were: Converts to Catholicism from Islam or from Judaism and their descendants; heretics and their descendants; unmarried women, unless accompanied by their parents or a close relative; all "foreigners," *i.e.*, every one not subject of Castile, Aragon, Navarre, Catalonia, or Valencia.[5] About 1707–1714, after the Bourbons had ascended the throne, a plea was made that the Catholic King relax the severity of the laws excluding the greater part of his subjects from America; and, about 1743, an otherwise highly sagacious commentator, Campillo y Cosio, made the absurd suggestion—never carried out, fortunately—that all Gypsies, jail-birds, and prostitutes be sent to America from Spain in the belief that the air of the New World would miraculously convert them into people of worth and respectability.[6] Throughout the colonial period the following regulations were in force: Married men going to America without their wives had to provide the Casa with written permission from their spouses and a bond of 1,000 ducats to ensure their return; married women, and presumably their children, could go to America to join husbands already there, but they had to be accompanied by a kinsman within the fourth degree of consanguinity; married officials going out to posts in America were supposed to take their wives and children. These, and all other regulations were frequently evaded and even the Crown itself sometimes overrode them in special cases.[7] In the curious and informative book of Don Bernardo de Vargas Machuca, which won enthusiastic praise from King Philip II in his last days (1598), there is an idealistic portrait of the military emigrant. He must be: Willing and able to work hard; a good Christian; noble in birth and in qualities; rich, in order to meet the heavy expenses none of which is met by the Crown; liberal towards his inferiors; diligent, prudent, affable, resolute, cautious, ingenious, and honest.[8] Obviously such a Paragon as this seldom trod the blood-soaked soil of Peru. The ideal, however, is morally admirable.

Turning from visions to facts we find that the racial character of Hispanic America is largely the outgrowth of the Casa's regulations regarding emigration. For one thing, they caused the number of Spanish women in Peru and elswhere to be much smaller than the number of men. The ladies, God bless them! often displayed an understandable reluctance to leave their comfortable homes in Spain and to venture into new and mysterious lands. Consequently, wives not seldom resorted to ingenious tricks in order to avoid going out to America, with the result that comparatively few Spanish wives and children did go out to join their men-folk.[9] Only very rarely do we hear of any large number of Spanish women emigrants to Peru such as that which accompanied the Viceroy Nuñez Vela. (See pages 85–86.) The conquerors and later settlers who, in high proportion, were deprived of mates of their own race, naturally sought for consolation in the arms of native women, whom they either married or maintained as concubines. The result was that the mestizo (white-and-Indian) element early became important and numerous. In this, more than anything else, does the racial aspect of Spanish colonization stand in contrast with that of the English.

Into the details of the Spanish colonial institutions resident in Spain we need not go further here because, through the operation of the geographic factor—the time-space complex—they were, for the people in Peru upon whom our attention must be focused, remote, shadowy, and all but impotent. The menaces and thunders of the Casa, those of the Council, even those of the King himself, were in the main things of theory only. Nevertheless, they produced, in course of time, one of the most astounding legal codes ever drawn up. The Compendium of Laws of the Kingdoms of the Indies (1681) was the tardy fruition and summary of an enormous mass of legislation of divers sorts and sundry origins—but all tracing back, of course, to the absolute authority of the Crown of Castile. Into that ponderous and imposing code—impos-

FIG. 9. An imaginary landscape showing types of costumes and of bridges, eighteenth century. *After Juan and Ulloa, 1748.*

FIG. 10. An obraje with one loom, note use of rollers, modern but same type as that used in eighteenth century.

Courtesy of W. V. Alford, Esq.

FIG. 11. Tapestry garment of Indian manufacture, sixteenth century.

Courtesy of the Museum of Fine Arts, Boston.

ing even in its factual futility—were woven many of the ordinances of Toledo and other rulers of Peru, as well as Royal decrees, orders in Council, and what not. The Recopilación de Leyes de los Reynos de Indias, when it came out in 1681, contained nine Books, with 218 Títulos and 6,377 Laws.[10]

Of far greater practical concern for us than any person or legal body resident in Spain is that great series of Spanish institutions which resided in Peru itself. Taken together they may be termed the "major government," which term should be understood to include all officials and bodies depending upon the King. The antithetical "minor government" will be described farther on.

At the pinnacle of the major government was the Viceroy, in his capacity of personal representative of the King. His powers of direction and of patronage were analogous to those of his master and, although he was surrounded with ceremonial and pomp commensurate with his position, he was expected to work hard in return for his salary of 30,000 ducats ($67,500 according to Bourne). Later on the salary of the Viceroy of Peru was 40,000 ducats or pesos de oro. His duties were multifarious, chief among them being: To be President of the Royal Audience of Lima; to be patron of all the appointive posts in State and Church which the King did not fill by his own nominees; to keep a close watch on the affairs of the Viceroyalty; to protect the poor, needy, and deserving; and particularly to safeguard the Indians. Theoretically the term in office was three years, but actually it was often much longer. At the close of his reign a Viceroy was supposed to hand to his successor a minutely detailed memorial on the state of the Kingdom of Peru, and these viceregal memorials throw a blinding light on the subject of colonial conditions. Theoretically, a firm rein was kept on the viceregal office by rendering each holder of it liable to a residencia or scrutiny of acts in office. Needless to say, so great an office was usually given either to some great nobleman or, especially under the Bourbons, to some man who had won renown by his own efforts—or had purchased a high nobiliary position.[11]

Immediately below the Viceroy was the Royal Audience of Lima and, less directly connected with him, there were the other Audiences. Those which concern us were as follows:

1. The Audience of Lima, created by Charles I, in the New Laws, 1542–1543. Originally there were four oidores or judges and a Fiscal or Crown prosecutor. In 1569, Philip II added a chamber of criminal jurisdiction with four more judges and another fiscal. This Audience belonged to the highest class, being normally presided over by the viceroy and having that of Mexico as its sole rival and equal.
2. The Audience of La Plata (alias los Charcas or Chuquisaca) was created in 1559 by Philip II, with a president, five oidores, and a fiscal. The president had the rank of a Governor and Captain-General. In 1778 this Audience was joined to the Viceroyalty of Buenos Aires.
3. The Audience of San Francisco de Quito, created by Philip II in 1563, with a president, four oidores, and a fiscal. In 1718 the Audience was suppressed and its territory given to the Audience of New Granada (now Colombia). In 1722, however, the Audience of Quito was refounded as part of the Viceroyalty of Peru and it remained so until 1740 when it was again joined to New Granada.
4. The Audience of Chile, created by Philip II in 1565, had a president, four oidores, and a fiscal. The president was also a Governor and Captain-General and was, to a large extent, independent of the Viceroy of Peru.[12]

The Viceroy, the Governors and Captains-General, and the Audiences are to be regarded as the topmost strata of the major government set up in Peru by the Crown of Castile. All of them were of purely Spanish origin. The Kings of Aragon had had Viceroys in Sardinia and in Mallorca as early as the middle of the fourteenth century. The Audiencia had its beginnings in the same century and by 1433 it had assumed practically the same form that it later had in America.[13]

Likewise purely Spanish was the vast array of functionaries known collectively as "los oficiales reales," the royal officials. Escalona, our chief source on this subject, shows clearly that, by the first half of the seventeenth century, the King regarded Peru primarily as a source of income. The royal officials were those men whose business it was to foment and collect the revenues. Every Peruvian province had a corps of them. They were much esteemed, were styled "ilustres," and were honored because they had to do with the very nerves and muscles of the monarchy. Their titles and duties may be described thus:

The contador was a recorder who set down the sums received into the royal chest of each city and who noted the sums paid out.

The tesorero, treasurer, was the custodian of the royal moneys. He made payments due from the royal estate.

The factor was supposed to seek out means of increasing the royal revenues. He had charge of the sale of goods received as tribute and also of arms and munitions belonging to the Crown.

The proveedor, purveyor, saw to the fitting out of the royal fleets and armies, and to the management of slaves belonging to the Crown.

There were also a pagador or paymaster, and a veedor, inspector, whose functions seem to have been vague.[14]

All these officials were to be bound together by "mancomunidad," a term expressive of fellowship and combined action. The ideal of the royal officials' character was scarcely less lofty than that of the military settlers' disposition already mentioned. They were to be: Faithful to the interests of the Crown; diligent in collecting the Royal revenue; vigilant in augmenting it; and intelligent, as well as scrupulously just, in administering it. Moreover, the integrity of the corps of royal officials was to be guarded by certain rules, viz.: Posts were not to be bought and sold; merchants were ineligible to appointment in the corps, as were also persons in debt to the Royal estate, infidels, and uneducated or lowly men; neither Judges nor Corregidores could be members of the corps; and, finally, there was a series of rules restricting the royal officials from doing any sort of private business with the Royal estate, and forbidding them to travel within Peru except under viceregal license or to leave Peru except under Royal license. On the other hand, the royal officials had recognized privileges: They took precedence over the regidores (aldermen) at cabildo (town or city government) meetings; and royal officials appointed by the King took precedence over those appointed by the Viceroy.[15] In short, the corps of royal officials—including both those resident in Spain, especially at the Casa, in Seville, and those resident in Peru—was designed to be a category of Crown servants most laudable in character and function. At the same time it is obvious that their several duties were ill defined, involving an immense reduplication of labor. Their work consisted largely of keeping numerous ledgers and records, in duplicate or even in triplicate, in which all matters relative to the King's revenues, debts to the Crown, the Royal share of treasure recovered from huacas (ancient tombs), and other such things had to be set down minutely.[16]

We can form some idea of the immensity of the affairs handled by the royal officials if we examine the statistics of mining. Although much will be said on the subject of mines and mining farther on, it is well to note here that Escalona tells us that: From the silver-mines at Potosí alone, between 1556 and 1576, silver to the value of 29,140,000 pesos was taken, of which the Crown's fifth came to 6,061,000 pesos; that, from 1579 to 1638, the yield of silver amounted to 236,128,000 pesos, of which the King received 53,451,000. Another economist of that period, Friar Thomás de Argüello, tells us that: From the discovery of the mines of Potosí in 1546 down to 1674 the yield in silver of Potosí came to the sum of 957,-320,500 pesos, of which the Royal fifth came to 191,464,100 pesos. The Friar adds that he does not count the yield of gold in Peru because it is uncertain.[17] Neither Escalona nor Argüello takes into account the gigantic revenues received by the Crown from tribute and from numerous imposts and taxes.

The treasure of the King was collected by the royal officials and placed in the royal chests in the divers cities of the viceroyalty, and these were cleared annually, their contents being sent to the Royal chests in Lima, whence they were duly despatched to Panama in the Armada of the South Sea. From there the treasure and merchandise from Peru were carried across to the great Fair of Porto Bello, and so to Spain.[18]

One receives the impression that, although the Crown was most eager to collect fat revenues from its American possessions, the machinery therefor was so much enwrapt in red tape that inefficiency and corruption had full play. A fundamental defect of the system was the fact that, while the colonists were everywhere subjected to regulations which made initiative almost criminal, nothing was done to foster well-being through new kinds of agriculture and industry. Only one form of wealth—hard cash or the metal wherewith to coin it—was understood; the manifold means of producing wealth from the country's natural resources were, for a long time, utterly ignored.

The oficios reales or royal officials were, of course, inferior to the Viceroy and the Audience, but in a special sense; for the King was directly their master, just as he was the Viceroy's, with the result that their dealings with the Viceroy had to do only with the fiscal routine of administering the King's money.

Hierarchically inferior to the Viceroy and Audiences, but still of great authority, came a rank of administrative officers styled Corregidores. This office had been important in Spain under Alfonso XI (1312–1350) who had instituted the corregidorial office as a means of counteracting the influence of the nobility and others inimical to the supremacy of the Crown. The power and usefulness of the office were much enhanced by Ferdinand and Isabella, holders of it being usually creatures of the Sovereign and drawn from the middle class.[19]

The office of corregidor as transplanted to America is described by Hevia Bolaños, a noted lawyer and economist. He tells that, once a man was duly appointed as corregidor by the King, he must write to the old corregidor, even if the term for which the latter was appointed had not expired, and must announce the new appointment. It was incumbent upon the old corregidor to give up the post without delay. The new man had to appear with his brevet of appointment before the cabildo and the old corregidor of his jurisdiction and, with considerable etiquette, receive from his predecessor the administrative functions. When a corregimiento was so large that it contained several towns the head-town received pre-eminence in all official announcements, regulations, and so on.[20]

Furthermore, the corregidor presided at meetings of the cabildos. He had no vote in them, however, unless there was an equal division of votes on any question; in that case he had a casting or deciding vote. We may observe, in passing, that the King's appointive power extended also to the regidores (aldermen), and to innumerable other secular and ecclesiastical offices.[21]

In Peru, as will appear in the next chapter, the office of corregidor underwent in practice inevitable perverse modifications. In spite of the fact that the corregidor was supposed to be the local representative of the King and, as such, a check both upon the democratic tendencies latent in the towns and upon the feudalistic proclivities of the surrounding landowners, he was, too often, a trader rather than an administrative officer, albeit this was specifically forbidden by the King's law.[22]

If a corregimiento (jurisdiction of a corregidor) were large, the corregidor might appoint lieutenants to administer sections of it. The corregidores and their aides were in far more intimate contact with the Indian peasantry than were any other members of the major government. This was due to the fact that their routine duties included the collection of tribute and taxes, the supervision of local trade, and the control of the mita, or corvée system of forced labor in mines and elsewhere.[23]

There were two classes of corregidores and two classes of towns wherein they had their headquarters. The Corregidores de Españoles (or Corregidores Reales) lived in the larger towns and cities, were presiding officers in their cabildos or town-governments, and were royal nominees; Corregidores de Indios lived in the smaller towns which had almost no Spanish inhabitants, presided over the cabildos there, and were vice-regal nominees.

In Peru a Spanish city or town was usually the foundation of some individual specially empowered thereto by the Crown

or by a Viceroy, Governor or Captain-General. After 1573 the
laying out of both Spanish and Indian towns was subject to
definite rules laid down by Philip II as a result of his personal
study of the matter. In both the plaza, the streets running
at right angles and at set distances, the plots of land for the
church, the custom-house (if any), the Royal treasury, the town
hall, and the private dwellings, as well as the best hygienic
arrangements then possible—water-supply, and drainage
through open channels through the centres of the streets—
were all provided for in the rules. There were also recognized
forms of local self-government, faint shadows of a nascent and
discouraged democracy. The first settlers of a Spanish town
were its first electors, and to their number new vecinos were
added from time to time. Indians, Negroes, and Mestizos
could not vote in Spanish towns.[24]

The Indian towns of Peru were modelled by Toledo and
later viceroys on the Spanish towns, in nearly all respects.
Nevertheless, we must remember that the Inca empire had
towns of varying size and importance whose social scheme was
adapted and worked into that of the Indian towns later
founded by the Spaniards. From the reign of Toledo onwards, the founding of Indian towns was favored by the
Crown because it made easier the Christianization and the
general control of the Indian population. The town of San
Francisco de la Victoria de Vilcapampa, established by Toledo
after the capture of Tupac Amaru I, typified the Indian town
of Spanish creation, wherein the officials subject to the corregidor were Christian Indians elected to office by the heads
of households but under purely Spanish rules, with little if
any reference to the ancient ayllu organization still in force
among the Indians in the rural districts and small hamlets
round about.[25]

Indian towns of a very different character were important
because of their great numbers. They would better be called
villages or hamlets than towns, being usually small. In many
cases they were pre-Hispanic, perhaps even pre-Incaic, in
origin. These were the villages which, owning a Spanish en-

comendero (or a large landowner) for their lord, still had a modified form of the ancient social organization, *i.e.*, the minor government, of which more will be said in the next section. One thing, however, holds true for all towns of whatever kind: The Church was invariably represented; in the largest cities by a cathedral with supplementary parish churches; in the towns and larger villages by churches; in the smaller villages by curacy chapels; and in the hamlets by at least a shrine before which Mass was said from time to time. The theory of the town, whether Spanish or Indian, was that the souls of the inhabitants must be saved.[26]

We must now consider that institution which, more than any other of those imported into Peru from Spain, influenced the daily lives of a high proportion of the native inhabitants. This was the encomienda.

Like the viceregal office, the audience, the corregidores, and the cabildos, the encomienda was of Spanish origin, albeit in Peru it combined with other institutions of native origin. Something similar to the later American encomiendas had been used by James the Conqueror, King of Aragon, as early as the thirteenth century, being employed then and later as a means of increasing the King's grip upon the nobles.[27]

In Peru an encomienda was a tract of land, often very large, conceded by the Crown to some individual for his lifetime and for one or two lives more. The land thus granted carried with it the usufruct of the tribute in money, in goods, or in labor, of the Indians upon the land. Only men between the ages of eighteen and fifty were tribute-payers. It was incumbent upon the encomendero to live within the province where his lands were and personally to supervise their temporal and spiritual welfare.[28] Francisco Pizarro, acting on Royal authority, granted the first encomiendas in Peru. Later, as we know, they were practically abolished by the New Laws (1542–1543), only to be revived by Gasca (1548–1550). The grants made by Pizarro were of immense size, and they carried with them the Indian social organization controlling the inhabitants of the soil.[29]

Considered as a political and sociological institution, the encomienda was, at least for a time, a deliberately fostered American recrudescence of that feudal system which the Crown had long been endeavoring to undermine in Spain. The paradox is explained by the fact that the Crown's experience had taught it only one way to hold alien peoples in subjection. This method, consisting of adapting native institutions to the purposes of the new régime, was made operative in Peru by Toledo.[30]

One of the major questions in Peru during the reigns of Philip II and Philip III was whether or not the encomiendas should be changed from grants of a temporary sort into permanent feudal fiefs wherein seignorial jurisdiction would belong to the grantee, who, in turn, would stand at the head of the encomienda's minor government made up of native institutions adapted to fit the new dispensation. The Church frantically opposed the change, partly because it could not hold encomiendas, partly because it feared that the Indians would thereby escape from spiritual control. Moreover, the Crown was reluctant to make a permanent gift of such importance to so turbulent a body as Peru's nascent landed aristocracy. Finally, the curacas (chiefs) and the mass of the Indian peasantry were opposed to the idea, dreading so great an increase in the power of the encomenderos.[31] Indeed, almost the only friends of the plan were the encomenderos themselves—and the most perspicacious lawyers in Spain. For a time it looked as though the proposal might go into effect; for Philip II was in great need of money during the early part of his reign and, apparently, he seriously considered the sale of the coveted perpetuity, together with seignorial rights, titles of nobility, and other honors, all in return for heavy recompense to himself.[32] The whole project fell to the ground, however, partly because the King's need of money grew less and partly because of the growth of the absolutist tendency in Spain.

We must remember that in theory the Crown itself was the fundamental and original owner of all lands in Peru and that, consequently, it owned directly vast numbers of encomiendas which were administered for it by bailiffs. Moreover, as encomiendas were forfeited, or as they lapsed in course of time, they returned to the Crown. In the last years of Philip II the Royal holdings had become enormous and the King ordered the Viceroy Marquis of Cañete to sell certain portions of the Royal lands, having due consideration for the interests of possible Indian purchasers, and taking care to provide for pastures and commons (ejidos). In this way private land-owning began gradually to supersede the encomiendas; but the process was a long one and encomiendas continued to be granted for many years after. In fact, they were not finally suppressed, by incorporation with the Crown lands, until June, 1720.[33]

The patronage aspect of the encomienda was intricate and important. The supreme patron in this, as in all other connections, was the Crown. Any encomienda that was granted to an individual was a reduction of the royal patrimony for the time being. Therefore the power to grant encomiendas was jealously guarded, and it was delegated to the servants of the Crown only under strict regulations of which the most significant was the rule that no two officials should have that power in any given locality. Thus, the Viceroy of Peru, in his capacity of Governor and Captain-General, could grant encomiendas, but neither the President of the Audience of La Plata (Charcas) nor the President of the Audience of Quito could do so as they were both strictly subordinated to the Viceroy of Peru. The Governor and Captain-General of Chile, on the other hand, being a practically independent officer, could do so, and frequently did.[34]

Categories of persons pronounced to be specially fitted to receive encomiendas were:

1. The discoverers and the conquerors of lands which later became appanages of the Crown of Castile.
2. The first settlers in such lands, particularly those who were active in establishing Spanish civilization therein.
3. Persons active in quelling subsequent disturbances therein.[35]

Conversely, certain classes of people were, theoretically, debarred from receiving encomiendas. These included:

1. Officers of the Royal Council of the Indies.
2. Their children and the wives or husbands of their children.
3. All other officers of the Crown.
4. All relatives within the fourth degree of Crown officers.
5. All persons already holding an encomienda or whose wives or husbands did so.
6. All churches, churchmen, monasteries, convents, and religious corporations; all monks and all nuns.
7. All persons whose habitual residence was not close to the land granted.
8. All Negroes and Mulattoes; all illegitimate Mestizos.[36]

It is not too much to say that, with the possible exception of the first, second, and eighth of these classes, theoretically debarred classes of persons did sometimes receive encomiendas; for the King often broke his own laws. It is specially true that members of the seventh class often received grants of lands-and-Indians from the King, by virtue of arbitrary exercise of the supreme Royal prerogative. This abuse became so common that Viceroys sometimes remonstrated with their master about it.[37]

In spite of such relatively rare distortions of the privilege of being an encomendero, it may be said, in general, that the encomendero, although not properly a government official, was in constant touch with the authorities comprised in the major government. At the same time, he was the pinnacle, or rather, one of the pinnacles—the other being the corregidor—of the minor government, which will now be described.

2. Institutions of Andean Origin

In Peru the final form of the colonial version of the native administrative hierarchy was largely the product of Toledo's activities. The minor government, as it is sometimes called, was an adaptation of the Incaic system, and it had for its pinnacle either an encomendero[38] or a corregidor de Indios. It is not possible to know exactly what proportion of the native element was on encomiendas (or on private estates) and what proportion under Indian corregidores in Indian towns. Conditions were continually changing, but it seems likely that about half the Indians were on encomiendas or on estates, that about one quarter were in Indian towns, and that the remaining quarter were in independent Indian communes.

During the years 1570–1575, the Viceroy Toledo made, or caused to be made, inquiries respecting the native institutions of Peru, and on the basis of the immensely varied and uncommonly complete data thus gathered he erected his perverted form of the ancient hierarchy and his adaptation of native institutions to the needs of colonial government.[39] The purpose of the whole thing was, of course, to wring as much hard work as possible out of the Indians.

The immensely intricate hierachy of the Incaic government[40] was reduced to a much simpler form under the Spaniards. On every encomienda or estate, and also in the Indian communes of which we shall take notice presently, there were two moieties or parcialidades, called Hanan-suyu and Hurín-suyu (Upper division and Lower division), exactly as there had been in Incaic times. Each of these had a curaca (chief) at the head of it, and the curaca of Hanan-suyu took the first place on all formal occasions. Under these curacas were at least two ranks of lesser chiefs, whom the Spaniards called Primeras Personas and Segundas Personas. Of these the first probably controlled each one an ayllu (tribe) or a village of some 500 families, and the second controlled 100 or so families. Below these, again, were still other chiefs who were called by the generic term of mandones (bosses).[41] Thus we see that the curaca of Hanan-suyu probably corresponded approximately to the Tucuiricuc (official in charge of 40,000 families), although it must be understood that, in colonial times, no curaca had any such large number of families under him.[42]

The effective survival of the native hierarchy, or minor government, was definitely provided for in the laws. It was specially provided that Indians who had been curacas or chiefs of any other rank, either they themselves or their ancestors, were to be continued in the privileges of their order and in the exercise of their duties; and the Audiences were enjoined to take cognizance of their rights and authority.[43] At the same time it was provided that the curacas—whom the Spaniards often style caciques—must not call themselves "señores" (lords) of their village, as that would infringe the King's paramount authority. In criminal matters the jurisdiction of caciques was limited to minor offenses. Although offices normally passed by inheritance, they could on occasion be filled by the corregidor's choice from three nominees of the Viceroy.[44]

The integrity of the Indian blood of the peasantry was desired by the Crown. Some of the laws on this subject were: That neither encomenderos nor any of their kinsfolk and slaves might reside upon the encomienda; the encomendero was bidden to build a solid mansion of stone or other durable material in the nearest city and to make his home there. In like manner, it was strictly prohibited that Mestizos, Spaniards, Negroes, and other non-Indians live on encomiendas or in Indian villages.[45]

The Royal intention to get as much profit as possible out of the Indians, with the saving proviso that their souls be cared for, is noticeable in the laws referring to Indian affairs. Encomiendas and repartimientos, whether in settled or in unsettled parts of the Indies, were to be established without injury to the existing rights of the Indians.[46] The building of towns for the Indians and, on the encomiendas, of villages or hamlets for them, was to be encouraged because it was a powerful aid in the process of Christianizing and Hispanicizing. Each recipient of an encomienda had to agree to support religious instruction among his Indians and to do everything possible to assist the spread of the Faith.[47] The bodies as well as the souls of the Indians were considered; for it was provided that Indian villages should be founded near the Indians' work of whatever kind, and that such villages should have hospitals where sick natives could be treated without charge.[48]

Laws such as these random samples display the intended benevolence of the Crown towards its Indian subjects. Other laws were expressive of tutelage: Indians were not allowed to ride on horseback; wine might not be sold to them; they might not hold dances and feasts without special permission.[49] The enforcement of the very numerous paternalistic laws designed to alleviate the condition of the Indians was entrusted by the Crown and the major government directly dependent upon it to the encomenderos and the minor government directly dependent upon them. Therefore, the minor government can best be defined as an adaptation—largely due to Toledo—of the Incaic system to Spanish requirements. Every encomienda or, later, every large landed estate privately owned as a result of purchase from the Royal patrimony, had its minor government, surmounted by the encomendero, landowner, or by the corregidor of the district.

Toledo himself provides interesting and concrete data on the relative importance of ordinary Indians of the tribute-paying, head-of-a-household sort and their chiefs. He does so in his instructions for the laying out of Indian towns, whether on encomiendas or elsewhere. These instructions were undoubtedly based upon the rules drawn up by King Philip II in 1573, and they were interpreted in a practical manner by Toledo very soon thereafter. The pertinent passages of Toledo's instructions to founders of Indian towns run thus:

You will trace the houses of the Indians in such a way that they shall have their doors upon the public streets, the house of each Indian being separate and without any door leading into the house of any other Indian.

You will trace out the house of the principal chief with a greater degree of spaciousness and with somewhat more of an air of authority than the houses of private Indians. This shall be done in such a way that there shall be a patio and an apartment large enough to permit the chief to assemble there the principal Indians, and the Indians of the repartimiento in general, whenever he has to discuss with them matters touching the public good and the government of the repartimiento. And, in addition to the said patio and apartment, you will endeavor to plan so that there shall be a parlor wherein the said chief may eat and be at his convenience. And to one side of the said parlor there shall be a chamber and an inner chamber, so that the chief and his wife may sleep in the chamber, whilst in the inner chamber their daughters and the other women who serve the wife of the said chief will sleep. And on the other side of the parlor there shall be two other rooms for the sons of the said chief and for the other Indians in his service; and there shall be no communication between these rooms and the apartment of the chief. And you will try to arrange so that, in addition to the rooms mentioned already, there shall be a kitchen and such yards as may be necessary for the service of the house.

And you will try to arrange so that in the houses of the private Indians the apartment of the wife, daughters, and women servants of the Indian shall be separate from the apartment of the sons and other Indian men who may be in the said house.[50]

All things considered, the domestic arrangements here set forth by the Viceroy are not bad, albeit they certainly do not appeal to our modern love of privacy except in so far as they tend to separate the sexes. Even so, the chief and his wife seem to have had more privacy than the rest—assuming that the instructions were carried out—although nothing is said about a doorway leading from the daughters' and women's room without going through the matrimonial chamber. A little farther on the document emphasizes the desirability of cleanliness in the house and it describes the kind of rude bedsteads which the Indians should be made to use instead of sleeping on the floor as had been the custom in ancient times.[51]

Matienzo conveys the impression that allotments of building-space for chiefs and private Indians were generous, for he speaks of the chiefs as receiving a whole square or at least half a square (that is, two solares or lots) and of private Indians as receiving one or two solares, according to the size of their households. According to him the corregidor's house was to have but one solar and that was to be on the plaza, with the jail beside it, while the tucuirico (as he spells it) was to have the two solares just behind. The tucuirico, one supposes, was the chief Indian functionary of the village. Respecting the size of villages, also, Matienzo is informative, telling us that the normal population was to be 500 tribute-payers (about 2,500 inhabitants) in each village, and that if there were 600 or 700 or more tribute-payers there were to be two villages, one for each parcialidad or moiety (Hanan-suyu or Hanan-saya, and Hurin-suyu or Hurin-saya).[52] In all of this we see the manner in which the once great empire, vertically welded to the paramount authority of the Sapa Inca through the official hierarchy in its numerous grades, was broken up into innumerable self-sufficient fragments.

In Figures 6 and 2 we have magnificent aerial photographs taken by the Shippee-Johnson Peruvian Expedition of 1931. In the first we have a wide view over a part of the Colca Valley with the typical Spanish-built Indian towns of Ichupampa and Yanque in the foreground and midground. In the second of these two pictures we have a more detailed view from the air, showing the town of Yanque. These towns show how Philip II's plans worked out in practice.[53] Moreover, they are well placed, on ground with good natural drainage. Note especially, in Figure 2, the position of the cemetery, in the lower right-hand corner, downhill from the town. All about the towns here shown stretch broad fields for the crops and, farther away, on the slopes of the mountains, we see the amazing agricultural terraces so typical of Peru, terraces which, in all likelihood, are many centuries older than the towns.

In great contrast with the two pictures just examined are two others, also air-photographs, by the Shippee-Johnson Peruvian Expedition. Figure 3 shows a typical ancient Indian town, now in ruins, with its irregular ground plan. On every side this town, also, is surrounded by agricultural developments, here entirely made up of carefully planned and painstakingly walled terraces. It is obvious, I think, that the Spanish type of town must have been more commodious, convenient, and salubrious than the ancient type of hamlet. In bringing the Indians to live under the new dispensation of things, the King and his Viceroy were undoubtedly doing them a good turn, notwithstanding the fact that the fundamental purpose was to get more work out of them. The Spaniards were not, however, invariably wise and successful in their town-planning, as Figure 7 shows. Here we see the ruins of a Spanish-type town in a state of total abandonment. The trouble here undoubtedly was a lack of good water and a want of tillable ground nearby. It is probable, also, that this settlement was made too high up on the mountainside to be healthful for permanent occupation. At present the only occupants of this forlorn spot are the dwellers in the hut which, with its corrales or yards, we see in the foreground.

An insight into the racial relationships existing in a typical rural region of Peru in the late sixteenth century is afforded by a document drawn up by Don Juan de Ulloa Mogollón, Corregidor of the Province of the Collaguas (in the Colca Valley). His Excellency Don Fernando de Torres y Portugal, Count of Villar-Don-Pardo and Viceroy of Peru, had received from King Philip II one of those very searching questionnaires by means of which His Majesty endeavored to acquire detailed and accurate information concerning his ultra-marine possessions, and this questionnaire the Viceroy duly circulated among the corregidores all over Peru. When it reached Juan de Ulloa Mogollón, at Yanque in the Colca Valley, he called together a number of Indians and Spaniards of his jurisdiction in order that they might provide the requisite information. The meeting took place at Yanque on January 20th, 1586. Those present were:

Don Juan Halanoca and Don Miguel Nina Taipe, Chiefs of the parcialidad (moiety) of Hanansaya in the Province of Yanqui Collagua.

Don Francisco Chacha, Don García Checa, and Don Francisco Inca Pacta, Chiefs of the parcialidad of Hurinsaya in the Province of Yanqui Collagua, which belongs to the Royal Crown.

Don Juan Caquia, Don Felipe Alpaca, and Don Juan Arqui, Chiefs of the parcialidad of Hanansaya in the Province of Lari Collagua, belonging to the encomienda of Francisco Hernández Retamoso.

Don Cristóbal Cusi, Don Marcos Guacallo, and Don Diego

Vaanqui, Chiefs of the parcialidad of Hurinsaya in the Province of Lari Collagua, belonging to the encomienda of Alonso Rodríguez Picado.

Don Luís Ala, Don Miguel Canauache, and Don Diego Ala, Chiefs of the parcialidad of Hanansaya in the Province of Cavana Conde, belonging to the encomienda of Diego Hernández de la Cuba.

Don Francisco Anti Ala, Don Juan Ala, and Don Pedro Ancas Cavana, Chiefs of the parcialidad of Hurinsaya in the Province of Cavana, belonging to the encomienda of Fernando de la Torre.

These, with the interpreter, an educated Indian named Diego Coro Inga, who was a scrivener and a schoolmaster, were the Indians. The Spaniards present were:

Father Diego Hernández Talavera, Priest of the villages of Huambo and Pinchollo, a man who had resided in the Province for more than twenty-four years.

Father Hernando Medel de la Feria, Curate of the village of Lari Collagua during six years past.

Gonzalo Gómez de Butrón, who had lived in the Province for more than twelve years.

Father Amador González, Priest of the village of Yanqui.

Various other Spaniards whose names do not appear in the document.[54]

We have here a very nice cross-section of the society, Indian and Spanish, of a typical rural region. Part of the land was in the hands of the Crown and had its minor government; the rest of the land was held in encomienda by Spaniards, whose names are given, each encomienda having its minor government. In these encomiendas the Indians all belonged, apparently, to one or the other of the two parcialidades or moieties. One small point is rather puzzling: All the Indians except the interpreter are given, in the document, the honorific title "Don," but none of the Spaniards is given it. The significance of this is a point which I commend to my fellow students for investigation.

Exact knowledge of the working out of the tasa or assessment of tribute to be paid by the Indians as planned by Toledo is given us by that great administrator himself. He describes a typical repartimiento or allotment of Indians, that of Sipesipe in the Audiencia of los Charcas (or la Plata). Sipesipe contained 819 tribute-payers, aged between 18 and 50. There were also 112 old Indian men, 846 Indian boys of less than 18, and 1,814 Indian women and female children. These 3,591 Indians were settled by Toledo in a village called Talavera de Sipesipe; formerly they were scattered in 52 hamlets in a countryside of 50 leagues. In Sipesipe there were four caciques who were exempt from tribute, so that 819 tribute-payers and their families were administered by that number of minor government functionaries. They were assessed to pay 5,255 pesos a year in money and 450 pesos' worth of maize for planting, or about 7 pesos a year per man. The chiefs, in addition to being exempt from taxes, received all their food, and all their household service free from women or from young men.[55] It is obvious that these obligations were not too onerous—or, rather, they would not have been so except for the extortions and abuses which became well-nigh universal in colonial Peru.

As already indicated, perhaps as much as a quarter of the entire Indian population dwelt, not on encomiendas or in towns, but as members of Indian communes which, owing either to their remoteness from towns where Spaniards congregated, or to the insalubrity of their lands, managed to survive into colonial and modern times. Such communes were their own masters in local affairs, albeit subject in law to the control of the corregidor in whose jurisdiction they were. The larger communes had several ayllus or tribes, the smaller only one or two. In many cases they were very old states under new names and existing under conditions described by Dr. Valdez de la Torre:

"The Incaic village communities or ayllus suffered considerable mutilation because of the wars between the conquerors, misery, epidemics, the assignment of repartimientos to the support of industries and public services, race mixture, and the arbitrary gathering of several ayllus into a single newly created village. The result of all these factors was the loss of the bond of fictitious kinship maintained until then by tradition. It came about that the Indian communes were deprived of their ancestor worship and of their feigned kinship, their common agrarian interests being now their sole bond save that forced upon them by the political and administrative machinery of the colonial government."[56]

This quotation from the little-known, but exceedingly important, book of Dr. Valdez de la Torre brings out the fact that, under the Spaniards, the minor government's chief object was that of getting the most possible work out of the natives. As a result of this the character of the ayllus—originally kinship groups of either real or feigned consanguinity—changed into a labor association in which the Indian officials came to be hardly more than bosses of workmen, or, in the higher ranks, collaborators with the corregidores in the extraction of tribute.[57]

The chief compensation—if, indeed, we can regard it as such—for the enforced modification of the spirit of the native officialdom was that, under the Spaniards, the ancient communal conception of property tended to give place to an understanding of and use of private property in the European sense.[58] This change resulted from the introduction of the money-complex, something wholly unknown in pre-Spanish days. The slight value of this "compensation" leaps to the eye when we consider how profoundly the spirit and purpose of the native hierarchy was altered for the worse as a result of it. In Incaic days every hatun-runa (grown man, i.e., head of a family) had to pay tribute to the Inca, either in the form of produce or in that of labor of different sorts. But two facts regarding tribute-paying under the Incas should be borne in mind, viz.: tribute was adjusted in such a way as not to be onerous; and, a very large proportion of the tribute resulted in benefits to society as a whole, not merely to the Inca or to the state religion.[59] Under the Spaniards, on the other hand, the wringing of money and of endless labor from the Indians became the principal purpose of the minor government. More-

over, the Spaniards assumed that the Indians would have to be
driven mercilessly in order to make them work, and so the
minor government was seized upon with avidity as an efficacious goad.[60] Its intolerable sharpness became all the worse
when Toledo obliged the Indians to cease paying their tribute
in produce of their farms and to pay it in silver instead. This
law of his contravened the expressed wish of the King, but it
went into force all the same. Toledo's chief purpose in making
the law was to oblige the Indians to go and seek for silver by
working in what Friar Rodrigo de Loaysa justly calls "that
accurséd hill of Potosí," where the royal silver-mines were.
There were two conspicuous evil results from this bit of Toledan legislation: agriculture fell into neglect so that prices
of foodstuffs rose enormously; and the former tendency of the
authorities to be lenient towards tribute-payers who paid in
produce, if natural conditions made the crops poor in any
given year, faded away.[61]

Enough has now been said concerning the salient features
of the minor government to show that it was a dolorous perversion of the noble administration of Incaic times. By it the
Indians of Peru were reduced to a universal misery which was
least among the Indians of the communes and worst among
the Indians who were under encomenderos, landowners, or
corregidores. The fact that the intentions of the Crown were
benevolent was but cold comfort; and that benevolence was,
in any case, rendered nugatory for the most part by the
Crown's own insatiable thirst for money.

A few words must now be said about the classes of Indians
who were ruled by the minor government's officials. These
classes were as follows:

The Hatunrunas. Under the Incas these were the heads of
households and tribute-payers. Under the Spaniards they
were the Indians who, dwelling either on encomiendas or on
estates, or under the direct rule of corregidores, were governed and supervised by their curacas. Some of these Indians,
called tindarunas in Spanish times, could be hired out for
work on public buildings, state undertakings, or even private

enterprises. Legally they could not be sent more than twelve leagues (thirty-six miles) from their homes. Applications for bodies of these workers were made to the corregidores, who then bade one or more curacas to supply the number required. As Friar Loaysa truly said, "The Hatunrunas are those who sustain the kingdom upon their shoulders. The gold and silver bars that go to Spain are their very sweat and blood."[62] The work of these Indians was subject to the mita or system of corvées, largely the creation of Toledo. It was largely bound up with the minor government whose officials furnished the mitayos or workers on the mita. The corvée system had existed, in non-oppressive form, under the Incas and all public works and public services had depended upon it.[63] Toledo, in taking it over bodily, did not intend to be oppressive. He ruled that from one seventh to one fifth of the Hatunrunas should serve for a wage in mines and in other kinds of work, for reasonable periods and under good conditions. The steady shrinkage of the Indian population rendered the mita far more onerous, however, than Toledo had expected.

The Yanaconas. The Inca Tupac Yupanqui, father of the Inca Huayna Capac, was the founder of this class. In the last two reigns of the Inca empire the members of it were an extra-social element whose rôle was perpetual and hereditary servitude without any of those dignified privileges and obligations which belonged to the Hatunruna who constituted the citizenry of the empire.[64] Under the Spaniards the term was applied to all Indians who seemed not to be subject to any special curaca or to belong to any special locality. Most of them had taken up their residence among the Spanish population. They were Christians, industrious and skilful workmen, were held in esteem by the Spaniards, and, in general, constituted a relatively small but comparatively fortunate class of Indians, having learned all the Spaniards' trades—and all their vices. Many of them worked on farms, the value of which depended on the number of their yanaconas, and they were there managed by a simple type of minor government. The owner of the farm gave a small parcel of land and a new

FIG. 12. The façade of the Cathedral of Cuzco.
Courtesy of W. V. Alford, Esq.

FIG. 13. Panorama from the road from Cuzco to Chincheros showing Cordillera de Vilcapampa in the centre and Urubamba Mountains on the right.
Courtesy of Dr. Hiram Bingham.

garment to each of them every year in return for a stipulated number of days of work. Other yanaconas worked as domestic servants in Spanish families of quality by whom they were usually well treated. Still others were mine-workers laboring for their masters on a commission basis. Some even worked mines for their own benefit with hired Indians, merely paying a royalty to the owner. Finally, some specially fortunate yanaconas worked on the coca-farms east of Cuzco, where they were subjected to a simple kind of minor government, receiving good wages and treatment because of the difficult and delicate nature of the work.[65]

It appears, in short, that the yanacona class which had been at the bottom of Incaic society retained that position in colonial society but, paradoxically, was somewhat better treated than the Hatunruna class which had formerly been the more respected. It should be remembered that, in theory, all labor by Indians of whatever class was supposed to be justly and mercifully managed. This point is emphasized by Escalona when he tells us that the legal hours for work in mines were to be from an hour and a half after sunrise to noon and from one o'clock to sunset. He adds that, from May to August, the winter months, metal washing—a cold kind of work—could be done only between ten and four. There were many other regulations of the sort, all in favor of the Indians, and Spaniards who broke them were liable to heavy fines, etc.[66]

3. The Church

Intimately interwoven with the secular and political institutions of the colony were the ecclesiastical. From the beginning of Castile's career in the New World a special obligation had been laid upon the King in spiritual matters, i.e., to bring the natives of America into the Catholic Church. This obligation was made all the heavier by the fact that Popes Alexander VI and Julius II, between them, had made the King of Castile as omnipotent in colonial church affairs as he was in colonial politics. The King thus became the supreme patron of the Church in Spanish America and likewise the recipient of important portions of the Church's revenues from many sources.[67] The Catholic Church in Spain's America was, therefore, hardly more than one of the appanages of the Crown. By 1610 the Holy Crusade of the Church against the pagan religions of America was neatly systematized in a manner that leaves us in no doubt as to the paramount position of the Crown.[68]

The soldiers of the Church Militant in its war against the Prince of Darkness were the clergy, who fell into two main categories: The secular priests and the regulars. The former were usually known as curas and their labors usually lay in the parish churches of the Spanish towns or in the Indian towns, in each of which the Church was present. The regular clergy, in Peru, were the members of the religious orders, namely, the Franciscans, the Dominicans, the Augustinians, the Mercedarians, and the Jesuits. Not only did all these orders have vast monastic establishments in the chief cities— as did the orders of female religious—but also they participated in the doctrinas among the Indian villages throughout the country. It was a fixed rule, however, that a secular clergyman and a regular clergyman could not be associated in one doctrina. Finally, the missions among the wild and backward Indians who occupied the outlying eastern regions were the special field of labor for the monastic orders, and the field which shows them at their best; for, in countless foci of instruction, they were pushing back and back the frontier of Spanish civilization, often with great heroism and sagacity.[69]

The Peruvian episcopate had its beginnings, as we know, in 1529 with the evanescent See of Tumbez conferred upon Father Luque. The second diocese was that of Cuzco, whose first bishop was Father Valverde (1534). When Friar Rodrigo de Loaysa was writing (1586) the vast territory whose history concerns us contained only four dioceses, those of Cuzco, Lima (Bishopric in 1540 and Archbishopric in 1545), Quito (1545), and Charcas or La Plata (1553). With reason Friar Rodrigo complained that they were not enough.[70] Subsequently, other bishoprics were founded: Santa Cruz de la Sierra (1605), La Paz (1606), Arequipa, Huamanga, and Trujillo (all 1611). Even after the foundation of these new Sees the territories forming the spiritual jurisdictions of the bishops were far too large for effective governance.

It is widely believed that the archbishops and bishops of the Church in Peru were almost always Spaniards. Study of the scanty available data reveals the fact that, with the exception of Lima, where all the archbishops seem to have been Spaniards, 53 out of 180 bishops were born in America and many of them in Peru.[71] It is a pleasure to demonstrate that the policy of the Crown with regard to ecclesiastical patronage in Peru did not exclude the sons of the New World from the episcopal office. It is to be understood, of course, that all prelates were of Spanish blood.

A natural consequence of the conditions under which the Church found itself in Peru—and elsewhere in America—was the ever-present necessity of combating the still strongly surviving pagan cults of the Indian peasantry. One of the most devoted and intelligent men of God who ever labored in Peru, Father Lope de Atienza (1537–1596), has drawn for us the ideal portrait of the proselytizing priest, showing forth all the virtues of discipline, moderation, prudence, mercifulness, and wisdom, which, in order to perform his heavy tasks, he ought to have.[72] He speaks with special emphasis of the fatherly love and sympathetic tenderness which should move those prelates of the Church whose work lies chiefly among the newly won converts from Indian paganism.[73] It is an ideal of moving loftiness, so much so that one is not surprised that it was very seldom incorporated in human flesh and blood. Nevertheless, and with pleasure, one can record the fact that there were numerous priests in Peru who studied the native language until they mastered it, who sought to understand the souls of their flocks, and who strove intelligently and vigorously to bring them to what they held to be the True Faith. Among the men of this category whose writings with reference to Christianizing the natives have come down to us are, besides Atienza: Archbishop of Lima, Don Pedro de Villa-gomez; Father Dr. Francisco de Ávila; Father Hernando de Avendaño; and Father Pablo José de Arriaga.[74] The published writings of these priests are important, not only as showing the problems and methods of the Church in the fight with paganism, but also as preserving, paradoxically, the best data regarding the native cults. This special group of ecclesiastical authors lived in the last half of the sixteenth and the first half of the seventeenth centuries. It is not necessary, I hope, to remind the reader that a high proportion of the Chroniclers of Peru were also churchmen.[75] Most of them lived and labored before 1650, giving impressive evidence of the intellectual powers to be found among the priesthood at that period. In the last half of the seventeenth century and, still more, in the eighteenth century, one perceives a distinct falling off in the mentality of the Peruvian clergy, at any rate in its lower ranks.

It is a satisfaction to be able to display here, albeit briefly, the creditable side of the priesthood in Peru. Nor must one forget that, among the very many benefices throughout the territory once occupied by Ttahua-ntin-suyu, there were hundreds of veritable men of God, true servants of Christ, men who spent their lives in obscure but honorable labor which never won them fame or remembrance. In later chapters I shall have to point out, however, that the company of the good was as nothing to the legion of the evil.

This brings me to the subject which, of all others, has brought the most contumely upon the Church in Spain and Spanish America, and which has occasioned more literary nonsense than any other. I refer, of course, to the Inquisition. Desiring not to run the risk of joining the ranks of those who have deliberately and otherwise misinterpreted this interesting Institution, I shall say very little about it here.

The emissaries of the Holy Office entered Peru for the first time with the Viceroy Toledo, in 1569. From the very first it was the rule that the Indians, in their character of neophytes and catechumens, were not within the jurisdiction of the In-

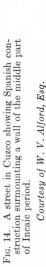

Fig. 15. An example of colonial Peruvian domestic architecture. Ground floor masonry Incaic, doorway and upper story sixteenth-century Spanish Cuzco.

Courtesy of Mrs. Myra Brady.

Fig. 14. A street in Cuzco showing Spanish construction surmounting a wall of the middle part of Incaic period.

Courtesy of W. V. Alford, Esq.

quisitors.[76] Previous to the arrival of the first Inquisitors the
episcopate had toyed a little with inquisitorial powers and
three autos de fé had been held in which heretics had been
punished by fire. Between 1581 and 1776 there were twenty-
nine autos de fé in Lima, whose victims by fire numbered in
all fifty-nine. If one be prepared to grant the rightness of
the Catholic point of view—and, in view of the present state
of the world, one inclines to do so—he must admit that the
Inquisition had its good points; for, contrary to the general
opinion among non-Catholics, there was nearly always good
reason for burning the victims, they being heretics, Jews,
witches, blasphemers, forgers, perjurers, and other poisonous
persons. In any case, the Inquisition in Peru was mildness
itself in comparison with what it was in Spain and elsewhere
in Europe. Nor should we of old New England stock shout
too loudly of intolerance among the Catholics of Spain. If
one regard the matter with some measure of detachment, he
must admit frankly that the worst result of the Inquisition's
activities was the stifling of intellectual enterprise and, especially, the banning of many thousands of good books which
were regarded as being morally dangerous simply on account
of their liberality. Nevertheless, certain forms of intellectual
activity were left unmolested for the most part, including
belles lettres, anthropology, geography, history, and several of
the natural sciences, all of which flourished in colonial Peru.[77]

Another point regarding Church history in Peru which re-
quires stressing here is the immense importance acquired by
the Jesuits through their educational and missionary labors.
Resentment was felt among the liberal element of the population because of the enormous real-estate holdings of the Society of Jesus. Nevertheless, it should be remembered that,
from beginning to end of their career in Peru, the Jesuits dedicated both their own strength and the vast material resources
of their Society to missionary and educational work in which
courage, intelligence, and thoroughness were salient features,
albeit, as the eighteenth century advanced, their methods and
tenets may have looked rather old-fashioned.[78]

The purpose of this chapter has been that of setting forth the chief aspects of the colonial government, lay and clerical, of Peru. Emphasis has fallen principally upon the state of affairs as it was supposed to be. In the next chapter we shall study an extensive array of evidence showing what conditions really ruled that period in history.[79]

NOTES TO CHAPTER VI

[1] Escalona, 1675, Pt. II, Bk. II, Ch. xx. Other editions of this work are: Escalona, 1647, and 1775. Dahlgren, 1909, pp. 1–7. Levene, 1918, pp. 20–22.

[2] Veitia Linage, Bk. I, Chs. i–iv, 1672, pp. 2–38. Gutiérrez de Rubalcava, 1750, Chs. iii–iv. Antuñez, 1797, pp. 4–6.

Piernas y Hurtado, 1907, 17–39. Dahlgren, 1909, pp. 7–9, 11–15. Moses, 1914, I, pp. 230–262. Levene, 1918, pp. 29–33. Haring, 1918, Chs. i–iii.

[3] Gutiérrez de Rubalcava, 1750, Ch. v. Haring, 1918, pp. 43–45, and 136.

[4] Haring, 1918, Chs. ii and vi.

[5] Veitia, 1702, pp. 107–109, 123–216. Haring, 1918, Ch. v.

[6] Monsegur, MS., 1714, p. 83. Campillo, 1789, pp. 260–270.

[7] Veitia, 1702, pp. 110–112. Haring, 1918, pp. 100–105.

[8] Vargas Machuca, 1599, fols. 6 verso to 30.

[9] Haring, 1918, p. 102, note. Teran, 1930, Ch. iii.

[10] Levene, 1918, pp. 75–78. See: Recopilación, 1681, 1756, 1774, 1791, 1841. The arrangement of títulos and laws is constant throughout the editions, new laws being inserted in such a way as not to disturb the order of the material in earlier editions.

For the benefit of those of my readers who may wish to study more fully the Laws of the Indies, I will here note down some of the chief materials for such a study. Previous to the Recopilación itself we have: Encinas, 1596; Aguiar y Acuña, 1628; Solórzano Pereira, 1629–1639, 1647–1648; Solórzano Paniagua y Trexo, 1639. (Solórzano Pereira was an Oidor in Lima, 1609–1627, and was later a member of the R. Council of the Indies; his son, Solórzano Paniagua y Trexo, supplemented his father's work in an important manner.) Particularly useful for the study of colonial law in Peru are Ballesteros, 1685 and 1752, in which much of Toledo's legislation will be found. The work of Ballesteros overlaps to a considerable extent the material in the Recopilación. Bourne, 1904, pp. 222–227.

[11] Material in the Recopilación (hereinafter cited as Recop.) referring to the viceregal office includes Bk. III, Tit. III, entire, 1841, II, pp. 15–29. Recop. III, III, vi, Ph. II, February 15th, 1566, specially marks out jurisdiction of Viceroys as including Auds. of Quito, los Reyes, and Charcas.

Madriga, 1906, pp. 86–87, says that the viceroy's salary was 40,000 ducats (about $90,000) to which were added 6,000 pesos more for expense-money, making the whole well over $100,000. See also: Caravantes, 1650(?), MS., especially folios 22–34. A gloomy picture of the viceregal office in the eighteenth century will be found in: Anonymous, 1741, pp. 180–182; Anonymous,

1742, pp. 1–17. Money, rather than military or political merit, was then the determining factor in the matter. Bourne, 1904, pp. 229–233. Moses, 1914, I, pp. 268–275. Dahlgren, 1909, pp. 9–10. Haring, 1918, pp. 93–95.

[12] Recop. III, III, xxx, Ph. III (as Prince regent), October 15th, 1597; Ph. III, January 15th, 1600.

Moses, 1914, I, pp. 263–267, 361. Cunningham, 1919, pp. 15–27. Ruiz Guiñazú, 1916, pp. 41–43, 106–117, 119–126, 127–145. Levillier, 1918, gives many documents. Quesada, 1881, Chs. i–iii. Barros Arana, 1884–1902, II, pp. 372–374, 381–382. Perez García, 1900, I, pp. 424–426. Bourne, 1904, pp. 227–234. González Suárez, 1890–1903, III, pp. 9–25 and V, pp. 1–10.

[13] Merriman, 1918–1925, I, pp. 230–232, 500, 505–507, II, 122–124. Chapman, 1918, pp. 155–156, 222, 292–293, 429–433.

[14] Escalona, Pt. II, Bk. I, Ch. i. This writer was born in los Charcas and educated in Lima. He served as Corregidor of Jauja, and later as Oidor in the Audiencia of Chile. See: Riva-Agüero, 1921, p. 115. Haring, 1918, Ch. iv, gives data on the Royal officials.

[15] Escalona, Pt. II, Bk. I, Chs. i–xx.

[16] Escalona, Pt. II, Bk. I, Ch. v.

[17] Escalona, 1775, Pt. I, Bk. I, Ch. xlv. Argüello, 1681, MS., folios 107–109. See: Haring, 1918, Appendix VI, for other statistics.

[18] An important and vivid account of all this appears in Haring, 1918, Ch. viii. See also: Bourne, 1904, Ch. xix; Scelle, 1906, I, pp. 44–53; Dahlgren, 1909, pp. 20–23.

[19] Chapman, 1918, pp. 116–119, 158–160, 198–199. Merriman, 1918–1925, I, pp. 233–235, II, pp. 147–149.

In Peru, as will be seen on later pages, corregidores were sometimes men of title, but they usually belonged to the part of the nobility which depended on the King for favors, not to the grandeeship. Grandees, of course, had to look to the King, also, but they were, as a rule, after bigger prizes than mere corregidorships.

[20] Hevia, Pt. I, paragraph iii, 1733, I, fols. 12–13. Other editions of this work are: Hevia, 1603, 1617, and 1783.

[21] Hevia, Pt. I, paragraphs i and ii, 1733, I, fols. 3 and 7.

[22] Persons forbidden to be traders or merchants were: Priests, soldiers, militiamen, judges (including oidores and corregidores), regidores (aldermen), jurisconsults, scriveners, minors, criminals, and slaves. Nobility did not, however, preclude a man from being a merchant, provided his business were on a large scale and that it were carried on by his employees rather than by himself. In the eighteenth century, as we shall see later, the nobility of Peru was very much "in trade." See: Hevia, Pt. II, Ch. i, 1733, II, pp. 1–6.

[23] Bourne, 1904, pp. 234–235. Mendiburu, 1874–1890, VIII, pp. 400–403, gives a list of the corregimientos existing in 1632. Among those whose holders were appointed by the King were: Quito, Cuenca, Loja, Piura, Cajamarca, Trujillo, Huamanga, Huancavélica, Castrovirreina, Tarma, Arequipa, Cuzco, Paucarcolla, La Paz, Potosí, Cochabamba, and Porco. Most of the rest— the total number in the three Audiences of Quito, Lima, and Charcas being 86—were appointed by the Viceroy.

[24] Moses, 1914, II, pp. 366–381. Ruiz Guiñazú, 1916, pp. 283–311. Nuttall,

1921–1922, pp. 743–753. For a careful study of Spanish colonial towns, see: Kirkpatrick, 1915, who explains that the territory dependent in various matters from a Spanish town was very large and included many corregimientos of Indians and their respective Indian towns.

25 Ruiz Guiñazú, 1916, pp. 283–311.

26 Blanco Herrera, 1888, Ch. xxvi.

27 Chapman, 1918, pp. 60 and 138. Merriman, 1918–1925, II, pp. 232–235.

28 Solórzano Pereira, 1647–1648, Bk. III, Ch. iii. González Suárez, 1890–1903, III, pp. 401–403. It should be remarked that the fact of tribute obligations being limited to men of between 18 and 50 is a direct survival of Incaic practice. Cf. Means, 1931, pp. 294–302. The Incas, however, limited tribute-paying to men of between 25 and 50.

29 Santillán, 1879, pp. 15–27, where he describes the Incaic system of tribute-administration; pp. 27–32, where he describes the effect of Spanish rule and of the encomienda. Valdez de la Torre, 1921, Ch. iv.

30 Cf. Suárez, 1920, pp. 147–153, where she analyzes the interracial aspect of the encomienda system.

31 Matienzo, Pt. I, Chs. xxviii–xxxii, 1910, pp. 52–61, advances powerful arguments in favor of perpetuating the encomiendas. So do León Pinelo, 1630, Pt. I, Chs. i–iii and v–xx, and Solórzano Pereira, 1647–1648, Bk. III, Ch. xxxii, pp. 478–491. I must again cite here the very rich data on the subject of perpetuating the encomiendas which will be found in *Nueva colección de documentos inéditos para la historia de España,* Vol. VI, pp. 28–105 and 268–274, Madrid, 1896. See also: Torres Saldamando, 1879–1880; Zurkalowski, 1919; and Riva–Agüero, 1922, pp. 57–67.

32 Riva-Agüero, 1922, pp. 61–62. Loth, 1932, Chs. i–v, makes it very clear how bitterly both Philip II and his father need money. In later chapters Mr. Loth shows how, if not less needy, Philip II became at any rate less anxious about money, in the sense, that is to say, that he spent more and more of it—largely in somewhat foolish undertakings.

33 Escalona, Pt. II, Bk. II, Ch. xx. Torres Saldamando, 1879, and 1879–1880, pp. 428–432. Riva-Agüero, 1921, p. 119.

34 León Pinelo, 1630, fols. 33 verso to 35 verso. Moses, 1914, II, Ch. iii. Amunátegui Solar, 1909–1910, I, pp. 59–76.

35 León Pinelo, 1630, fols. 51 recto to 52 verso. Solórzano, 1647–1648, Bk. III, Ch. vi, pp. 278–288. Suárez, 1920, pp. 149–151. Torres Saldamando, 1879–1880, pp. 428–431.

36 León Pinelo, 1630, fol. 56 recto. Solórzano, 1647–1648, Bk. III, Ch. vi, pp. 278–288. In Ch. xvii, pp. 357–370, and in Chs. xxii–xxiv, pp. 393–415, Solórzano describes minutely the rules for the inheritance of encomiendas and especially the part of women therein. Torres Saldamando, 1879–1880, pp. 428–431.

37 Two of the most exhaustive studies of the Peruvian encomiendas are Torres Saldamando, 1879–1880, reprinted in Cabildos, II, pp. 92–158. See especially pp. 428–429 and 436–437 of the former, and p. 119 of the latter, where Torres gives a list of men and women to whom the King arbitrarily gave encomiendas in Peru. The list includes: Two dukes and one duchess; three marquises; four counts; and four countesses. Not one of these nobles ever

did an hour's service in America or for Peru. They were merely friends of the absolute King, Philip II or Philip III. Incidentally, they were absentee landlords of the worst description.

38 In the case of absentee landlordism, whether because the King himself was the encomendero, or because he had granted the encomienda to some one resident away from Peru, a bailiff or steward represented the encomendero on the ground and acted as pinnacle of the minor government on that particular encomienda. In the case of large estates bought by private persons from the Royal patrimony, the landowner found himself at the summit of the minor government on his property.

39 Toledo, 1924, pp. 142–160.

40 For purposes of comparison see Means, 1931, pp. 291–293, on the Incaic hierarchy, and pp. 306–308, on the subdivisions into moieties or parcialidades.

41 Matienzo, Pt. I, Chs. vi–viii. Montesclaros, 1859, pp. 19–20. Loaysa, 1889, pp. 586–589. Mendiburu, 1874–1890, VIII, p. 26. Valdez de la Torre, 1921, pp. 29–35.

42 Matienzo, Pt. I, Ch. xiv. Valdez de la Torre, 1921, pp. 57–67.

43 Recop. VI, VII, i—Philip II, February 26th, 1557. Recop. VI, VIII, iii—Ph. III, July 9th, 1614; Ph. IV, February 11th, 1628. Recop. VI, VII, entire is important in this connection.

44 Recop. VI, VII, v—Ch. I, February 26th, 1538; VI, VII, xiii—Ch. I, December 17th, 1551, Ph. II, December 19th, 1558. Montesclaros, 1859, pp. 18–20. Recop. VI, VI, concerns an office called Protector de Indios, which, however, seems to have been a mere gesture.

45 Recop. VI, IX, xi, Ph. III, October 10th, 1618; VI, IX, xiiii, Ch. I, April 24th, 1550, Ph. III, October 10th, 1618; VI, IX, x, Ph. II, March 31st, 1583; VI, VII, vi, Ph. II, January 11th, 1576; VI, III, xxi, Ph. II, May 2nd, 1563, Ph. IV, December 17th, 1646; VI, IX, xv, Ch. I, December 17th, 1541, Ph. II, September 3rd, 1580.

46 Recop. IV, XII, vii, Ph. II, April 6th, 1588.

47 Recop. VI, III, i, Ch. I, March 25th, 1551, Ph. II, May 20th, 1578; VI, III, iiii, Ph. III, October 10th, 1618; VI, III, vi, same day; VI, III, v, Ph. II, October 8th, 1560.

48 Recop. VI, III, x, Ph. III, November 24th, 1601.

49 Recop. VI, I, xxxiii, Ph. II, July 19th, 1568; VI, I, xxxvi, Ph. II, May 15th, 1594, Ph. IV, April 5th, 1637; VI, I, xxxviii, Ph. II, November 2nd, 1576. Loaysa, 1889, pp. 584–586, emphasizes the King's benevolence and underscores the part which all officers of the Crown were supposed to take in giving it practical expression. Solórzano, 1647–1648, Bk. II, Chs. i–iii, cites many laws designed for the Indians' welfare.

50 Toledo, 1924, pp. 164–165.

51 Toledo, 1924, pp. 165–166.

52 Matienzo, Ch. xiv.

53 Compare Nuttall, 1921–1922, where the King's rules are given.

54 Ulloa Mogollón, 1885, pp. 38–39. Yanque and Yanqui both occur.

55 Toledo, 1924, pp. 204–205, 214–216. Bourne, 1904, pp. 239–242.

56 Valdez de la Torre, 1921, p. 101.

57 Matienzo, Pt. I, Ch. vii. Loaysa, 1889, pp. 586–589.

58 Valdez de la Torre, 1921, p. 49.

59 Means, 1931, pp. 298–302.

60 Matienzo, Pt. I, Chs. iv and v. A vivid description of conditions among the Indians of Peru just prior to Toledo's coming will be found in the Memorial which Friar Bartolomé de Vega presented to the Royal Council of the Indies in 1563. See: Vega, 1896. The evidence therein makes it clear that heavy payments in goods and oppression by officials of the minor government were already sources of misery to the Indians before Toledo came. But, as we shall see, he systematized existing abuses.

61 Loaysa, 1899, pp. 590–596.

62 Loaysa, 1889, pp. 586, 589–590. Matienzo, Pt. I, Ch. ix. Solórzano, 1647–1648, Bk. II, Ch. iii.

63 Means, 1931, p. 298. Valdez, 1921, p. 66.

64 Means, 1931, pp. 296–297, 302.

65 Matienzo, Pt. I, Chs. viii and xlix–xl. Loaysa, 1889, pp. 603–605. Solórzano, 1647–1648, Bk. II, Ch. iv. King Philip III wrote a letter to the Viceroy Marquis of Montesclaros from Aranjuez on May 26th, 1609, in which he shows that he shared the general belief that the Indians had to be forced to work. He had decided to continue the mita in order to insure their doing so. If, however, the number of free paid laborers, other than Indians, or that of Negro slaves, should increase enough to maintain society, or if the Indians themselves should develop a zest for toil, the repartimientos and the mita are to be given up little by little. The kinds of work mentioned by the King are: Agriculture, animal husbandry, mining, and the cloth factories or obrajes. (I owe my knowledge of this letter to the courtesy of Messrs. Maggs Brothers, of London, who, in March, 1922, allowed me to make copious notes from it.) See: Valdez de la Torre, 1921, Ch. xii.

66 Escalona, Bk. II, Pt. II, Ch. i, 1775, pp. 127–129.

67 Recop. I, VI–XVII. Vélez Sarsfield, 1919, Chs. i–iv. Bourne, 1904, pp. 302–304. Haring, 1918, pp. 130–133.

68 Perez de Lara, 1610. Vélez Sarsfield, 1919, Chs. vi–xi.

69 Recop. I, XIII, ii, Ph. II, May 23rd, 1559. Also, in general, Recop. I, XIII. Loaysa, 1889, pp. 568–569. Bourne, 1904, pp. 304–306. S. Suárez, 1920, Chs. iii–iv.

70 Loaysa, 1889, pp. 559–560. Important data on the bishoprics of Peru will be found in: A. de Alcedo, 1812–1815, under the several names of the dioceses; Rada y Gamio, 1917, Ch. xi.

71 There may have been more American bishops, as some are not known about. On the other hand, a given man often held two or more sees (at different times) with the result that there may be some duplication. It is plain, at any rate, that there was a fairly high percentage of American-born bishops.

72 Atienza, 1931, Pt. II, entire. See also: Loaysa, 1889, Chs. ii–xxvi.

73 Atienza, 1931, Pt. II, Ch. ix.

74 Villagomez, 1649. Arriaga, 1621. Avila, 1873. Avendaño, 1648. Atienza, 1931. Information on these priestly writers will be found in: Means, 1928, pp. 299–310.

75 Means, 1928, studies the lives and works of forty-five Chroniclers of

Peru (writers of before 1700), of whom twenty-two were churchmen. Of the latter number were the four to whom I am referring specially as enemies of paganism. Of the remaining eighteen, at least six may be counted as being in the first rank of authorities.

[76] Recop. I, XIX, contains the Laws about the Inquisition. VI, I, xxxv, Ph. II, February 23rd, 1575. Medina, 1887, I, pp. 19–28. Lea, 1908, p. 332. Bourne, 1904, pp. 312–313.

[77] Authorities on the Inquisition in Peru include: Medina, 1887; Palma, 1863 and 1897; Lea, 1908; Moses, 1914, I, pp. 327–335; Bourne, 1904, pp. 311–314; Verrill, 1931, pp. 286–327.

[78] When the Society of Jesus was expelled from Peru in 1767, it had eighteen establishments, mostly educational, in its Lima jurisdiction (which included most of modern Peru), and there were fifteen in what is now Ecuador as well as thirteen in what is now Bolivia. Contrary to the belief general among Protestants, the Jesuits were not monks and they were not cloistered. They were a militant ecclesiastical society which dedicated itself chiefly to the purposes here indicated. See the folio MS. in the Library of Congress (Ac. 958) entitled "Noticia de los Colegios Residencias y Misiones que tubieron en Yndias é Yslas Filipinas los Regulares de la Compañía. . . ."

[79] Peru produced three Saints! They were: Don Toribio Alfonso de Mogrovejo y Robles, born at Mayorga, in León, on November 16th, 1534, of noble parentage. After studying at the Universities of Valladolid and Salamanca, he became, although still a layman, an official of the Inquisition of Granada, perhaps in a theologico-legal capacity. Oddly enough, he was still a layman when, in 1579, he was appointed to be Archbishop of Lima, and his consecration as a priest did not take place until 1580. Accompanied by his sister, Doña Grimanesa de Mogrovejo de Quiñones, and her husband, who were to make a home for him, he sailed from San Lucar de Barrameda late in 1580 and reached Lima on May 24th, 1581—a quick journey. On August 15th, 1582, he opened the session of the Third Council of Lima (two earlier Councils having been held by Archbishop Loaysa) to which he had summoned the Bishops of Panama, Nicaragua, Popayán, Quito, Cuzco, La Plata (alias Charcas or Chuquisaca), Santiago de Chile, Imperial, Tucumán, and Paraguay. The attendance was not all that he had hoped, for the first three named did not come on account of the distance, and the Bishop of Quito, Don Pedro de la Peña, died in Lima while the Council was in session. Nevertheless, this Council—which lasted until mid-October, 1583, was very active and did much to regulate ecclesiastical affairs, especially missionary work. Archbishop Mogrovejo also held the Fourth Lima Council, January to March, 1591, and the Fifth Lima Council, April to June, 1601. In very truth this admirable Prelate was a man of deep and practical piety. Unremittingly he devoted himself to the duties of his high office, taking great pains to learn Quechua so that, in the long journeys which he made throughout his too-vast archdiocese, he could converse with the Indians and so learn of their needs from their own words. He lived as austerely as the bishop in *Les Misérables* and as laboriously as that other exemplary churchman in Willa Cather's *Death Comes for the Archbishop*. Most of his money he gave to good works, especially to hospitals. He died at Saña, in the

cura's house there, while on one of his journeys, on March 23rd, 1606. Most justly, Holy Mother Church honored this noble son: He was beatified on June 28th, 1679, by Innocent XI, and was canonized by Benedict XIII on December 10th, 1726. See: Mendiburu, 1874–1890, VII, pp. 221–245; Markham, 1892, pp. 168–169; León Pinelo, 1653; García Irigoyen, 1906–1907.

Non-Catholics, and heathens like myself, find Peru's second Saint far less comprehensible. Isabel Flores y Oliva, better known as Saint Rose of Lima, was the daughter of a sergeant in the Viceregal Guards. Born in Lima on April 20th, 1586, she spent her amazing youth in that city. While still a child she cut off her beautiful hair because her brother taunted her with vanity. Our Lady, in the Rosary Chapel of St. Dominic's Church, bade her to call herself Rosa de Santa María. Her mode of life was as uncomforting to the senses as she could make it; her diet consisted of bitter herbs, gall, ashes, and orange-pips; her bed, on which she reposed only two hours in the twenty-four, was made of rough logs and was strewn with broken glass and earthenware. She was borne up, however, by recurrent visions of her Divine Spouse, Jesus Christ. She worked for her mother, and did it well, during ten hours each day, and prayed in a small hut in the garden during the remaining twelve hours. In 1597 she moved, with her parents, to Quivi, in the province of Canta (north of Lima) and there she was confirmed by Archbishop Mogrovejo. Returning to Lima some years later, she became, in 1606, a nun of the Third Order of St. Dominic. According to Catholic tradition in Lima, her appeals to the Virgin and to Christ saved the city from the Dutch pirates in late August, 1615. (But by that time the corsair, Spilberghen, was far north of Lima, see p. 233, so that this myth appears not to have much solid substance in it.) The holy girl died after a long illness on August 24th, 1617. She was canonized, and made patron Saint of the Americas, by Clement X, in 1672. See: Mendiburu, VII, pp. 211–216; Anonymous, 1896; Capes, 1899, and Note 57 on p. 287, below.

Peru's third Saint is easy to understand and to revere. Francisco Solano y Jiménez was born near Córdoba, in Spain, on March 10th, 1549, and twenty years later he became a Franciscan. In 1589 he went to Peru with the Viceroy Marquis of Cañete. During many years thereafter he toiled with absolute devotion among the Indians of Tucumán and Paraguay. Towards the end of his life he became Guardián of San Francisco, in Lima, and in that post he died on July 14th, 1610. He was beatified by Clement X on January 25th, 1675, and was canonized by Benedict XIII in 1726. See: Mendiburu, 1874–1890, VII, pp. 357–359.

CHAPTER VII

THE REALITY OF THE COLONIAL RÉGIME IN PERU

1. Affairs of the State

IT has been made clear that the intentions of the Crown
towards its American subjects were characterized by self-con-
scious benevolence partly arising from an authentic desire to
fulfil what were supposed to be moral obligations laid upon
the King by the Pope and partly arising from a belief that
good treatment would be more lucrative to the Crown than
would bad. In actual fact, however, the King's laws were
mere paper, ink, and wind, with the result that, beyond doubt,
the outstanding fact of the colonial régime in Peru and elsewhere in Spanish America was evasion of the law. It was an
evasion so universal and so various, so much a part of the
life of all classes—except that which, being the largest and the
lowest, supported all the rest—and so multifarious in its manifestations that it puts into the shade our own little attempts
at law-breaking on the grand scale. The texture and purpose
of the two evasions—the colonial Peruvian and the modern
North American—are very different. The former had for its
chief aim the oppression of the Indians for private gain in
spite of the official Royal benevolence towards them; our
evasion of the law—barring a few side lines such as murder
and robbery—has for its purpose the maintenance of human
dignity and personal liberty in the face of legislation wholly
lacking in common sense. The systematic non-observance of
the law in colonial Peru had, however, at least two aspects,
one good and one bad. It was "a liberating force when it concerned the evasion of the absurd proscriptions relative to commerce and to such matters as the too-heavy taxation, the

eradication of 'foreigners' and the publication and diffusion of books; but it was a deep-rooted evil when it tended to vitiate the juridical organization and to corrupt the administration and governance of the Indians."[1]

Beginning at the top of the colonial Peruvian tree, we find that even the Viceroys and the Audiences were sometimes institutions imperfect in their working. Friar Rodrigo de Loaysa, writing in 1586, speaks feelingly of the incessant wrangles between the Viceroys and the Audiences, all of which, so he says, could be avoided if only each would keep within the proper sphere of action. He urges that the viceroy be made powerless to imprison and otherwise humiliate the oidores. Moreover, he recommends that appointees to the viceregal office be men young and vigorous enough to inspect the country personally, as Toledo did, and, like Toledo before him, he suggests that it would be well for the Viceroy to dwell in Cuzco. Finally, this intelligent Friar hints that it might be wise to abolish the viceregal office altogether and to cause the land to be ruled by a Governor or by the President of the Royal Audience, the post to be held by a letrado (usually a lawyer) such as Vaca de Castro, Gasca, or Lope García de Castro, rather than by some great nobleman who would receive a far larger salary than a letrado would require.[2]

Respecting the oidores Friar Rodrigo is no less severe. He says that they should be protectors of the Indians and that, in legal matters, they should do their business quickly and so avoid running up the expenses of the Indian litigants. He thinks that they, also, should inspect the country personally, but that in doing so they should not take with them so many servants that every village they stop in is "devoured" in a few days. Finally, he suggests that the doings of Viceroys and oidores be inspected secretly from time to time by special emissaries of the King and of the Royal Council of the Indies.[3]

These remarks and suggestions convey the impression that the Spanish colonial government in Peru was decidedly wormy even at the top. All this, however, is as nothing in comparison to the harm caused by the corregidores. Enough has been said of the corregidorial office to show that it might easily be changed from the necessary and laudable thing it was intended to be into a thing quite different, if, that is to say, it were abused by ill-disposed men holding it. It was so abused, apparently, not merely sometimes, but very nearly always. In fact, the corregidores, by reason of the dominant position held by them in political, social, and economic matters and by reason of their almost universal misuse of their powers, came to be not only the focal point of the Indians' complaints and hatreds but also the target for the curses of all right-thinking Spaniards.

Although the Viceroys and the Oidores were very frequently earnest in their efforts to carry out the King's laws, the iniquity of the majority of corregidores could operate without great danger from them because of the fact that immense tracts of difficult country, almost devoid of rapid and incorruptible means of communication, lay between them in their provinces and the higher authorities in Lima or in Spain. Each corregidor, especially in the seventeenth and eighteenth centuries, was a veritable king in his own corregimiento; for the encomenderos had ceased to be an effective counterpoise, partly because many encomiendas had lapsed to the Crown, partly because their holders—and the big landowners after them—were leagued in self-interest with the exploiting corregidores.

Formal protests against the methods of the corregidores began to be made as early as 1586, within twenty-four years of their introduction into the country.[4] Among the first of the disinterested criticisms of the corregidores were those of the already much-cited Friar Rodrigo de Loaysa, who, we must remember, was addressing King Philip II himself, through the mediation of the private secretary, Don Mateo Vazquez. In his opening chapter Friar Rodrigo says that the cupidity of the corregidores and the negligence of Viceroys, Governors, and Audiences have been such that "those miserable indians . . . are being finished and consumed with the greatest speed."[5] Elsewhere he adds that, if Toledo's regulations had been strictly observed, the corregidores would not be a burden upon the Indians; but that, in cold fact, they think only of making money and so come into collision with the parish priests, who also think only of making money. The corregidores, so says Friar Rodrigo, now commit all the crimes which the encomenderos ever did, and more besides. He avers that this sad situation could be rectified if only the Viceroy and the Oidores would inspect affairs properly. A particularly sane suggestion made by Loaysa is that, instead of corregidores sent out from Spain, there should be corregidores chosen from among the men of the country.[6]

Specially odious was the general practice of making the Indians wear their hair long because it served as a convenient rope for dragging them about. The treatment which the Indians received cowed them so thoroughly that they rarely dared to complain of any abuse given to themselves, their wives, or their children. In their desolation and despair many Indians committed suicide or killed their children to spare them suffering. At the same time they often declared that they wanted not to go to Heaven if the Spaniards go there, because the demons in Hell would treat them better; and they sometimes resisted religious instruction on the ground that they wanted no God so cruel as He who suffers the Spaniards.[7]

By 1594 the corregidores had become habitual despoilers of the Indian peasants to such an extent that the Viceroy Marquis of Cañete found himself obliged to formulate severe charges and ordinances against them. Both the corregidores of the larger and richer jurisdictions where there was an important Spanish element and those corregidores whose subjects were predominantly rural or small-town Indian peasants having their native chiefs over them were oppressive and frequently violated the letter as well as the spirit of the King's laws. Some of the leading charges made by Cañete are:

That the corregidores forced not only the proper tribute-payers (heads of families, between eighteen and fifty years old) to work, but also their women and children, whom the law exempted from tribute-paying. This abuse was carried to such length that the Indians had no time and no strength for the requirements of the Faith.

That the Indians were systematically overworked, with the natural result that their holdings of land, their cattle, and their other sources of money for themselves and for their tribute fell into complete unproductiveness.

That persons other than Indians, especially Mestizos, Negroes, Mulattoes, and Zambos (offspring of Negroes and Indians), all which racial groups were forbidden to come into contact with the Indian peasants, were suffered by the corregidores to wander at will through the country and to settle wherever they chose, to the great harm of the pure-blooded Indians.[8]

Early in the seventeenth century there was made an effort to abbreviate the powers of the corregidores by giving to the alcaldes ordinarios (justices of the peace) of the municipalities a large part of their authority. The plan met with slight success. A document in the British Museum describes the amazing inefficiency and venality prevailing in municipal governments throughout the Andean region. Justice was boldly tampered with. The officials connived at short measure in the sale of bread and other commodities. A shameless raising of the price of necessities was often enforced for the benefit of alcaldes and other city officials. If any such owned farms near the city, they arbitrarily took more than their proper share of the irrigation water, to the fatal injury of their Indian neighbors, and they would follow this up by selling the produce of their farms at high prices in the city market. The rule, in short, of the alcaldes being fully as bad as that of the corregidores, it had to be given up.[9]

Valuable data on the conditions surrounding the Indian laborers in the mines are provided by Don Diego de Luna, who, during five years, served the King diligently in the post of Protector-General of the Indians of the Kingdom of Peru. In his Memorial to the King (about 1629 or 1630) Luna uses language which is a striking combination of the servility then customary in addressing the Lord's Anointed with the utmost boldness and sagacity both of ideas and of recommendations. It is clear that Luna had profound convictions on the subjects of which he treats.

From Luna we learn that Don Luís Gerónimo de Cabrera y Bobadilla, Count of Chinchón, and Viceroy of Peru from 1629 to 1639, was deeply interested in matters pertaining to the mines and their operatives. Knowing that evils existed, the Viceroy resolved to make improvements and to draw up a new arrangement with the mine-owners of Huancavélica relative to labor conditions there. The negotiations were entrusted to a triangular commission made up of the Oidor Don Alonzo Perez de Salazar, representing the Viceroy; lawyers who represented the owners; and Don Juan del Campo Godoy, acting for the Indian laborers' interests. Luna was present *ex-officio* to see that there was fair play.

Finding that some of the proposed provisions of the new arrangement were prejudicial to what he considered the best interests of the Indians, Luna, in his official capacity, prepared a memorial or memorandum which he intended to lay before the Viceroy so that he might be guided by it at the final meeting of the commission in which the Viceroy would examine all the evidence and determine the final form of the new arrangement. Of that earlier memorandum Luna sent a copy to the King in order that he might be truly informed as to the conditions.

Luna boldly set forth his belief that the mita or corvée system of forced labor in mines and elsewhere, as it then existed in Peru, threatened the Indians with absolute extinction and the Kingdom with utter ruin. Cynically he remarks that as the remedies proposed in the past have not been carried into effect there is but little hope that those now to be proposed will be effectual. In vigorous language he urges the King to abolish the mita. Already, so he says, there remains but one third of the number of Indians who were originally set apart (by Toledo) for working the mercury mines of Huancavélica.

So terrible are the abuses still practiced that the remaining mita Indians are rapidly dying out.

Specific points regarding the Indian laborers at Huancavélica are emphasized by Luna:

The Indians have no means of obtaining legal advice in their civil and criminal lawsuits, nor have they any effective legal protection against the rapacity of the lesser officials (the corregidores and the curacas).

Every one, from corregidores and priests down to the vilest Mestizo or Negro, regards the wretched mita Indians as mere prey, making it a common practice to despoil them of their wives and daughters and of their poor fragments of property. The habitual and general plundering of the Indans came to such a point in 1629 that they seemed destined soon to be totally destitute and forsaken.

The last part of Luna's account of conditions at Huancavélica—a mining-centre typical of all the rest—is taken up with the fact that the officials whose duty it was to safeguard the Indians were on the point of resigning their posts because their salaries had not been paid for a long time, the arrears amounting to 40,000 pesos ensayados (between $80,000 and $120,000). To remedy this situation, Luna proposes that the tribute be increased somewhat for a time, but only to a small part of the reduction of the tribute which had been granted by the Viceroy Don Martín Enríquez, Viceroy from 1581–1583.[10] We shall return presently to this matter of labor at Huancavélica.

A Viceroy who was especially diligent in his efforts to improve the condition of the Indians was Don Pedro de Toledo y Leyva, Marquis of Mancera, in office from 1639 to 1648. With stark truth he says that "the worst enemies of these poor Indians are the greed of their Corregidores and the cupidity of their priests and caciques (chiefs), who are all intent upon growing rich by the sweat of the Indians."[11] A little later, Mancera shows that the corregidores, the caciques or curacas (chiefs), and also the priests, were active in disobeying the laws which forbade the sale of wines and other intoxicants to the Indians.[12]

We will now examine the evidence given by an engaging but rascally swashbuckler of the type very common in those days. This was a Portuguese gentleman named Don Manuel Ribeiro Teixera de Morais. He was known to the man who was destined to be the all-powerful minister of King Philip IV, Don Gaspar de Guzmán, Count-Duke of San Lucar and Count-Duke of Olivares. As early as 1605, in the reign of Philip III, Guzmán had advised Ribeiro to enter the service of the King of Spain. In 1606, after some preliminary adventures in battles with the Dutch, Ribeiro went to America, arriving at length at Porto Bello. Having proceeded thence to Peru, he applied to the Viceroy Marquis of Montesclaros (ruled 1607 to 1615) for the command of a company with which he might go to the wars in Chile. Although for some reason or other his request was not granted, he was given instead the post of administrator of the Indian commune of Paucarcolla, formerly held by the Corregidor Count of la Gomera, who had acted through lieutenants. These men, according to Ribeiro, who was certainly a humbug, were consuming the wealth, such as it was, of the unfortunate Indians. Rather naïvely he goes on to say that he himself bought and sold produce, as many other "good people" did, and that he searched for gold and silver ore.[13]

Among the specific charges made by Ribeiro against the corregidores may be noted the following:

That the corregidores overwork the Indians by making them carry wine to and fro for sale.

That they pitilessly exploit the Indian spinners and weavers, obliging them to work by day and by night in badly kept rooms and yards, and not allowing them to sow their crops nor attend to other urgent matters.

That they despoil the Indians by collecting their tribute twice or oftener in a given year, frequently doing so in collusion with the caciques (chiefs in the minor government).

That the corregidores forcibly take the produce of the Indians' farms and either pay for it with bad wine (forbidden by law to the Indians), or else not paying for it at all.

That the caciques co-operate with the corregidores in the mulcting of the Indians, doing so in order to gain favors for themselves from their superiors.

For these and countless other abuses Ribeiro could suggest but one remedy and that an unsavory one: Espionage. In this he goes further than does Friar Rodrigo de Loaysa; for, it will be remembered, he also suggested espionage, but in a mild form. Ribeiro, on the other hand, recommended the use of spies and informers such as those maintained by the worst of the Roman emperors and by certain equally deplorable democratic governments of our own day.[14]

We derive further information concerning conditions at Huancavélica, Potosí, and other mining centres from Don Juan Estévanez de Azebedo, who, in 1650, wrote a detailed report for Don García Sarmiento de Sotomayor y Luna, Count of Salvatierra, and Viceroy of Peru from 1648 to 1655.

Estévanez corroborates the evidence already given by Don Diego de Luna (see above, pages 181 and 183), as to the serious diminution of the Indian population from which Huancavélica drew its labor. In 1650, he says, there were but one third as many Indians available for those mercury mines as there had been when Toledo made his original assignments of mita Indians. He adds that, in 1650, the tribute paid by the Indians in that district was not sufficient to pay the salaries of the corregidor and other officials. Estévanez goes on to say that the silver mines of Potosí drew their labor from an immense territory that included the following corregimientos:

1. Urcos
2. Canas and Canches
3. Azángaro and Asillo
4. Cavana and Cavanilla
5. Paucarcolla
6. Copacavana
7. Chucuito
8. Pacajes
9. Sicasica
10. Carangas
11. Challacollo
12. Cochabamba
13. Chayanta
14. Porco
15. Chichas

In other words, the whole country from twenty-five miles southeast of Cuzco down to and around Lake Titicaca and thence in a broad strip running southeastwardly along the eastern side of Lake Poopó or Aullagas down to and around the Imperial Town of Potosí was subject to social drainage on behalf of the silver mines at Potosí.

How dire were the effects of that drainage is indicated by Estévanez in his description of the conditions which he found in the provinces of Chucuito and Pacajes. He tells us that the population of those two provinces was much smaller than it had been in Toledo's day, but that it was still the densest to be found in the fifteen provinces mentioned. Estévanez describes the frauds practiced upon the unfortunate Indians by the officials in charge of the mita system. Two months previous to the date when the year's quota of mitayos must begin work in the mines, all the caciques of the fifteen provinces were warned to have their men in readiness. A functionary called "captain of the mita" was sent by every corregidor to each village in his province to collect the mitayos into gangs and take them to the mines. Inasmuch as the curacas (caciques or chiefs) were strongly averse to having any of their subjects even temporarily removed from their control, they were wont to buy exemption for as many Indians as possible of those whom the luck of the lottery had appointed to go to the mines. The price of a year's exemption was 350 pesos per man. It was often raised by the help of the priest and was paid to the captain of the mita. When, at last, this official was satisfied that he had got all the money he could for that time, he marched off the unransomed ones to his corregidor, reporting that the men missing from the quota had run away.[15]

The severity to which those Indians who could not avoid the mita were subjected is harrowingly described by Estévanez. He says that they dreaded it so much that, in some localities, they were daily escaping in large numbers into the eastern forests where they would be beyond the officials' reach. If things continue in this way, he remarks, the land will soon have to be conquered anew or else mining will have to be discontinued.[16]

Fig. 16. A travelling hammock or litter, eighteenth century. *After Frézier.*

Fig. 17. A travelling litter and Indian houses on the Peruvian coast. *After Juan and Ulloa, 1748.*

Fig. 18. The river navigation on the Isthmus of Panama. *After Juan and Ulloa, 1748.*

Bad though the situation was, it might have been still worse had not a high official here and there striven to remedy matters. In 1633, Don Juan de Carvajal y Sandi, President and Visitador (Inspector) of the Audience of La Plata, forced a number of mine-owners to give up their Indians and to close down their mines because of their atrocious treatment of their workers. This act led Estévanez to suggest that, in any case, there were too many privately owned mines at Potosí. If some of them were sequestrated on account of abuses the remaining mine-owners would treat their Indians better.[17] An official such as President Carvajal y Sandi is like a ray of sunlight falling suddenly into the murk and horror of a torture chamber—and, unhappily, as rare.

Although it is noteworthy that Estévanez does not, like Luna, recommend the abolition of the mita, he does urge that it be made as mild and as just as possible and that all possible means be taken to ensure the spiritual salvation of the Indians through the activity of the priests of Potosí's fourteen parishes.[18] In those days this was doubtless regarded as a panacea and as an example of great liberality.

An important account of things Peruvian was given by Don Lorenzo de las Llamosas in 1692. He was a devoted servant of Don Melchor de Navarra y Rocaful, Duke of La Palata, and Viceroy of Peru from 1681 to 1691. His Epistle on the services of that high official was addressed to the Queen, María Ana of Neuburg, who, in 1689, had married that pathetic and epileptic monarch, King Charles II, called "The Bewitched."[19] Mother Spain was now in the deepest of shadows, with her Royal house in appalling decay and every part of her being mouldy with all manner of corruption. Yet La Palata was a great ruler, an infinitely better man than his piteous master. Such is the background of Llamosas.[20]

Llamosas speaks of the friction between the corregidores and the parish priests, referring to a cédula of February 20th, 1684, on that very subject. He states that priests were wont to complain of the tardiness with which the corregidor paid their salaries out of the tribute-money. To correct this, the

Viceroy Duke of La Palata ruled, on May 4th, 1684,[21] that the priests might collect their stipends directly from the caciques of their parishioners, the corregidores being bound to take the receipts for money thus paid as part of the annual tribute. The idea behind this measure was that, once the priests were fully paid, they would cease to squabble with the corregidores and to wring money out of the Indians by force.[22] We may have our doubts as to how it worked in practice.

Llamosas then points out that the chief sources of the Royal revenue in Peru were: The tribute paid by the Indians;[23] the Royal fifth of the products of the mines; taxes, such as the alcabala (sales tax), almojarifazgo (customs duties), avería (convoy tax on shipping), monopolies (gunpowder, salt, tobacco, and mercury), church tithes (in part), and other imposts.[24] As Llamosas observes, the Indians bore the brunt of the first two. He corroborates Luna and Estévanez, saying that the number of Indians in the provinces whence Potosí drew its labor had so much diminished that the number of workmen in the mines at a given moment had declined from 4,000 under Toledo to 1,400 under La Palata. This condition resulted in extra hard work for those who were left and in a diminution of the output of the mines. Alarmed by this situation, the King, in a cédula dated May 28th, 1681, ordered that, if need were, other provinces could be made to contribute to the mita service at Potosí.[25]

There follows a passage of truly enchanting naïveté in which Llamosas shows us the happy-go-lucky manner in which even the most important affairs of the Viceroyalty were conducted. He explains that, when La Palata received the 1681 cédula mentioned, he decided to begin work by taking a census. In order to avoid the necessity of paying special census-takers, the Viceroy Duke decided that the job should be done by the caciques, parish priests, and corregidores. The Duke reasoned that another advantage of this plan would be the fact that those officials, moved by selfish reasons of their own, would understate the true number of Indians rather than exaggerate it, and that the result would be favorable rather than unfavorable to the Indians, so that there would be an additional number of Indians to share the labor apportioned in reference to the figures in the census. One little point seems to have escaped the Duke's notice, however, namely, that the corregidores, priests, and caciques would know the true number of the Indians and would probably overwork them in any case. Nevertheless, the Duke believed this measure to be the only way to save the mining industry of Peru from untimely extinction.[26]

The taking of this comical census began on October 1st, 1683, and every precaution was taken not to count any individual more than once! As though this were not enough protection for the Indians, the Viceroy deducted forty per cent from the totals in order to reach a figure favorable to the Indians in the manner described. The work was completed in the area drawn upon by Huancavélica and it would have been finished in that of Potosí had not the great earthquake of October 20th, 1687, at Lima, thrown the entire government of Peru out of gear.[27]

An increase in the amounts paid as tribute was an unexpected result of the census taken at Potosí. The mercury mines at Huancavélica were the prime source of both Royal and private wealth in Peru; for, without the mercury produced there, the silver mines at Potosí and elsewhere could not be worked profitably; and without mining, there would be no Royal fifths nor, according to the economic dogma of that day, any other wealth. Llamosas goes on to say that the mines of Huancavélica had been so misused that one of the chief lodes was "buried in its own ruins," which means, presumably, that the galleries leading to it had collapsed. La Palata strove to remedy all this, and, at the same time, he bought out two mine owners, using such tact that they were content to be recompensed with five years apiece in the office of corregidor.[28]

This brings us to the end of the Hapsburg period in the Viceroyalty of Peru. Into the intricate dynastic aspects of the matter and all the European strife arising from them we need not enter here. We need only remember the fact that, ever since the last decade of Philip II, ever since the ghastly passing of that monarch—so graphically described by Lytton Strachey in *Elizabeth and Essex,* page 175—the Hapsburgs have been a degenerating family, typifying well the vast, loose-jointed, gilded, mouldy, and badly lubricated coach of state whose drivers, at any rate in theory, they were. When, in 1700, the Bourbons, in the person of Philip, Duke of Anjou, obtained the throne of the Spains a new period began for Peru. To many people it will seem a fantastic suggestion that the Bourbons were enlightened and progressive sovereigns; yet such they certainly were, at least in comparison with their immediate predecessors. With Philip of Anjou's coming to Spain as Philip V, there came also a change from the traditional Spanish type of court-life—glum, etiquette-smothered, and religious beyond measure—to the more gracious and elegant ways of the Bourbons of France. The weak character of Philip V made him the tool first of that admirable woman, the Princess des Ursins, camarera mayor (mistress of the robes) to the Queen (María Luisa of Savoy), and, from 1714 onwards, of his horrible but clever second wife, Elizabeth Farnese of Parma. It is not too much to say that these three women, in their different ways, ensured the establishment of the Bourbons in Spain, doing so in spite of the lamentable weakness of Philip V himself.[29]

The period of dynastic change is bridged, for Peruvianists, by one of the most stalwart and intelligent critics of the Spanish régime in the Indies. This was the Marquis of Varinas, who, on occasions, was ably seconded by his wife. By reason of his long wanderings in America and his varied experiences there, Varinas was peculiarly well versed in the facts of affairs in Spain's America.[30]

Although the Varinas evidence deals chiefly with commerce, and so will be noticed further on, the Marquis, no less than other daring men, severely censures the corregidores. Speaking of the time at the close of the seventeenth century, he makes grave accusations against them, saying that:

The corregidor who has paid ten or twelve thousand pesos for his post buys about 20,000 pesos' worth of stuffs and general merchandise which he forces his Indians to purchase at six or eight times the proper price. At the same time, he forces them to sell to him at one fourth of the fair price the produce of their lands and of the local manufactures (chiefly textiles). In this way he not only gets back his money but also quickly makes a fortune besides. To this he adds:

That the corregidores make it a custom to exempt the caciques from forced purchases, thus securing their complacence. The common Indians of the villages, including the widows, the agéd, and the unfortunate, are compelled by the caciques to buy goods that are either useless to them or else forbidden by law, such as wines and saddle-horses, at the corregidor's price.[31]

Elsewhere Varinas refers to the general inefficiency of the colonial administration and then proceeds vividly to describe the outrageous cruelty of the mita as it was at the end of the seventeenth century. Then, as in former years and in later, mines depended upon the mita for their operatives; and, in addition to that, the mita had become of great importance to cattle-estates, obrajes (cloth-factories), and even privately owned farms. It had had a disastrous effect upon the population. The Marquis states that in the more than 200 leagues of country between Lima and Paita, wherein more than 2,000,000 Indians had dwelt in the early days of the colony, there were hardly 20,000 to be found in his day.[32]

The coming of the Bourbons to the Throne did not, in actual fact, alter for the better the conditions under which the desolate Indians of Peru lived out their joyless lives. This fact was due, not to any lack of good intentions on the part of the Kings and of many of their higher officials, but to the pernicious workings of the money-hunger among corregidores, priests, and Indian functionaries of the minor government, all this being aided, as before, and as in later times, by the fatal operation of the geographic factor, the time-space complex. There is no need, I think, to examine the details of the available descriptions of conditions in the eighteenth century; their tenor is in general the same as those which we have already examined. Still, for the benefit of any reader who may wish to delve into the lugubrious details, I will enumerate here, very briefly, some of the most important sources.

Don José del Campillo y Cosio was born in 1695, of noble but impoverished parents. In 1715 he became page or clerk to Don Francisco de Ocio, superintendent-general of the customs. Soon after he was patronized by the reforming minister Don José Patiño, by whom he was transferred to the naval department in 1717. During many years thereafter, Campillo studied American affairs, both in Spain and in America. In 1741 he became for a time prime minister, and in 1743 he died. He left behind him a great book entitled *Nuevo sistema de gobierno económico para América*. In it he drew up an elaborate and highly intelligent scheme for the reform of American affairs, the crux of which was the desirability of making the American peasants rich and prosperous so that they could become powerful as sustainers of commerce. The fact that this book was not published until 1789 reveals the small degree of attention which Campillo's excellent ideas commanded from his contemporaries.[33]

Equal obscurity was the fate, for many years, of one of the chief works of Don Jorge Juan y Santacilia and Don Antonio de Ulloa. The first of these distinguished colleagues was born at Novelda, near Alicante, in 1713. From 1729 to 1734 he was an officer of marines and saw service in the Mediterranean. In 1734, Philip V, acting in conjunction with Louis XV, chose Juan y Santacilia as one of the two officers whom he was sending to Quito as colleagues for the French Academicians whom the King of France was sending out to measure an arc of meridian on the Equator. The other officer chosen by King Philip was Antonio de Ulloa, also an officer of marines, who had had some experience in America already. Thus these two highly educated, extremely intelligent, and most industrious young men went to Peru with the French scientists, La Condamine, Bouguer, and Godin, in 1735, when Juan was only twenty-two and Ulloa but nineteen years old. They remained in the Viceroyalty of Peru until 1745, being engaged in multifarious labors of a scientific and of a politico-sociological nature. They saw samples of nearly every aspect of life in Peru at that time, and in their later years each received many honors in Spain, England, and France, all of which they fully merited. Juan died in Madrid in 1773 and Ulloa at Cadiz in 1795. More estimable men were never produced by any land.

The portion of the work of Juan and Ulloa which was deemed publishable with political safety in their day will be found in one of their works.[34] But their comments—not to say strictures—on the conditions in what are now Ecuador and Peru were embodied in a report to the minister Marquis of la Ensenada and by him laid before King Ferdinand VI. This report being as it is a candid revelation of the state of things in Peru, remained unknown to the world until it was tardily printed in London in 1826.[35] The First Part of this classic work is taken up with a detailed account of the military, political, and commercial aspects of Peru and other regions as the authors found them to be. In Part Two there is a devastatingly vivid account of the governmental and sociological conditions. Together the two Parts made a report which must have been profoundly depressing to any conscientious King or minister. It is a fair guess that that truly enlightened sovereign, King Charles III (reigned 1759–1788), knew something of these pages and based upon them certain of his reforms. When, at long last, the *Noticias Secretas* were published in England they were soon translated into English and various editions were printed on both sides of the North Atlantic with the result that many readers were given good reason to rejoice that the Spanish-American lands had won their freedom. Such, of course, was not the purpose of the authors; rather it was their aim to provide their King with materials for knowing the facts of his overseas possessions in order that he might ameliorate them.

Highly informative concerning life in the Audiencia of

Quito in the 1740's are two little books by the Academician
Charles Marie de La Condamine, published soon after his return to France.[36] Their evidence as to the degree of polish
and decency among the people in those parts is far from being of the most cheering sort. The popular tumult at Cuenca
on August 29th, 1739, in which the French Academicians' sur-
geon, Seniergues, was murdered, is vigorously set forth by La
Condamine in the second of the works cited, and it shows
clearly the rowdy character of the gentry in that city at that
time.

Before concluding this section of this chapter, I must say
something about the information contained in three "sources"
of much importance. The first is the work of Don Miguel
Feyjoo de Sosa, sometime Corregidor of Trujillo, by appointment of King Charles III.[37] It appears that that enlightened
monarch, the best of the Spanish Bourbons, was desirous of
acquiring detailed information regarding Trujillo, then the
curled darling of Peruvian regions. It is well, therefore, to
note what Feyjoo said of it in his book, which is dedicated to
the King and printed by the press of the Council of the Indies.

One of the three valuable maps provided by Feyjoo shows
the Valleys of Chicama, Chimu or Moche, Viru, and Chao,
with a part of the Valley of Santa. The Chicama Valley was
then the seat of notable industrial development, having in its
lower part, where cane-fields abounded, seventeen or more
trapiches (sugar-mills), worked by human strength or by
horse-power. In the upper parts of the valleys there were
many obrajes (cloth-factories) scattered among the hills
where wool from the highlands and cotton from the coast
could be brought with equal facility by mule-trains. In all
parts of the valleys haciendas (estates) devoted to general agriculture were numerous. The province of Trujillo produced
all sorts of vegetables, fruits, meats, and game-birds. Sugar
was raised and exported in important quantities. The people
were "decent" in all classes and very cultivated and urbane in
the upper class.[38]

All this sounds paradisiac. We soon discover, however, that

Trujillo province was almost empty of people. In the city of Trujillo there were: Negro and Mulatto slaves, 3,650; Mestizos, 2,300; Whites (including nobility, clergy, and nuns), 3,050; Indians (divided among three parishes), 289; not very grand total, 9,289.[39]

Other statistics are given by Feyjoo which show the far from prosperous condition of this, one of the most prosperous provinces of Peru. Speaking of the Chimu Valley he tells us that there were five Indian villages therein whose total population, counting both sexes and all ages, was 1,333 Indians and 269 Mestizos (Indian and White mixture), most of the latter being in one village.[40]

Feyjoo then treats of the Chicama Valley in like manner. He tells us that there were four Indian villages whose total population came to 854 Indians and 287 Mestizos.[41] And in the Viru Valley the only Indian village therein had but 326 Indians and 34 Mestizos.[42]

Thus we perceive, with sorrow, that in these three famous and fertile valleys, where every circumstance of Nature favors human welfare (if we except the occasional earthquakes), there were only 2,513 Indians and 590 Mestizos, a most lamentable showing, especially when we consider how thickly peopled these same valleys had been in pre-Spanish and early Spanish times. The decay here made evident was typical of all Peru in the eighteenth century.

The figures just given do not, however, account for quite all the population; for, scattered through Feyjoo's pages, there are copious data on the haciendas (landed estates) of these valleys and on their population of Negroes—both slaves and freefolk—and of Indians. The latter were extremely scarce; and to the former we shall return in a later section.

In general, these Indians lived by agriculture, with some attention to the mechanical and liberal arts such as home-manufactures, handicrafts, and also, in some villages, fishing and lighterage. Their sole language was Castilian, at any rate near to the coast, those further inland being generally more backward and still speaking native dialects. The author says that the people in the lowlands are intelligent and tractable. The political conditions of the minor government in these villages was not uniform. Santa Lucía de Moche had no cacique of its own, his place being taken by a tax-collector appointed by the Royal officials of Trujillo. San Juan Bautista de Symbal had a cacique but, at that time, the post was in litigation between Don Agustín Alexandro Enríquez Llaczacondor and Don Joseph Maxo. The Indians of Symbal were lucky in that their tribute of five pesos and two reales per year was paid for them out of funds left by Doña Florencia de Mora, daughter of the Conqueror Don Diego de Mora. This noblewoman, though married, had no children, and so she left most of her wealth for this cause. A most rarely noble woman! The tribute of the Indians of San Salvador de Manciche and of Guanchaco was also paid for them from the moneys produced by certain lands anciently set aside for the purpose. The cacique of these villages was Don Antonio Chayhuac Casamusa, whose ancestors had been chiefs in that region before the Conquest, and in whose veins ran also the blood of the Inca Pachacutec. Don Antonio resided in Lima, exercising his functions through a deputy, and his noble descent was fully recognized by the viceregal government.[43]

All this makes it seem that the lot of the Indians in the Trujillo valleys was not bad, albeit their numbers were small. It is a comfort to note that at least some of them were still ruled by their ancient curacas' descendants, whose position and rights were properly acknowledged.

Representing the last years of the period discussed in this book are two other important documents, both connected with the Viceroy Don Manuel de Amat y Junient.[44] They show the state of the Viceroyalty just prior to the rebellion of Tupac Amaru II, in 1780.

The condition of the Indians is described as being practically one of slavery under the rigid control of the corregidores. The Royal wish to be benevolent is referred to; the Indians' character is described as deserving of good treatment; but it is made clear that neither the King's compassion nor their own intrinsic worth could enable the Indians to escape terrible hardships and oppression of many kinds.[45] The later of the two documents speaks in detail of various uprisings of the Indians. In connection with one which took place in the provinces of Sicasica and Pacajes, in 1770, Amat says:

"I have already observed to your Excellency [his successor, Don Manuel de Guirior] that the object of the Corregidores of the kingdom is not the administration of justice, nor the preservation of peace, nor the safe-guarding of the people in their charge; but rather it is their purpose to trade with and have dealings with them, using for that end the authority inherent in their position which serves them as a guarantee in their undertakings. Because of this it frequently happens that the Peace is disturbed, for traffic of such kind cannot fail to make the magistrates depart from the rectitude which should govern their acts."[46]

Amat then tells us that some provinces were so large that they required twelve lieutenant-corregidores. The men who held those posts purchased them at high prices from the corregidor himself, and they were wont to resort to all sorts of malfeasance in order to recoup their outlay and build up a fortune. Cruelties were the rule, and the exasperated Indians, not so mild and cowed in what is now Bolivia as were the Peruvian Indians further north, frequently rebelled. One such uprising took place in the villages of Chupa and Chilimani in 1771, when 3,000 Indians revolted against the atrocious misrule of the Corregidor Marquis of Villa Hermosa. The movement was promptly crushed, however, and after many Indians had been killed their mutilated bodies were hanged on the very gibbets which the rebels had prepared for their Spanish oppressors.[47]

2. Affairs of the Church

The servants of God were no less iniquitous during the colonial period than were the servants of the King. On this subject I shall say as little as possible because the tenor of the evidence is uniform, and everywhere we hear of avarice and unrighteousness, rampant and implacable.

The splendid *Historical Compendium of the State of the Indians of Peru,* by Father Lope de Atienza, has lately been brought out entire in an excellent edition by Don Jacinto Jijón y Caamaño, Ecuador's leading archæologist and historian.[48] Although every page of that work is replete with rich data, we shall notice here only certain points. In Part One, Father Atienza gives an exact idea of the problems arising from the Indians' character and customs, problems which missionary priests must be prepared to solve. In Part Two, Father Atienza points out that, if the priests are to hold the respect of their neophytes (converts), they must be well disciplined, moral in their lives, not given to trade and money-getting, and, above all, they must know the native languages.[49] The gist of Atienza's message to the prelates of the Church is that they must forget the pomp and majesty of their position and, without abandoning their authority, must go down among the people in order to understand their spiritual and mundane requirements and so learn how best to serve them. Father Atienza says, bluntly, that bishops willing and able to do this have been sadly lacking.[50]

To the same period as Atienza belongs our old friend, Friar Rodrigo de Loaysa. He informed the King's private secretary that it was very necessary to provide the right sort of men to be bishops; for, he avers, too many bishops are negligent of their duties and unfit to perform them.[51] Loaysa goes on to warn against the evil arising from the giving of bishoprics merely as rewards for services elsewhere. Like Father Atienza, Loaysa emphasizes the need of keeping the bishops and other priests out of commerce, and he says that a trafficking bishop should be made to bear heavy penalties and also Papal censure. Again, like Father Atienza, he wants the bishops and other clergy to know the native languages, because a bishop who does not is a bishop deaf and dumb.[52]

Friar Rodrigo says that bishops ought to go out to Peru with no idea of going home again. If they can hope to return to Spain their covetousness becomes very great, and he thinks that if that hope were removed they might "become more moderate in acquiring wealth and more generous in giving alms." He goes on to tell of some bishops' peculiar use of their money: Bishop Solano, of Cuzco, took to Rome 150,000 pesos which could have been used much better in his diocese; a Bishop of Quito spent more than 20,000 pesos building fine houses for the Inquisitors in Lima, forgetting his own poor Indians. And so on.[53]

One particularly wise suggestion was made by Loaysa: He urged that the Peruvian clergy be chosen from among the best students at the University of San Marcos, in Lima.[54] It was well known that men born and brought up in the country were less avaricious and abusive than men sent out from Spain with the knowledge that they would go home after a time.

Scores of recommendations of like tenor were made by the good Friar Rodrigo. A true servant of God himself, he was saddened by the smallness of the number of worthy priests in Peru. He cites, with justifiable pleasure and pride, the donation of Archbishop Loaysa—perhaps a kinsman of his—who left all his money to found a magnificent hospital for natives in Lima.[55]

Turning now to a time some twenty years later, we find that a document in the Vatican throws a blinding light on the post-mortem treatment of the Indians. It is a decree by that admirable Pontiff, Paul V (Camillo Borghese), dated at Rome on February 16th, 1607. In it His Holiness forbids monastic orders in New Spain and other parts of the Indies to demand more money for burials in their land than is demanded by parish priests for burials in the cemetery, and, conversely, it is forbidden that parish priests charge more for burials than monastic orders do. This dual pontifical order—which the Pope felt called upon to issue notwithstanding the fact that the King was supposed to attend to Church affairs—indicates a tendency on the part of both secular and regular clergy to mulct the poor Indians even after they were dead.[56] It also indicates that the Pope did what he could to remedy the King's neglect.

We have already noted, on pages 167 and 168, that various

churchmen devoted much energy to the extirpation of the ancient native cults. Those clergymen mentioned in that place acted, on the whole, reasonably and commendably, at any rate from the Catholic point of view. But such activities could be carried too far, as the fanatical Don Gonzalo de Ocampo, Archbishop of Lima, proved. Between 1625 and 1630 he caused many Indian villages to be destroyed by fire and their inhabitants to be moved arbitrarily to new homes in the expectation that this strenuous treatment would induce them to abandon the local cults to which the Archbishop objected.[57] Do we see in all this an imitation of the Incaic practice of moving whole tribes into new homes in order to render them more docile?[58]

The Portuguese gentleman-adventurer, Ribeiro Teixera de Morais, whom we have already cited, at one time in his checkered career played the incongruous rôle of missionary priest. In that capacity he saw enough of the ways of too many clergymen to make him abandon holy orders. Among his charges are these:

That the clergy do not observe the rules of their calling, nor attend the synods of their bishops.

That they are Christians in name only and are, in reality, more depraved than the heathen. The laxity of the bishops permits indiscipline and corruption to flourish among them.

That the clergy maintain slaughter-houses which bring them much wealth, and that they participate in and favor even the most wrongful doings of the corregidores.

That out of 1,040 priests with whom he had to do, only five were perfect in their mode of life and in their performance of their duties.[59]

During the middle years of the eighteenth century, the condition of the clergy fell to the lowest depths of moral and psychological degradation, characterized by extraordinary and general lewdness among both seculars and regulars. The monasteries throughout the kingdom had fallen so far below their ancient standards that monks shamelessly kept their concubines either in rented rooms or in their cells and, for the ladies' amusement, held drunken revelries with much indecent dancing in the sacred precincts of their monasteries.[60] Even the nuns, though perhaps not given to sexual immorality, were extremely rowdy in their ways and frequently indulged in unseemly brawls about conventual elections and other matters. These feminine wars often reached such a pitch that not only the prelates but also the constables had to intervene in order to restore the cloistral peace.[61]

True to his character of a great reformer, the minister Campillo y Cosio advocated drastic reforms in the Church. He held that the dioceses were too large, being planned to give the bishops huge incomes rather than to ensure proper pastoral supervision. He urges that, instead of a large diocese with an episcopal stipend of 50,000 pesos or so, there should be two or three smaller sees each capable of being properly managed by its bishop who would receive not more than 12,000 pesos. To this he added the remark that there were far too many priests in the land.[62]

One serious manifestation of the decline in moral and intellectual values during the eighteenth century was the chaos into which the educational system, such as it was, had fallen. Even the venerable University of San Marcos, founded by Charles I in 1553 and improved by Philip II in 1572, had decayed to such an extent that there were more instructors than students, and the doctorate was often conferred upon shamefully ignorant men.[63] Universities and colleges at Cuzco, Arequipa, Trujillo, and Huamanga—two of them for noble Indians—also suffered a parallel decline at this period. Only among the Jesuits in their colleges was education still preserved in its purity and a decent if rather archaic standard maintained among both teachers and pupils.[64]

Fatally, however, the expulsion of the Jesuits from Spain and all Spanish possessions was decreed by Charles III in 1767. It was something which had been preparing for many years. In France, under Louis XV, the unremitting attacks of Jansenism and of the Parliament led to the suppression of the Jesuits in 1764; in Portugal the Society was suppressed by

the Marquis of Pombal in 1759–1760. In Spain, in the opening months of 1767, the Jesuits were suppressed by Charles
acting through his minister Count of Aranda. In all this we
see the result of the spread of the new liberal ideas voiced by
the Encyclopædists and other progressive elements.[65]

In Peru, as has been said, the Jesuits had been a force for
good, but their mediæval type of teaching was not considered
consistent with the spirit of the time. So they had to go—
steered out of the country by Viceroy Amat. Although it
might be rash to attribute to their going the quickened pace
which showed itself in Peru during the last third of the eighteenth century, it is quite safe to say that there were no Jesuits
in the country when that quickened pace showed itself.

3. The Non-Indian Classes; the Nobility

Thus far, in this chapter and in the preceding one, our attention has been given chiefly to those facts of the colonial
period in Peru which refer to the Indians and to their governance by the white invaders, often acting through the minor
government made up of Indian chiefs of various grades. I
propose now to give the reader at least a slight idea of the situation in which other races and classes in the state found
themselves.

The African or Negro Race may truly be said to have come
into Peru at the same moment that horses, firearms, money-
hunger, and Catholicism did. All through the early days of
the Hispanic ascendancy in Peru we keep catching glimpses
of Negroes, usually in the rôle of servitors.[66] By 1600, the
African element in society was fairly large, particularly on the
coast, and it was notorious for its licentiousness and tumultu-
ousness. The Crown, wishful to preserve the racial integrity of
the Indian peasantry, passed many laws designed to keep the
Indian and African races from crossing and to preserve the
natives of the land from contact with the Negroes. This policy was both sound and merciful, and it was underscored by

Fig. 20. The exterior of the Jesuit Church, Quito, mid-eighteenth century.

Fig. 19. In the Cloister of La Merced, Cuzco.

Courtesy of Mrs. Myra Brady.

other laws whose purport and tenor were that the Indians were free-born subjects of the Crown whose labors were to be paid for at a just wage and that the Negroes were slaves.[67]

The history of the trade in African slaves to all parts of Spanish America has been exhaustively studied by M. Scelle, who has shown that the first period, down to 1580, was one in which the Spanish government licensed the traffic; the second, 1580 to 1640, was one in which Portugal (then subject to Spain) played a dominant part; and the third, 1640–1700, was one in which the Dutch were important.[68] Finally, during most of the eighteenth century, the slave trade was carried on under asiento treaties by the Spanish government in conjunction, at different times, with the French, Portuguese, English, and Dutch.[69]

So much for the slave trade to America in general. The only figures relative to the importation of African slaves into Peru that I have been able to discover are those of Ribeiro Teixera de Morais, who tells us that between 100 and 150 slaves were registered annually as going to Peru from Africa but that the real number taken was between 700 and 800, most of whom were smuggled so as to escape the duties.[70]

Peru, therefore, acquired a considerable African element between the time of the Conquest and the end of the colonial period. As we have noticed, the Indian population of the coast had shrunk to miserable proportions by 1760. Negroes, chiefly slaves, had come in to take the place of the natives and to supply the necessary labor, not only in the plantations, but also in the nascent industries of the coast—sugar-mills, called trapiches, and such. At the present time the lower classes of the coast are far more African in race than they are Indian. In the Department of Piura, for example, I did not discover any communities which I could describe as truly Indian west of the Andean foothills, and even in the mountains around Huancabamba there is much evidence of Negro blood, albeit families obviously pure Indian abound also.

Our old friend, Don Miguel Feyjoo de Sosa, supplies us with valuable data on the part played by Negroes in the Trujillo region about 1760. In the briefest possible form I will present his materials regarding various properties in those valleys:

As displayed by Feyjoo, the landed properties of the four valleys of Chicama, Chimu or Moche, Virú, and Chao were very moderate in proportions, yield, and worth. Worked, when worked at all, chiefly by Negro slaves, they supported only small numbers of these operatives. The properties listed are of three kinds: Trapiches or haciendas trapiches (estates with sugar-mills); haciendas (estates without their own sugar-mills), and haciendas de pan-llevar (estates chiefly given to raising food-crops). Some of the lands in question were owned by the Church and rented to private persons for small annual rentals (from 90 to 200 pesos a year, according to circumstances). Several other estates belonged to the Indians of the various villages, and were likewise rented.

In the Chimu or Moche Valley there were 38 estates of the different kinds mentioned whose cultivable area came to 1,627 fanegadas (a fanegada being 1.59 acres). The smallest estate was that of Doña María Ana de Torres, close to the village of Guamán and so near the mouth of the Chimu or Moche River, which estate had only two fanegadas of land. It had three Negro slaves, raised alfalfa and food-stuffs, and was worth, without the slaves, 200 pesos. The biggest estate was the hacienda trapiche of San Isidro de Galindo, three leagues from the city of Trujillo, which was owned by Don Francisco Javier de la Torre. It had 239 fanegadas of land, 40 slaves of all ages, and produced 2,000 arrobas of sugar a year. (An arroba is 25 pounds.)[71] The value of this estate was 46,000 pesos, not counting the slaves. The biggest number of slaves on any estate in the Chimu Valley was 73. This was the estate of San Nicolás del Paso, less than two leagues from Trujillo, an estate of 79 fanegadas belonging to Dr. Don Gaspar Antonio de Remirez y Laredo, who had bought the estate at auction for 30,528 pesos, its yield being 917 pesos annually. On most estates that had slaves there were usually less than 25 of all ages, and estates that had no slaves were worked, when worked at all, by hired day laborers.[72]

In the Valley of Chicama there were several interesting properties. One, the hacienda trapiche de Chicama, contained 133 fanegadas of land and 29 slaves. It produced yearly 1,200 arrobas of sugar and 300 arrobas of olive oil. This estate was the first one in Peru to grow sugar-cane, although, as Feyjoo duly notes, Garcilaso says that the first sugar estate was near Huánuco.[73] This estate of Chicama had belonged to Don Diego de Mora, one of the first conquerors, and already mentioned in these pages. The estate was bought at public auction in 1755 by Don Juan Joseph Ruiz Cazo for 23,000 pesos, including the 29 slaves. A bargain, one would say.

Another very interesting property in the Chicama Valley was the vínculo (entailed estate) founded in the seventeenth century by Don Juan de Herrera. It was made up of the estates named Nuestra Señora del Rosario de Chiclín, Exaltación de la Cruz, and San Juan Beautista de Fachén or la Guaca. When Feyjoo wrote, this important vínculo or entailed estate belonged to its third owner, the Marquis of Herrera and Valle-Hermoso. It had 319 fanegadas of land, and produced yearly 5,000 arrobas of sugar, 300 arrobas of olive oil, and some food crops. Up the Chicama Valley some six leagues was the hacienda of Santo Domingo de Zauzál, with 70 fanegadas of land. This was also a part of the vínculo of the Marquis of Herrera. The production of sugar at Zauzál came to 2,000 arrobas. A final series of properties belonging to this relatively fine and rich landed estate lay still further up the river and consisted of the lands called Chala Baxa, Chala Alta, Xaguey, and Cogitambo. These were chiefly given up to cattle raising. The Marquis owned also 115 Negro slaves. The total value of the lands of the vínculo was 125,000 pesos.[74]

Still another estate of interest was the hacienda de Catabio, belonging to the heirs of Don Valentín del Risco and administered for his children by their Tutoress, Doña Isabel de Alvarado. This estate contained 314 fanegadas of land, but had only 12 Negro slaves. It grew maize, wheat, rice, and other food-crops. Its value, including the slaves, was only 18,000 pesos.[75]

On the northern bank of the Chicama River was another set of estates all belonging to one owner. These were the hacienda trapiche of Mocoyope and the estates of la Viña, Santa Ana, San Juan de Buenaventura, and Fallape or Vizcaino. They were bought at auction by Don Joseph Alfonso Lizarzaburu for 77,700 pesos. They had 799 fanegadas and 76 Negro slaves. These properties produced 5,000 arrobas of sugar and much rice, maize, and wheat.[76]

In short, the properties in the Chicama Valley were much larger and much better provided with slaves than those in the Chimu Valley. Even so, there were various large holdings in that valley which were suffering from general decay, and one property of 300 fanegadas, when put up for auction, commanded no price whatever. The cultivated land in the Valley of Chicama came to 11,848 fanegadas (including land owned by the four Indian villages). The slave population on the 44 haciendas of the valley was about 1,000.[77]

In the Virú Valley, also, there were some large properties. Doña Francisca Santoyo, Marchioness of Bella-Vista, had the hacienda of Santa Elena with 788 fanegadas and 30 slaves. On that estate maize, beans, vegetables, and alfalfa were grown and also goats, cows, and horses. She also owned the haciendas of San Juan and San Ildefonso, with 52 and 98 fanegadas, respectively; and the hacienda trapiche of Tomavál, with 131 fanegadas, including the four lands called Caray, Guacapongo, Mallasco, and Susanga, with 72 slaves. The Marchioness thus owned 1,069 fanegadas of land, and 102 slaves. Her property was valued at 80,000 pesos, including the slaves. At the same time, Don Joseph Muñoz, first Marquis of Bella-Vista (husband of the above-mentioned lady) owned the hacienda de Buena-Vista, including the lands of San Francisco de Lunar, with 300 fanegadas of land growing maize, wheat, and vegetables. There were no slaves here but 24 Indians and 5 Mulattoes lived on the property. Another estate of the Marquis was the hacienda of Guadalupe or Tambo Real, near the mouth of the Santa River. It had 300 fanegadas of land growing alfalfa and hay, and had 6 or 8

Negro slaves. The Marquis also had a cattle-ranch called San Bartolomé de Chao, which was 3 leagues long and ¾ league wide.

The hacienda of Puito, in the Chao Valley, was owned by a noble Indian named Don Lorenzo Tuzñán and his brothers. It had 180 fanegadas and grew maize, wheat, beans, and cotton. There were no slaves, but 22 Indians of all ages and 21 Mestizos and 1 free Mulatto lived on the property. There seem to have been very few Negroes, slave or free, in the Virú and Chao Valleys.[78]

I have presented these data because they show exactly the state of affairs in this, the most fertile region of Peru. The picture which Don Miguel Feyjoo de Sosa draws for his King, and for posterity, shows a diminished Indian population living mainly in its villages, and a by no means impressive number of Negro slaves and mixed-blooded people living on private estates. The yield of land and the value of it was, on his showing, pitifully small, the only properties of respectable proportions being those of the Marquis of Herrera and Valle-Hermoso and those of the Marquis and Marchioness of Bella-Vista.

A part of the lamentable condition, perhaps a very large part, was due to the earthquakes which had afflicted the Trujillo region, as also Lima and other parts of Peru, at different times. Feyjoo gives graphic details of three great quakes which gravely injured Trujillo, those of February 14th, 1619, January 6th, 1725, and September 2nd, 1759. At the time of the last-named disaster, Feyjoo was Corregidor of Trujillo, and he seems to have proceeded with diligence and good sense in doing everything possible to remedy the sad situation of the people. On September 10th, 1759, he wrote a long and detailed letter to the Viceroy Count of Superunda in which he narrates the extent of the damages suffered by the churches, public buildings, and private houses of Trujillo.[79] Harm was wrought by earthquakes not only in the destruction of edifices and the terrifying of the people, but also in the sterilizing effect they had upon the soil, putting it into such a condition that many food-crops would not grow, although sugar, grasses, and some vegetables would.[80]

Turning now to the white element in Peru we find that, in spite of the presence of two darker-skinned races in the country, there were also white men, mostly Spanish, who occupied humble places in the social scale. There were pedlars, and there were other Spaniards who lived as they could, wage-earners, booth-keepers, and the like.[81]

A very high percentage of the pure Spanish blood in the country was found, naturally, in the upper classes. There was, however, an invidious and ludicrous distinction drawn between Chapetones or Spaniards born in Spain, and Criollos, Creoles, persons of pure or nearly pure Spanish blood born in America. To understand this highly important and very cruel and meaningless distinction we must remember that a high proportion of the Spaniards who came into Peru in the sixteenth century were of gentle or of noble blood in Spain. Some of them came, indeed, from the bluest blood that country possessed, being, for the most part, younger sons of noble houses. As already shown, many of these young blades perforce married or mated with Indian women of rank, there being an insufficiency of white women in the country during the early days. But this tincture of Indian blood did no more harm to the portion of the Peruvian gentry which had it than was received by the numerous descendants of Pocahontas among ourselves. It was, in fact, a very good mixture, and, as we have seen, on pages 110 and 134, ladies of the blood imperial of the Incas were deemed fit wives for Spanish men of the loftiest birth. Moreover, as time wore on, an increasing number of Spanish women of quality came into Peru. Therefore, by about 1600, there was a very important gentry in the country whose blood was either Spanish and high-caste Indian or else pure Spanish. These were the nucleus of the creole gentry. Had not Gonzalo Pizarro's—or rather Francisco de Carvajal's —plans for making Peru an independent monarchy (1544– 1548) fallen through, they would have constituted an excellent nobility; again, had not the plan to convert the encomiendas into feudal fiefs in perpetuity fallen through (1555–1720), they would have composed a respectable land-owning and politically important aristocracy.

As things were, however, the creoles came to be a gentry, indeed, but one bereft of political importance. To a large extent they were excluded from the higher offices of the colonial state. Dr. Moses tells us that out of 754 viceroys, captains-general, and governors who held office in Spanish America during the colonial period only 18 were creoles.[82] There were, as we have noted in the preceding chapter, some, but not enough, Peruvian bishops who were born in America. In the uppermost classes of the creoles there were many men who could have filled ably even the post of Viceroy, and certainly that of Oidor; yet from these and from other high posts they were excluded by a cédula of Philip III dated March 16th, 1609.[83] Never was there snobbery of more senseless cruelty. The situation was aggravated during the seventeenth and eighteenth centuries by the constant arrival of low-caste Spaniards who, being nothing at home, ventured to place themselves on an equality with the highest of the creoles. This pretentiousness on their part nurtured a growing hatred in creole breasts for the chapetones, a hatred destined, ultimately, to aid powerfully in the final break with Spain. Being usually very skilful at money-grubbing and at place-grabbing, these low-born Spaniards frequently managed to marry into the noblest creole houses. Their children, however, were creoles, and they often displayed a virulent hatred towards their chapeton fathers.[84]

Thus we see that, in colonial times, Peru had a very definite creole aristocracy. During the seventeenth and eighteenth centuries a part of it became a true nobility. Wealth was its bulwark, derived from mines, lands, and commerce; for, in Peru, it was specially ruled that large-scale commerce was not incompatible with the quality of nobility.[85] The descendants of families of wealth were, notwithstanding the Crown's laws against creoles holding high posts, flattered and favored by the Crown, at first with knighthoods in the military orders of

Spain, later with mayorazgos or entails which ensured the preservation of estates, and finally with titles in the nobility of Castile. The first such title was that of Count del Puerto, granted in 1632 to Don Juan de Vargas Carvajal.[86] In the Audiencia of Lima alone, without considering the Audiencias of Quito, La Plata, and Chile, in all which titles of Castile were also granted, there were innumerable mayorazgos (entails), besides 1 duke, 58 marquises, 44 counts, and 2 viscounts.[87]

These nobles were not, however, a great source of strength to the colony. True, a high proportion of the best land belonged to them, as well as many of the largest commercial fortunes, but for the most part they were too town-loving, seldom going to their estates and almost never developing them wisely. Highborn ladies in their youth were usually lovely creatures who were very prone to frivolous adventures in which their peculiar habit of being enveloped, all save one eye, in impenetrable black mantles aided them not a little; in their old age extreme religiosity and obedience to the confessor swept down upon them. As a rule, the minds of gentlewomen were but little trained through formal education. They lived in a secluded fashion, taking the air in the shuttered balconies of their mansions, or, if more libertine, in outings which were surrounded by mystery and systematic anonymity designed to avert scandal. Betagh, who was in Lima in 1720, emphasizes the decorum which prevailed outwardly and comments both on the sobriety of the men and on their extreme dedication to amorous matters. He says that they were effeminate and adverse to "manly sports," one of their favorite pastimes being to go out in a calash-for-two with the shutters up and to halt in some quiet spot where passion could be discreetly savored within the roomy carriage. Our own flaming youth, it seems, did not invent that brand of tender dalliance which is indulged in while the vehicle stands still.[88]

For the rest, there were many evening parties, especially in the Bourbon period, made gracious by the undeniable wit of the women, then, as now, delightful. These characteristics

are chiefly attributable to the political insignificance forced
upon the nobility, and partly also to the then prevalent custom of entrusting the young children to slaves and foster
parents whose habits, in too many cases, were depraved.[89]
Having thus haphazardly grown to boyhood, the young Peruvian nobleman went to some Church school, then to the
University, receiving such education as was then available.
Afterwards there was very little to occupy his energies save
going into the militia, into the Church, into the Law, or into
commerce. Not one of these could absorb the vitality of even
a lazy young man, with the result that idleness had full play
upon his character.

The function—if it can be called that—of the nobility was,
therefore, chiefly decorative. Society was a pageant, sometimes a badly mildewed one, but at other times—particularly
when some viceroy was making his state entry—very gorgeous. At the pinnacle of society stood the viceroy and the
vicereine, the archbishop standing discreetly on the highest
step of their dais. Just below were the oidores and their wives,
and then came the phalanx of royal officials and the colonial
nobility, to lend a somewhat deceptive brilliance to the whole.
In the provincial capitals the corregidores had their "courts,"
made up of the local royal officials and the neighboring landowners. In all this, picturesque though it was, little scope was
offered to beneficial activities of young men. The vapidness
of polite life must have been almost painful.

As yet the middle class was merely embryonic, composed
chiefly of persons of mixed blood in modest or lowly callings,
and of creoles engaged in the smaller government posts or in
professional and mercantile pursuits, without being rich
enough to maintain the state of gentlehood.[90] To these groups
which, in the colonial period, contributed to make the nucleus
of a middle class should be added that section of the Indian
population which was already being led away, by the circumstances of its life and labor, from the peasanthood natural to
it and was being inducted into a condition resembling that of
an industrial proletariat. A true peasantry, as we all know,

lives by agriculture—or by animal husbandry—amid surroundings of a rural sort. Village life, or farmstead life, or pastoral life, coupled with ancient usages and institutions, are characteristic of peasantries the world over, and they are especially present in the Indian peasantry of the Andean countries. Still other peasant characteristics, this time of a psychological import, are extreme love for and devotion to the soil, and a deeply rooted conservatism. These traits, also, have been conspicuous in the Andean peasantry from time immemorial—and they are so to this day.

Proletarianism—by which term I here mean detachment from the soil as a means of livelihood—and industrialization —by which term I indicate labor of the regimented and mechanized type—together distinguish the lower ranks of a middle class. They enter into the lives of peasants when these are first torn loose from the ancestral glebe and when they are first obliged to engage themselves in highly systematized and mechanical occupations. In colonial Peru, the occupations in question were: First of all, mining; secondly, the obrajes or cloth-factories. In some of these factories, particularly in those which belonged to private individuals, the Indian workers began as voluntary laborers receiving daily or weekly wages; but very soon, because of the tyrannical attitude and methods of the owners, they became permanently proletarian and industrial workers—wage-slaves and debt-slaves—whose original and natural peasant character was superseded by that of landless, regimented, and mechanistic day-laborers forming the lower stratum of a nascent middle class. For any one who admires and respects the peasant character the process of this change was bad enough; but the cruelty with which it was carried out made it a thousand times worse than it needed to be.[91] In the eighteenth century the obrajes had become the prisons wherein a groaning and violated proletariat labored long hours with slight if any rewards and always within sound of the overseer's whishing lash. The obrajes, to which Indians were often dragged by the hair of their heads tied to the tails of horses, were worse than the traditional galleys of Europe.

As early as 1664 the conditions in the cloth-factories were so horrible that the Viceroy Count of Santistéban and the Royal Audience of Lima drew up elaborate, just, and merciful laws designed to benefit their operatives. But that effort had no noticeable result, because of the fatal interposition of the time-space complex which separated the benevolence of the Viceroy from the malevolence of the obrajes' managers.[92]

Thus, amid blood, sweat, and anguish, the obrajes were drawing Indian peasants from the land and making them into industrialized proletarian workers. A parallel process was going on in the mines, conspicuously at Potosí, and, from 1657 to 1669, at Laicacota, in the province of Paucarcolla,[93] as well as in many less noted mining centres. Here, also, as we have seen on page 165, the Royal benevolence sought to ameliorate conditions of work, but with the usual lack of solid results. A proletarian industrial class, largely Indian in blood, but with other racial strains present also, was gradually formed through the progressive disruption of the original peasant character of those Indians who were caught in the toils. This process went on irresistibly, against the King's twofold intention that the Indians be treated well and that the racial integrity of the Indian peasantry be maintained. This intention rested upon the King's complete understanding of the multifarious harm that Indians were certain to receive if Spaniards, Mestizos, Mulattoes, and Negroes dwelt among them.[94]

In this way, during the colonial period in the Andean countries, materials were prepared upon which, subsequently, the Industrial Revolution could work in its special way.

NOTES TO CHAPTER VII

[1] Levene, 1918, pp. 81–82. Cf. Loaysa, 1889, pp. 584–586. Ruiz Guiñazú, 1916, p. 263, where he quotes from E. S. Zeballos, a passage most eloquently stressing the contrast between the Royal intention and the facts as they were.

[2] Loaysa, 1889, pp. 573–576. Both Loaysa and Bourne, 1904, p. 230, tell us that the viceregal salary in Peru was 30,000 ducats, which, according to Bourne, was equal to about $67,500. As already stated, it was later increased to 40,000 ducats.

[3] Loaysa, 1889, pp. 576–580.

[4] The first corregidores were established in office by Governor the Licentiate García de Castro, about 1565. Markham, 1892, p. 148.

[5] Loaysa, 1889, pp. 555–556.

[6] Loaysa, 1889, pp. 581–584.

[7] Loaysa, 1889, pp. 586–590.

[8] Cañete, 1594.

[9] Anonymous Manuscript entitled Los daños e ynconvenientes, etc. Brit. Mus. Add. MSS. 13,977, folios 242–247. Dated at Lima on January 10th, 1628. (For fuller title, see Bibliography.)

[10] Luna, 1630. This document, in the British Museum, Add. MSS. 13,976, fols. 356–357, verso, is dated at Lima on February 1st, 1630. Luna informs the King that he has been in his service for 45 years and that he is now old and poor. Chinchón, 1871, throws much light on the matters treated by Luna.

[11] Mancera, 1648, paragraph 15. See also Mancera, 1896.

[12] Mancera, 1648, paragraph 17. In spite of his laudable activities, this Viceroy was accused of peculation and other misdemeanors while in office. But the twenty-one charges preferred against him in 1648 by the Oidor Don Pedro Vazquez de Velasco and printed in Mendiburu, 1874–1890, VIII, pp. 81–84, do not shake my conviction that he was an efficient and intelligent servant of his King.

[13] Ribeiro Teixera de Morais, ca. 1635. This MS. work, in the British Museum, is dedicated to Guzmán, Count-Duke of San Lucar (and of Olivares), Lord Chamberlain to the King. See also: Montesclaros, 1859, pp. 18–19. For splendid data on Philip IV and Olivares see: Hume, 1907.

[14] That of the late dictator, Leguía, for example.

[15] Estévanez, 1650, fols. 1v–2v. This writer, whose work is practically unknown, dedicated it to the Viceroy Count of Salvatierra. On his title-page he states that he was a native of Trujillo, in Estremadura, and a vecino of Potosí.

[16] Estévanez, 1650, fols. 2v–3r.

[17] Estévanez, 1650, fols. 6r–7v.

[18] Estévanez, 1650, fols. 6r–10v.

[19] The farcical marriage of Charles to the Austrian princess, within a year of his French wife's death, was engineered by the Queen Mother, María Ana of Austria, and it was intended to strengthen the power of the Austrian party at Court in its plans to give the reversion of Charles's kingdom to the House of Austria. In fact, however, it strengthened the French party, because of the unpopularity of the war with France which began in 1689. See: Chapman, 1918, pp. 268–271.

[20] Llamosas, 1692. This work is cited by Palau, IV, p. 305, but otherwise appears to be unknown. A copy of it was formerly in my library, but developments in the Stock Exchange in the autumn of 1929 obliged me to part with it and with many other priceless bibliographical items. The book is divided into three "Puntos" of which the second, entitled Noticia de las Materias Universales del Reyno del Perú is the most important (fols. 3 recto to 18 verso). The first and third "Puntos" consist chiefly of flattering passages on the career of the Duke of La Palata and on his death at Porto Bello, in 1691.

21 Probably this should be 1685.

22 Llamosas, 1692, fols. 3v–4r.

23 A hundred years earlier the tribute of 311,257 Indians in the jurisdictions of Los Reyes (Lima), Trujillo, Huamanga, Huánuco, Piura, and Cuzco had only come to 1,434,420 pesos. This is stated in a document drawn up at Lima in 1592 by the Bursar Luís de Morales Figueroa. Brit. Mus. Add. MSS. 13,977, fol. 80. It is to be doubted if the King received, in the 1690s, more than 5,000,000 pesos of tribute from all Peru, per year.

24 Bourne, 1904, pp. 239–240. These imposts would not have been unduly onerous if they had been justly administered.

25 Llamosas, 1692, fol. 5r.

26 Llamosas, 1692, fols. 5r–5v.

27 Llamosas, fol. 5r.

28 Llamosas, fols. 6v–7r. In spite of his somewhat weird methods in census-taking, the Viceroy Duke of La Palata was an able, honest, and commendable viceroy. Good modern accounts of his reign are: Markham, 1892, p. 183; Moses, 1914, II, pp. 188–205.

29 Chapman, 1918, pp. 368–382.

30 Varinas, 1899. Further data on Varinas will be found on pp. 242 to 244 below.

31 Varinas, 1899, pp. 237–246.

32 Varinas, 1899, pp. 203–204.

33 Campillo, 1789.

34 Juan and Ulloa, 1748.

35 Juan and Ulloa, 1826.

36 La Condamine, 1745 and 1746.

37 Feyjoo de Sosa, 1763.

38 Feyjoo, 1763, pp. 12–18.

39 Feyjoo, 1763, pp. 28–31.

40 Feyjoo, 1763, pp. 79–83.

41 Feyjoo, 1763, pp. 103–108.

42 Feyjoo, 1763, pp. 129–130.

43 Feyjoo, 1763, Ch. viii, pp. 74–100.

44 Amat-Parish, 1775 and 1776. I style these two documents thus because the first of them was prepared for Amat's use in connection with his official report to his successor, in 1775. It was copied in 1830–1831 by Sir Woodbine Parish, H.B.M. Minister in Buenos Aires. This copy, in the British Museum, Add. MSS. 19,573, is the one here used, under the symbol "Amat-Parish, 1775." Its title will be found in the Bibliography. The second document is by Amat and was also copied by Sir Woodbine Parish, its date being 1776. It is in the British Museum, Add. MSS. 19,572, and I cite it as "Amat-Parish, 1776."

45 Amat-Parish, 1775, fols. 30v–34r.

46 Amat-Parish, 1776, fols. 123v–124r.

47 Amat-Parish, 1776, fols. 124r–126v.

48 Atienza, 1931.

49 Atienza, 1931, Pt. II, Chs. i–iv, and vii.

50 Atienza, Pt. II, Ch. ix. (Atienza wrote in 1583.)

[51] Loaysa, 1889, pp. 556–557.

[52] Loaysa, 1889, pp. 557–560.

[53] Loaysa, 1889, pp. 560–562.

[54] Loaysa, 1889, pp. 563–564.

[55] Loaysa, 1889, pp. 560–562. Mendiburu, 1874–1890, V, pp. 30–62.

[56] Pope Paul V's decree is in the Vatican Secret Archives, Arm. 42, t. 52, folios 222–223. (At least, that was its signature in 1922; it may be different now.) The tone of indignation in the document (which is in Latin) is characteristic of that admirable, if also somewhat pugnacious, Pope. Cf. Hayward, 1931, pp. 296–299.

[57] Luna, 1630.

[58] Such colonies were called mitmac-cuna. See: Means, 1931, pp. 343–347.

[59] Ribeiro, ca. 1635, MS.

[60] Juan and Ulloa, 1826, Pt. II, Ch. viii.

[61] Castel Fuerte, 1859, p. 74. Moses, 1914, II, pp. 312–315.

[62] Campillo, 1789, pp. 36–50.

[63] Castel Fuerte, 1859, p. 126.

[64] Markham, 1892, pp. 168–171. Moses, 1914, II, pp. 315–316.

[65] Altamira, 1913–1914, IV, sections 816–817. Chapman, 1918, pp. 448–452. Brucker, 1919, pp. 795–823. Markham, 1892, p. 189.

[66] Markham, 1892, p. 165. Prado, 1894, pp. 142–150. Romero, 1905.

[67] Recop. Bk. VI, entire, sets forth the legal position of the Indians. Prado, 1894, pp. 150–162. Moses, 1914, II, pp. 63, 203–205, 396–405. Ruiz Guiñazú, 1916, pp. 264–265.

[68] Scelle, 1906, I, Bks. I–III.

[69] Scelle, 1906, II, Bks. IV–VI. Haring, 1918, pp. 118–119, 134–135, 270–271. The Crown received from thirty to forty ducats per slave, in the middle of the seventeenth century. By the asiento treaty of 1713 the contracting English slave-dealing company was bound to take 4,800 slaves to America per year, or a total of 144,000 in thirty years' time, and to pay \$33.33 per head for them to the government. This is according to Moses, 1914, II, pp. 266–267. See also: Chapman, 1918, pp. 370–371.

[70] Ribeiro, ca. 1635, MS.

[71] I assume that Feyjoo's figures for the yields of sugar refer to sugarcane, not to the finished product.

[72] Feyjoo, 1763, Ch. viii.

[73] Garcilaso, Pt. I, Bk. IX, Ch. xxviii, says that he knew the gentleman who introduced sugar planting into the Huánuco region. He tells a quaint story about it: A servant of that planter, seeing that his master's sugar commanded a poor price because of the importation of sugar from New Spain (Mexico), advised his master to send a ship-load of sugar to New Spain for sale so that the people there would learn that Peru had sugar of its own and would cease to send theirs. See: Feyjoo, 1763, pp. 108–110, where he says that Garcilaso was mistaken. Cobo, Bk. X, Ch. xxxii, gives some general data on sugar in Peru, saying that it was introduced early in the colonial period from Spain by way of Hispaniola and that it grows best on the Peruvian coast. He tells us also that, after the cane was crushed, it was dried and became an excellent fuel for boiling sugar-juice.

[74] Feyjoo, 1763, pp. 110–111. At the present time the hacienda of Chiclín, one of the best administered in all Peru, belongs to my highly esteemed friend, Don Rafael Larco Herrera, descendant by his mother's side, from the above-mentioned Don Juan de Herrera. See Riva-Agüero, 1921, p. 132.

[75] Feyjoo, 1763, p. 114. Catabio now belongs to a North American commercial house.

[76] Feyjoo, 1763, p. 117. These lands once formed the Marquisate of San Juan de Buenaventura (seventeenth century). It seems to have decayed and the title went to a family in Cuzco. See: Riva-Agüero, 1921, pp. 134–135.

[77] Feyjoo, 1763, Ch. ix.

[78] Feyjoo, 1763, Ch. x.

[79] Feyjoo, 1763, pp. 140–148.

[80] Moses, 1914, II, pp. 196–198.

[81] Betagh, 1813, p. 21. Moses, 1914, II, pp. 203–205, 396–399.

[82] Moses, 1914, II, p. 398.

[83] Solórzano y Velasco, 1652. This writer was a creole of aristocratic blood.

[84] Juan and Ulloa, 1826, p. 417.

[85] Hevia Bolaños, Pt. II, Ch. ii, 1733, II, pp. 1–6. Riva-Agüero, 1921, pp. 93–150, gives a clear account of the Peruvian nobility, much of which was in trade.

[86] X. Y. Z., 1879, p. 206.

[87] X. Y. Z., 1879, pp. 205–207. Courte de la Blanchardière, 1751, pp. 126–128. Rezabal y Ugarte, 1792, pp. 147–178. Córdova y Urrutia, 1839, pp. 147–149. Prado y Ugarteche, 1894, pp. 111–116.

[88] Betagh, 1813, pp. 7–12.

[89] Moses, 1914, II, pp. 402–405, has much to say about slaves in Peruvian households. Interesting data on the sociology of Quito will be found in Juan and Ulloa, 1748, Bk. V, Ch. v. See also: Prado, 1894, pp. 104–113, and 142–150.

[90] Moses, 1914, II, p. 405.

[91] León Pinelo, 1660, fols. 6 recto to 7 verso, and 38 recto to 45 recto. Juan and Ulloa, 1826, pp. 275–279. Moses, 1914, II, pp. 177–178, and 327–329. Ruiz Guiñazú, 1916, pp. 266–267.

[92] Juan and Ulloa, 1826, pp. 279 and 288. Moses, 1914, II, pp. 177–178.

[93] Mendiburu, 1874–1890, III, pp. 224–227. Moses, 1914, II, pp. 174–177. Alcedo, 1812–1815, IV, pp. 72–73.

[94] Recop. VI, I, i—Ph. II, December 24th, 1580; VI, III, xxi, Ph. II, May 2nd, 1563, Ph. IV, December 17th, 1646; VI, X, xxiii, Ch. III, n.d.; VI, XII, i, Ch. I, February 22nd, 1540, Ph. III, November 23rd, 1601; VII, IV, v, Ph. II, February 11th, 1581. Laws relative to Negroes and Mulattoes will be found in: Recop. VII, V, entire. Ruiz Guiñazú, 1916, pp. 271–273.

CHAPTER VIII

COMMERCE AND FOREIGN ENVY

1. The Spanish Colonial Commercial System

ALTHOUGH a little has been said on earlier pages, and especially at the beginning of Chapter VI, regarding the commerce of colonial Peru, it is well that the subject be examined now more fully.

To begin with, it might well be remarked that the so-called Spanish colonial system would be more accurately described by the term European colonial system in Late Renaissance times. Not only did the Portuguese and the Spaniards erect strictly monopolistic systems of colonial commerce, but so did the French, Dutch, English, and other northern countries, in somewhat later periods. In the case of the Spanish system there was a general discrepancy between the results hoped for by the Crown and the results actually obtained in practice, this discrepancy being due, as we shall see, to three chief causes.

Not only was Spanish colonial trade monopolistic in the sense that it was designed to concern only the mother country and her overseas possessions, but it was also monopolistic in the still narrower sense that, at the Spanish end, the sole port was Seville, with its dependencies, Cadiz and San Lucar de Barrameda.[1] Seville remained the seat of the Casa de Contratación and of the Consulado, as mentioned on pages 140 and 141, there being more or less constant rivalry and friction between Seville and Cadiz. In this struggle an important aid to Cadiz's pretensions was the slow silting-up of the Guadalquivir River, which, coupled with the gradually increasing size of merchantmen, resulted, in 1717, in the transference to Cadiz of the Casa and almost all the rest of the commercial administrative machinery. From then until 1749 there was a period when Seville was trying, desperately but vainly, to regain her ancient supremacy.[2]

The method whereby Spanish colonial commerce was carried on, for more than 200 years, was that of shipments by fleets, not by single vessels. As early as 1522 sporadic ships had been forbidden, ships in groups of two, three, or more being encouraged instead, for safety's sake; and in 1537 the first great merchant fleet with a warship convoy went to America from Spain. After 1550 the system of fleets with convoys, sailing (at least in theory) at stated times, was definitely established; and, with vicissitudes which we need not trace, the system lasted until 1748.[3] At first, the armed convoy consisted of four galleons of 250–300 tons, and of two caravels of 80–100 tons, there being in this convoy 360 soldiers with their officers. Every merchant fleet was conducted across the Atlantic from San Lucar to Havana by the convoy, and at the latter port the merchant ships dispersed to their destinations while the galleons with Havana as their headquarters, were supposed to scour the adjacent waters for corsairs. At the end of three months the merchantmen rejoined the convoy at Havana and thence returned to Seville. The whole process was supposed to take about nine months, beginning in March or April (but with great variations and delays in actual practice). The passage from San Lucar to the Antilles, under favorable circumstances, took about 30 days at a speed of 25–30 leagues (75–90 miles) a day.[4]

These defensive measures grew in energy and desperation in proportion as the dangers from corsairs[5] mounted. Those dangers arose, in Antillean and Mexican waters, as early as the 1520s, when French corsairs began their depredations against the Spanish shipping, and they were increased as English and Dutch buccaneers joined in the gory game.[6] On this subject much more will be said in the next section.

As time wore on and perils increased, a tendency grew up to carry merchandise in the galleons (men of war), so that the fleet which went to Porto Bello with merchandise destined for Peru came to be called "the Galleons." This fleet, after leaving Havana, called first at Cartagena, where it would pause for a week or more. On its arrival there a small, swift ship was immediately sent ahead to Porto Bello, bearing news of the fleet's approach and correspondence for the officials at Panama and for those in Peru. From Porto Bello a courier bore the packets to Panama where they were handed to the highest official, who, in his turn, would at once send a dispatch boat to Paita, whence messengers would carry the packets down the coast to Lima by road. Other messengers would go overland from Panama or Cartagena to Santa Fé de Bogotá, Popayán, and even, in case of need, to Quito and down into Peru. The route from Cartagena to Peru consisted of 200 leagues of river and 300 leagues of trail. Although perfectly safe, it was used only in times when the usual route via Panama and Paita was dangerous on account of freebooters.[7]

The Viceroy at Lima, having received news of the arrival of the galleons at Cartagena or Porto Bello, sent orders to Potosí and other mining centres, and to all royal officials throughout the southern parts of the kingdom, bidding them to send the royal treasure to Arica so that, in due course, the products of the mines and other merchandise could be put on board the South Sea Fleet, which made a preliminary voyage to that port and back to Callao. Having been richly laden and made ready, the fleet would sail northwards, stopping at Huanchaco (for goods from Trujillo and north-central Peru), at Paita (for northern Peru), and at or near Guayaquil (where a special ship bearing gold and merchandise from the Audience of Quito joined the fleet), and so to Panama. From that place the contents of the ships were taken on mule-back over to Porto Bello, which dank and lugubrious spot was annually transformed for a brief while into a scene of frenzied commercial activity. The unsalubrious surroundings wrought havoc among the traders, so that all the signs of mercantile and metallic wealth were but a veneer covering much squalor, bad health, and misery. The fair being concluded in a fortnight or a month, the galleons took their stately way to Cartagena and Havana, where the convoy and the fleet from Vera Cruz were joined, and so home. The South Sea Fleet, southbound, carried goods that had come from Spain via Panama with the Peruvian ports as their destinations.[8]

Such, almost incredibly cumbersome though it seems to us, was the normal and legal method of carrying on trade between Spain and Peru. Various other routes were used in addition, for the most part illegally, or at best with grudgingly conceded permission from the Crown. There was, for example, a lively trade to Buenos Aires and up the River Plate from Oporto and Lisbon, a trade which shows how imperious necessity must and will override an absolute monarch's laws, particularly when those laws rest upon no better moral basis than the selfish dictation of monopolistic merchants.

Founded permanently in 1580, Buenos Aires was long regarded as being in a remote corner of the world; certainly the vested interests of Seville did their best to keep it so. If they had had their way, all merchandise from Spain would have gone by the galleons to Porto Bello, thence to Callao, and onwards by land into Peru, La Plata, and what is now northern Argentina, as far as Buenos Aires, a course which would inevitably result in the commodities so carried attaining to prices eight or ten times those paid for the same goods in Spain. In 1599, when Buenos Aires was not yet twenty years old, the Governor, Don Diego Rodríguez de Valdez y de la Banda, urged the King to open up the River Plate to trade from Spain by way of Brazil. In 1602, Philip III made a small concession to this demand by giving a six-year permission to Buenos Aires to trade with Brazil, but not directly with Spain via the Atlantic, and above all not with the country to the west and northwest of Buenos Aires. The merchants of Seville and Lima fought this nascent tendency all through the next century and a half, and so successfully that, except for a "permission-ship" of not more than 200 tons a year via the Atlantic, the Porto Bello-Panama-Callao-overland route was the sole legal one.[9]

Meanwhile, the people of Buenos Aires were quietly arranging matters for themselves better than the King would or could do it for them. The first move towards the foundation of a flourishing illicit trade was made in 1586, when Friar Francisco de Victoria, Bishop of Tucumán, sent a ship laden with Potosí silver down to Brazil where a second ship was bought, the two returning up the River Plate with cargoes of sugar, conserves, and general merchandise. Unfortunately a damper was put on the enterprise by Thomas Cavendish, who captured the Bishop's ships when they re-entered the River Plate in February, 1587.[10] The quaint figure of the contrabandist bishop is typical of the chaos prevailing in Spain's America.

In 1595, however, the Buenos Aires trade, still illicit, was revived, but with a difference. Peruvian merchants, apparently hostile to the legal route, had gone down the River Plate and so to Brazil and had there begun a commerce carried in small, swift barks of only 30–40 tons. To make the round trip from high up in the River Plate drainage to Brazil and back took only four or five months; the down-cargoes were silver and the return-cargoes were miscellaneous commodities which were sold along the route and in southern Peru so profitably that 100 ducats became 1,200–1,300 by a single trip.[11] In this way a splendid, if illegal, commercial outlet was developed in the River Plate provinces and all along its banks. By the end of the first decade of the seventeenth century there were as many as 200 illicit ships a year plying between Portugal, Brazil, and the River Plate region, whence goods were carried overland to Chile, La Plata, La Paz, Potosí, and into Peru, even as far as Lima. The goods carried were largely silks, linens, and woollens of English, Flemish, and French manufacture, all strictly prohibited by law.[12] In like manner, illegal trade was carried on between the Philippines (whither Oriental goods were brought by Chinese merchants in junks) and New Spain and Peru. In this way there was a constant flow of Asiatic stuffs, porcelains, spices, etc., into Peru during the colonial period.[13]

There is no need to go into details regarding the nature of the goods carried, legally or otherwise, during colonial times. In general it may be said that merchandise going from Spain to the Peruvian markets consisted chiefly of woven fabrics of the more luxurious categories—linen, woollen, silk, and metallic stuffs—to which should be added not only such luxury articles as watches, firearms, glassware, but also such things as iron and steel, knives, nails, general hardware, wines, drugs, and fine olive-oil. The consuming power of colonial Peru in these directions seems to have been amazing, especially when we remember that such things as most of those here indicated could concern only a small percentage of a not very large population.

The return-cargoes consisted, first and foremost, of precious metals, coined or uncoined, and secondly of such raw materials as vicuña wool, tobacco, cacao, sugar, quinine, coca, hides, dye-woods, and cotton. It may be stated as a general principle that manufactured articles went only one way—Spain to Peru—but that, in proportion as the industries of the mother country were squeezed to death by insensate taxation and regulation, analogous industries tended to grow up in the Indies, especially in Peru and in New Spain, but not so much for purposes of export as for fulfilling the needs of the colonies themselves.[14]

If the Crown's subjects had all been angels of unswerving rectitude, superlative intelligence, and uncompromising integrity; and if all the other nations of Europe had been wholly wanting in envy and malice; and if God Almighty had been pleased always to restrain the raging of His winds and waves whenever a ship put out to sea, the commercial system set up by the Crown of Castile might have worked well. As matters stood, however, it worked, on the whole, very badly. This was largely due to three major groups of causes just now indicated which demand further comment.

Acts of God, not only storms at sea and casting away on reefs and land-masses, but also all factors related and contributory thereto, accounted for terrible losses of lives, goods, and

vessels. The naughtiness of men—to say nothing of their native stupidity and invincible avariciousness—led to such practices as building the superstructures of ships so high as to
make the craft top-heavy and as overloading them with
freight and overcrowding them with passengers. Sr. de Artíñano has shown that the naval construction of the Spaniards,
particularly those of Bilbao and other northern shipyards
prior to 1588 (the Invincible Armada), were as good as any
then known, albeit they, like the commerce with America and
like the economic state of Spain herself, suffered a grave decline
during the seventeenth century. One trouble was that new
ships were commonly used in the mild Mediterranean and that
only in their old age were they put to work in the stormy Atlantic and Caribbean waters. Furthermore, crews and officers
were often below the proper standard of preparedness for their
duties. The Royal regulations to correct all these dangers to
passengers and goods were generally evaded as were all other
laws. In short, as between the wrath of God and the im-
perfection of man, the chance of a safe voyage out and back
was not much more than fifty per cent.[15]

Fraud and contraband together constitute the second of the
three major foes of the Royal commercial system. Under this
heading are included all those artful dodges which aimed to rob
His Majesty of his rightful income. They ranged from simple
jugglery in the matter of book-keeping up to elaborate hid-
ing of goods 'tween decks and to carefully planned clandestine
traffic such as that described on pages 221–223. The fatal results of frauds are best shown by a few figures. Gasca, when
he returned to Spain from Peru in 1550, brought home
1,500,000 ducats (over $3,000,000) for the King; in 1578,
the Royal fifth from mines in America came to 800,000 pesos
($1,600,000 or more); in 1579, the sum was about 1,000,000
pesos; and in 1585 it was over 1,500,000 pesos. Later, chiefly
because of fraud, the Royal receipts shrank to 500,000 a year,
albeit the amount of silver and gold (particularly silver, from
Peru) was mounting steadily throughout the reign of Philip
II. It was under his Hapsburg successors that the great decay

FIG. 21. The main stairway in the Monastery of La Merced, Cuzco.

FIG. 22. Interior of the Cathedral of Cuzco.
Both by courtesy of Mrs. Myra Brady.

set in, to which contrabrand powerfully contributed.[16] Between 1567 and 1600, the most prosperous period of legitimate trade (under the Hapsburgs), the annual registered tonnage of merchandise sent out to Peru was only some 15,000, according to good judges.[17]

The third and most malignant of the three chief enemies of the Castilian commercial system was foreign envy resulting in attacks both piratical and authentically warlike. This subject is so intricate and so important that I shall postpone discussion of it to the next section.

Thus far we have been considering chiefly the commercial system as it was under the Hapsburgs. We must now turn to the eighteenth century, when the Bourbons were ruling. The relative liberality of the new dynasty's commercial policy will be apparent. During the eighteenth century not only commerce itself but also the ships in which goods were carried drew away from the antiquated modes of the Hapsburg period and nigh to those of modern times.

In August, 1708, Philip V caused to be drawn up a new code of laws relating to commerce, the gist of it being that foreign merchants might consign their goods in Spanish ships going in fleets to America, and that they might do so without fear that an outbreak of war would imperil their goods or their moneys. In doing this the King was undoubtedly acting under pressure from France, whose people had long participated in the trade carried by the galleons, as had also the merchants of England, Holland and Flanders, Hamburg, and even Genoa, all of which were represented in the marts of Seville where the Spanish merchants acted as their carrying and selling agents. Another manifestation of the pressure brought to bear on Spain was the cédula of January 11th, 1701, wherein the Queen Dowager opened colonial ports to French ships desirous of revictualing there; and, again, a proposition made, about 1708, or a little earlier, by an anonymous economist, strove to win the privilege for French ships to conduct trade in Spain's America with the proviso that only one quarter of the cargo be French, the rest being Spanish.[17]

The growth of English and Dutch colonies in America was a great factor in the progressive corrosion of the traditional commercial policy of Spain, as were also France's untiring efforts to win a good footing for herself. This last factor was long fought desperately by Spanish officialdom and by Spanish traders who did not see that the new dynasty had any right to alter the monopolistic position so long held by them. The tendency of the times was too strong for them, however, and in 1748 the fleet system was finally abandoned, being replaced by single ships sailing when their owners willed. In 1762 the English captured Havana and held it for less than a year, during which brief period over 720 merchant ships entered that harbor and drove a lucrative trade in the city. This lesson was not wasted on King Charles III, who, in 1765 and 1768, greatly liberalized Spanish and West Indian trade by opening sundry ports to Spanish vessels. In 1774, the King abolished the old restrictions on coastwise trade in the Pacific from New Spain to South America.[18] The amazingly swift change from the ancient style of highly restricted monopolistic trade to a type of commerce almost modern in character is wholly due to the enlightened King and to his intelligent ministers, all of them influenced by the new ideas then burgeoning in France. The decree of free commerce, dated October 16th, 1765, was amplified on February 2nd, 1778. At the latter date not only was Buenos Aires opened up to commerce —in Spanish ships—with the privilege of being a port of entry for her hinterland, but also the coastwise trade and the general trade of Peruvian and Chilean ports was much liberalized. The Spanish ports which might now conduct direct trade with any of the authorized ports in America were: Seville, Cadiz, Málaga, Alicante, Cartagena, Barcelona, Santander, Coruña, Gijón, Palma de Mallorca, and Santa Cruz de Tenerife.[19] This represents the Spanish Bourbons at their best and sanest.

The land communications by which commerce was aided and by which rulers maintained their control—such as it was —of their jurisdictions must now be examined briefly. The chasqui or relay post-runner system of the Incas, together with the system of beacon fires and the roads, road-houses, storehouses, and bridges, formed the mechanism of communication which had held the Inca empire together.[20] It was a mechanism which compelled the admiration of all beholders. In adapting it to their own uses, the Spaniards did not improve it. Bridges, to judge by Figure 9, remained as primitive and scary as ever, and the introduction of horses or mules instead of the traditional running relays of well-trained chasquis, did not speed things up. Moreover, the postal system set up under the Hapsburgs and continued under the earlier Bourbons had various quaintnesses which did not enhance its efficiency.

For one thing, the office of Correo Mayor de las Indias, or Postmaster General of the Indies, was conferred upon Dr. Don Lorenzo Galíndez de Carvajal by King Ferdinand in May, 1514, and it was confirmed to him by King Charles I on October 27th, 1525. In other words, the absolute King conceded to a private individual and his descendants all that part of the Royal power which concerned postal matters and income, doing so in such a way that the recipient of the grant and any subsequent holder of it could rent out or even sell important jobs and contracts within the postal organization.[21] It is by no means clear why Dr. Galíndez de Carvajal, erudite lawyer though he was, should have been considered specially fitted for the onerous task of creating a postal service to Spain's America. Nevertheless, the Crown granted to the Postmaster General numerous prerogatives and privileges, guarantees and protection. The office became a hereditary possession in the family of its first holder, and the Peruvian part, at least, of the post-office was held and managed by seven successive descendants of Galíndez de Carvajal, all of whom resided in Lima. Not until 1768 did King Charles III merge the postal system of the Carvajals with the appanages of the Crown.[22]

An important agreement was reached in 1599 between the Viceroy Don Luís de Velasco and the fourth Correo Mayor, Don Diego de Carvajal Vargas y Ortiz (in office 1593–1631) whereby the roads formerly used by the Incaic chasquis were taken over and the traditional running relay-messengers were replaced by mounted Spaniards or other non-Indians. Thereafter the letter-service was maintained, at least in theory, between Lima and the chief places throughout the Viceroyalty. The charges varied from two to three reales an ounce for ordinary letters, but special delivery cost 3 reales per league; official mail was franked. At least sometimes, perhaps usually, postage was paid in advance and the sum paid was clearly marked on each letter. One can imagine that there was a good deal of corruption practiced in all this, but he is surprised to note that there was no improvement in speed as against that of the chasquis; for it took twenty-eight days to exchange letters between Lima and Potosí.[23]

Ordinary journeys were much slower. A highly placed man who, we may suppose, enjoyed all the available facilities, travelled along the main highway from Cuenca to Lima between Thursday, August 28th, and Friday, November 20th, of a year between 1747 and 1767.[24] In other words it took nearly three months to go about 750 miles, or an average speed of less than 10 miles a day.

2. Foreign Envy—and Its Results

In this section I shall discuss briefly the third and most potent of the above-mentioned three chief foes of the Spanish commercial system. Throughout the whole of the conquest and colonial periods Spain was the object of implacable hatred and jealousy on the part of other European powers which craved the rich lands of the Crown of Castille in America. For example, the distrust and envy felt towards Spain in England, not only by Henry VIII and by Elizabeth (not to mention the weird matrimonial interlude of Bloody Mary and Philip II), but also by many of their subjects, are well known to every schoolboy in Britain and in North America—who all too often sympathize therein. My purpose here is first to trace the history and to describe the complexion of that now ancient antipathy, and second to outline the results of it during the period here studied.

As we know, Bishop Friar Bartolomé de las Casas was the indefatigable publicist of the more unseemly events in the Spanish conquest and settlement of America. Something has already been said on pages 82–85 about his methods in his writings. To that one need only add here the remark that the extreme sensationalism of his printed outbursts—replete as they were with gruesome chatter about tyrants, massacres, rapes, and every other atrocity—won for them a widespread diffusion among nations only too happy to hear and believe evil of the Spaniards. The objurgations of Casas on the subject of his compatriots' deeds in America were published in English, French, Dutch, German, Italian, and Latin, a degree of renown almost equal to that afterwards accorded to Mrs. Stowe, with her Uncle Tom and Little Eva.[25]

Altogether, one may safely say that Casas contributed heavily to the foreign enmity towards Spain. That his publications were having this effect was perfectly understood by at least some of his contemporaries and compatriots; this is made clear by a long passage in the Anonymous Letter of 1571 in which it is eloquently pointed out that the defamatory bishop was bringing the Spanish monarchy and its people into disrepute among non-Christian and heretical nations.[26]

Casas was not, indeed, the sole source of information regarding Peru and the rest of Spain's America early possessed by the world at large. Saner, sounder and, at the same time, more alluring pictures of Peru and its grandeurs were drawn by such chroniclers as Acosta, Cieza, Garcilaso, and Zárate, to mention only the four most prominent. They were widely read in Europe, both in Spanish and in translations published between 1550 and 1700.[27] These works, although they lacked the denigratory comments on the Spaniards which pepper the pages of the furious bishop, none the less whetted the appetites of other nationalities which hungered for the possessions of Spain, doing so by describing with unction all the greatnesses therein contained.

The English reaction to all this stream of varied suggestion is typical of the reaction elsewhere. Sir Walter Raleigh is a case in point. He once remarked, "By the abundant treasure of that country (Peru) the Spanish King vexeth all the Princes of Europe, and is become in a few years from a poor King of Castile the greatest monarch of this part of the world."[29]

The hankering which then irked all Englishmen shrieks in these words. Nor did Sir Walter Raleigh content himself with merely envying the Spanish King. He *could* not stop there; for, truth to tell, that King was making a most infernal nuisance of himself to all the chief nations of Europe, not only in a religious way, but also in political and commercial ways. There was, therefore, a natural justification for the attitude of northern nations which explains, if it does not excuse, their actions.

To go on with Raleigh, he strove to give his jealousy a practical turn. Firmly believing—as did many others—that the ancient Peruvian empire was refounded and reconstituted in the hinterland of Guiana, he sought to acquire it for his Queen. On this subject he wrote, about 1595, concerning an inland empire whose golden capital city was called Manoa and whose people, the Epuremei, were subject to an "Inga" descended from the ancient Emperors of Peru, described by "Cieca" (Cieza de León). The polity by which this illimitably aureate realm was governed was the same as that formerly established in Peru. True, he admits that he has never seen these wonders, but he quotes at length from Chapter cxx of López (de Gómara) in which the golden glitter of "Guaynacapa's" (Huayna Capac's) court and his garden of gold on the Island of Puná are described. He avers that Guaynacapa was "auncestor to the Emperour of Guiana."[30]

On this basis, Raleigh had the audacity to conceive of a plan for uniting Manoa and its empire to the English crown. There were, he thought, two ways of doing it. One was to expel the "vsurping Inga" from Guiana by title of his subjects' consent, and taking possession of the "Tassell royall" (the Incaic llautu or imperial fillet) and turning it over to the use of Her Majesty and her successors. (Here we may well pause to cosset our fancies with a picture of the figure of fun Good Queen Bess would have been had she added a llautu to all the vast cargo of baubles and gew-gaws that the excellent woman habitually wore.) The other plan, more favored by Raleigh, was to win the Inga as an ally and vassal of Queen Elizabeth, this to be done, if you please, with the idea that the Inga aid the English in conquering Peru away from its Spanish oppressors. There follows much pious palaver about the holiness of Christianizing the "Guianians"—and de-Catholicizing Peru.[31]

Needless to say, naught came of this daring project; but the quaint belief in the marvels of Manoa persistently teased the English to at least as late as 1613, and the French until as late as 1654.[32]

Sir Walter Raleigh's projected incursion into Inca Land from the side of Guiana was but one indication of the national attitude. Other symptoms of it were plentiful. For example, Sir George Peckham, in his essay on "The Western Planting" (1583), refers to the fact that many exploits of the Spaniards in America have been made available in English and have "been accounted a fantasticall imagination, and a drowsie dreame." He goes on to urge his countrymen to awake to their opportunities, to know and to serve their Creator. Speaking first of the ease with which the Spaniards conquered Mexico, he goes on to say, "And in like maner in the Countrey of Peru, which the king of Spaine hath now in actuall possession, Francisco Pysarro, with the onely ayd of Diego de Almagro and Hernando Luche, being all three but private gentlemen," had managed to raise a small force wherewith Peru was conquered. He then gives a tolerably accurate account of the conquest of Peru, all to the end that his compatriots be incited to go and do likewise.[33]

Turning now to the practical results arising from Casas's propaganda we find that he was largely responsible for the active hostility from which Spain and her America suffered. In the maritime incursions—ranging from barefaced piracy to authentic naval warfare—of which we shall study various examples, envious greed was the chief motive, but it was, in many cases, powerfully seconded by Protestant zeal which delighted to worry a great Catholic enemy. As time wore on, however, the religious aspect of the matter gradually yielded before the growing desire for economic advantages in those rich Peruvian regions, culminating in the South Sea Bubble which, for sheer commercial audacity and folly, makes the hocus-pocus of Wall Street bankers in contemporary South America look like the petty doings of so many juvenile delinquents.

As mentioned above, on pages 132–133, Drake's raid on Peru in 1579 was the first affair of the kind. One should remember of him the fact that, from the English point of view, he was no mere pirate; he was a warrior of the seas fighting his liege lady's battles, and having her approval. This, however, did not make him look any the prettier to Spanish eyes. The chief consequence of Drake's advent was the attempt of Captain Pedro Sarmiento de Gamboa and others to found a colony in the Strait of Magellan in order to prevent further invasions of the South Sea by that route. Leaving Callao with two ships on October 11th, 1579, by way of the Strait he went to Spain, arriving there in mid-August, 1580. Sarmiento reported to Philip II at Badajoz and, in spite of the opposition of the Duke of Alva and others, won the King's backing for his project. He fitted out 23 ships at Seville, with 3,500 people, and sailed on September 25th, 1581. But a gale forced the expedition back to Spain after a loss of 5 ships and 800 people. In December, 1581, a new fleet, with 16 ships, and fewer people, left Seville. They arrived at Rio de Janeiro on March 24th, 1582, and wintered there until November, 1582, after which, in spite of further mishaps and losses, the colony went on to the Strait, where its subsequent sufferings were terrible. On his way home, in 1585, Sarmiento was captured by English rovers who took him to England, where Queen Elizabeth was kind enough to converse with him in Latin and send him on to Spain with 1,000 crowns as a remembrance.[34]

Between the end of Drake's invasion of Peru and 1743 there were many armed intrusions by maritime foreigners, some of whom were "authorized" by their own governments either to fight against the Spanish colonies in America or else to trade with them; others were out-and-out pirates whose sole authorization was their own avarice. All were equally unwelcome to officialdom in Spanish America. In the history of piracy in Peru there are distinct periods, with distinct tendencies and meanings, which I shall now indicate briefly.

The first English period, beginning with Drake, in 1579, and continuing with Thomas Cavendish, in 1586–1588, and with Sir Richard Hawkins, 1593–1594, marks the time when Good Queen Bess was wont to stick at nothing in order to annoy and injure her Catholic brother-in-law and enemy, Philip II. Cavendish, who sacked and burned Paita and Guayaquil, May–June, 1587, boasted on his return to England using these proud words: ". . . I made great spoiles: I burnt and sunk 19 sailes of ships, small and great. All villages and towns that I ever landed at, I burnt and spoiled."[35] He, then, was a corsair who had some success. Hawkins, on the other hand, was captured by the Peruvian fleet under Don Beltrán de Castro (July 2nd, 1594), and only through the Peruvians' courtesy did he eventually make his way home.[36]

There followed a Dutch period beginning in 1598–1601 with an expedition under Olivier van Noort which coasted along Chile and Peru, but accomplished uncommonly little. In 1614–1615 Admiral Joris van Speilbergen, "authorized" by the Netherlands government, sailed along the same coast. On July 16th–17th, 1615, there was a great sea-battle with the Peruvian fleet under Don Rodrigo de Mendoza in which the Dutch won because of the superiority of their artillery. They were prevented from landing at Callao, however, by the shore-batteries, and on August 10th they plundered Paita with but small results. In 1623–1624, a large fleet under Admiral Jacob l'Heremite, with 294 guns, over 1,600 men, and good equipment, was sent by the Netherlands government to Peru for the avowed purpose of depriving Philip IV of some of his territories and income. L'Heremite died of prolonged illness on June 2nd, 1624, in Callao harbor, or on San Lorenzo Island, and he was succeeded by Schapenham. In spite of its grand pretensions and preparations this expedition, like the preceding Dutch attempts, accomplished very little, its high-spots being two rather profitless raids on Guayaquil.[37]

The poor results obtained by these raids gave Peru a reputation for impregnability. There followed a period of nearly sixty years, 1625–1684, in which Peru was not seriously troubled by sea-rovers. That was, however, a period of fierce piracy in the Atlantic waters and on the mainland at Porto Bello, Panama, and elsewhere during the course of which rich plunder was won by the filibusters and immense harm was done to the colonists, all of which reacted upon Peru indirectly.[38]

From 1684 to 1687 there was a period in which completely unauthorized freebooters, English under Edward Davis, and French under Grogniet, Picard and others, acted sometimes together and sometimes separately. Davis, in November, 1684, burned Paita because the Spanish authorities would not ransom it. In April–June, 1685, the combined corsairs strove unsuccessfully to capture a very rich South Sea Fleet sent northwards from Callao by the Viceroy Duke of La Palata; but it eluded them and safely landed its cargo at the Isthmus. Two years later the French pirates captured Guayaquil and, while trying to obtain ransom for it, accidentally burnt part of it. An enormous booty in money and jewels was taken, pleasant interludes with the ladies of Guayaquil were enjoyed, and, after the spoils had been amicably divided, the corsairs separated into national parties each of which went its way.[39]

Of the English and French corsairs who were involved in these operations none possessed any sort of legality even in their own countries. In 1670 there had been made a treaty between Spain and England which ended the pseudo-legality enjoyed by the earlier English corsairs; and, from 1664 onwards, Louis XIV had been discountenancing piracy by his subjects, partly because he was hoping to capture the Crown of the Spains, and partly because he and Colbert had entered the business themselves with their Compagnie des Indes Orientales, whose field of projected monopolistic commerce included all lands bordering on the Pacific.[40]

Between 1687 and 1697 there was a general repatriation of French filibusters who, on their return home, filled the minds of all their listeners with thoughts about the commercial opportunities along the Pacific coast of America. All this helped to engender a new period, one in which commercial aggression by French merchants protected by the King of France is the salient feature.[41] In 1698, the Nouvelle Compagnie, better known by its later title of Compagnie Royale de la mer Pacifique (or du Sud), was founded under the patronage of Louis XIV and his minister of marine, Count de Pontchartrain. In short, the enticing tales which French pirates had brought home from Peru had combined with conditions arising out of the peace of Ryswick (September–October, 1697) to induce the Sun King to go into ultramarine brigandage in a big way. In order to carry out his plans Louis availed himself of the ambitions of two rich merchants, Noël Danycan de Lépine, of St. Malo, and Jourdan de Grouée (or Groussey), of Paris. Together, these two were, in effect, the Compagnie Royale aforesaid.

In 1698 to 1701, and again from 1701 to 1703, there were French expeditions to Peru financed by the Company primarily for commercial purposes, but also with some idea of gaining territories by means of bellicose aggression. The advantages taken of the change of dynasty, and particularly of the already mentioned cédula of January 11th, 1701, in which French ships were given permission to take on supplies in Spanish colonial ports—but *not* to trade—were of dubious taste, to put it mildly. When, in June, 1703, after very lucrative trade in Chile and Peru, the homebound French ships were forced into the Spanish port of la Coruña, their arrival produced a contest between the francophile King, Philip V (backed up by Mme. des Ursins and other admirers of Louis XIV) and the purely Spanish Council of the Indies which was burning to avenge itself on the returned French traders for their infractions of Spanish law. There arose, therefore, a conflict between the King and his Spanish officials which the well-disciplined subjects of Louis XIV found to be shocking and incomprehensible.[42]

In general it may be said that there was much vacillation in the policies of both the French and the Spanish governments, fluctuating between absolute prohibition of foreign commerce (1701–1705) and plans for commercial co-operation between the Spanish and French crowns (1704–1706) with a second period of absolute prohibition (1711–1713). Official arrangements had, however, but little effect on realities; for, during this period, French trade in western South America went merrily on. Although officials tried to check it, the merchants of Peru did business with the interlopers under the authorities' noses. In the year 1712, for example, at least nine French ships visited and traded in Chile and Peru.[43]

French intrusion in Peru was not confined to commercial activities during these years. Two justly celebrated French scientists visited and studied the country and, in their books, made all its principal features and treasures known to the world. These men were: Father Louis Feuillée, in Chile and Peru from 1708 to 1711, and A. F. Frézier, who was there from 1712 to 1713. The return of these learned men to their native land was followed by a rancorous squabble between them which has close kinship with modern disputes between pundits.[44]

A second period of pseudo-legal English activities in Peru is marked by two voyages both of which were backed by English merchants. The first, 1703–1704, was led by William Dampier, whom the British, for no discoverable reason, idolize; the second was led by a better man, Woodes Rogers, in 1708–1711. One should observe in passing that Alexander Selkirk, the original of Defoe's immortal Robinson Crusoe, was left on Juan Fernández by the first of these expeditions (October, 1704) and that he was picked up by the second (February, 1709). The only result of these two expeditions was a small amount of plunder and a fairly sizeable ransom for Guayaquil (April, 1709).[45]

The grand climax of all these enterprises, French and English, was, in France, the Mississippi Bubble—or, more accurately, John Law's system of high finance—and, in England, the South Sea Bubble, fathered by Robert Harley, Earl of Oxford. Briefly stated their significance, for us, was as follows:

The death of Louis XIV heralded a period which lasted from 1716 to 1721 during which the grandiose projects of the unfortunate Danycan and the Compagnie Royale de la mer du Sud faded into nothingness amid a crowd of lawsuits and attempts at regularization. Against a background of forensic and financial tumult the "system of Law" had its brief day of deceptive optimism. In 1716 John Law opened his bank under the protection of the Regent Duke of Orléans, and in 1718 it became a "Royal Bank" which was going to make everything successful and solvent forever. All the world rushed to buy shares, and by 1719 the paper value of the shares was eighty times greater than the amount of all the specie current in France. The utterly impracticable Mississippi scheme was one basis for all this and another was a Company fleet of twelve or fourteen ships which was sent out to Peru in 1719 and early in 1720. Before its return, Law's system had collapsed like the pricked bubble that it was, leaving widespread ruin and despair behind it. Law himself was exiled from the land of his adoption in 1720. The fleet, when it came back to France a little later, did nothing to lighten the gloom. Spanish authority in Peru and Chile had been strong enough to deprive the intruding merchants of all gain. Thus ended French efforts to win a part of the Peruvian trade.[46]

It can be said with truth that French commerce in Peru had not been brilliant in its results and that it never wore the aspect of dignified and legitimate enterprise, such mild successes as it won being all obtained through trickery and injustice.

Equally divorced from ethics and from sound business were

the contemporary efforts of the English to gain a part of Peru's trade. Britannia's incursions in those parts, like those of France, had been of dubious financial success. In 1710 it was made known that the national debt of England was £9,-000,000 or more and that the financial condition was appalling. In May, 1711, Robert Harley, Earl of Oxford, Lord Treasurer, galloped a bill through both Houses of Parliament whereby all the creditors of the government were formed into a Company which was to pay interest at six per cent a year, the shares thereof to be redeemable—under conditions—after the end of 1716. The shares were to be secured by the duties on wine, vinegar, tobacco, East India goods, wrought silk, whalebone, and other articles. So far, perhaps, the scheme was reasonable enough. But Oxford wished to make it still more alluring. In the bill of 1711 it was specifically stated that the Company was to have sole right to trade with the coast of America from the mouth of the Orinoco to Tierra del Fuego and thence up the Pacific coast to the northernmost part of America. The bill exempts the territories held by the crown of Portugal or by Holland, but includes trade "into, unto, and from all countries . . . which are reputed to belong to the crown of Spain."[47] Greater impudence was never known.

Almost the entire English nobility, gentry, and plutocracy went completely mad over stock-jobbing (having been headed in that direction for some time past), and the South Sea Company enjoyed not only the patronage of Royalty but also that of much that was noblest, highest, and greediest in the nation. Oxford was the first Governor of the Company, and from 1715 to 1718 the Prince of Wales (later George II) was Governor, being followed by His Majesty King George the First, a fact which called forth ribald comment from the Duchess of Ormonde, Dean Swift's friend and correspondent.[48]

Meanwhile, publicity work and propaganda equal in general unsavoriness to the worst that our contemporary public-relations counsel can perpetrate was being carried steadily forward. Not every one was gulled, to be sure; for Dean Swift

and Daniel Defoe solemnly yet satirically warned their compatriots. The latter, who through his work on Robinson
Crusoe (Alexander Selkirk) had some knowledge of the true
conditions, pointed out that the fundamental weakness of the
South Sea Scheme lay in Spain's absolute determination to
squelch trade by foreigners in her ports.[49]

In 1713 Philip V granted to Queen Anne and the Company
the famous Asiento for 4,800 Negro slaves yearly for 30 years,
a few very limited trading rights, and permission for a 500-ton
ship each year, one-fourth of whose profits were to go to him
together with five per cent on the remainder.[50] On this modest
basis the backers of the Company erected a stupendous fabric
of deceit, leading their victims to suppose that the King of
Spain would concede to the Company real and solid privileges
in his American possessions. A Babel of baseless chatter concerning Peru and Mexico deafened the ears; skullduggery in
the form of many scores of silly schemes of the wild-cat variety flourished; England—except for a few obstinate souls
who remained sceptical and sane—went mad with a desire to
get rich without honest toil. There was plenty of precedent
for our own madness prior to September, 1929, a madness
which, however, was sanity itself in comparison with the
financial plans of the bubble period.

From having been at 76 when Swift took his flyer, the South
Sea stock rose, in the winter of 1719–1720, to more than 1,100.
The grand deflation, preceded by the collapse of Law in
France, took place in August–September, 1720, and innumerable other bubbles burst at the same time. Thousands of
households throughout Great Britain entered upon a period
of retrenchment and readjustment very like that which we,
for the good of our souls, are enjoying at the present time.[51]
We may thank our stars that we have not to be thrown into
debtors' prisons as so many thousands were in those days.

At the very moment when the English were indulging their
greed with the South Sea Bubble, an English corsair named
Shelvocke was conducting illicit traffic and committing depredations in Peru. He burned Paita on March 21st, 1720, be-

cause a $10,000 ransom was refused. It was there that Betagh, already cited, was set ashore.

The final chapter in the history of piracy in Peru relates how Commodore George Anson, another of England's inexplicable idols, with a grand fleet heavily armed—but manned in part by poor old fellows dragged from the Chelsea Hospital, none of whom ever saw his native land again—assaulted a number of Spanish ships either unarmed or else much less well prepared for fighting than his fleet was, and also how his brave men raided Paita on November 10th, 1741, and, with great courage, took off with them most of the clothing and jewels of the inhabitants, many of them women. The heroic Anson then burned defenceless Paita to the ground because, as usual, the Spaniards would not ransom it. Booty worth 1,500,000 pesos was taken. Anson's typically British heroism was rewarded in a typically British way: He was elevated to the company of those whom a flunkey-minded nation addresses as "Me Lud."[52]

Study of the history of piracy—of divers types—in Peruvian waters reveals the fact that, as a rule, the prizes gained by it were of moderate worth. Moreover, it becomes apparent that the Peruvians not seldom successfully defended themselves from their enemies, both on the sea and by using their shore-batteries. The practice of refusing to ransom towns or individuals was also general and did much to lessen the success of the interlopers. Nevertheless, piracy did do much harm to Peruvian colonial trade, partly through the apprehensions which it awakened in Peruvian minds, but chiefly through the very serious havoc wrought by pirates in Atlantic waters where the principal nerves of the commercial system were concentrated.

3. Criticisms by Spanish Subjects

Having shown at any rate the main features both of the theoretical or official commercial system of Spain with regard to her colonies and the forms and effects of foreign envy thereby awakened, I shall now speak briefly concerning various suggestions which were made by Spanish subjects with a view to aiding the King to maintain the official system. Before doing so, however, it is well to point out the fact that, in spite of the recurrent menace of foreign piratical or bellicose intrusion, the commercial life of colonial Peru was carried on with some degree of success. An anonymous document of about 1640 or a trifle earlier serves us well in this connection.[53]

We learn, for example, that Manta, on what is now the coast of Ecuador, was a centre for the manufacture of tackle and ropes for ships and that Guayaquil, the chief port for the Audience of Quito, had important ship-yards as well as an active ship-chandlery business and an excellent general trade. The city was a focal point of intensely European culture, represented by well-supplied shops and an upper class of rich and cultivated Spaniards and Creoles. In 1687 Raveneau de Lussan found this situation still to be true, and in or about 1740, Don Dionisio de Alcedo y Herrera spoke in like terms of Guayaquil.[54] The Anonymous author gives an equally satisfactory account of Trujillo as it was in his day before the decay noted above on pages 194–208 set in.[55]

With regard to Lima the Anonymous writer tells us much. At that time it had some 40,000 Negroes, mostly slaves, and there was also a large Indian population in and close to the city whose occupations included tailoring, shoemaking, carpentry, silver-working, and handicrafts in general. The upper class led a gay and charmingly libertine life, their great love of finery being amply satisfied in the Calle de Mercaderes (Merchants' Street), where more than 40 shops were filled with fine goods from all parts of the world. Some of this, if not most of this, mercantile wealth had come, as we know, through illegal channels; but, at any rate, it was there for the enjoyment of any one who could pay the price. Some of the merchants had fortunes of 1,000,000 pesos or more; many had 500,000 pesos; and others rich, but not so rich, were very numerous.[56] For the rest of the Viceroyalty a similar picture could be drawn.

The importance of all this is that foreign envy, far from
ruining Peru, contributed incidentally to its well being. Yet it
would be folly to maintain that foreign envy did not also constitute a menace, and a grave one, albeit not the only one.
Avarice on the part of officials and private persons was equally
hostile to the economic and political health of colonial Peru,
as was also a series of extravagant abuses which had come into
being by the middle of the eighteenth century. I shall now
discuss a few criticisms by Spanish subjects of these matters.

One of the most outspoken, and at times one of the sanest,
of Spain's critics in regard to colonial affairs was Don Gabriel
Fernández de Villalobos, Marquis of Varinas and of Guane-
Guanare,[57] whom I have already cited above on pages 190–191.
He was born in Castile about 1642, of noble but impoverished
parents, and he went to the Indies when about twelve years
old. His career in America was stormy and varied; for, at one
time or another, he served as a skipper in dubious navigations,
as a slave-dealer, as an agent for contrabandists, and as a soldier; he was shipwrecked many times, and for a while he was
a slave in the Barbadoes. From that position he was rescued
by some Dutch merchants who made him serve them in their
illegal dealings between Curaçao and the Spanish possessions
nearby. He was invited, in flattering terms, to go to the Court
of Spain so that his wide knowledge of colonial affairs might
be put at the disposition of the government. When he arrived
at Madrid in 1675 he gave himself out as a Captain of the
Indies deeply versed in the secrets of colonial government and
affairs. Fernández de Villalobos had, one gathers, an unfortunate boastfulness of manner which won him numerous and
powerful enemies, among them the President of the Council
of the Indies, the Count of Medellín. Nevertheless, he won a
certain following, which included the Duke of Medinaceli, the
Infanta Sor Mariana de la Cruz, and, to a certain extent, the
Queen-Mother, Mariana of Austria. In November, 1685, he
was, after lesser and earlier honors, made Marquis of Varinas
and of Guane-Guanare. He married a lady named Madera de
los Ríos y Alfaro, whose brother, Don Martín Madera, was a

high official at Caracas. The Marchioness was a faithful and enthusiastic helper of her husband, much to his credit and to hers. Fernández Duro points out, with needless acerbity I think, that Varinas took too high and too omniscient a tone in his writings addressed to the King and various other lofty persons. A graver fault was his verbosity; for, between 1683 and 1689, he sent over 5,000 pages of good advice to the King and others. Inasmuch as he never hesitated to damn up and down innumerable high officials, and, at the same time, to solicit for himself the post of President of the Casa de Contratación, it is not remarkable that, in 1688, he was imprisoned, first at Cadiz and later at Orán. By that time he was nearly blind, but he managed, in February, 1698, to break out of his prison, and to make his way in a fishing boat to Algiers where he made his home among the Moors of Mostagán until his death, after 1702.[58]

It is quite clear to me that Varinas, in spite of his somewhat bombastic and pretentious manner, and in spite, also, of his rather dubious early career, of his occasional self-seeking and of his attempts at enlisting interest at the Court of France, was a man of economic and political clear-sightedness far ahead of his time and wholly admirable in any age. He was a great finder of flaws and frailties in the governmental mechanism set up by Castile in her colonies, but his constant efforts to point out remedies were met with either indifference or with active opposition. Even so, his reports had some effect; for, in 1677, a special commission was formed in the Council of the Indies for the purpose of studying the propositions made by him. The Duke of Medinaceli, then President of the Council, stood at the head of the commission, and before it Varinas made many sane recommendations about the fortifying numerous ports in America, among them Guayaquil, all as a means of keeping out the corsairs. He had much to say about methods of checking the contraband trade (as to which he was well informed by experience). Concerning Lima and its defence he gave good advice, saying that a large and well-trained cavalry would do much to protect the city. This last remark piqued the ire of one of the Commissioners, the Marquis of Mancera, whose father had been Viceroy of Peru, and he made a sneering but not very intelligent rejoinder to it. Varinas met with warm approval, however, when he recommended that the Pope be asked to forbid the religious orders to acquire more property than the vast amount they already had.[59]

In 1688, the Marchioness of Varinas wrote a long letter to the King (who, it will be remembered, was practically an idiot, and untidy at that) in which she points out that, through the non-adoption of her husband's recommendations, more than 50,000,000 pesos have been lost to the Crown. She goes on to say, doubtless under inspiration from her spouse, that if foreign commerce were suppressed the Crown would receive a profit of 6,000,000 pesos a year from its colonies. She adds that the wickedness of corregidores and other officials has been the death of some 12,000,000 Indians in Spain's America.[60]

In that part of the published papers of the Marquis of Varinas which is called "Vaticinios de la Perdida de las Indias" ("Prophecies of the Loss of the Indies") the author points out, among other things, how the population of the Indies, and especially of Peru, has diminished. He addresses the King with most daring, but most merited, sharpness, revealing all the manifold harm done by oppression, corruption, and official stupidity.[61] Again, in the "Mano de Relox que muestra y pronostica la ruina de América" ("Watch-hand which points out and foretells the ruination of America") the Marquis of Varinas, in still bolder and more indignant terms, chides the King for the abject condition to which avarice, unintelligence, and irreligion have brought his monarchy, and he foretells that some day England, France, and Holland will seize Spain's American possessions.[62] Not even Varinas could foretell the birth of the Latin American republics within a century and a quarter of his own death.

The second and last of the critical commentaries on the Spanish régime in Peru which I shall notice here is addressed by an unknown writer to King Philip V.[63] Its leit-motif is the sins of the colonial officials and, especially, of the viceroys who were the vice-patrons royal. There is much injustice, I believe, and no little exaggeration, in this document; but there is much common sense, as well.

The author begins by tracing the progressive decay of the viceregal office, distinguishing therein three periods. The first was in the time of the earliest viceroys (from Nuñez Vela to Toledo, inclusive) who accomplished the duty of bringing the Indians, still mourning the loss of their Incas, to obedience. The second state of the viceregal office came into being when the Castilians became more numerous than they had been and the Indians lost in strength. At this time the Spaniards forsook their ancient and heroic military prowess and gave themselves up to vile, mechanical occupations such as mining and commerce. The third state of the viceregal office is that which prevailed in the writer's time. In it the viceroys were restive under Royal authority and frequently evaded it in order to serve their own purposes. To this the author adds that the office of oidor suffered a parallel decay.[64]

As an example of the deterioration in the politico-economic morality of the viceroys, the anonymous writer or, as he describes himself, the loyal and zealous vassal, points out the fact that, by law, the arriving viceroy was bound to go all the way to Callao by sea. The object of the law[65] was the saving of time, expense, and endless trouble for the officials and for the Indians of the districts through which the viceregal retinue would have to pass if it went by land from Paita to Lima. The "zealous vassal" tells us that the land-journey of 230 leagues from Paita to Lima made necessary the provision of 56 stopping places along the route. Two of these are cities, two are towns, eleven are Indian villages, and the remainder are rustic shelters constructed at set distances in the midst of deserts. To each of these halting places vast amounts of food, water, fuel and other supplies, as well as adequate numbers of Indian servants, have to be brought from long distances and even from up in the mountains in order to give the viceroy and his numerous entourage a proper degree of comfort, or as near an approach thereto as possible. All of this entails a huge amount of unnecessary and costly labor. According to this author the earliest viceroys obeyed the law; those of the second group went by land from Paita to Lima under the conditions just indicated, but they made a gesture towards obedience by sending home medical certificates showing that their health required that the journey be made by land; the third group omitted even that slight formality.[66]

In all this the writer is inaccurate, if not unjust; for, of the earlier viceroys, Nuñez Vela landed at Tumbez and went to Lima from there by land; the elder Marquis of Cañete landed at Paita, and so did the Count of Nieva and Toledo. It looks to me, therefore, as though the precedent had been established by Nuñez Vela, the first viceroy, and maintained ever since his day. It is true, of course, that the practice was an extravagant one which took much time, sometimes three months, and that the journey by sea would have been altogether more sensible.

The "zealous vassal" goes on to relate the various forms of graft practiced by viceroys in connection with the use of the King's money and with the selling of official posts, often at the expense of the King's own appointees.[67] In like sense he speaks of the oidores of the audience whose office was designed to be a counterpoise and complement to that of the viceroy. In this author's day the oidores were almost always rich merchants or their sons, with the result that they tended, in legal cases, to favor their own class at the expense of litigants of other social groups. In this perverse behavior the viceroys and the oidores too often acted in co-operation with one another for money's sake.[68] To all this the loyal and zealous one adds the remark that, even the best of the viceroys—and he admits that there have been some moderately good ones—cannot contend successfully against the systematic practice of corruption long since sanctified by custom. He likewise deplores the fact that wealth is become the chief criterion of nobility, so that titles and honors which should have gone to the first settlers and their descendants go too often to men who are rich and

FIG. 23. The pulpit in San Blas Church, Cuzco, Churrigueresque style, seventeenth century.
Courtesy of Mrs. Myra Brady.

no more.[69] In this we see, I think, a late flickering of that feudal spirit which, in the sixteenth and seventeenth centuries, had striven to convert the encomiendas into permanent feudal fiefs with primary or seignorial jurisdiction over the Indian vassals. (See above, pages 150–152.)

Having, in vigorous language, laid before the King the far from pretty state of affairs in Peru, the loyal and zealous vassal proceeds to outline two projects for reform, one of which, as he seems to suspect, is far more sensible than the other. The first and less sane of the two is, briefly, as follows:

In the first place, the writer points out that the King pays 48,000 pesos a year for the maintenance of 100 mounted soldiers at a salary of 40 pesos a month each, but that even this tiny force has been suffered by the viceroys and oidores to decline and to become riddled with corruption.[70] Aware that there is no effective armed force in the realm, the author suggests that an army be created to the number of 8,000 troops, half infantry, half cavalry. The wages of the former are to be 20 pesos a month and of the latter 35 pesos. These figures are based on the fact that the infantry garrison of 600 men at Callao, a force distinct from the above-mentioned "army," had been receiving 15 pesos a month. He says that, although the proposed new army would cost over 3,000,000 pesos a year, it would end corruption and all illegal doings and so would more than pay for itself. The force of 8,000 men would be distributed thus: Chile would have 2,500 troops; Panama, 600; Guayaquil, 300; Paita, 100; Potosí, 1,000; and Lima (headquarters of the army), 3,500. A special function of the new army would be that of squelching the all too flourishing contraband trade. It should be noted in passing that it was something like this that poor, despised Varinas had had in mind fifty years earlier.[71]

To these perfectly reasonable recommendations (except that the pay proposed for the soldiers was much too small) the author adds a suggestion that cannot fail to seem to modern folk absurd, namely, that the viceroys should all be bishops who, for good service, would be rewarded with the cardinal's hat, and that the oidores should be ecclesiastics also, as a means of keeping them out of trade.[72] He goes on to say that, under proper conditions, the participation in and control of commerce by corregidores is not bad because they can act as capitalists and as recipients of money due for merchandise much better than private merchants resident far from their bucolic customers could do. In order to improve the character of the corregidores and of their lieutenants he suggests that the latter, as well as the former, be directly appointed by the Crown at a salary of 8,000 pesos, selection being made from among the nobility or from among the retired soldiers of the realm. He would have them be men of education and would give them the title and duties of judges. They would thus cease to be mere servants and appointees of the corregidores and would act as a powerful check upon them.[73] This, again, is not a bad idea, if it could have been carried out.

At one place the "loyal and zealous vassal" boldly rebukes the King because of his never having troubled to set foot in his American possessions, which he left entirely to servants of his to administer.[74] It is quite true that, until the Infanta Eulalia went to the Chicago World's Fair in 1893, no member of the Spanish royal family ever trod the soil of the New World in an official capacity. And by that time it was a trifle too late to do any good! Had the Kings of Castile made it a habit to send their heirs, or at any rate near kinsmen of theirs, on a grand tour through the Indies, it could not have failed to benefit both the visitors and the visited.

The second and more important suggestion made by this author is as follows: Because the King receives from Peru only about 3,500,000 a year, something must be done to improve his income and make it more nearly equal to the vast sums which his corrupt officials and other subjects enjoy at his expense. The author recommends that a Royal Commercial Company be formed for the entire management of Peruvian business. To the Company the King will subscribe 500,000 pesos, and every one in Lima with more than 20,000 pesos to his fortune will subscribe 5 per cent thereof. As there are at

least 50,000,000 pesos of private fortunes in that city the
Company will start off with upwards of 2,000,000 pesos of
capital, and more will speedily come in from other parts of the
kingdom. The author then proceeds to say that there are at
least 6,000,000 people in the viceroyalty and that well-paid
labor by 10 per cent of these would yield, from mines alone,
50,000,000 pesos a year, of which the Company would get one-
tenth. In addition to the profits from mining on a new and
sound basis (each mine-owner being obliged to have at least
200,000 pesos of capital for the purchase of machinery and incidental expenses), there would be a large income arising out
of the suppression of contraband trade and the augmenta-
tion of general commerce so that the King, in addition to his
dividends from the Company, would have vastly increased returns from the usual taxes. The Company would have to
maintain and administer the "annual" fleet (which sometimes
went eight or nine years without sailing) and it would have
also to fight off such intruders as Admiral George Anson, who,
in 1740, did immense injury to Peruvian trade. Moreover,
commerce was to be encouraged in every possible way and
trade all along the Pacific coast from one colony to another
was to receive official sanction and help. Finally, the author
draws an exciting and, in the main, a reasonable picture of all
that the proposed Company could do to foment and expand
Peruvian commerce in such a manner as to make full use of
the immeasurable natural wealth of that land both of a min-
eral sort and of agricultural and pastoral kinds. The huge dis-
crepancies between the value of the trade actually carried on
through illicit channels and that which followed the official
routes and paid the rightful taxes to the King would cease;
popular misery would dwindle and terminate so that the consuming power of the Peruvian public would rise;[75] the swell-
ing income produced by the proper management of the Company would choke the leakage of money into foreign lands
and would correspondingly augment the benefits to the Crown
both from its investment in the Company and from its receipts of taxes. The loyal and zealous vassal concludes his

convincing argument with a plea for free commerce, by which he means the abolition of the fleet system and the opening up to Spanish commerce of many ports both in Spain and in America.[76] It was precisely this type of free commerce that was introduced some twenty-three years later by King Charles III, as explained above on pages 225–226.

Strangely enough, a British contemporary of the writer whose work we have just examined largely confirms the ideas set forth by him. The British writer harps upon the corruption and the stupidity of the Spanish colonial officials and the failure of the Spanish Government to foster wholesome trade in all the myriad products of those realms.[77] The British author's purpose is, however, very different from that of the Peruvian. The former, after comparing Spain to a sieve which, whatever it receives is never the fuller, all because of the wasteful and corrupt practices prevailing, goes on to point out the immensity of the contraband trade carried on and to urge his countrymen to force the Spaniards—whom he openly despises—to open up their possessions to a proper international trade.[78]

I have now traced the chief aspects of the history and manifestations of foreign envy in regard to the Spanish colonial commercial system. In conclusion I will simply observe that, if the counsels of Varinas, Campillo, and the anonymous Peruvian writer (1742) and of many others had been followed out more fully the Spanish monarchy might not have lost its overseas possessions so soon. True, the enlightened King, Charles III, did his best to liberalize the prevailing system, but he came too late. The seeds of political and economic misery had already begun to grow into the strong tree of a desire for complete independence.

NOTES TO CHAPTER VIII

[1] Between 1529 and 1573 there was a period when Bayona, Coruña, Avilés, Laredo, Bilbao, and Santander, on the Atlantic and Biscayan coasts, and Málaga and Cartagena on the Mediterranean coast, could send ships to America. But as all ships had to re-enter Spain through the Seville port

before going on to their home ports, and as copies of all registers of cargo and passengers had to be sent from those ports to the Council of the Indies, the liberty was more apparent than real, and it was but little availed of. See: Encinas, 1596, IV, p. 133; Haring, 1918, p. 15.

[2] Antuñez, 1797, pp. 9–10, and appendices 1–3. There is a very informative volume, anonymous, but dated 1743, in the Bodleian Library, Oxford. (Arch. ∑ 122.) The various tracts therein include one by Don Miguel de Berria wherein various efforts to liberalize commerce are described. See also: Arias y Miranda, 1854, pp. 17–66; Bourne, 1904, Ch. xix; Scelle, 1906, I, pp. 35–53; Dahlgren, 1909, pp. 3–29; Artíñano, 1917, pp. 19–73; Haring, 1918, pp. 14–17.

[3] Antuñez, 1797, pp. 102–103. Bourne, 1904, p. 296. Dahlgren, 1909, pp. 17–21. Haring, 1918, p. 71.

[4] Veitia Linaje, 1672, II, pp. 88–96 and 158–159. Dahlgren, 1909, pp. 19–21. Artíñano, 1917, pp. 75–94. Haring, 1918, pp. 71–73. All the expenses of the convoy were supposed to be paid out of the avería, a tax of 1½ per cent to 5 per cent on the value of the protected merchandise carried. See: Encinas, 1596, III, p. 174; Haring, 1918, pp. 76–77.

[5] The words corsair, pirate, filibuster, freebooter, buccaneer, and pechelingue are all used to designate the picturesque maritime brigands who, in various ways, preyed upon Spain's legitimate commerce. They are quite different from smugglers and contrabandists on the one hand and from privateers (who carried letters of marque from their respective sovereigns) on the other. The Spaniards, of course, eschewed fine distinctions and regarded all of them as pirates. See: Anonymous, 1741, p. 289, for English attitude in this matter.

[6] Artíñano, 1917, pp. 177–231. Haring, 1918, pp. 16, 68–71, 231–235, 240–241, 248–251.

[7] Vaz, 1904, p. 236. Raleigh, 1905, p. 52. Because of wind conditions and ocean current conditions, it usually took about two months to go from Panama to Callao, and only half that time to return. Artíñano, 1917, p. 81. Dahlgren, 1909, p. 57. Haring, 1918, p. 189.

[8] Anonymous, 1741, p. 229. Scelle, 1906, I, pp. 63–65. Dahlgren, 1909, pp. 20–23. Artíñano, 1917, pp. 80–86. Chinchón, 1871, p. 101, leads us to believe that haulage by land was done by contractors who bid for the job.

[9] Bourne, 1904, pp. 290–291. Moses, 1914, I, pp. 199 and 203, II, pp. 129–138. Haring, 1918, pp. 140–143.

[10] Haring, 1918, pp. 140–141.

[11] See the letter written, in 1596, by Francisco Suares in Rio de Janeiro to his brother Diego in Lisbon, wherein this new trade up the Plate is described. (In Hakluyt, 1903–1905, XI, pp. 39–43.) See also: Merivale, 1861, p. 16.

[12] Scelle, 1906, I, pp. 53–57. Haring, 1918, pp. 117–118.

[13] Haring, 1918, pp. 143–151.

[14] Arias y Miranda, 1854, pp. 66–67, tells how the once thriving worked-leather industry of Spain was legislated to death, and on pp. 73–76 he gives an admirable account of the vicious system of taxes bearing on woollens, silks, iron, wine, sugar, salt, meat and other necessities, with the result that the woollen and silk industries were crushed. (Pp. 77–78 and 153–154.) Compare what Dahlgren, 1909, pp. 57–67, says on the same general subject. I venture

to think, however, that this great Swedish savant has understated the importance in colonial Peru of those arts and manufactures in which the Indians and their peculiar æsthetic and technological ideas took an interesting and vital part. (P. 63.) To this point we shall revert, on pp. 264–268. Further valuable data on this subject will be found in Artíñano, 1917, pp. 154–158 and 303–318. Also see: Haring, 1918, pp. 124–129; Cappa, 1889–1897, Vol. VII–X, inclusive, and particularly VII, pp. 39–44, 66–68; Means, 1932, pp. 27–28.

[15] Haring, 1918, Chs. xi and xii, especially pp. 272, 276–277, and 292–297. Artíñano, 1917, Ch. vii; and 1920, entire, in which magnificent monograph he gives vivid information about shipbuilding. La Roërie and Vivielle, n.d., may be used to advantage in this connection, their monograph being also magnificent, for one desirous of studying shipbuilding in general.

[16] Varinas, 1873, pp. 239–240. Guerra y Céspedes, 1868. Dahlgren, 1909, pp. 26–50. Artíñano, 1917, pp. 158–162. Haring, 1918, pp. 166–167.

[17] Artíñano, 1917, pp. 136–138.

[18] Two documents of special importance in this connection will be found in the Bibliothèque Nationale, Paris (MS. Department), under signatures Esp. 152, fols. 57–80, and fols. 91–97 verso. A third document, Esp. 152, fols. 85–88, is also interesting. A vivid account of the foreign merchandise carried in Spanish ships is given in Anonymous, 1741, pp. 291–306. But the best possible study of the whole matter will be found in Dahlgren, 1909, pp. 76–122 and 321–357, where the enormous values of the foreign goods carried by Spanish ships are indicated.

[19] Bourne, 1904, pp. 294–297. Merivale, 1861, ascribes the King's liberality to necessity arising from smuggling.

[20] Real Decreto, 1778. Bertrand, 1929, I, pp. 338–341.

[21] Alcazar, 1920, pp. 36–41. Means, 1931, pp. 329–340.

[22] Alcazar, 1920, pp. 50–51.

[23] Alcazar, 1920, pp. 51–58. It seems that, although the Carvajals retained the title of Correo Mayor de las Indias, they either sold a part of their monopoly to other Postmasters General (in Mexico and elsewhere) or else let it be filched from them; for, from 1599 to 1768, they were in reality only Postmasters General of Peru. See: Alcazar, 1920, pp. 60–61 and the various documents and laws which he gives in his book.

[24] Chinchón, 1871, pp. 88–95, gives an array of data on this and connected matters. Mancera, 1896, pp. 21–22, or 1648, paragraphs 63–65, says that he reduced the time for the round-trip between Lima and Potosí from four months to twenty-six or twenty-four days, this being done by replacing the Indian chasquis with mounted messengers. Excellent statistics on the post-office will be found in J. Arriaga, 1771–1774, pp. 107–110. In the Juicio de Límites entre el Perú y Bolivia (Barcelona, 1906), Vol. III, pp. 232–250, will be found a minute (eighteenth-century) account of the mail-route from Lima to Chuquisaca or La Plata by way of Huamanga (Ayacucho), Cuzco, Puno, La Paz, Oruro, and Potosí, a distance of 449 leagues, with more than 65 stopping-places along the way where new beasts and supplies could be obtained. We are told that a messenger who took more than 32 days for the round trip was received in the jail at Lima on his return and afterwards shipped to Chile. See also: Montesclaros, 1859, pp. 25–26; Alcazar, 1920, pp. 58–60 and

78–81; Moses, 1914, I, pp. 388–391; Haring, 1918, pp. 34–35. For purposes of comparison see the speeds of the Incaic chasqui relay-runners at p. 334 of Means, 1931.

25 Royal Library, Copenhagen (Ny Kongl. S. 4to, 568). The year of this MS. narrative is fixed by internal evidence as being between 1747 and 1767. The author mentions seeing some Jesuit property, from which the Society would have been absent after 1767, and one of his visitors at Lima was the Count of San Javier, whose title dates from 1747, according to Riva-Agüero, 1921, pp. 132–133.

26 My friend, Mr. Lewis Hanke, of Harvard, has shown me for my use here a MS. of his in which he points out that Casas may be considered the first great modern propagandist. "His most popular tract, the *Brevísima Relación de la destruyción de las Indias* (Seville, 1552), wherein he denounced Spain's 'bloody deeds' in the New World, was quickly seized upon by Spain's enemies abroad and translated into English, French, Dutch, Italian, German, and Latin for the greater defamation of Spain." The tracts went through many editions in those languages during the sixteenth to eighteenth centuries. The titles given to many of these throw a blinding light—and a lurid glow it is—on the underlying purposes of their publishers. Sir Walter Raleigh, of whom more very soon, was one who frequently cited Casas and his chatter about the "sighes, grones, lamentacions, teares and bloud of so many innocent men, women, and children afflicted, robbed, reviled, branded with hot irons, roasted, dismembered, mangled, stabbed, whipped, racked, scalded with hott oyle, suet, and hogsgrease, . . ." all this being Raleigh's version of what Casas said (see Raleigh, 1928, pp. 143–144). On the manner in which Casas's writings, in the original and in translations, worked against Spain abroad, see: Juderías, n.d., pp. 302–307. Even our New England settlers, when they left Holland for these shores, were filled with horror of Spain and of its "Popery," having seen the Dutch editions of Casas's works, with their horrendous illustrations. And, finally, Raleigh, if not Casas himself, was subsequently cited in England as justifying the acquisitive plans of the South Sea Company.

27 Anonymous Letter of 1571, 1848 edition, pp. 439–445. It is well to observe also that Ginés de Sepúlveda cast serious doubt on the soundness of Casas's ideas during the Apostle's lifetime, and that León-Pinelo, 1630, and Solórzano Pereira, 1647–1648, contain valid refutations of innumerable statements by Casas. See especially: Solórzano, 1647–1648, Bk. I, Chs. viii–xii.

28 See: Palau's data on each of these, and the rich material in the John Carter Brown Library Catalogue, in Leclerc, and in the amazingly informative catalogues of Messrs. Maggs Bros., of London, and also the various articles in Means, 1928.

29 Raleigh, 1905, p. 52. This is the modern Walter Raleigh, who quotes from his ancestor, Sir Walter.

30 Raleigh, 1928, pp. 17–18, 53, and 70–71. I am greatly indebted to Mr. Walter Briggs, of the Harvard College Library, for his kindness in bidding me to read this magnificent volume with its able Introduction by Mr. Harlow.

31 This scheme is set forth in a MS. in the British Museum (Sloane MSS. 1133, fols. 45 ff.), which Mr. Harlow prints in Raleigh, 1928, pp. 140–141. If

the scheme had been carried out it would have constituted an invasion of Peru from the east. It would not, however, have been the first occasion upon which Peru was approached by Europeans from the east or southeast. As early as 1522 one Alejo García, at the head of a force of Chiriguanos, came near to invading the Inca Empire from the east. See: Nordenskiöld, 1917; Means, 1917. Again, when Francisco Pizarro appeared at Court, in 1529, he was unconsciously heading off Sebastian Cabot, Hernando Calderón, and Roger Barlow (English), who, in 1527–1528, had been near the eastern side of Peru, in the region now called Paraguay. See Dr. E. G. R. Taylor's remarks on pages xxxviii–lxiii of his edition of Barlow's work, Barlow, 1932. On page lv of the same volume Dr. Taylor mentions that the Earl of Warwick, in 1550, considered, with Cabot and Roger Barlow, an attack on Peru from the eastern side, to be carried out on behalf of Henry VIII. As these matters are curious rather than important, I relegate them to this note, mentioning them merely for the sake of completeness.

[32] Robert Harcourt, in 1613, sent his cousin, Fisher, to look for Raleigh's Manoa. (Harcourt, 1928, p. 119.) A very fine map by P. du Val d'Abbeville, Geographer to the King (of France), was published at Paris in 1654. It shows "Lac Parime" and adds, below it, "En ces quartiers se sont retirés les successeurs des Incas du Perou." Above the lake appears "Gvaiana ou Roiavme du Roy doré," and at the northwest corner of the lake we find "Manoa El Dorado." It is shown as a walled city. The map is reproduced at p. 140 of Harcourt, 1928. The map made by the Jesuit Father Samuel Fritz in 1707 and published by Dr. Edmundson in Fritz, 1922, shows "Parimé Lago" as a large, rectangular lake on the Equator east of the Río Negro but it makes no reference to Manoa, el Dorado, or the Incas. Thereafter, during the eighteenth century, the myth of Manoa, the golden kingdom, began to melt away. The last chapter in the long story of the myth's exposure is told us by Sir Everard Im Thurn who, in the 1870s or 1880s, visited its supposed location. Just after sunrise he beheld a strange cloud-formation which looked like a city with temples, towers, and golden spires or minarets. As the sun rose higher, and the clouds melted into nothing, the vision vanished. The "lake" was nothing more than a vast plain which grows soggy at the wet season. Im Thurn, 1883, pp. 36–37. In reality "el Dorado" was not a golden kingdom, but a gilded man. A chief of the Chibchas, in what is now Colombia, was annually covered with unguents and gold dust which he ceremonially washed off in the mountain tarn of Guatavita. Markham, 1912, pp. 24–27. Harlow, on pp. xlv–lxxxiii of Raleigh, 1928, gives ample data on the el Dorado myth. See also: Alcedo, 1812–1815, II, pp. 442–443; Zerda, 1883; and Moses, 1914, I, pp. 42, 75, 150 and 285.

[33] Hakluyt, 1903–1905, VIII, pp. 95–96 and 124–126.

[34] Sarmiento, 1895. Burney, 1803–1817, II, pp. 1–57.

[35] Burney, II, pp. 64–94. Wycherley, 1928, pp. 103–134.

[36] Medina, 1916b, describes a very rare work, printed in Lima, in 1594, by Antonio Ricardo, formerly of Turin, the first printer in Lima. The work in question is by an unknown author who describes in a lively manner the Hawkins affair as seen with Peruvian eyes. See also: Burney, II, pp. 118–133; Riva-Agüero, 1919.

[37] Speilbergen, 1906. Anonymous Greek Soldier, 1625. Burney, II, pp. 206–224 and 328–352; III, pp. 1–37. Riva-Agüero, 1919. Markham, 1892, pp. 175–176.

[38] Burney, IV, pp. 38–131. Wycherley, 1928, Chs. vi–vii.

[39] Raveneau de Lussan, 1930, pp. 79–87 and 196–230. Burney, IV, pp. 150–187 and 188–284.

[40] Dahlgren, 1909, pp. 72–75 and 108–109. In the latter place M. Dahlgren explains that the Company formed in 1664 was not very active, but that it served as a parent for later undertakings of analogous sort.

[41] Dahlgren, 1909, pp. 111–114, gives a vivid idea of the barefaced insolence of the French attitude towards the Spanish authorities in Peru.

[42] Burney, IV, pp. 375–383. Dahlgren, 1909, pp. 114–120, 123–146, 247, 251–255 and 288–293.

[43] Burney, IV, pp. 487–500. Dahlgren, 1909, pp. 661–703.

[44] Feuillée, 1714. Frezier, 1716 and 1717. Burney, IV, pp. 455–456 and 500–505; also, 505–507.

[45] Burney, IV, pp. 430–447 and 457–484. Wycherley, 1928, pp. 235–250 and 266–293.

[46] Dahlgren, 1909, pp. 210–233.

[47] Melville, 1921, pp. 1–3. Botsford, 1924, pp. 164–165. As both these excellent books are amply documented I feel it unnecessary to cite original sources.

[48] Melville, 1921, p. 27.

[49] Melville, 1921, pp. 11–14. Botsford, 1924, pp. 165–166. Dean Swift, according to his *Journal to Stella,* took a flyer in the South Sea Company in 1711, paying £380 for £500 of its stock; but he did it with his eyes open. Defoe's pamphlet, *An Essay on the South Sea Trade,* came out in 1712 and *Robinson Crusoe* in 1719.

[50] Scelle, 1906, II, pp. 523–582. Melville, 1921, p. 14. Botsford, 1924, p. 166.

[51] Melville, 1921, Chs. iii–vi, inclusive. Botsford, 1924, pp. 166–170. Burney, IV, pp. 553–555.

[52] Burney, IV, pp. 519–544, V, pp. 38–88. Wycherley, 1928, pp. 361–419.

[53] This document, Anonymous, ca. 1640, is in the Bibliothèque Nationale, Paris (Fonds Espagnol, 280), is undated, but as the author mentions witnessing two earthquakes, one in November, 1605, at Ica, the other in October, 1609, in Lima, I have dated it as being of 1640 or earlier.

[54] Anonymous, ca. 1640, MS., pp. 1–6. Raveneau, 1930, p. 211, speaks of the magnificence of the Governor's house and of the charms of the ladies of Guayaquil. Alcedo, 1741, and 1915, pp. 36–37.

[55] Anonymous, ca. 1640, MS., pp. 13–14.

[56] Anonymous, ca. 1640, MS., pp. 42–43, 80–81, 108–114. Through the kindness of Miss Irene Wright, of Sevilla, Spain, I have lately obtained a copy of one year (1631) from the Diary of the Count of Chinchón during his term as Viceroy of Peru. This document, quite distinct from his Memoria (Chinchón, 1871) has never been published. It is in the archives of the Indies, in Seville, and it throws a vivid light on life in colonial Peru in its quotidian aspect.

[57] Don Cesáreo Fernández Duro, in his Introduction to Varinas, 1899, p. 7, gives the title as Barinas y de Guane-Guanare, and the same spelling, Barinas,

is used by Haring, 1918, pp. 143, 152, and 250. Varinas, however, is undoubtedly more correct, and this is the spelling generally used by Señor Fernández Duro, the greatest authority on this man's career. It was likewise the spelling most often used by Varinas himself. Barinas (or Varinas) is a city in Venezuelan territory, and so is Guanare, the history of both being treated of by Father Jacinto de Carvajal, in his *Relación del descubrimiento del río Apure*, written in 1648 and published by the officials of León (Spain) at León in 1892, from the original MS. which was found in the provincial archives of León by Don Pascual de Gayangos. Barinas (or Varinas) is about 110 miles southeast of the southeastern corner of the Lagoon of Maracaibo in northern Venezuela. See: Alcedo, 1812–1815, I, pp. 142–143, and II, p. 195; Bingham, 1909, pp. 59–70.

58 These data on Varinas are gleaned from Fernández Duro's Introduction and from various documents in Varinas, 1899. This interesting reformer is all but forgotten in our day, and one rarely finds mention of him in encyclopædias or in books.

59 Varinas, 1899, pp. 17–37. Also 1873.

60 Varinas, 1899, pp. 57–63.

61 Varinas, 1899, pp. 193–324. The date of the "Vaticinios" is 1685.

62 Varinas, 1899, pp. 327–386. At some time after 1666 a gentleman named Don Balthazar Pardo de Figueroa, who had had a career in Peru, Chile, and others parts of America almost as varied as that of Varinas, drew up an elaborate report in which he urged Louis XIV of France to conquer Spain's American possessions. Pardo not only told the King of France all about the bad conditions prevailing in Spanish America, but also exactly how to go about the proposed conquest. See Pardo de Figueroa, 1841. Had not Louis XIV and his minister, Colbert, among whose papers Pardo's Mémoire was found, been busy in Europe something might have come of the suggestion.

63 Anonymous, 1742.

64 Anonymous, 1742, pp. 1–3.

65 Recop. seems to say nothing on this subject. But see: Anonymous, 1742, pp. 2–4.

66 Anonymous, 1742, pp. 4–5.

67 Anonymous, 1742, pp. 6–13.

68 Anonymous, 1742, pp. 13–17, 20–27.

69 Anonymous, 1742, pp. 17–20.

70 Anonymous, 1742, pp. 6–7. He says that all the captains in this microscopic "army" are friends and dependents of the viceroys and that any soldier who wishes to begin receiving his stipend of 480 pesos a year has to pay them 200 pesos or, in the case of squad-leaders, 400 pesos. This is typical of what went on in the viceroyalty's officialdom.

71 Anonymous, 1742, pp. 27–33.

72 Anonymous, 1742, pp. 34–38.

73 Anonymous, 1742, pp. 40–47.

74 Anonymous, 1742, pp. 52–53.

75 Compare this with Campillo y Cossio's ideas, cited above on p. 192.

76 Anonymous, 1742, pp. 53–90. The authorship of this powerful and intelligent pamphlet in which is erected a scheme which might have saved the

Indies for the Spanish monarchy is not surely known. Charles Leclerc, in his *Bibliotheca Americana* (Paris, 1878), lists the work under the name of Vitorino Montero, mentioning under No. 1801 a manuscript which was copied in Lima in 1783 by Don Pablo Saavedra, apparently from either the author's original manuscript or from a printing of it. It seems that the name of Don Vitorino Montero and the date 1744 appear on the original from which Saavedra made his copy. Under No. 2575 Leclerc cites a printed edition of this work which also exists in the Harvard College Library. That edition is dated, in the dedication which it contains to Don Joseph de Carvajal y Lancaster, Governor of the Council of the Indies, April 30th, 1747. The printing which I have used is without either title-page or colophon, and it lacks the dedication. It is quite different in make-up from the 1747 edition, but the contents are practically the same with occasional variations in the phraseology. This copy, which I own, speaks on p. 40 of events which befell in the year 1742, using the present tense in that connection. Therefore, not knowing whether the author really was Don Vitorino Montero—whoever he may have been— and finding the edition internally dated 1742, I have cited it as Anonymous, 1742.

[77] Anonymous, 1741, pp. 74–80. This writer, whose book is sometimes cited with the title *A Compleat (not Concise) History of Spanish America,* was almost certainly John Campbell.

[78] Anonymous, 1741, pp. 291–319.

CHAPTER IX

INTELLECTUAL LIFE IN VICEREGAL PERU, 1530–1780

In spite of the prevalence in viceregal Peru of such untoward facts as tumult, political and social and economic corruption, there were enough people left who were interested in the arts of peace to enable colonial Peru to produce some noteworthy architecture, industrial arts, and literature. It is to points such as these that our attention will be directed in this chapter.

1. Architecture

Elsewhere I have said enough about native Peruvian architecture to convey at least a general idea of what it was during various pre-Spanish periods.[1] Study of this subject convinces one that, although there was much which was imposing and much that was technologically interesting in native architecture, there were only a few features of it suitable for blending with Spanish architecture when the latter arrived on the scene. Certain native architectonic forms such as the pyramid, the tapering niche-, window-, and door-outlines with monolithic lintels, such also as the mortarless ashlar and polygonal masonry, and as the thatched roofs, were all so alien to Spanish ideas that they afforded no inducements to the newcomers for their adaptation. Conversely, certain architectonic forms which, during many centuries, had been integral parts of the Spanish architecture, were wholly absent from native architecture and remained always alien to it. The forms here in question included: the arch, the vault, the dome. Buildings having these elements in their structure were often imposed upon native edifices that lacked them; but the two never blended, the line of cleavage, racial in its character, being clearly visible, as in Figures 5 and 14.

There is no need for me to go into details here regarding architectural history in Spain. It suffices to point out the main trend:

By the time of the Spaniards' entry into Peru the highly decorated Plateresque (Silver-smith) style of architecture, in which vast expanses of plain wall are relieved by intense ornamentation concentrated around doors, windows, and structural lines, was already in the vogue, and it lasted until the end of Charles I's reign (about 1555). Plateresque architecture, containing as it did the last traces of Gothic and Arabic influence combined with elements derived from the Low Countries, Germany, and Italy, was appropriate to the reign of that cosmopolitan monarch, Charles.

In strongest possible contrast to the Plateresque style was that of the succeeding period, down to about 1650. This was the so-called Greco-Roman or Herreran style[2] whose fundamental characteristic was austere classicism coupled with impressive bulk and a coldness and paucity of ornamentation. The finest and most celebrated example of it is the Monastery-Palace of San Lorenzo el Real, commonly called the Escorial, a building whose proportions are enormous, but so perfectly balanced as to produce an impression of mathematical harmoniousness.[3]

The classical severity of the Herreran style was always foreign to the true taste of the Spaniards, and from about 1650 to about 1750 the natural love of intricate ornamentation reasserted itself in that Spanish version of the so widespread Baroque style which, in Spain, is called the Churrigueresque style, after José Churriguera and his sons. The traveller in Spain is continually finding examples of this family's handiwork, some of which is far too ornate to make sense for most of us, but some of which is very pleasing, albeit expressive of a loss in strength characteristic of its period, the doldrums of Spanish history.

The last Spanish style to be important in connection with architecture in Viceregal Peru was that usually called Neo-Classical or French Academic. It was the gift of the Bourbons to Spanish architecture, and its vogue lasted until the Napoleonic invasion. In both the Churrigueresque style and the French Academic the underlying structure is usually closely akin to the Herreran, being inspired by Roman-Classical ideas of construction, but on this basis the Churrigueresque style applies richly ornate conventional decorations and the French Academic applies lighter, "prettier," and more naturalistic ornamentation of the well-known eighteenth-century French style.[4]

Certain features once dominant in the architecture of Spain, notably the Gothic influence and the Moslem influence, were almost absent in the Plateresque style and fully so in the Herreran. As a result, neither Gothic nor Moslem taste ever played any real part in the architecture of colonial Peru, albeit some have claimed that balconies such as that in Figure 15 and an occasional bit of tile-work are due to Moslem influence, a dictum which seems to me far-fetched.

When Pizarro led his men into Cuzco in 1533 he found a city which commanded admiration and which demanded only minor modifications in order to adapt it to Spanish and Christian requirements. Neither at that time nor for some thirty years afterwards were circumstances propitious to the development of a hybrid colonial architecture derived from both the native and the intrusive cultures. As a result, the Spaniards contented themselves with taking existing Incaic buildings, usually low, and adding to them upper stories built of rather crude masonry (whose stones were very often derived from native buildings) covered over with whitewash and embellished by adventitious elements such as balconies, towers, and arcades.

Naturally enough, more care was taken with public buildings, and especially with churches, than with private houses. Cuzco Cathedral, for example, shows the influence of the Herreran style very decidedly. See Figures 12 and 22. It was begun in March, 1560, and finished in July, 1654, so that it coincides well with the dates of that period in Spain. The successive architects of the cathedral were Don Juan Miguel Velamendi, Don Juan Correa, and the Prebend Dr. Don Diego Arias de la Cerda.[5] Both outside and inside the structure of the cathedral of Cuzco displays strong influence by the Herreran style with, here and there, touches which may be later suggesting the Churrigueresque style. There are, in the choirstalls (Figure 22), a number of influences, running all the way from a hint of the Gothic tradition (in the human figures behind and above the stalls) to Churrigueresque (in the columns overlaid with ornament). There is here no trace of Indian influence; these carvings are purely European and Christian in inspiration.[6]

It seems that there had been a pro-cathedral in some other part of the city. The inauguration of the magnificent new cathedral of course awakened the liveliest interest in all classes, as is made clear by a charming episode showing Peruvian colonial life at its best. It befell thus:

The many decades of labor upon the church had naturally buried its floor deeply in miscellaneous rubbish. The task of removing the mounds of débris was begun by the chapter of the cathedral who started to haul away the trash in leather sacks. In that heavy labor they were soon joined by the Corregidor of Cuzco, Don José de Idiaquez, and by his principal gentlemen. Their example was contagious, and presently all the religious in the city, and all the Spaniards, whether noble or plebeian, including the ladies, were hard at work "with such great devotion and so much Christian zeal that they gave a splendid example to the Indians and, very quickly, cleared the church and made it quite neat."[7] On August 14th, 1654, the cathedral was consecrated with appropriate splendor.[8]

Cuzco is rich in interesting and beautiful buildings. In Figures 19 and 21 we see the Monastery of La Merced, one of the sightliest buildings in all Peru. It was built after the already mentioned earthquake of 1650, replacing an earlier monastery of this Order which was shattered by the shocks.

The present edifice, built with money afforded by Don Diego de Vargas Carvajal and his wife, is fundamentally of the Herreran style, but it is richly ornamented in many places with overlaid Churrigueresque embellishments which may be somewhat later than the basic construction. The main stairway, however, is pure Herreran, and nothing more austerely dignified is to be found even in the Escorial itself.[9]

In the Frontispiece and Figure 5 we see two views of the Church of Santo Domingo, also in Cuzco. This, it will be remembered, was the monastic establishment which acquired the Coricancha, or Temple of the Sun, early in the Spanish period of Cuzco. With Christian zeal the monks did their best to obliterate the pagan fane whose new owners they were; but, as shown in Figure 5, they could not wholly destroy the marvellous masonry of the Incaic builders. They could only add their own structures above it, as we see. It is probable that what we now behold, somewhat nondescript in style for the most part, was erected after 1650, the original Santo Domingo having been destroyed in that fatal earthquake. The sightly tower shown in the Frontispiece seems at first glance to be Herreran in the main. One might better call it neo-Incaic, however, at least as far as the shaft is concerned, because most of the stones there were undoubtedly cut by the Incas' masons for Coricancha and only re-located here after the Spanish period began. The two doorways and the body of the church are clearly Herreran, but the top of the tower is certainly Churrigueresque.[10]

Arequipa, strangely enough, is rich in the super-ornate sort of Churrigueresque architecture, for example the façade of the Jesuit Church. In all likelihood work of this kind was executed by Indian artisans acting under Spanish direction. The Argentine architect, Angel Guido, finds in these heavily ornamented façades, and in others like them, strong influence from the native art which, so he claims, has blended with Hispanic art to form what he calls Hispano-Indigenous architecture. On this subject Sr. Guido has much to say, regarding both decorative details and arrangement of lines and masses. He points out that, in opulent decorative designs such as these there occur numerous motifs derived from the natives' experience through the channel of their traditional art—Indian men and women; sun, moon, and stars, patently related here to the ancient sun-cult; pumas, llamas, serpents, viscachas, and other animals peculiar to the country; and likewise such things as ears of maize, coca leaves, cotton flowers, and the cantut blossom.[11] It is true that these elements occur frequently not only in Andean Churrigueresque designs but also in post-Conquest Andean designs in other media than the architectonic, being introduced therein perhaps through the pleased appreciation of Spanish designers rather than through any intentional self-expression on the part of native workers. In short, one fails to discover that native architecture has deeply influenced that which the Spaniards brought into the country. Nor is Sr. Guido's eloquence on the subject of the rhythms, alternations, repetitions, antitheses, and balances which, so he says, are native art's other great contribution to colonial architecture, convincing; for such factors in design are not peculiar to any one type of architectonic pattern. They are universal.[12]

The last-mentioned of the great classes of Spanish architecture, that is the Neo-Classical or French Academic style, also occurs, though rarely, in the Andean area during the viceregal period. The finest example of it is the façade of the Church of the Jesuits in Quito, seen in Figure 20. The Society of Jesus and all the other religious corporations in the Audience of Quito, had a career during colonial times which was even more lurid and scandalous than in other parts of viceregal Peru. In spite of repeated Royal efforts to control the religious orders and to keep their worldly wealth within bounds they became exceedingly rich and equally undisciplined. The Society of Jesus did not decay in morale so conspicuously as the monastic orders; it did, however, wax enormously rich during the late seventeenth and the eighteenth centuries. This voluptuously ornate façade was a tangible evidence of the Society's mundane position. Begun in 1753 it was not finished in 1767 when, as we know, the Society was expelled from Spain and

Spanish America. Even so, the façade had already cost 42,000 pesos, a vast sum in those days.[13] In this structure the only decorative element even faintly suggesting influence from native traditions and art is the sun-motif which we see above and beside the central doorway, and even this is rendered in such a manner that it suggests le Roy Soleil fully as much as it does Inti. On the whole one may safely say that this façade is as thoroughly European as that of the cathedral of Murcia in Spain, which it resembles in general aspect.

In my opinion native Andean architecture and art contributed in only two ways to the architecture of the colonial period: First, they provided Spanish builders with a certain amount of building material—either *in situ* or in the shape of wrought stones torn from their original places and re-used elsewhere; second, in the matter of decorative motifs of the kinds already indicated. In connection with these last it is well to remember that most of them were derived from media other than architecture, their ancestral forms having occurred chiefly on pottery and in textiles.[14]

2. *Other Arts in Viceregal Peru*

If the contribution made by native art to architecture was slight, that made to other forms of art during the colonial period was relatively much more considerable, especially in the earlier part of the period, *i.e.*, before about 1700. For example, there is the textile art. In my earlier book I said something about the genius of the Andean people for weaving, and in a more recent work specimens of Indian, or at any rate Peruvian, fabrics of the colonial period were described.[15] Such webs as those to which I refer now were usually produced in cloth-factories of the sort called obrajes (or obrages) which were very simple in their equipment and general aspect, but which, both in the most ancient times known to us and ever since then, have frequently produced exquisitely designed and manufactured fabrics. An obraje might have only one loom, as in Figure 10, or it might have many; but in either case it represented a direct and very important survival of the ancient culture into colonial and modern times.

Elsewhere, on pages 212–213, I have referred to the politico-social aspect of the obrajes. I wish now to consider them and their productions from the æsthetic angle. The chief contribution of Spanish culture to the textile art of the colonial period was in the matter of new materials. To the cotton, the llama- and vicuña-wool, and certain rarer fibres anciently used in the Andean area the Spaniards added sheep-wool, linen, and silk. Likewise they added numerous decorative motifs which were frequently combined most felicitously with native motifs, giving rise to a bi-racial textile art which is a true blend. At first this process of building up a really admirable industry was not opposed by the Crown; but later, under Philip III and Philip IV, especially, the government did its best to hamper the development of Peruvian cloth factories which would tend to lessen the consumption of Spanish-made fabrics.[16] Nevertheless, in obedience to imperious necessity such as that which caused the Buenos Aires trade to flourish in the face of Royal opposition (see pages 222–223), obrajes did exist throughout the viceregal period. A high proportion of their output consisted of coarse stuffs of wool and cotton destined to the use of all save the highest classes; but fine fabrics of cotton, sheep-wool, llama-wool, vicuña-wool, linen, silk, and silver or gold tissue were likewise made for the use of the highest ranks, both for wearing and for the adornment of their houses and public buildings.

In Figure 11 we see, for instance, a splendid piece of tapestry in which the handicraftsmanship could not be better. In it we see a perfect blending of decorative motifs derived from both the native and the Spanish repertoires of æsthetic ideas. This sort of blending is observable also in many of the early colonial paintings which show how the post-Conquest Incas modified their apparel by adopting various ideas from the Spaniards.[17] For one thing, the traditional tunic of the Incas, with or without sleeves, was retained for ceremonial use during a long period, but was gradually replaced by the poncho, which has a hole for the neck but which is not closed at the sides.[18] There is an interesting class of finely made tapestry, both for garments and for other uses, in which the majority of the motifs are pure Incaic but the remainder are Spanish—such things as stringed musical instruments, cornets of Spanish type, and even firearms or bits of Spanish armor. In Figure 24 we see a lacquered wooden cup or quero in the traditional Incaic shape but decorated in such a way as to display most clearly the influence of Spanish culture, albeit the motifs near the bottom are pre-Conquest, as are also the yuca flowers in the upper part.[19]

Turning now to household furnishings we find that, in the sixteenth century, there was a large amount of furniture made by Indians for the use of Spaniards. Although somewhat crude in execution it was often very attractive, consisting largely of pieces that had Spanish shapes—vargueños, cabinets, desks, wardrobes, tables, chairs, etc.—decorated with inlaid or carved designs in which native decorative motifs played a large part.[20] The old Spanish families of Cuzco and other parts of Peru still have in their houses innumerable lovely specimens of this class of furniture.

As time wore on, however, the influence of native ideas faded away. This is brought out very clearly by the splendid collection of Peruvian colonial furniture and art formed by Mrs. Frank Barrows Freyer during her years in Peru with Captain Freyer, then chief of the American Naval Mission to that country. Mrs. Freyer's collection has been on view at several art museums in this country, and at present (July, 1932) is at the Catholic University, D. C. Not only is the collection the best one of the sort ever to be seen in our museums, but also it has been the subject of the only article of which I know wherein Peruvian furniture is described with penetrating good sense and without silly condescension.[21]

In Figure 27 we see several of Mrs. Freyer's Peruvian antiquities as they appeared in her house in Washington after her return to this country (1925). The bed with its accessories, the little stool beside it, the wall-shelf, the paintings

Fig. 24. Sixteenth-century wooden cup decorated with designs whose pigments are inlaid in mastic and then lacquered.

Courtesy of the American Museum of Natural History.

Fig. 25. A "Frailero" or chair of wood and leather, seventeenth century.

Courtesy of Mrs. F. B. Freyer.

Fig. 26. A Peruvian settee, showing influence of Thomas Chippendale designs with French Academic style in the carving along the top, latter half of eighteenth century. The wall bracket holds three sixteenth-century carvings.

Courtesy of Mrs. F. B. Freyer.

and their frames all represent the finest furniture of Peru in the seventeenth century. Their style is pure Spanish of the Churrigueresque type, but in all likelihood they were made in Peru and by Indian workmen. Minor technical points and a few oddities of workmanship make this clear. Particularly interesting is the so-called pineapple-motif combined with acanthus-motif, on the bed. The pineapple was not native to Peru, but the chirimoya, which superficially resembles it, was. Therefore the degree to which Indian ideas were influential in the confection of this design depends upon whether the pineapple or the chirimoya inspired it.[22] We may note, in passing, that this motif, or one very like it, occurred also in architecture, as, for instance, in Figure 19.

Representative of the most intricate Churrigueresque design is the celebrated pulpit of the church of San Blas, in Cuzco, shown in Figure 23. This amazing piece of carving dates from about 1680[23] and so represents the Churrigueresque style at its apogee. Although many architects and designers would say that it is thoroughly decadent and bad, the very delicacy of the workmanship—in which I fail to discern any Indian influence—commands one's respect, albeit he wonders how the heavy canopy manages to stay in its place. Certainly it looks weak, structurally.[24]

Characteristic of the early and middle part of the seventeenth century is the chair shown in Figure 25. It is closely akin to the type of chair called in Spain "frailero" (friar's chair). This specimen, however, is certainly Peruvian. A certain not unpleasing roughness in the woodwork, the fact that it is made of "white" mahogany or Peruvian cedar, not of walnut, the absence of a richly wrought front stretcher all differentiate it from its Spanish prototype.[25] Moreover, the rich tooling of the leather seat and back contains motifs derived from flowers native to Peru—yuca or amancæ blossoms, it is hard to say which.

The Neo-Classical or French Academic style (eighteenth century) made itself felt in Peruvian furniture as well as in architecture. The table in Figure 28 displays it well. Here, as in the chair already mentioned, there is a roughness of execution which, though not displeasing, indicates that the table was made by Indians working with native tools. The design, however, is quite European in character. The settle, shown in Figure 29, is likewise of the Academic French style, its color being a soft green touched up with gilding. It is a delightful piece of work.

The interiors of Spanish colonial houses, like those of mansions in Spain, combined a spaciousness and a tendency to bareness with exceedingly rich embellishment in furniture, paintings, hangings and other adventitious elements. It was a type of house admirably adapted to the country and its upper classes. It will surprise those who have not read Mrs. Crenshaw's article, already cited, to learn that distant Peru felt the influence of that master-designer, Chippendale. In Figure 26 we behold a delicately wrought settee obviously inspired—no matter how indirectly—by him. The shell-motif along the top is, however, French Academic and is more elaborate than what Chippendale would have put in that place.[26]

All that has been said here regarding furniture refers, of course, to the Spanish and Creole upper classes. The great bulk of the population dwelt during colonial times in its villages, whether of the type shown in Figures 2 and 6, where the influence of Philip II and of Toledo is apparent, or in villages of far more ancient type, like that in Figure 8, where the Church is the one building to represent Spanish culture, and where the priest and, perchance, the landowner (occasionally) are the only representatives of the Conquistadores.

3. The Sciences

The more rabid non-Catholics blame the Inquisition for the dwarfing which the intellectual life of viceregal Peru undoubtedly suffered. This distortion was produced, however, by the conditions in which the Church as a whole found itself rather than to the Inquisition in particular. That tribunal was only an instrument for the choking of all things which might be inimical to the natural conservatism of the Church.[27] At the same time, we should not lose sight of the fact that things opposed by the Inquisition, including nearly all books of foreign origin, romances and books of chivalry (lampooned to death, in any case, by Cervantes), and persons of "dangerous" tendencies—heretics, and, above all, Jews—were not thereby excluded from Peru because of the ineradicable tendency of human beings to bootleg whatever is denied them without sound reason.[28] Banned books were as plentiful in Peru, relatively, as in Boston or Tennessee; and the Jews grew fat and prosperous under the very noses of the Familiars.[29]

Furthermore, the Church itself was far from uniform in its way of thinking; there was, during the sixteenth century, a prolonged battle between the school of thought represented by Bishop de las Casas and that represented by Ginés de Sepúlveda. (See pages 82–84, above.) It turned chiefly upon the question of whether or not the Indians were rational beings with rights which should be respected. The philosophic basis of the facts presented in Chapters VI and VII is this: Casas and his school, standing for mercifulness towards the Indians, gradually won theoretical and official supremacy; Sepúlveda and his co-thinkers, maintaining that the Indians were irrational creatures and consequently fit only to be worked remorselessly for the production of lucre, gradually became factually (but nevertheless illegally) supreme.[30]

Thought, therefore, had to conform to the Church's doctrines, but there were confusing and debilitating sets of doctrines at war with one another within the Church. The University of San Marcos had begun its career in 1551 as a Dominican school under the patronage of Charles I, but between 1574 and 1580 the University was separated from monastic control and set up in specially prepared quarters (still occupied) as a secular institution under the patronage of Philip II. Its finances soon fell into disorder and, in 1613, the Viceroy Marquis of Montesclaros valiantly endeavored to restore it to prosperity. The University suffered cruelly, however, from the competition of the schools maintained by the monastic orders (prone to squabble the one with the others) and by the Jesuits, and, in 1636, the University was fain to fill its empty lecture-rooms by permitting the divers religious corporations to found chairs for the teaching of this or that brand of theology, with the proviso that they bring their scholars thither to hear lectures. As a result of this the University degenerated into a mere theological seminary which was too often disturbed by brawls between the various monkish clans.[31]

In the eighteenth century financial depravity added itself to the older evil forces and venality came to rule the giving of degrees. A servile snobbery, which Sr. Barreda describes most pungently, filled the University in all its functions. One form of it was the custom of giving to quite ordinary men who chanced to be viceroys high degrees and loads of fulsome flattery set forth in abominable poetry. Various efforts were made to raise the tone of the University by excluding from it all save persons of pure Spanish blood and legitimate birth. This movement began under the Viceroy Count of Castellar (reigned 1674–1678), but Mestizos and persons of Negro blood continued to flock to San Marcos, especially to its courses in medicine. The racial restriction was repeated, however, by the Viceroy Count of la Monclova (1689–1705) and by the Viceroy Marquis of Villagarcía (1736–1745), and, all that failing to win obedience, Royal decrees were issued in 1752 and 1768 which had for their purpose the exclusion of all but white folk of legitimate birth.[32] These efforts, as to whose intrinsic excellence it is difficult to judge, had but little effect, partly because some of the highest in the land had Indian blood in their veins, partly because, in any case, anthropological determinations were vague and racial prejudice not rancorous.

The background of intellectual life, whose history I have endeavored to outline, was not precisely stimulating. There was, as I have indicated, a general opposition to all new ideas, so that independent thinkers from Roger Bacon and Ramón

Lull down through Bruno, Descartes, Leibnitz, and Newton to the Encyclopædists, met strenuous opposition from the orthodox teaching orders which, of course, still quarrelled among themselves on theological questions of profoundest unimportance.

There are, however, bright spots even in the general intellectual gloom of the viceregal period. Two Jesuits, Father José de Acosta (in Peru from 1569 to 1583) and Father Bernabé Cobo (in Peru, 1599–1657), were wholly admirable men moved by an authentically scientific spirit. The first-mentioned was, in addition to being a great historian and a student profoundly versed in such Natural History as was available in his time, a celebrated teacher of the young. Father Cobo, besides being one of the four best Chroniclers of Peru, enriched the world with permanently valuable accounts of the animal and vegetable kingdoms as represented in Peru and other American regions which, in his long journeys, he visited.[33] Two men such as they would have adorned any country of their day.

There was also a pleasant calendrical incident set on foot by Pope Gregory XIII (Ugo Buoncompagni) in a Bull dated February 13th, 1582, wherein he ordered that the Julian calendar be abandoned in favor of a new calendar, which we use today. This was made necessary because the Julian calendar had got sadly out of kilter with the movements of the sun and the moon. The first piece of printing ever issued in Peru was produced by Antonio Ricardo, in 1584, at Lima, and it was Philip II's Pragmatic, dated from Aranjuez on May 14th, 1583, in which His Majesty ordered obedience to the Pope's commands. The Pragmatic reached Lima on April 19th, 1584, and it was proclaimed on April 26th, Ricardo's printed edition being a part of the publication of the reform. In accordance with Pope Gregory's ideas, King Philip ordered his subjects to omit the dates between October 4th and October 15th, 1583, passing directly from the first to the second of those dates. He knew, however, that time and distance would prevent his American subjects from doing this in 1583, and so he ordered that they do it at the corresponding time in 1584. Nothing could have been more sane.[34]

Father Cobo was the last important naturalist to flourish in Peru for a century after his death. Even so simple a thing as the circulation of the blood, demonstrated by William Harvey in 1628, and long since accepted in Spain, was not recognized in Peru until 1723. Against the deep-rooted, but moribund, scholasticism of the Church not even such able naturalists as Cosme Bueno (1711–1798) and José Eusebio de Llano Zapata (about 1720–1790), both of whom went to Nature for their facts rather than to musty volumes bound in vellum, could make any real headway. These two were, however, harbingers of a new day whose dark dawning concerns us not at present. Symptomatic, also, was the expulsion of the Jesuits in 1767, whose going left the monastic orders to crumble into the dust of the ancient pundits to whom they had clung too closely and too long.[35]

4. Belles Lettres

Belles Lettres, particularly poetry, formed an integral and rather important part of colonial life. Already I have quoted, on page 21, the rather feeble doggerel which inaugurates Peruvian poetry. I hope some day to study the literary history of viceregal Peru in full, but at present I can do no more than to present a very brief outline of its main trend.

In the sixteenth century most of the verse was religious or laudatory—and extremely dull. There was, besides, some vigorous martial poetry, notably the little known "Nueva obra y breve . . . sobre la muerte del . . . Adelantado Don Diego de Almagro."[36] It is a stirring and virile, if also rough-hewn, composition by a fervent adherent of Almagro, and it is redolent of battle-fields and of camp life. Written in the 1540s or a little later, it was never printed until modern times.[37] Besides this poem there were many other soldierly verses, mostly short and sententious, by Carvajal and various other bold spirits who sang of the warlike events in which they took part.[38]

Some decades later there was written a more ambitious poem in three books, entitled "El Marañón." Its author was Don Diego de Aguilar y Córdoba, who lived in Huánuco, but who, in 1603 and 1607, was corregidor of Huamanga. Although finished in 1578, the poem was given a new introduction dated 1596. The subject-matter is the series of heroic and tragic events which befell during the various expeditions into the Amazon country. The poem itself has not been published, but some of the laudatory stanzas which precede it, notably an exquisite sonnet by Father Cabello de Balboa, have been printed. Cabello, in addition to being a great historian, was an able literary man, author of two poetic or perhaps dramatic pieces called "La Comedia de el Cuzco" and "La Vazquirana," both much praised in his day, but since lost.[39]

A writer of considerable renown in the first years of the seventeenth century was Don Diego de Ávalos y Figueroa, a native of Écija in Spain but long resident in Peru. He wrote the "Miscelánea Austral" and the "Defensa de Damas," printed by Antonio Ricardo in Lima in 1602. The first of these works is a miscellany, partly in prose, partly in verse, in which colloquies between Delio (Ávalos) and Cilena (his wife, Doña Francisca de Briviesca y Arellano) are sustained wherein they treat of subjects so various as love, the origin of finger-rings, music, bezoar-stones, the architecture of the Incas, the meaning of dreams, and the bird-life of Peru; these are interestingly, and often very beautifully, described.[40]

Among the poets of the early seventeenth century Don Diego Mexía de Fernangil is most typical of his time. He wrote a poetical work in two parts called "Parnaso Peruano" of which only the First Part has been published, the Second Part being still in manuscript.[41] Born in Seville about 1565, Mexía went to America about 1585 and, after some preliminary wanderings, settled in Lima as a bookseller. Between 1596 and 1599 he made an exciting journey to Mexico and back again to Lima, during which time, we may suppose, he finished Part One and sent it to Seville for publication. About 1609 he lost a good proportion of his considerable wealth and, as was so natural in those days, he went up to Potosí to repair his fortunes. He remained there until 1617, and, among other activities, he was controller of the book-trade for the Inquisition. It was there that he finished Part Two and dedicated it to the Viceroy Prince of Esquilache.

Part One of the "Parnaso Peruano" is a series of paraphrases or adaptations of some of Ovid's less lewd lucubrations; the Second Part is far more thrilling for modern readers because it is less "classical" and far more rich in matters referring to Peruvian history than the First Part, albeit there is much heavy piety in it as well. Nevertheless, my examination of it convinces me that, in spite of dreary passages, it contains much of great value and likewise a deal of real poetic beauty.[42]

Associated with Mexía was a writer known to fame as "Clarinda" who composed a long, but readable, panegyric in verse wherein famous writers ancient and recent were lauded, Mexía himself included. This "Discurso en loor de la Poesía" makes it plain that its author possessed great erudition. Until 1899 no one questioned the femininity of Clarinda, whose work precedes the First Part of Mexía in the 1608 edition of the "Parnaso Peruano." The current belief is that Mexía wrote the Discurso himself, pretending that it was by a woman, thereby indulging a very human tendency towards auto-laudation.[43]

If "Clarinda" was, after all, Mexía and so of the male sex, "Amarilis" was certainly a woman. She lived in Huánuco, a descendant of the first settlers of that city, and from there she wrote an Epistle to the great Lope de Vega entitled "Amarilis a Belardo." It is full of platonic, but not always particularly tepid, admiration for the famous Spaniard, and it is a charming piece of work in which, with girlish candor, she tells the object of her interest all about her belovéd sister, Belisa (Isabel), and all about herself. Nothing could be more exquisitely feminine than this fair disciple of the Muses. Her verse, in addition to being gracious and polished, is highly entertaining.[44]

At the very end of the best period of Peruvian colonial literature comes a very interesting writer named Don Rodrigo de Carvajal y Robles. He was of gentle birth and a native of Antequera, in Spain. Arriving in Peru about 1599, he devoted himself during many years to the service of his King, chiefly in military matters but also in administrative posts. His career being what it was, we need not be surprised that his most celebrated work, "Poema Heroyco del Assalto y Conquista de Antequera," first published by Geronymo de Contreras in Lima in 1627, should be of a martial and virile tone. A later work of his, "Fiestas que celebró la Ciudad de los Reyes del Piru, al nacimiento del Serenissimo Principe Don Baltasar Carlos de Austria . . .," was printed by Contreras in Lima in 1632, at the expense of the city government. It also is a vigorous and interesting work.[44a]

It is well now to take a brief look at letters as they were in the northern and southern portions of the area which concerns us during the first century or so of Spanish occupation. In the region of Quito, then, the first important writer was Don Lorenzo de Cepeda, brother of the celebrated Santa Teresa de Jesús. He lived in Quito from 1550 to 1567, holding high office there. His wife, Doña Juana de Fuentes, was a native of Trujillo in Peru. Although of the pietistic sort, his verse is excellent and possesses a quality of fervent mysticism enriched by philosophy altogether becoming to the brother of a Saint.[45]

The people of the Audience of Charcas (alias La Plata or Chuquisaca—now Bolivia) were so taken up with hunting for sudden wealth in mines that one can hardly expect much literature from them. Nevertheless, at least two distinguished authors did live among them. One, Don Enrique Garces, a native of Portugal, lived many years in Potosí, dividing his energies between mining and such labors as translating into Spanish the "Lusiads" of Camoens, the songs and sonnets of Petrarch, and the work of Francisco Patricio, who, in 1519, had written a book in Latin on the subject of government.[46] Garces, as was natural, took much interest in matters connected with mining, and in a poem modelled on Petrarch and addressed to Philip II, he complains of the vexations suffered by the colonists in the mining centres, particularly emphasizing the impurity of the silver money due to too great admixture with baser metals. He also addressed, in November, 1574, two letters on the same subject to the Viceroy Toledo and, as the great man paid no attention to them, he sent copies to the Council of the Indies—which paid no attention to them, either.[47]

Of much greater literary merit are the "Sagradas Poesías" of Don Luís de Rivera or Ribera, a Sevillean dwelling in Potosí. They were written for his sister, Sor Constanza María, a Conceptionist nun living in Seville. The verse of Rivera is chaste, and accurate in measure, and is devoted chiefly to religious or moral themes. In its way it is very good.[48]

Although the justly celebrated epic poem, "La Araucana," by Don Alonzo de Ercilla y Zúñiga may be regarded as a most important representative of viceregal Peru's literature, I mean to say naught of it here beyond stating that the First Part, written in Chile during the warfare against the Araucanians, is, to me, by far the most vigorous and most beautiful. Ercilla wrote it in the field, using whatever crude substitutes for paper came his way, and in the midst of desperate military adventure. The leader of the enterprise was Don García Hurtado de Mendoza, son of the Viceroy Marquis of Cañete, and the time was from 1556 to 1561.[49]

Naturally enough Ercilla, who enjoyed great and well-deserved fame in his own day and ever since, had many imitators. Of these I shall mention only one, Don Juan de Miramontes Zuázola, author of "Armas Antárticas." It was dedicated to the Viceroy Marquis of Montesclaros (reigned 1607–1616) and its chief merit, aside from its splendidly vigorous versification, is the liveliness of its subject matter; for it deals in a most informative way with the Incas, the Conquistadores, the Pirates, Volcanoes, and the "Lutheran" enemies of Spain. The history of Peru, poetically treated, is the very substance of this epic which contains many really beautiful passages.[50]

Also belonging to that period was the author of a superbly emotional, but very uneven, epic. The poet was Friar Diego de Ojeda (or Hojeda), and his poem is "La Cristiada." Very young he came to Peru against his parents' will and in the humble guise of a peddler. In 1591, in Lima, he was made a monk of Saint Dominic, and he remained in Peru—at Lima, Cuzco, and Huánuco—until his death at Huánuco on December 24th, 1615.[51]

"La Cristiada" is undoubtedly a splendidly fervent and sincerely pious epic, interpretative of the Catholic conception of Christ's personality and significance. In it there are innumerable deeply felt passages of real beauty. At the same time there are other passages which are either arid and prosaic or else of regrettable taste, albeit produced by the religious attitude of the time. In one such place Queen Elizabeth is described as being born of abominable incest and of schismatic blood, which is quite as unpleasant in one way as Spenser's bracketing of the same lady with the Godhead is in another. Yet, on the whole, the good in the poem far outweighs the bad, and it may be regarded as one of the best religious poems in the Spanish language.[52]

In 1630 the literary disease variously known as Gongorism, Culturanism, or Conceptism, and comparable in some ways with the *préciosité* which affected French literature or with the Marinism which harmed Italian letters, entered Peru. Gongorism and its congeners spring, I think, from the same psychological foundation as Baroque architecture, and, like the latter, spread far a very uninvigorating influence. As for Gongorism in particular, it is well to remark here that it had its roots in the work and ideas of Fernando de Herrera (?1534–1597) and that it was brought to its final form by the Cordovan poet Luís de Argote y Góngora (1561–1627) who, in his later works, deliberately employed an intricate, metaphorical, and esoteric style of phraseology intended to be understood only by the initiate, that is, the upper class as contrasted with the ordinary run of humanity. Góngora—he preferred to be known by his mother's name—exercised a deplorable influence over Spanish letters for more than a century.[53]

As can be readily imagined, viceregal Peru offered to Gongorism a soil in which that noxious plant could run wild once it took root. And it did! The ominous crop was first sown in a poem by a Franciscan, Friar Juan de Ayllón, entitled "Poema de las fiestas que hizo el convento de San Francisco de Jesús, de Lima, a la canonización de los veyntitres Martyres de Xapon . . ."—the rest of the endless title may be omitted in the name of common sense.[54] This hideously unreadable composition has all the faults of high-flown metaphor, obscure imagery, pseudo-erudition, and bombastic diction which characterize other works influenced by the worst in Góngora's productions. That influence, taking no account of Góngora's lovely and comprehensible earlier work, but only of his lamentable later manner, cast a blight over Peruvian letters which lasted for more than a century.

By a strange paradox which always astonishes students of Peruvian literature Góngora's chief champion in Peru was Don Juan de Espinosa Medrano, called "el Lunarejo" (Fellow-with-a-spot-in-his-face), whose own style was clear as a mountain brook. Espinosa was born in the remote sierra province of Aimaraes (west of Cuzco) in 1632, and at the age of thirty he published his celebrated "Apologético" in favor of Góngora. Well written itself, it defended the worst of pedantic poetry and its sole result was to confirm and strengthen the rising harvest of execrable verses.[55]

Only one important poet of the century or more following the advent of Gongorism demands attention here. He was Don Juan del Valle y Caviedes, usually known by his last name. He lived from about 1653 to 1694. Unlike the writers hitherto noticed, he made no pretensions to learning nor even to conventional respectability. Born of decent parents, from whom he had a considerable fortune, he led a riotous life in the course of which he acquired a venereal taint. He married in spite of it, and his wife died young. After that, beginning about 1681, he was tenant of a booth for the sale of cheap

FIG. 27. Bed of the seventeenth century in the Churrigueresque style; pictures, wall shelf and stool of same period.

FIG. 28 (*above*). Low table of carved Peruvian cedar, brown in color, eighteenth century.

FIG. 29 (*below*). A settee in French Academic style, green and gold, eighteenth century.

All three by courtesy of Mrs. F. B. Freyer.

trifles, one of those squalid stalls which at that time lined the front of the viceregal palace, dimming its splendors not a little. He was the first of those bitterly hating, witty, vitriolic, scurrilous, but brilliant satirical writers of whom Peru has had so many since his day. His literary roots were Quevedo and the picaresque (criminal class) novel, although he did not know it, being uneducated. His phobias were many —a detestation of doctors even more sharp than that of Molière being among them. He was a thorough low-lifer, a drunkard, and all kinds of a reprobate; but his poetry is a thousand times more vital and more readable (adults only!) than all the rest of Peruvian colonial literature put together. In the satirical portion of his work, entitled "Diente de Parnaso" (Tooth of Parnassus), and dedicated "To Death," appear those peppery and savage verses in which he flayed society in general and the medicine men in particular. Most of his verses would be banned in Boston, as it were.

In the second group of Caviedes's poems, the "Poesías diversas", the japing horse-laugh is present still, but with it there are some entirely different verses which show that the man was more than a salacious clown. His stanzas on his wife's death have a deep and reverent tenderness. His anguish when he cries, "My Sun! My Sun has died!" is very moving. Again, in "Lamentaciones sobre la vida en pecado" (Laments for a Life of Sin) there are exquisite verses in which he shows how brooks, mountains, flowers, fishes, birds, and animals are all his superiors in worth because they have praised God, and he never has done so. Saint Francis of Assisi would have rejoiced in such a poem of humility and repentance.[56]

Caviedes represented that dolorous age wherein the Hapsburg monarchy of the Spains, feebly headed by the almost-imbecile Charles II, was rushing towards the blackest of shadows. As already indicated, the advent of the Bourbons and of French culture brought a renewal of vigor to Spain and her colonies, in both political and economic ways as well as cultural. The new influences did not, however, immediately make themselves felt in Peruvian letters; indeed, during the early decades of the eighteenth century, some of the silliest and most wearisome rubbish ever written was produced in Lima. The perpetrators of it were, among others, the Viceroy Marquis of Castell-dos-Rius and his "Academy" of cronies whose highly artificial and pedantic lucubrations are set forth in the already cited "Flor de Academias." The Viceroy was wont, during 1709 and 1710, to hold Monday-evening assemblies in the palace where he and his aristocratic or erudite guests diverted themselves and a select society with exercises in versification that were unmatched for general idiocy. The sad part of all this was the fact that, had they been spared the calamitous influence of Gongorism, some of the Academicians might have been fairly praiseworthy men of letters.

Even as it was, two of the group demand some notice here. Don Luís Antonio de Oviedo Herrera y Rueda, Count of la Granja (1680–1717), wrote two poems which, amid the gloom of imbecility surrounding them, shine with some lustre. The earlier was "La Vida de Santa Rosa de Santa María," a long poem which purposes to describe the terrestrial career and celestial ecstasies of Isabel Flores y Oliva, known to hagiology as Saint Rose of Lima, patroness of the Americas.[57] Incidentally, the poem of Granja contains many striking references to pirates and various events in Peruvian history. Granja's other poem, "Poema Sacro de la Pasión de Nuestro Señor Jesucristo," is a frightfully long and prosaic effort vastly inferior to "La Cristiada" of Ojeda.[58]

The other important member of the Viceregal Academy was a man of more than usual capacity in several directions, Don Pedro de Peralta Barnuevo (1663–1743). In a way he was a tragic figure, a Leonardo da Vinci lost and stifled in the miasma of bad taste which choked the intellectual life of Lima in his time. His linguistic attainments were remarkable: He knew Italian, French, English, Latin, Greek, and Quechua perfectly. Also he had wide knowledge of mathematics, astronomy, metallurgy, civil and military engineering, nautical science, and history. In all this he resembles that other and even more versatile intellectual figure of the eighteenth century, Count Gianrinaldo Carli, of Capodistria, and, like the amazing Italian, he is almost forgotten by the modern world of narrow-visioned specialists. I call Peralta a tragic figure because it is clear that, if he had been born either in the expansive and virile atmosphere of the Italian renaissance or anywhere in Europe a century after his day, he would have impressed his personality indelibly on the page of history.

As a poet Peralta is noticeable chiefly because his Muse—albeit fat with collops of Gongorism (the malady is catching!)—was infinitely more vivacious than those of his poetaster contemporaries. Poems of his which should be named here are: "Lima Triumfante" (1708), a wearisome literary concourse at the University, typical of the snobbery mentioned above; "El Templo de la Fama vindicado" (1720), and "Historia de España vindicada" (1730), both intensely dull and Gongoristic. Least forgotten and best of his poems is "Lima Fundada."[59] It seeks to do what Miramontes had done in "Armas Antárticas" more than a century earlier. The older poem is much better, "Lima Fundada" being abominable as poetry and unreliable as history. In this we see a part of Peralta's tragedy—he aspired to be a poet, but could not because of the Gongoristic poison which worked within him all uncomprehended by himself. Still worse, his poetical ambitions somehow managed to obscure his undeniable gifts in other directions, so that he gained but little lasting renown from them.

Near the end of his life he published his "Pasión y triunfo de Cristo" (1738) which caused him to be haled before the Inquisition. Although, during the legal process which followed, he was dubbed "a presumptuous liar," he was not jailed—there being naught in the poem for which to imprison him—and, in 1743, he died, embittered and disillusioned.[60]

One more poet of viceregal Peru claims our attention, Don Pablo de Olavide y Jáuregui (1725–1803). In him, at last, we perceive that a new day was dawning, even in Peru. At seventeen he was already a Doctor of Canon Law and Oidor of the Audience of Lima. It was the great earthquake of October, 1746, which sealed him to fame; for, amid all the horror and grief thereupon attendant, he played the part of an active and merciful official, doing all that he could for the victims and handling vast sums of charitable moneys with utter integrity. Not long after his noble work in that connection he was summoned to Madrid where his brilliant and distinguished person won him not only powerful friends but also a very rich wife. He found a patron in the liberal minister, Count of Aranda, and for many years the Olavides held a salon where liberal ideas from France ran freely. At the end of the period which here concerns us he was in France, among the Encyclopædists, having been made to suffer greatly by the Inquisition. There I shall leave him—until another occasion. Olavide is important for us in that his life bridged the gulf between traditional, viceregal Peru and the new Peru which blossomed after 1780.[61]

Notes to Chapter IX

[1] Means, 1931, pp. 80–83, 108–113, 124–126, 192–197, 200–202, 228–229, and 524–535.

[2] "Greco-Roman" is a misnomer as there is no perceptible Greek influence in it. "Roman" and "Roman-Classical" would be better terms. On the whole, however, it is more convenient to call it the "Herreran" style, after Juan de Herrera, chief architect of the Escorial.

[3] The Escorial was built between 1563 and 1584, its first architect being Juan Bautista de Toledo, who was followed, after his death, by his disciple, Juan de Herrera.

[4] Readers desirous of going more thoroughly into the subject of Spanish architectural styles may find the following citations to be of help: Lampérez y Romea, 1908–1909, especially, II, pp. 622–653; Lampérez, 1915 and 1922; Haupt, 1927, pp. 126–146; Byne and Stapley, 1917; Briggs, 1913, Ch. xiv, and Briggs, 1929; Sedgwick, 1925, Ch. xxii.

[5] H. Fuentes, 1905, pp. 161–163.

[6] H. Fuentes, 1905, pp. 163–165, tells us a little about the history of this building. Still more data will be found in Anales del Cuzco, 1901, especially at pp. 123–125, where, under date of July, 1654, we are told that the finishing of the long-delayed work was due to the Bishop Dr. Don Juan Ocón and to Dr. Arias de la Cerda, whom the Viceroy Marquis of Mancera had appointed as head of the works, in February, 1641.

[7] Anales del Cuzco, 1901, p. 125.

[8] Anales del Cuzco, 1901, pp. 125–126. The church was so well built that

the terrible earthquake which devastated Cuzco on March 31st, 1650, did it no harm. It was a very costly edifice, however, among the sums going to defray the expense being six annual donations of 150,000 ducats (over $300,000), a total of close on $1,800,000, derived in equal parts from the King's moneys, from the encomenderos, and from the Indians of the diocese. One of the viceroys is said to have remarked that it would have been cheaper to make the cathedral out of silver!

9 Fuentes, 1905, pp. 174–176. Anales del Cuzco, 1901, p. 104.

10 Anales del Cuzco, 1901, pp. 98–109. Fuentes, 1905, pp. 153–154.

11 Guido, 1925, Chs. vi and vii.

12 Here and there throughout the Andean countries and in those adjacent to them one finds modern buildings, whether public or private, deliberately planned along bi-racial lines, that is, with æsthetic elements derived from both the native and the intrusive architecture. Almost always they are hideous beyond measure, being neither one thing nor the other. Nevertheless, it may come to pass some day that architects deeply versed in both arts may arise and may, with good taste based on authentic knowledge, work out a harmony between the two arts so that their offspring shall be, not a mongrel, but a blend.

13 González Suárez, 1890–1903, IV, pp. 422–454, VII, pp. 128–131.

14 The reader will understand, of course, that in these brief remarks on colonial architecture I have touched only on the broad outlines of the subject. Throughout the length and width of the Andean area (Ecuador, Peru, Bolivia, and adjacent parts of Argentina and Chile) there are scores of buildings, public and private, clerical and secular, which reveal the architectural activities of the people there during the colonial period. Some day, let us hope, they will be adequately studied and described, and their contents, too —pictures, carvings, furniture, objects of art.

15 Means, 1931, Ch. xi; 1932. Full documentation will be found in these publications.

16 Recop. IV, XXV, i; IV, XXV, vi; VI, IX, xviii. (These are laws of Philip III and Philip IV, between 1602 and 1628.) See also: Cappa, 1889–1897, Vol. VII.

17 There are innumerable paintings throughout Ecuador, Peru, and Bolivia, mostly in churches but also in private houses and public buildings, which show the changes in the Incas' dress produced by the influence of the Spaniards. Those in the Jesuit Church and in the Church of Santa Ana, in Cuzco, are particularly interesting. It will be remembered that the Inca Titu Cusi, when receiving the Spanish envoy, Rodríguez, in 1565, wore garments made of blue damask and of crimson velvet, as well as others of more ancient type. (See pp. 111–114.)

18 Montell, 1925, and 1929, pp. 237–244, gives valuable data on this subject.

19 The quero or cup has been studied and described by Saville, 1929.

20 Owing to the bubble-like trend of the Stock Market in the Autumn of 1929—and ever since—I no longer own the small but choice collection of such pieces that I formerly had. Some of my things were long displayed in the Museum of Fine Arts, Boston, where they were much admired, but all my

efforts to trace them to their present owners in the hope of obtaining photographs have failed. I particularly regret a magnificent bed-spread of cotton tapestry (with over 300 weft threads to the inch) decorated with charming painted designs in sepia (perhaps intended to be embroidered).

21 Crenshaw, 1928. It was my privilege, in days gone by, to wander at will through the extremely beautiful Lima palace of my old friend, Dr. Don Javier Prado y Ugarteche. A score or more of large and stately rooms were judiciously filled with Peruvian antiquities representing all periods from the earliest to the dawn of the republican era. There was, besides, an unsurpassed library of books on Peru among which, with that noble and generous hospitality so universal in Peru among all classes, Dr. Prado allowed me to browse during many happy hours. The apartments furnished with colonial objects made an impression of overwhelming magnificence. I particularly remember a huge wardrobe from Cajamarca, of the late sixteenth or early seventeenth century, whose front was a mass of amazingly intricate and beautifully executed carving. The design, as I remember it, was a perfect blend of Indian and Spanish embellishment. There were scores of other impressive examples of Peruvian art during the viceregal period—furniture, silver, paintings, carvings, fabrics, and objects of art in general. Unfortunately this superb assemblage of exquisite things was destroyed.

22 Cobo, Bk. IV, Ch. xvii, describes a plant called achupalla in Quechua and chulu in Aymará (Colla) which closely resembles the Spanish piña or pineapple. In Bk. VI, Ch. vii, he describes the chirimoya. See also: Acosta, Bk. IV, Ch. xix. On the whole, I think it is likely that either the achupalla or the chirimoya inspired this charming motif, in which case the Indian influence was decidedly present.

23 H. Fuentes, 1905, p. 180.

24 The bad condition of the paintings beside the pulpit, the chicken-coop-like glass screen in front of it, and the utterly tasteless disposition of the electric lights are all typical of the treatment given to works of art in Peru in far too many instances. If that country would but enter upon a well-planned programme for the proper care and presentation of her immense treasures of beauty and interest, she would have a much larger—and more lucrative—tourist traffic than she now does.

25 Crenshaw, 1928, legend for Figure 4.

26 Poor Chippendale! The Encyclopædia Britannica rightly says that his ideas were "remorselessly plundered." So they were, far and wide, for I have seen an almost exact replica of this settee in Palma de Mallorca, where it had been made by a local craftsman from plans acquired God knows how. This suggests an interesting possibility: It was said above, on p. 226, that, as a result of Charles III's liberal commercial policy, Palma was one of the ports empowered to ship goods to Spanish America. (See also: Bertrand, 1929, I, pp. 338–341.) It is at least conceivable—although not provable—that Mrs. Freyer's Peruvian-Chippendale settee and the Mallorcan-Chippendale settee which I saw were both made in Mallorca. But, in the absence of certain knowledge, it is well to assume that the settee here shown was made in Peru.

27 All this is revealed by a careful reading of the Cédula of January 25th, 1569, whereby Philip II established the Inquisition in Peru. See: Medina,

1887, I, pp. 19–28. The first Inquisitors arrived in Panama on August 15th, 1569, reached Paita on September 16th, and Lima November 28th. By early February, 1570, they had begun their labors. See: Moses, 1914, I, pp. 331–333. We have here an exact measure of the time-space complex: it took a full year for the King's will to make itself active in Peru.

28 See: Moses, 1914, I, pp. 371–374.

29 Moses, 1914, I, pp. 348, 376–377.

30 Barreda y Laos, 1909, pp. 75–106. One of the upholders of the rights of the Indians was Father Francisco de Victoria, author of various theological works in the 1550s and 1560s, all listed by Palau. This was not the same man whom we noticed above, on p. 222, as broadmindedly combining the functions of a bishop with those of a contrabandist.

31 Prado, 1894, pp. 87–97; 1918, pp. 35–48. Barreda, 1909, pp. 142–160 and 197–225. Moses, 1914, I, pp. 328–329, and II, pp. 315–316.

32 Barreda, 1909, pp. 290–304.

33 Barreda, 1909, pp. 111–141. Means, 1928, pp. 287–295, 349–357.

34 Medina, 1916. Hayward, 1931, pp. 289–290.

35 Mendiburu, 1874–1890, II, pp. 91–92; V, pp. 109–114. Barreda, 1909, pp. 305–326.

36 It is printed on pp. 369–389 of Enríquez, 1889. See: Menéndez y Pelayo, 1911–1913, II, pp. 135–137; L. A. Sanchez, 1921, pp. 19–21.

37 Menéndez, in the place cited, tells us that the original MS. is in the Archives of the Indies.

38 Menéndez, II, pp. 137–141. Sanchez, 1921, pp. 21–24.

39 The MS. of "El Marañón" was seen by Don Marcos Jiménez de la Espada in 1875, in the house of its then owner, Sr. Soto Posadas, of Asturias. Where it is now I know not. See: Mendiburu, 1874–1890, VIII, p. 412; Menéndez, II, pp. 141–143; García Calderón, 1914, p. 309; Sanchez, 1921, pp. 24–28; Means, 1928, pp. 320–321.

40 Medina, 1904–1907, I, pp. 57–63. Menéndez, 1911–1913, II, pp. 178–179. Palau, I, p. 135. Riva-Agüero, 1921, p. 87. Sanchez, 1921, pp. 47–49.

41 Part One of the "Parnaso Peruano" was published by Alonzo Rodríguez Gamarra at Seville, in 1608. Part Two, dated 1617, exists in the Bibliothèque Nationale, Paris (Espagnole, 599). García Calderón, 1914, p. 311, mis-dates it 1647.

42 Arana de Varflora, 1791, No. 1, p. 85. Menéndez, 1911–1913, II, pp. 165–170. García Calderón, 1914, pp. 310–311. Riva-Agüero, 1915, by far the best study of Mexía and his work. Sanchez, 1921, pp. 52–61.

43 Don Ricardo Palma, in his Introduction to the "Flor de Academias" (1899—see Note 56, below), expresses grave doubts as to the sex of this writer and the one next to be mentioned. Menéndez, 1911–1913, II, p. 152, accepts the femininity of the poet. Riva-Agüero, 1905, pp. 276–277, and Prado, 1918, p. 48, take a middle ground. García Calderón, 1914, pp. 310–311, suggests that Mexía invented the lady, and Sanchez, 1921, pp. 61–66, accepts this idea.

44 The Epistle, "Amarilis a Belardo" and Lope's rejoinder, "Belardo a Amarilis," were published in 1621 with Vega's "La Filomena" (Madrid, Viuda de Alonso Martín). The two Epistles were edited by Dr. M. A. Valdizán at

Lima in 1834. Menéndez, II, pp. 153–163, suggests that the authoress was Doña María de Alvarado, a descendant of Gomez de Alvarado who was brother to Pedro de Alvarado. Sanchez, 1921, pp. 136–145, with much more convincing argument, maintains that she was Doña María Tello de Lara y de Arévalo y Espinosa.

44a Our only source for the life of Carvajal y Robles is a paper drawn up by him at Lima on February 15th, 1624, now preserved in the Archives of the Indies and printed by Medina. Carvajal there tells us of his many services to the King and asks for the post of corregidor at Arica, Ica, Collaguas, or Paita. Later, he received the corregimiento of "Colesuyo," as it is called on the title-page of his later work; probably in truth it was Condesuyo, in the province of Arequipa. See: Medina, 1904–1907, I, pp. 258–261, 283–286; Menéndez y Pelayo, II, pp. 178–181; Sanchez, 1921, pp. 133–135.

45 Menéndez, 1911–1913, II, pp. 80–82.

46 Garces's translations of these three authors were brought out in Madrid in 1591, the Camoens and the Petrarch by Guillermo Droy, the Patricio by Luís Sanchez. Palau lists them all under the original authors' names.

47 Menéndez, 1911–1913, II, pp. 270–272, where important data on mining literature are given.

48 The "Sagradas Poesías" were first published by Clemente Hidalgo, in Seville, 1612, and again by Diego Flamenco, in Madrid, 1626. Both these early editions are exceedingly rare. Many of the poems were reprinted by Don Justo de Sancha in Biblioteca de Autores Españoles, XXXV, pp. 56–67 and 277–289 (Madrid, 1855). Arana de Varflora, 1791, No. 3, p. 92, incorrectly calls them "Rimas Sagradas." See: Menéndez, II, pp. 273–274.

49 The First Part of "La Araucana" was published in Madrid in 1569, the Second Part in 1578, and the Third Part in 1589. The first collected edition came out the next year. The definitive edition is the magnificent one edited by Don José Toribio Medina, Santiago, 1910–1918, in five volumes, with a superb biography of Ercilla and much valuable auxiliary material. For further data on Ercilla see: Menéndez, II, pp. 293–309. Sanchez, 1921, pp. 67–70; Moses, 1922, pp. 158–188.

50 The original MS. of "Armas Antárticas" is in the Biblioteca Nacional, Madrid (MS. No. 3,946), and there are copies of it in the Biblioteca Nacional, Lima, and in the library of Don Jacinto Jijón y Caamaño, in Quito. This scholar has brought out a charming edition (only 200 copies) of the poem in two volumes, Quito, 1921. Otherwise it has never been published in full that I know of. The best general study of Miramontes and his poem is that of Coronel Zegarra, 1879, first four instalments. See also: Menéndez, II, pp. 185–186; Sanchez, 1921, pp. 92–104; Moses, 1922, pp. 386–387.

51 Sanchez, 1921, pp. 105–128.

52 In addition to Sanchez, see: Arana de Varflora, 1791, No. 1, p. 85; Menéndez, II, pp. 169–171; Riva-Agüero, 1905, pp. 277–292; Rada y Gamio, 1917b. The first edition of Ojeda's (or Hojeda's) "Cristiada" was brought out at Seville by Diego Perez in 1611. It is extremely, rare. Various modern editions are cited by the authors already referred to. The best modern edition is that edited by Don Francisco Miquel y Badia, Madrid (Calpe), 1896, a sumptuous folio.

53 The sanest and clearest discussion of Gongorism known to me is that of Mérimée and Morley, 1930, pp. 224–234, where very ample citations are given. See also: Sedgwick, 1925, pp. 222–223; Entwhistle, in Ch. iv of Peers, 1929.

54 First edition, Lima, March, 1630, printed by Francisco Gómez Pastrana. See: Medina, 1904–1907, I, pp. 267–269; García Calderón, 1914, pp. 318–320; L. A. Sanchez, 1921, pp. 146–151, and 1927, p. 8.

55 Espinosa Medrano died in 1688. The first edition of the "Apologético" was published at Lima in 1662 by Juan de Quevedo y Zárate. In addition to that work, Espinosa, who lived at Cuzco for a time as rector of the cathedral, wrote three comedies in Quechua and Spanish and translated at least some of Virgil into Quechua. The best biography of Espinosa is Matto de Turner, 1887. See also: Mendiburu, 1874–1890, III, pp. 73–74; Sanchez, 1921, pp. 166–169.

56 The best edition of Caviedes's two groups of work will be found in "Flor de Academias," edited by Don Ricardo Palma, Lima, 1899, pp. 333–474. In that volume Palma includes an able study of the poet by Don Juan María Gutiérrez originally written for an earlier but less good edition, that in Don Manuel de Odriozola's *Documentos literarios del Perú*, Vol. V, Lima, 1873. Palma's edition of Caviedes is based on a MS. bought by the National Library of Lima from Don Felix C. Coronel Zegarra in 1898. See also: Menéndez, II, pp. 191–198; García Calderón, 1914, pp. 330–335; Prado, 1918, pp. 69–74; Sanchez, 1921, pp. 186–200; Moses, 1922, pp. 335–338.

57 In addition to the materials on the Academy provided by Palma in the "Flor de Academias" see: Menéndez, 1911–1913, II, pp. 198–203; García Calderón, 1914, pp. 344–345; Sanchez, 1921, pp. 205–213. A full bibliography—276 works—on St. Rose was prepared by Don Felix Coronel Zegarra and printed in the "Concurso literario en honor de Santa Rosa de Lima," Lima, 1886, pp. 61–133. The best study of Granja and his poem is Riva-Agüero, 1919.

58 Coronel Zegarra, 1879, pp. 597–613. Menéndez, II, pp. 203–207. Sanchez, 1921, pp. 214–248. Moses, 1922, 333–335. The first edition of the "Vida de Santa Rosa" was published in Madrid by Juan García Infanzón in 1711. The best modern edition is that edited by Manuel González de la Rosa, Lima, 1867, with a critical notice by Don Ricardo Palma. The first edition of the "Poema Sacro" was brought out in Lima by Francisco Sobrino, in 1717. See: Medina, 1904–1907, II, pp. 287–291.

59 Published in Lima by Francisco Sobrino y Bados, 1732, two volumes. Palau lists editions of all Peralta's works.

60 Mendiburu, 1874–1890, VI, pp. 264–267. Menéndez, 1911–1913, II, pp. 207–213. Riva-Agüero, 1910, pp. 291–345. García Calderón, 1914, pp. 340–345. Sanchez, 1921, pp. 249–264. Moses, 1922, pp. 383–386.

61 Mendiburu, 1874–1890, VI, pp. 136–145. Menéndez, 1911–1913, II, pp. 221–230 and 232–236. Sanchez, 1921, pp. 297–298. García Calderón, 1914, pp. 347–352.

CHAPTER X

CONCLUSIONS

THERE can be no doubt, I think, as to the relative practical merits of the Incaic system in Peru and of the Spanish colonial system which followed upon it. No one who examines the evidence regarding the two can fail to arrive at the conclusion that the subjects of the Incas were more free from oppression and misery than were their descendants under the Hapsburgs and the Bourbons.

Beyond doubt, the underlying explanation of this contrast was the money-complex—absent among the Incas and their subjects, omnipresent among the subjects of Spain. In previous pages I have accused the Kings of Spain and the Spaniards themselves of money-greed. I wish now to enlarge upon this point by saying that, although all the forms of avarice which money engenders in manifold ways were theirs, they were not theirs alone. They were and are common to all people whose civilization turns upon the money-complex as upon an axis, to all peoples who regard money as the sum of good and as the sole seriously-to-be-desired thing. True, when one passes in review the relations between the divers European nations and the several sorts of Indian societies with which they came in contact in America he sees the working of the money-complex at its most malignant development in Spanish America. But that fact is due, in my belief, not to any special covetousness on the part of the Spaniards, but simply to the accidental circumstance that the natives with whom they came in touch were at once the furthest advanced in civilization and the best provided with precious metals and precious stones. Any one who has travelled in Spain with an open mind and with a gracious attitude towards its people and their culture will agree with me in saying that nowhere has he encountered more kindly and more generous people, more dignified and considerate treatment, more general eagerness to make him feel at home, than he found in Spain. With the single exception of their attitude towards animals—which is one of indifference rather than downright cruelty and which existed also among the English until recent times—the Spaniards of all classes are people of almost universal kindliness, generosity, and uprightness in all their dealings. They have shown these qualities splendidly in the great political change through which they have recently passed and in the manner of their meeting the grave problems which still confront them.

Yet the ancestors of those same Spaniards, when plunged as Conquerors among the subjects of the civilized states of America, too often acted the part of vultures; so much so, indeed, that one wonders if their characters did not suffer some sort of sea-change by going to America. But, when he reflects upon certain phases of the relations between Christians and Moslems in Spain itself, one sees that money-lust and religious passion together explain the state of mind pre-induced among the Spaniards when brought into relationship with the Aztecs and the Incas.

At the same time, one perceives that the English, the Dutch, and the French would have been affected in much the same way as the Spaniards in like circumstances. Of all the European nations to colonize in America only the Swedes seem to have been relatively free from mercenary and fanatically religious motives, and their career in America, unhappily, was both short and of narrow scope.

As to the religious aspect of Spanish colonization in America one can only say—as all fair-minded historians have said—that there was much therein which was heroic and profoundly magnanimous. The missionary efforts of the Spaniards in America were at least as systematic and efficient as those which any other European folk would have been able to make. The endeavors of the Spanish churchmen—particularly of the period prior to about 1650—to bring the Peruvians into what they held to be the true Faith were earnest and surprisingly successful. True, the Christianity which they gave to their catechumens was often no more than a veneer, as indicated on pages 166–168, and is so still, but it was at any rate a more triumphant campaign than anything of the sort in English America.

Down to the middle of the seventeenth century, or, more accurately, to the end of Philip IV's reign (1665), there was a definite religious zeal on behalf of the Indians, both on the part of the Kings and their representatives in Peru and on that of the Church, a zeal which was, however, increasingly at odds with corruption arising from one aspect or another of the money-complex. This conflict concerned the Kings themselves; for, although Charles I and Philip II were prolific in legislation designed to foster Catholicism among their American subjects, they were equally prolific in measures designed to extract money from their ultramarine possessions. In short, they and their officials were perennially torn between the impulse towards Christian benevolence and the impulse towards wealth-collecting. The former was vigorously sustained by such noble and intelligent churchmen as Friar Rodrigo de Loaysa, Saint Toribio de Mogrovejo, Saint Francis Solano, and Father Bernabé Cobo—not to mention countless other devoted men who never won fame—but, among the clergy as a whole, there was a rising tide of laxity, greed, and misrule which caused the conditions described in Chapter VII to come into being and which, under Philip III and Philip IV, gradually engulfed most of the laudable activities of the Church in Peru.

Parallel with that laxity among the clergy there was an analogous laxity among the Crown's officials of all ranks, a laxity which existed side by side with ideals of the highest moral quality. These ideals have been concretely described on at least three occasions in this book, viz.: on pages 141–142, where Vargas Machuca's sketch of the ideal for the soldiers of the Indies is set forth; on pages 144–147, where Escalona y Agüero outlines the obligations of the Royal officials;

and pages 197–198, where Father Atienza's remarks on the peculiar responsibilities of the clergy are mentioned. Moreover, in Chapters VII to IX there are numerous adverse criticisms of the conduct and methods of Spanish functionaries, from viceroys and prelates down to corregidores and parish priests, criticisms which, being mainly the utterances of Spaniards, indicate that political and ecclesiastical ideals were by no means wanting among the more reflective Spaniards.

As Don Julián Juderías has observed in his powerful book, "La leyenda negra" (The Black Legend), there has been for centuries a flood of denigratory comment about Spain, her people, and their civilization, a flood proceeding from both non-Spanish and Spanish sources. The fact which I wish to stress here is one which Sr. Juderías seems largely to overlook, namely, that as fast as Spaniards committed crimes and blunders in America other Spaniards brought them—or tried to do so—to the government's attention. Nor were the exposers of abuses usually of the frenzied type represented by Bishop de las Casas. Other churchmen, far more serene in their judgments and much more practical in their suggestions, Friar Rodrigo de Loaysa, and Lope de Atienza, begin in these pages the long series of Spanish critics of Spanish rule in Peru. They, and most of those critics who came after them, were men moved not only by a desire to chastise evildoers, but also —and more especially—by a wish to improve the methods and conditions of government. The reasons why critics of the sort indicated did not more often succeed in producing practical and beneficial results can be set forth under various headings.

First of all there was the character of the leaders and men who took part in the Conquest. In the early days leaders were too often of low social origins who, from having been nobodies and possessors of nothing at home, found themselves outstanding figures and owners of great wealth in Peru, with the consequence that they were enabled to act in the unpleasant ways typical of parvenus everywhere. Moreover, the conquerors and later settlers, whether of low or of high birth, were nearly all in Peru for one purpose only—the sudden acquisition of as much money as possible no matter by what methods. In earlier periods the energies of martially minded and fortune-seeking men had been absorbed by the wars of the Reconquest and by the campaigns of Charles in Italy and North Africa; but, on arriving in Peru, they found an alien folk of smaller powers of resistance and of unimagined wealth, so that they became more tyrannical in proportion as they learned to control the native Andeans and to rid them of their gold. At the same time, partisan strife between sundry groups of acquisitive invaders fomented vindictiveness and cruelty on the part of Spaniards against other Spaniards, thus giving rise to the deplorable internecine strife described in Chapters III and IV.

In the second place there was the lamentable contrast between the theory and the facts of colonial government. The Crown, at any rate theoretically, opposed all forms of abuse of the Indians. But its opposition thereto was partly vitiated by the Kings' own incessant demands for money and partly by the Crown's inability to give a practical interpretation to its will in colonial affairs. It is this last point which I wish to stress now. Scattered through these pages are references to what, for want of a less doctrinaire term, I have called the space-time complex. Here and there throughout the book will be found materials wherewith to measure its proportions and significance. Here I will say merely that the absolute King in Spain was separated from his subjects in Peru not only by some 7,000 miles of space but also by at least 8 months of time. This brings us to the fundamental weakness of the Hapsburg-Bourbon system in America. The Kings of those dynasties regarded Spain's possessions in America as their personal property, to be ruled precisely as they willed even in the minutest details. In other words, the Kings of Castile widely separated from the realms in question, pretended to rule as absolute monarchs vast territories and complicated populations which they never saw and which they never really understood. True, in actual practice, portions great or small of the absolute monarch's all-inclusive authority were delegated to various bodies and officials, as shown in Chapter V; but the Crown permanently alienated no part of its power and, in any case, continued to direct—or to try to direct—the multifarious business of colonial administration. Because of the inescapable functioning of the space-time complex, neither the King in Spain nor even his viceroy in Peru could maintain a well-informed and efficacious control over the affairs of that country. In truth, the self-styled "absolute" Kings of Castile were far from being absolute. Never were sovereigns more consistently set at naught by their servants and their subjects than were they. Sheltering behind the impenetrable wall afforded by the space-time complex, officials and settlers alike in Peru allowed full play to all the abuses arising from their ineradicable money-worship.

In the third place we must consider how great was the contrast between that condition and the one which had existed under the Incas. That peerless dynasty was far more truly absolute than any Hapsburg or Bourbon ever was even at home. The Inca Empire, before it grew overlarge (see Chapter I), was not only happy in being without the money-complex and its attendant sorrows, but also in being administered through an official hierarchy based on the soundest common sense and surmounted by a verily absolute sovereign rightly looked up to as superior to mankind in general.

Against those laudable emperors who, even to the end of their career, under the usurper Atahualpa, were justly held by their subjects to be worthy of all obedience, we must balance the sordid and money-needing figures of Charles I and Philip II, who were flouted by their subjects much oftener than they were obeyed. Add to these the later Hapsburgs, Philip III and Philip IV, stupid and impotent monarchs forever badgered by a lack of funds and ruled by unscrupulous ministers or favorites under whose misguidance glorious Spain decayed with increasing rapidity until, under that pitiable degenerate, Charles II, it reached the nadir of its fortunes.

Add, finally, the Bourbons, who, beginning with the woman-ruled Philip V, managed to ameliorate somewhat conditions both in Spain and in Spanish America, a process culminating in the reign of Charles III, who was at once the most liberal and the most intelligent of Spanish kings, a sovereign of whom any nation might well be proud. But even he, though he accomplished much, was incessantly hampered by that old enemy of absolutism, the space-time complex.

Adding all these Spanish kings together and weighing them against their mighty predecessors in Peru, how very greatly do the latter, moneyless and godlike, overbalance the former as regards civic virtue, social intelligence, and administrative efficiency! Indeed, the only European autocrat who even remotely approached the governmental competency of the Incas was Napoleon—and Fate willed that he be but one man, not a dynasty.

Not even the best of the viceroys of Peru, although present in the country, succeeded in ruling the land as well as the Incas had done; for they, also, were impeded in their efforts to govern well by the pervasive time-space complex. On pages 226–228 it was shown how signally the Spaniards failed to maintain communications equal in speed and binding force to those of the Incas. Moreover, the viceroys who followed upon the great Toledo lived almost entirely in Lima without making serious attempts to study the country at first hand, and the oidores were as negligent. The result was that corregidores generally did as they pleased in their own bailiwicks without fear of interference from Lima. Very rarely do we hear of condign punishment as being given to an erring corregidor by a viceroy or by an audience. The one case of the sort that comes to mind is that of Don Diego González Montero, Corregidor of Cañete, who, in January–February, 1631, was suspended from office and heavily fined for malfeasance, as set forth in the Diary of the Viceroy Count of Chinchón already referred to on page 255. Bright spots indicative of an occasional, but too rare, righteousness on the part of corregidores are: That excellent man who acted well in the matter mentioned on page 187; and the Corregidor of Cuzco who, with his people, helped to put the new Cathedral into good order, as told on page 261.

On the whole, however, it is clear that absolutist—or rather pseudo-absolutist—rule of the Spanish sort was not what Peru needed. The term "pseudo-absolutist" is here justified, not by the presence of anything even faintly resembling a parliamentary factor such as that which was increasingly potent in the England of Henry VIII, Elizabeth, and the Stuarts, or such as that in the Spain of Charles I and Philip II where parliamentarianism was progressing towards desuetude, but by the universal and systematic contumacy of the subjects of the would-be absolute kings.

What, then, would have served the people of colonial Peru better than the system of centralized control which the Hapsburgs and the Bourbons strove so unsuccessfully to maintain? The answer is, I think, feudalism, that is to say, a social system in which encomiendas converted into permanent feudal fiefs, whose lords would have possessed full seigneurial jurisdiction, would have given to the bi-racial society of viceregal Peru exactly what it required.

Let me illustrate this point with historical facts. What the Indians of Peru enjoyed under the Inca Emperors, whose memory they cherished so wistfully and so long after the Conquest, was paternalism. To be happy, Indians need a mode of life wherein work is reasonably proportioned to relaxation, both being governed by an intimate knowledge of the conditions on the part of the administrators. Had the encomienda become a permanent institution, they would have enjoyed anew paternalism of the kind best suited to them. Each encomendero would have been as an Inca in little to the people on his lands, ruling them through a hierarchy of officials benevolently modelled on that of the ancient Incas. Because the need for hurrying to acquire wealth—the major evil of the short-term encomienda—would have been absent from permanent fiefs, the whole attitude of the grantee towards his people would have been altered for the better. On receiving land and Indians from the Crown as a permanent guerdon, the encomendero would have perceived, and soon, that his fief in itself constituted great wealth and that the prosperity of his vassals was an integral part of his own. This principle was recognized as sound by the two greatest students of the matter, Don Antonio de León Pinelo and Don Juan de Solórzano Pereira, as well as by an imposing number of other well-informed men.

That pseudo-absolute monarch, Charles I, intensely unintelligent as he was in all that concerned the culture native to Peru (see pages 52–53), feared to be generous to the men who had won him Peru and its riches and so, allowing himself to be swayed by that insensate fanatic, Casas, prototype of the prohibitionist among our unhappy selves, he endeavored to abolish, or at least greatly to limit, the encomienda, thus drawing the Indians of Peru away from those who might easily have become their most vigilant protectors and bringing them into the Crown's direct control wherein the Indians inevitably suffered all the multitudinous wrongs arising from the improbity of the Crown's servants, money-hungry and protected by the space-time complex. As we have seen, Charles I was obliged to re-establish encomiendas, but both he and his successors did everything possible to render them impotent for good. Encomenderos who, if they had been permanent lords of vassals, would have dwelt among and benignly ruled their Indians, were not allowed to live in villages on their estates, nor to spend more than one night there at a time. They were bidden to reside in the nearest city. (Recopilación, Bk. VI, Titulo IX, Laws ix–xiv, laws of Charles I, Philip II and Philip III.)

Twice in the viceregal period of Peru a paternalistic system based upon permanent feudal fiefs came near to being established. The first occasion was when Gonzalo Pizarro seemed like to weld Peru into an independent monarchy in whose destiny both races would have shared. (See pages 81–96.) That opportunity slipped by, however, because Gonzalo lacked the requisite audacity and because the King recommenced the granting of short-term encomiendas. The second occasion lasted longer, namely from the reign of Philip II to that of Philip V, or from 1555 to 1720, at any moment of which long period the system of permanent fiefs could have been created. That salutary change was not made, because of the ever-increasing greed for power and wealth on the part of the Kings, none of whom had wit enough to perceive its merits.

The results of the change would have been these: The creole upper class, or at least an influential portion of it, would have become a territorial aristocracy of great political and social significance. The nobles, each one on his estate, would soon have learned the desirability of fostering the agriculture and the animal husbandry of their Indian peasants. These, in their turn, would have been made as industrious as their ancestors had been, knowing that, with the exception of a justly apportioned tribute to their lords, the product of their toil would go to their own betterment with naught to be feared from the rapacity of the Crown's servants. Under such conditions they would have become the great sustainers of commerce which Campillo and others (pages 192–193) wished to make them. Legitimate trade, subject to reasonable taxation, would have flourished and contraband trade would have been starved out of existence.

The Kings of Castile, being the imperfectly informed and unimaginative men most of them were, could not accept the judgments of their many advisers who urged this course upon them. The minor government (pages 153–165), instead of becoming the paternal instrument of permanent lords of productive lands and thriving peasants, became a goad in the hands of extortionate encomenderos and corregidores, each one out for all the pelf he could acquire during his short term in office, and each one daily betraying the distant king who was his theoretical master.

The change would have been so easy to make, would so greatly have strengthened those very Kings who dared not to make it, and came so near to being made against their wills that one cannot regard calmly its not having been made. In this tragic failure of the Crown to avail itself of the opportunity presented lies the great practical lesson of the colonial period. In the epoch following that examined in these pages the Indian question continued—and continues to this day— to be the crux of Peru's and her neighbors' problems. Today the Indian peasants of the Andean republics suffer as acutely from artificial and unnatural democratic or pseudo-democratic forms of government as ever they did from pseudo-absolutism. They still require that paternalistic governance which made the Inca dynasty shine forth among the rulers of all times. Perchance on some future occasion it will be possible for me to enlarge upon this point.

BIBLIOGRAPHY

BIBLIOGRAPHY

NOTE: This Bibliography is not designed to meet the requirements of Bibliophiles whose chief interest lies, not in the knowledge contained in books, but rather in the trifling details of dates, formats, types, colophons, collations, watermarks, etc. Intended primarily to be a list of the works cited in the foregoing pages, this Bibliography seeks also to aid students of history in finding the best sources of information regarding all aspects of the Viceroyalty of Peru, 1530–1780. The older sources have, as a rule, been indicated here by citing an early edition, usually the first edition, and by then citing one or more good and accessible modern editions. In those cases where older writers' works were not published until recent times the writers' approximate dates are indicated. In citing MS. material, whether still unpublished or not, I have endeavored to tell where it now abides. I have not attempted to list all editions of the various books and works, nor have I striven meticulously to reproduce the typographical vagaries of their title-pages, colophons, etc. Finally, it is well to mention here that the abbreviation, "Lic.," which precedes some authors' names, stands for Licenciado or Licentiate, a title borne by members of the legal profession and sometimes by other learned men.

ABBREVIATIONS OF PUBLICATIONS
(PERIODICALS AND OTHER SERIALS)

AA	*The American Anthropologist.*
BSGL	*Boletín de la Sociedad Geográfica de Lima.*
CDI	*Colección de documentos inéditos . . . del archivo de Indias.* (Madrid.)
CDIHE	*Colección de documentos inéditos para la historia de España.* (Madrid.)
CLDHP	*Colección de libros y documentos referentes a la historia del Perú.* (Lima.)
CLDRHA	*Colección de libros y documentos referentes a la historia de América.* (Madrid.)
CLERC	*Colección de libros españoles raros o curiosos.* (Madrid.)
GR	*Geographical Review.* (New York.)
HAHR	*Hispanic American Historical Review.* (Durham, N. C.)
JAP	*Journal de la Société des Américanistes de Paris.*
NCDIHE	*Nueva colección de documentos inéditos para la historia de España y de sus Indias.* (Madrid.)

NGM   *National Geographic Magazine.* (Washington.)

NYPL   *New York Public Library.*

RGI   *Relaciones Geográficas de Indias.* (Madrid.)

RH   *Revista Histórica.* (Lima.)

RMLP   *Revista del Museo de La Plata.* (La Plata, Argentina.)

RMN   *Revista del Museo Nacional.* (Lima.)

RP   *Revista Peruana.* (Lima.)

TCAAS   *Transactions of the Connecticut Academy of Arts and Sciences.* (New Haven.)

LIST OF WORKS

ACOSTA, Father José de:

1590   *Historia natural y moral de las Indias.* Seville. (Juan de León.)

1604   *The Naturall and Morall Historie of the East and West Indies.* Translated by E. G. [Edward Grimston]. London. (Edward Blount and William Aspley.)

1880   *The Natural and Moral History of the Indies.* (A re-issue of Grimston's translation.) Edited by Clements R. Markham. London. (Hakluyt Society.)

AGUIAR Y ACUÑA, Rodrigo de:

1628   *Sumarios de la Recopilacion general de las Leyes . . . para las Indias Occidentales . . .* Madrid. (Juan Gonzalez.)

AITON, Arthur Scott:

1927   *Antonio de Mendoza, First Viceroy of New Spain.* Durham, N. C.

ALBENINO, Nicolao de:

1549   *Verdadera relacion delo sussedido enlos Reynos eprouincias dl peru . . .* Seville. (Juan de León.)

1930   *Verdadera relacion* etc. Edited, and reproduced in facsimile of 1549 edition, by José Toribio Medina. Paris. (Institut d'Ethnologie.)

ALCAZAR, Cayetano:

1920   *Historia del Correo en América.* Madrid.

ALCEDO, Antonio de:

1812–1815   *The Geographical and Historical Dictionary of America and the West Indies.* Translated and edited by G. A. Thompson. London. 5 vols.

ALCEDO Y HERRERA, Dionisio de:

1741   *Compendio histórico . . . de Guayaquil.* Madrid. (Manuel Fernández.)

1915   *Descripción geográfica de la Real Audiencia de Quito.* Introduction by C. A. González Palencia. Madrid. (Hispanic Society of America.)

ALMANAQUE DE "LA CRÓNICA":

1918   Lima.

ALSEDO Y HERRERA, Dionisio; see ALCEDO Y HERRERA.

ALTAMIRA Y CREVEA, Rafael:
1913–1914   *Historia de España y de la Civilización Española.* Third edition, enlarged and improved. Barcelona. 4 vols.

ALVARADO, Pedro de:
1884   *Carta del Adelantado Pedro de Alvarado dando cuenta de la muerte de Pedrarias Dávila, e rafyriendo su expedición de Nicaragua al Perú.* (Dated at Puerto Viejo, 10 March, 1534.) CDI, XLI, pp. 513–518. Madrid.

AMAT–PARISH:
1775   *Relación histórica del Perú.* (The original of this document was prepared for the use of the Viceroy Don Manuel Amat y Junient in 1775 and it was copied by Sir Woodbine Parish, H. B. M., Minister in Buenos Aires, in 1830–1831. This copy is in the British Museum, Add. MSS. 19,573.)

1776   *Relación del estado del Perú en el gobierno del Exmo. Sor. Virrey Don Manuel Amat y Junient.* (Original document dated 1776 and copied by Sir W. Parish in 1830–1831. Copy in British Museum, Add. MSS. 19,572.)

AMUNÁTEGUI, Miguel Luis:
1862   *Descubrimiento i Conquista de Chile.* Santiago de Chile.

AMUNÁTEGUI SOLAR, Domingo:
1909–1910   *Las encomiendas de indíjenas en Chile.* Santiago de Chile. 2 vols.

ANALES DEL CUZCO, 1600–1750:
1901   Edited by Ricardo Palma. Lima.

ANDAGOYA, Pascual de: (Ca. 1490–1548.)
1865   *Narrative of the Proceedings of Pedrarias Dávila in the Provinces of Tierra Firme or Castilla del Oro.* Translated and edited by Clements R. Markham. London. (Hakluyt Society.)

ANDERSON, C. L. G.:
1911   *Old Panama and Castilla del Oro.* Washington.

ANONYMOUS:
1534   *Nouvelles certaines des Isles du Peru.* Lyons. (Françoys Juste.)

ANONYMOUS:
N.D.   *Noticias Chronologicas de la Gran Ciudad del Cuzco.* (Unpublished MS. in NYPL.)

ANONYMOUS:
1896   *St. Rose of Lima.* London. (Catholic Truth Society.)

ANONYMOUS CONQUEST:
1534   *La Conquista del Peru.* Seville. (Bartolome Perez.) (Unique printed copy in NYPL.)

ANONYMOUS CONQUEST (1534):
1929   *The Conquest of Peru.* (Reproduced in facsimile from 1534 edition and translated by Joseph H. Sinclair.) New York. (NYPL.)

ANONYMOUS CONQUEST (1534):
1930   *La Conquista del Peru . . .* Edited by Alexander Pogo. Proc. Am. Acad. Arts & Sci., LXIV, No. 8, pp. 177–286. Boston.

ANONYMOUS GREEK SOLDIER:
1625   *Casos notables, sucedidos en las costas de la ciudad de Lima . . . desde Iunio deste año passado de 1624.* (Extremely rare printed document of 4 pages in the Yale University Library.) Madrid. (Juan González.)

ANONYMOUS LETTER OF 1571:
1848   (Written from "Incai," i.e., Yucay, to a high official in Spain on March 16th, 1571.) Edited by Miguel Salvá and Pedro Sainz de Barranda. CDIHE, XIII, pp. 429–469. Madrid.

ANONYMOUS MANUSCRIPT (1628):
Los daños e ynconvenientes que a esta Ciudad de los Reyes se siguen de ser governados por Alcaldes Hordinarios y no por Corregidor como antiguamente lo havia son los siguientes . . . (Dated Lima, January 10th, 1628.) Br. Mus., Add. MSS. 13,977, fols. 242–247.

ANONYMOUS MANUSCRIPT: (ca. 1640.)
Discrición general del Reyno del Piru, emparticular de Lima. Bib. Nat., Paris, MSS., Esp. 280.

ANONYMOUS (i.e., John Campbell):
1741   *A Concise History of the Spanish America.* London.

ANONYMOUS:
1742   *Estado político del reyno del Perú.* (No title-page, nor colophon. P. 40 reveals date as 1742. See Note 76 on page 256.)

ANTUÑEZ Y ACEVEDO, Rafael:
1797   *Memorias históricas sobre la legislación, y gobierno del comercio de los españoles con sus colonias en las Indias Occidentales.* Madrid. (Sancha.)

ARANA DE VARFLORA, Fermín:
1791   *Hijos de Sevilla* . . . Seville. (Vazquez é Hidalgo.) (The real name of this author was Fernando Diaz de Valderrama.)

ARGÜELLO, Friar Thomás de:
1681   (Five tracts about *Moneda de vellón*—silver or copper money.) Bib. Nac., Madrid, MS. 9475.

ARIAS Y MIRANDA, José:
1854   *Examen crítico-histórico del influjo que tuvo en el comercio, industria y población de España su dominación en América.* Madrid.

ARRIAGA, Friar Julián de:
1771–1774   *Nuevo Gazofilacio real de el Perú.* (MS. in Yale University Library. Written in obedience to a Royal Order dated May 4th, 1769.)

ARRIAGA, Father Pablo José de:
1621   *Extirpación de la idolatría del Piru.* Lima. (Geronymo de Contreras.)

ARTÍÑANO Y DE GALDÁCANO, Gervasio de:
1917   *Historia del comercio con las Indias durante el Dominio de los Austrias.* Barcelona.

1920   *La Arquitectura Naval Española.* Madrid.

ATIENZA, Father Lope de: (1637–1596.)
1583   *Compendio Historial del Estado de los Indios del Perú.* (Original MS. in the library of the Cathedral of Palencia. Copy made for J. B. Muñoz in the Academia de Historia, Madrid. Two other copies in NYPL.)
1931   *Compendio,* etc. Edited by J. Jijón y Caamaño. Quito.

AVENDAÑO, Father Hernando de:
1648   *Sermones de los misterios de nuestra Santa Fé Católica, en lengua Castellana y la general del Inca.* Lima. (Jorge López de Herrera.)

ÁVILA, Father Francisco de: (Ca. 1565 to 1647.)
1873   *A narrative of the false gods, and other superstitions and diabolical rites in which the Indians of Huarochiri lived in ancient times.* In *Rites and Laws of the Yncas.* Translated and edited by Clements R. Markham. London. (Hakluyt Society.)

BALLESTEROS, Tomás de:
1685   *Tomo primero de las ordenanzas del Perú.* Lima. (Joseph de Contreras.)
1752   *Tomo primero,* etc. Lima. (Francisco Sobrino y Bados.)

BANDERA, Damián de la: (Flourished about 1557.)
1881   *Relación general de la disposición y calidad de la Provincia de Guamanga* . . . Edited by Marcos Jiménez de la Espada. RGI, I, pp. 96–104. Madrid.

BARLOW, Roger: (Writing 1540–1541.)
1932   *A Brief Summe of Geographie.* Edited by E. G. R. Taylor. London. (Hakluyt Society.)

BARREDA Y LAOS, Felipe:
1909   *Vida intelectual de la colonia.* Lima.

BARROS ARANA, Diego:
1884–1902 *Historia jeneral de Chile.* Santiago de Chile. 16 vols.

BAUDIN, Louis:
1928   *L'Empire socialiste des Inka.* Paris. (Institut d'Ethnologie.)
1930   *François Pizarre.* Paris.
1931   *L'empire des Incas d'après quelques écrivains français des XVIe, XVIIe et XVIIIe siècles.* In *Revue de l'Amérique Latine,* XXI, pp. 22–29. Paris.

BENZONI, Girolamo:
1565   *La Historia del Nuovo Mondo.* Venice. (Francesco Rampazetto.)
1857   *History of the New World.* Translated and edited by Rear-Admiral W. H. Smyth. London. (Hakluyt Society.)

BERTRAND, Jean Toussaint:
1929   *Histoire de l'Amérique Espagnole.* Paris. 2 vols.

BETAGH, Captain (William): (In Peru 1720–1721.)
1813   *Observations on the country of Peru and its inhabitants.* (Published in vol. XIV, pp. 1–29, of John Pinkerton's *A General Collection of the best and most interesting Voyages and Travels in all parts of the World.* London, 1808–1814, 17 vols. According to Palau, there was an edition of Betagh's work in London, 1744, but I have not seen it.)

BETÁNZOS, Juan de:
1551   *Suma y narración de los yngas que los yndios llamaron Capac-cuna* . . . (The original MS. is now lost. An early copy of part of it is in the library of the Escorial under the signature L. J. 5.)
1880   *Suma y narración*, etc. Edited by Marcos Jiménez de la Espada. Biblioteca Hispano-Ultramarina, II. Madrid.
1924   *Suma y narración*, etc. Edited by Drs. H. H. Urteaga and Carlos A. Romero. CLDHP, 2nd ser., VIII. Lima.

BINGHAM, Hiram:
1909   *The Journal of an Expedition across Venezuela and Colombia, 1906–1907.* New Haven and London.

1910   *The Ruins of Choqquequirau.* AA, n.s., XII, pp. 505–525.

1912   *Vitcos, the Last Inca Capital* Worcester, Mass. (American Antiquarian Society.)

1913   *In the Wonderland of Peru.* NGM, April, 1913, pp. 387–573.

1922   *Inca Land.* Boston and New York.

1930   *Machu Picchu, a Citadel of the Incas.* New Haven.

BLANCO HERRERO, Miguel:
1888   *Política de España en Ultramar.* Madrid.

BOTSFORD, Jay Barrett:
1924   *English Society in the Eighteenth Century.* New York.

BOURNE, Edward Gaylord:
1904   *Spain in America.* New York and London.

BRIGGS, M. S.:
1913   *Baroque Architecture.* London.

1929   *Spanish Architecture and Sculpture.* (Chapter VII of Peers, 1929.)

BRUCKER, Father Joseph
1919   *La Compagnie de Jésus.* Paris.

BURNEY, James:
1803–1817   *A Chronological History of the Discoveries in the South Seas or Pacific Ocean.* London. 5 vols.

BYNE, Arthur; and, STAPLEY, Mildred:
1917   *Spanish Architecture of the Sixteenth Century.* New York. (Hispanic Society of America.)

CABELLO DE BALBOA, Father Miguel:
1586   *Miscelánea Antártica.* (The original MS. is lost; but a good copy of it, dating from about 1700–1725, is in the NYPL, and to that copy all references in this volume refer.)

CABERO, MARCO A.:
1906   *El corregimiento de Saña y el problema histórico de la fundación de Trujillo.* RH, I, pp. 151–191, 336–373, 486–514.

CABILDOS DE LIMA: See: LIBRO PRIMERO DE CABILDOS DE LIMA.

CALANCHA, Father Antonio de la:
1638   *Coronica Moralizada del Orden de San Augustin en el Peru.* Barcelona. (Pedro Lacavallería.)

CALVETE DE ESTRELLA, Juan Cristóbal: (Mid-Sixteenth Century.)
1889   *Rebelión de Pizarro en el Perú y Vida de D. Pedro Gasca.* Edited by A. Paz y Mélia. Madrid. 2 vols.

CAMPBELL, JOHN: See: ANONYMOUS, 1741.

CAMPILLO Y COSIO, Joseph del: (Writing in 1742–1743.)
1789   *Nuevo sistema de gobierno económico para la América.* Madrid. (Benito Cano.)

CAÑETE, García Hurtado de Mendoza, Marquis of:
1594   *Ordenanzas que el Señor Marqués de Cañete Visorey de estos Reynos del Piru mando hazer para el remedio de los excessos que los Corregidores de Naturales hazen en tratar, y contratar con los Indios,* . . . Lima. (Antonio Ricardo.)

CAPES, F. M.:
1899   *The Flower of the New World: Being a Short History of St. Rose of Lima.* London.

CAPPA, Father Ricardo:
1889–1897   *Estudios críticos acerca de la dominación española en América.* Madrid. 20 vols.

CARAVANTES, Lic. Mathías de:
1650 (?)   *Poder ordinario del Virei del Piru.* Br. Mus., Add. MSS. 28, 448.

CARTAS DE INDIAS:
1877   Published by the Ministerio de Fomento. Madrid.

CASAS, Bishop Friar Bartolomé de las:
1552   *Brevissima relacion de la destruycion de las Indias.* Seville. (Sebastián Trugillo.) (Sometimes, but most rarely, this tract occurs bound up with eight or seven others printed by Trugillo in the same year or in 1553.)

1583   *The Spanish Colonie, or Briefe Chronicle of the Acts and gestes of the Spaniardes in the West Indies, called the newe World, for the space of xl. yeeres:* . . . Translated by M. M. S. London. (Printed by Thomas Dawson for William Broome.)

1875–1876   *Historia de las Indias.* Edited by the Marquis of la Fuensanta del Valle and Don José Sancho Rayón. CDIHE, LXII–LXVI. Madrid.

1892   *De las antiguas gentes del Perú.* Edited by Marcos Jiménez de la Espada. CLERC, XXI. Madrid.

CASTEL FUERTE, José de Armendariz, Marquis of:
1859   *Relación del estado de los reynos del Perú.* In *Memorias de los Vireyes,* III, pp. 1–369. Lima. (This document was signed at Lima on January 14th, 1736.)

CHAPMAN, Charles E.:
1918   *A History of Spain.* New York. (Based on Altamira, whom see.)

CHINCHÓN, Luís de Cabrera y Bobadilla, Count of:
1871   *Relación del estado en que* . . . *deja el gobierno del Perú.* In *Relaciones de los Vireyes y Audiencias,* II, pp. 65–128. (Signed at Los Reyes—Lima—January 26th, 1640.)

CHURCH, George Earl:
1912   *Aborigines of South America.* Edited by Sir Clements R. Markham. London.

CIEZA DE LEÓN, Captain Pedro de:
1553   *Parte primera Dela chronica del Peru.* Seville. (Martin de Montesdoca.)

1554   *La Chronica del Perv, . . .* Antwerp. (Martin Nucio.) (Two other editions of Cieza's First Part were brought out in Antwerp in 1554, one by Juan Steelsio, the other printed by Juan Lacio for Juan Bellero.)

1555 (?)   *Relación de la sucesión y govierno de los Yngas . . .* MS. in the same volume as Betánzos and Santillán, whom see, in the library of the Escorial, signature L. J. 5. (This is Part Two of Cieza's Chronicle.)

1864   *The Travels of Pedro de Cieza de León,* A.D. 1532–1550, contained in the First Part of his Chronicle of Peru. Translated and edited by Clements R. Markham. London. (Hakluyt Society.)

1877   *La Guerra de Quito.* Edited by Marcos Jiménez de la Espada. Biblioteca Hispano-Ultramarina, I. Madrid. (This is Pt. IV, Bk. III, of Cieza's Chronicle.)

1880   *Segunda Parte de la Crónica del Perú.* Edited by Marcos Jiménez de la Espada. Biblioteca Hispano-Ultramarina, II. Madrid.

1883   *The Second Part of the Chronicle of Peru.* Translated and edited by Clements R. Markham. London. (Hakluyt Society.)

1913   *The War of Quito.* Translated and edited by Sir Clements R. Markham. London. (Hakluyt Society.) (This is Part IV, Bk. III, of Cieza's Chronicle.)

1918   *The War of Chupas.* Translated and edited by Sir Clements R. Markham. London. (Hakluyt Society.) (This is Part IV, Bk. II, of Cieza's Chronicle.)

1923   *The War of Las Salinas.* Translated and edited by Sir Clements R. Markham. London. (Hakluyt Society.) (This is Part IV, Bk. I, of Cieza's Chronicle.)

COBO, Father Bernabé:
1653   *Historia del Nuevo Mundo.* MS. in the Muñoz Collection in the Academy of History, Madrid.

1882   *Historia de la fundación de Lima.* Edited by Manuel González de la Rosa. Lima.

1890–1893   *Historia del Nuevo Mundo.* Edited by Marcos Jiménez de la Espada. Seville. (Sociedad de Bibliófilos Andaluces.) 4 vols.

CORBETT, Julian S.:
1898   *Papers relating to the Navy during the Spanish War, 1585–1587.* London. (Navy Records Society.)

CORDOVA Y URRUTIA, José María:
1839   *Estadística histórica, geográfica, industrial y comercial de los pueblos que componen las provincias del departamento de Lima.* Lima.

CORONEL ZEGARRA, Felix Cipriano:
1879   *Tres poemas del coloniaje.* RP, III, 291–305, 340–354, 414–427, 506–517, 593–613. Lima.

CORRADO, Friar Alexandro M.:
1884   *El Colegio Franciscano de Tarija y sus Misiones.* Quaracchi (near Florence, Italy).

COURTE DE LA BLANCHARDIÈRE, l'Abbé René:
1751   *Nouveau voyage fait au Pérou.* Paris.

CRENSHAW, Mary Mayo:
1928   *Some Peruvian Furniture.* In *Antiques,* XIV, pp. 313–318.

CÚNEO–VIDAL, Rómulo:
1925   *Historia de las guerras de los últimos Incas Peruanos contra el poder español.* Barcelona.

CUNNINGHAM, Charles Henry:
1919   *The Audiencia in the Spanish Colonies.* Berkeley. (University of California.)

DAHLGREN, E. W.:
1909   *Les relations commerciales et maritimes entre la France et les côtes des l'Océan Pacifique au commencement du XVIIIe siècle.* Paris. (Champion.)

DIAZ DEL CASTILLO, Bernal:
1908–1916   *A True History of the Conquest of New Spain.* Translated and edited by Alfred P. Maudslay. London. (Hakluyt Society.) 5 vols.

DIAZ DE VALDERRAMA, Fernándo: See: ARANA DE VARFLORA.

EATON, George F.:
1916   *The Collection of Osteological Material from Machu Picchu.* In *Memoirs of the Connecticut Academy of Arts and Sciences, V.* New Haven.

EGUIGUREN Y ESCUDERO, Víctor:
1895   *Fundación y traslaciones de S. Miguel de Piura.* BSGL, IV, pp. 260–268.

ENCINAS, Diego de:
1596   *Provisiones, cédulas, capitulos de ordenanzas . . . tocantes al buen govierno de las Indias.* Madrid. 4 vols.

ENRÍQUEZ DE GUZMÁN, Alonso: (In Peru during the Civil Wars.)
1862   *The Life and Acts of Don Alonso Enríquez de Guzmán.* Translated and edited by Clements R. Markham. London. (Hakluyt Society.)
1889   *Libro de la vida y costumbres.* CDIHE, LXXXV. Madrid.

ESCALONA Y AGÜERO, Gaspar de:
1647   *Arcae Limensis. Gazophilatium regium Perubicum.* Madrid. (Imprenta Real.)
1675   *Gazophilatium Regium Perubicum.* Madrid. (Antonio González Reyes.)
1775   *Gazophilacium Regium Perubicum.* Madrid. (Blas Román.)

ESPINAR, Manuel de:
1900   *Relación hecha por el Tesorero Manuel de Espinar al Emperador de lo sucedido entre Pizarro y Almagro.* In *Libro Primero de Cabildas* (which see), III, pp. 189–216. Lima. (Signed at Lima June 15th, 1539.)

ESTETE, Miguel de: (In Peru at the time of the Conquest.)
1872   *The narrative of the journey made by . . . Hernando Pizarro . . . from the city of Caxamalca to Parcama, and thence to Xauxa.* Translated and edited by Clements R. Markham. London. (Hakluyt Society.) (See Xerez.)

1918   *El descubrimiento y conquista del Perú.* Edited by Carlos M. Larrea. Quito.

ESTÉVANEZ DE AZEBEDO, Juan:
1650   *Práctica de repartición y buen uso de Indios y azogues.* Lima. (Jorge López de Herrera.)

FALCÓN, Lic. Francisco:
1580 (?)   *Representación sobre los daños y molestías que se hacen a los Indios.* MS. in the Bib. Nac., Madrid.

1918   *Representación,* etc. Edited by Drs. H. H. Urteaga and Carlos A. Romero. CLDHP, XI, pp. 133–176. Lima.

FERNÁNDEZ, Diego:
1571   *Primero, y segvnda Parte, de la Historia del Perv, . . .* Seville. (Hernando Diaz.)   Both Parts bound in one volume.

1913–1916   *Primera Parte de la Historia del Perú.* Edited by Lucas de Torre. Madrid. 2 vols.

FERNÁNDEZ DE OVIEDO Y VALDES, Captain Gonzalo:
1535   *La Historia general delas Indias.* Seville. (Juan Cromberger.)
1557   *Libro. XX. Dela segunda parte de la general historia delas Indias.* Valladolid. (Francisco Fernández de Córdova.)

1851–1855   *Historia general y natural de las Indias, Islas y Tierra Firme del Mar Océano.* Edited by José Amador de los Ríos. Madrid. 4 vols.

FEUILLÉE, Louis:
1714   *Journal des observations physiques, mathématiques et botaniques, . . . faites sur les côtes orientales de l'Amérique méridionale . . . depuis l'année 1707 jusques en 1712.* Paris.

FEYJOO DE SOSA, Miguel:
1763   *Relación descriptiva de la ciudad, y provincia de Truxillo del Perú.* Madrid. (Imprenta del Real y Supremo Concejo de las Indias.)

FISKE, John:
1892   *The Discovery of America.* Boston. 2 vols.

FORONDA Y AGUILERA, Manuel de:
1914   *Estancias y viajes del Emperador Carlos V.* Madrid.

FRÉZIER, Amedée François:
1716   *Relation du voyage de la Mer du Sud, aux côtes du Chily et du Pérou, fait pendant les années 1712, 1713 et 1714.* Paris. (Nyon.)

1717   *A voyage to the South Sea, and along the coasts of Chili and Peru, in the years 1712, 1713, and 1714.* London. (Joseph Bowyer.)

FRITZ, Father Samuel:

1922   *Journal of the Travels and Labours of Father Samuel Fritz in the River of the Amazons between 1686 and 1723.* Translated and edited by Rev. Dr. George Edmundson. London. (Hakluyt Society.)

FUENTES, Hildebrando:

1905   *El Cuzco y sus ruinas.* Lima.

FUENTES, Manuel A.:

1866   *Estadística general de Lima.* Paris.

GARCÍA CALDERÓN, Ventura:

1914   *La Literatura Peruana.* In *Revue Hispanique,* XXXI, pp. 305–391. New York and Paris.

GARCÍA IRIGOYEN, Carlos:

1906–1907   *Santo Toribio.* . . . Lima. 4 vols.

GARCILASO DE LA VEGA, el Inca:

1609   *Primera Parte de los Commentarios reales, qve tratan del Origen de los Yncas, Reyes qve fveron del Perv,* . . . Lisbon. (Pedro Crasbeeck.)

1617   *Historia general del Perv.* Córdoba. (Viuda de Andrés Barrera.) (This is Part Two of the Royal Commentaries.)

1869–1871   *The First Part of the Royal Commentaries of the Yncas.* Translated and edited by Clements R. Markham. London. (Hakluyt Society.) 2 vols.

1918–1920   *Los Comentarios Reales de los Incas.* Edited by Dr. H. H. Urteaga, with an Elogio by José de la Riva-Agüero. Lima. 5 vols. (This edition is the best one for general use. It contains Part One and Part Two.)

GONZÁLEZ SUÁREZ, Archbishop Federico:

1890–1903   *Historia general de la República del Ecuador.* Quito. 7 vols. and Atlas.

GUERRA Y CÉSPEDES, Francisco de: (Flourished 1663.)

1868   *Relación que se envía á S. M. y á su Real Consejo de Indias de cosas tocantes á su real hacienda.* CDIHE, LII, pp. 484–492. Madrid. (Signed at Lima April 30th, 1603.)

GUIDO, Angel:

1925   *Fusión hispano-indígena en la arquitectura colonial.* With a Preface by Martín S. Noel. Rosario, Argentina.

GUTIÉRREZ, José Rosendo:

1879   *Mancio Sierra de Leguizamo.* RP, II, pp. 25–32, 88–98, 181–187, 250–258. Lima.

GUTIÉRREZ DE RUBALCAVA, Joseph:

1750   *Tratado histórico, político, y legal de el comercio de las Indias Occidentales* . . . Cadiz. (Imprenta Real de la Marina.)

GUTIÉRREZ DE SANTA CLARA, Pedro: (In Peru during Civil Wars.)

1904–1910   *Historia de las Guerras Civiles del Perú.* Edited by Manuel Serrano y Sanz. CLDRHA, II, III, IV, and X. Madrid. 4 vols.

HAKLUYT, Richard: (Sixteenth Century.)
1903–1905   *The Principal Navigations Voyages Traffiques and Discoveries of the English Nation.* Glasgow. (J. MacLehose and Sons.) (Also Hakluyt Society.) 12 vols.

HARCOURT, Robert:
1613   *A Relation of a Voyage to Gviana.* London. (Printed by John Beale, for W. Welby.)

1928   *A Relation,* etc. Edited by Sir C. Alexander Harris. London. (Hakluyt Society.)

HARING, Clarence Henry:
1918   *Trade and Navigation between Spain and the Indies in the Time of the Hapsburgs.* Cambridge. (Harvard University Press.)

HAUPT, Albrecht:
1927   *Geschichte der Renaissance in Spanien und Portugal.* Stuttgart.

HAYWARD, Fernand:
1931   *A History of the Popes.* New York.

HELPS, Sir Arthur:
1855–1861   *The Spanish Conquest in America.* London. 4 vols.

HERRERA Y TORDESILLAS, Antonio de:
1601–1615   *Historia General de los Hechos delos Castellanos en las Islas i Tierra Firme del Mar oceano . . .* Madrid. (Juan Flamenco and Juan de la Cuesta.) 4 vols.

HEVIA BOLAÑOS, Juan de:
1603   *Cvria Philippica.* Lima. (Antonio Ricardo.)

1617   *Laberinto de Comercio terrestre y naval.* Lima. (Francisco del Canto.) (This is the first edition of Hevia's Part Two.)

1733   *Curia Filipica. Primero, y Segundo Tomo.* Madrid. (Manuel Fernández.)

1783   *Curia philipica, Primero, y Segundo Tomo.* Madrid. (Josef Doblado.) (There are many other editions of Hevia Bolaños. These are the ones which I have consulted. See: Palau, IV, pp. 34–35.)

HUME, Martin:
1907   *The Court of Philip IV.* London.

IM THURN, Sir Everard:
1883   *Among the Indians of Guiana.* London.

JUAN Y SANTACILIA, Jorge; and ULLOA, Antonio de:
1748   *Relación histórica del viaje a la América meridional hecho de orden de S. Mag. . . .* Madrid. (Antonio Marin.) 4 vols.

1826   *Noticias secretas de América.* Edited by David Barry. London.

JUDERÍAS, Julián:
N. D.   *La leyenda negra.* Barcelona.

JUICIO DE LÍMITES ENTRE EL PERÚ Y BOLIVIA. PRUEBA PE-RUANA.
1906   Edited by Victor M. Maúrtua. Barcelona. 12 vols.

KIRKPATRICK, F. A.:
1915   *Municipal Administration in the Spanish Dominions of America.* In Transactions of the Royal Historical Society, 3rd ser., IX, pp. 95–109. London.

LA CONDAMINE, Charles Marie de:
1745   *Relation abrégée d'un voyage fait dans l'intérieur de l'Amérique Méridionale.* Paris.

1746   *Lettre a Madame * * * sur l'émeute populaire excitée en la Ville de Cuenca au Pérou, le 29. d'Août 1739 contre les Académiciens des Sciences,* . . . Paris. (These two works often occur in one binding.)

LAMPÉREZ Y ROMEA, Vicente:
1908–1909   *Historia de la Arquitectura Cristiana Española en la Edad Media.* Madrid. 2 vols.

1915   *Una evolución y una revolución de la arquitectura Española.* (1480–1520.) Madrid.

1922   *Arquitectura Civil Española.* Madrid. 2 vols.

LA ROËRIE, G.; and VIVIELLE, J.:
1930   *Navires et marins de la rame à l'helice.* Paris. 2 vols.

LARRABURE Y UNÁNUE, Eugenio:
1893   *Monografías histórico-americanas.* Lima.

LEA, Henry Charles:
1908   *The Inquisition in the Spanish Dependencies.* New York and London.

LEGUÍA Y MARTÍNEZ, Germán:
1921   *Don Francisco de Toledo.* In *Mercurio Peruano,* VI, pp. 86–101. Lima.

LEHMANN-NITSCHE, Robert:
1928   *Coricancha, el Templo del Sol en el Cuzco.* RMLP, XXXI, pp. 1–260.

LEÓN PINELO, Ľ Antonio de:
1630   *Tratado de Confirmaciones Reales de Encomiendas,* . . . Madrid. (Juan González.)

1653   *Vida del ilvstrissimo i Reverendissimo D. Toribio Alfonso Mogrovejo.* Madrid.

LEÓN PINELO, Diego de:
1660   *Mandó que se imprimiese este escrito* . . . Lima. (Printer unknown.)

LEVENE, Ricardo:
1918   *Notas para el estudio del derecho indiano.* In *Anales de la Facultad de Derecho y Ciencias Sociales,* XIX, pp. 1–131. Buenos Aires.

LEVILLIER, Roberto:
1918   *Audiencia de Charcas—Correspondencia de Presidentes y Oidores* (1561–1579). Prologue by A. Bonilla y San Mártín. Madrid.

1922   *La Correspondencia de la Audiencia de Lima.* 1549–1564. Prologue by José de la Riva-Agüero. Madrid.

1929   *Ordenanzas de Don Francisco de Toledo, Virrey del Perú.* Madrid.

LIBRO PRIMERO DE CABILDOS DE LIMA:
1888–1900   Edited by Enrique Torres Saldamando, Pablo Patrón, and Nicanor Boloña. Lima. 3 vols. (In the text of the present book this work is cited as "Cabildos.")

314 BIBLIOGRAPHY

LIZÁRRAGA, Friar Reginaldo de: (Ca. 1540–1611.)
1908   *Descripción y población de las Indias.* Edited by Carlos A. Romero. Lima.

LLAMOSAS, Lorenzo de las:
1692   *Relación en que se tratan las principales materias del Reyno del Perú.* Place of printing unknown.

LLANO Y ZAPATA, José Eusebio de:
1759   *Preliminar y cartas qua proceden al tomo I de los Memorias histórico-physicas, crítico-apologéticas de la América Meridional.* Cadiz. (P. J. de Requena.)

LOAYSA, Friar Rodrigo de: (Latter half of Sixteenth Century.)
1889   *Memorial de las cosas del Perú tocantes a los Indios.* CDIHE, XCIV, pp. 554–605. Madrid.

LÓPEZ DE GÓMARA, Father Francisco:
1552   *La historia de las Indias.* Zaragoza. (Agustín Millán.)

1922   *Historia general de las Indias.* Madrid. (Calpe.) 2 vols. (Palau, IV, pp. 264–265, cites many editions of this work.)

LOTH, David:
1932   *Philip II of Spain.* New York.

LOZANO, Father Pedro:
1733   *Descripción chorographica del terreno . . . del Gran Chaco . . .* Córdoba, Argentina.

LUNA, Diego de:
1630   *Memorial . . .* Br. Mus. Add. MSS. 13,976, fols. 356–357, verso. (Dated Lima, February 1st, 1630.)

MACKEHENIE, C. A.:
1909–1913   *Apuntes sobre Don Diego de Castro Titu Cusi Yupanqui Inca.* RH, III, pp. 371–390, V, pp. 1–13.

MacNUTT, Francis Augustus:
1909   *Bartholomew de las Casas.* New York.

MADRIGA, Pedro de:
1906   *Description of the Government of Peru.* In Speilbergen, 1906, pp. 86–97, which see.

MAGGS–HUNTINGTON:
1925   *From Panama to Peru. The Conquest of Peru by the Pizarros. The Rebellion of Gonzalo Pizarro, and the Pacification by la Gasca.* London. (This is a long and highly important series of abstracts of original documents. The documents were assembled and described by Messrs. Maggs Brothers, of London, and were afterwards bought by the Henry E. Huntington Library and Art Gallery, San Marino, California, where they now are.)

MANCERA, Pedro de Toledo y Leyva, Marquis of:
1648   *Relación del estado del govierno del Perú . . .* Lima.
1896   *Relación,* etc. Edited by José Toribio Polo. Lima.

MARKHAM, Sir Clements Robert:
1892   *A History of Peru.* Chicago.
1910   *The Incas of Peru.* London and New York.

1912 *The Conquest of New Granada.* London. (Sir Clements Markham also edited many of the chronicles which appear in this list.)

MAS LATRIE, Count Louis de:
1889 *Trésor de Chronologie, d'histoire et de géographie.* Paris.

MATIENZO, Lic. Juan de: (Flourished 1565–1572.)
1910 *Gobierno del Perú.* Edited by José Nicolás Matienzo. Buenos Aires.

MATTO DE TURNER, Clorinda:
1887 *Don Juan de Espinosa Medrano o sea el Doctor Lunarejo.* Lima.

MEANS, Philip Ainsworth:
1917 *A Note on the Guarani Invasions of the Inca Empire.* GR, IV, pp. 482–484. New York.

1919 *The Rebellion of Tupac Amaru II, 1780–1781.* HAHR, II, pp. 1–25.

1920 *Indian Legislation in Peru.* HAHR, III, pp. 509–534.

1925 *A Study of Ancient Andean Social Institutions.* TCAAS, XXVII, pp. 407–469. New Haven.

1928 *Biblioteca Andina. Part One, The Chroniclers* . . . TCAAS, XXIX, pp. 271–525. New Haven.

1931 *Ancient Civilizations of the Andes.* New York and London. (Scribners.)

1931b *A Re-examination of Prescott's Account of Early Peru.* In *New England Quarterly,* IV, pp. 645–662. Portland, Me.

1932 *A Study of Peruvian Textiles.* Boston. (Museum of Fine Arts.)

MEDINA, José Toribio:
1887 *Historia del Tribunal del Santo Oficio de la Inquisición de Lima.* Santiago de Chile. 2 vols.

1904 *La Imprenta en Quito.* Santiago de Chile.

1904–1907 *La Imprenta en Lima.* Santiago de Chile. 4 vols.

1913–1914 *El descubrimiento del Océano Pacífico, Vasco Nuñez de Balboa.* Santiago de Chile. 2 vols.

1916 *La primera muestra tipográfica salida de las prensas de la América del Sur.* Santiago de Chile.

1916b *Un incunable Limeño hasta ahora no descrito.* Santiago de Chile.

MELVILLE, Lewis:
1921 *The South Sea Bubble.* London.

MEMORIAS DE LOS VIREYES QUE HAN GOBERNADO EL PERÚ.
1859 Edited by Manuel A. Fuentes. Lima. 6 vols.

MENDIBURU, General Manuel de:
1874–1890 *Diccionario histórico-biográfico del Perú.* Lima. 8 vols.

MENÉNDEZ Y PELAYO, Marcelino:
1911–1913 *Historia de la Poesía Hispano-Americana.* Madrid. 2 vols.

MÉRIMÉE, Ernest; and MORLEY, S. Griswold:
1930 *A History of Spanish Literature.* New York.

316   BIBLIOGRAPHY

MERIVALE, Herman:
1861   *Lectures on Colonization and Colonies.* London. (These Lectures were delivered at Oxford 1839–1841.)

MERRIMAN, Roger Bigelow:
1918–1925   *The Rise of the Spanish Empire in the Old World and the New.* New York. 3 vols.

METRAUX, Alfred:
1930   *Études sur la civilisation des Indiens Chiriguano.* In *Revista del Instituto de Etnología de la Universidad Nacional de Tucumán,* I, pp. 295–494. Tucumán, Argentina.

MINNAERT, Paul:
1925   *Les institutions et le droit de l'Empire des Incas.* Ostende.

MOLINA, Abbé Juan Ignaciode:
1788–1795   *Compendio de la historia geográfica, natural y civil del Reino de Chile.* Pt. I (Vol. I) translated from the Italian by Domingo de Arquellada Mendoza. Pt. II (Vol. II) translated by Nicolás de la Cruz y Bahamonde. Madrid. (Antonio de Sancha.) 2 vols.

1809   *The Geographical, Natural, and Civil History of Chili.* London. 2 vols.

MONSÉGUR, Captain:
1714   *Nouveaux mémoires touchant le Mexique ou la Nouvelle Espagne* . . . MS. in Bib. Nat., Paris. (Français 24,228).

MONTELL, Gösta:
1925   *Le vrai poncho, son origine postcolombienne.* JAP, XVII, pp. 173–183.
1929   *Dress and Ornaments in Ancient Peru.* London.

MONTESCLAROS, Juan de Mendoza y Luna, Marquis of:
1859   *Memorial* . . . In *Memorias de los Vireyes,* I, pp. 1–69. Lima. (Signed at Chácara de Mantilla, near Lima, December 12th, 1615.)

MONTESINOS, Father Fernando de:
1640   *Avto de la Fe celebrado en Lima a 23. de Enero de 1639.* Madrid. (Imprenta del Reino.) (Palau, V, p. 231, cites an edition of this work as of Lima, 1639, printed by Pedro Cabrera. I have not seen it.)
1906   *Anales del Perú.* Edited by Victor M. Maúrtua. Madrid. 2 vols.

MOREL–FATIO, A.:
1879   *Lettres écrites de Madrid en 1666 et 1667 par Muret.* Paris.

MOSES, Bernard:
1898   *The Establishment of Spanish Rule in America.* New York.
1914   *The Spanish Dependencies in South America.* New York and London. 2 vols.
1922   *Spanish Colonial Literature in South America.* London and New York. (Hispanic Society of America.)

NAHARRO: See: RUIZ NAHARRO.

NOBILIARIO DE CONQUISTADORES DE INDIAS.
1892   Edited by A. Paz y Mélia. Madrid. (Sociedad de Bibliófilos Españoles.)

NORDENSKIÖLD, Baron Erland:
1917   *The Guarani Invasion of the Inca Empire in the Sixteenth Century: An Historical Indian Migration.* GR, IV, pp. 103–121.
1920   *The Changes in the Material Culture of Two Indian Tribes under the Influence of New Surroundings.* Göteborg, Sweden.

NUTTALL, Zelia:
1914   *New Light on Drake.* London. (Hakluyt Society.)
1921–1922   *Royal Ordinances concerning the Laying Out of New Towns.* HAHR, IV, pp. 743–754, V, pp. 249–254.

NYPL CHRONICLE. See: ANONYMOUS CONQUEST OF 1534.

OCAMPO CONEJEROS, Baltasar de:
1907   *Account of the Province of Vilcapampa and a Narrative of the Execution of the Inca Tupac Amaru.* Translated and edited by Sir Clements R. Markham. In Sarmiento, 1907, pp. 203–247, which see. London. (Hakluyt Society.)

OLIVA, Father Juan Anello: (1572–1642.)
1895   *Libro Primero del manuscrito, "Historia del reino y provincias del Perú."* Edited by Juan Francisco Pasos Varela and Luís Varela y Orbegoso. Lima. (For data on this writer and his work see Means, 1928, pp. 416–423.)

OVIEDO, Friar Gabriel de: (Flourished about 1571.)
1907   *Relación* . . . Edited by Carlos A. Romero. RH, II, pp. 65–73. Lima.

OVIEDO: See: FERNÁNDEZ DE OVIEDO Y VALDES.

PALAU Y DULCET, Antonio:
1923–1927   *Manual del Librero Hispano-Americano.* Barcelona and London. 7 vols.

PALMA, Ricardo:
1863   *Anales de la Inquisición de Lima.* Lima.
1897   *Anales,* etc. Madrid. (This is the third and best edition.)
1893–1896   *Tradiciones Peruanas.* Barcelona. (Montaner y Simon.) 4 vols.
1906   *Mis últimas Tradiciones Peruanas.* Barcelona. (Maucci Hermanos.)

PARDO DE FIGUEROA, Balthazar:
1841   *Mémoire présenté à Louis XIV . . . pour l'engager à entreprendre la conquête du Pérou.* Edited by H. Ternaux-Compans. In *Archives des Voyages,* II, pp. 241–296. Paris. (From the MSS. of Colbert.)

PEERS, E. Allison:
1929   *Spain.* New York.

PEREZ GARCÍA, José:
1900   *Historia natural, militar, civil y sagrada del Reino de Chile.* Santiago de Chile. 2 vols.

PEREZ DE LARA, Lic. Alonso:
1610   *Compendio de las Tres Gracias de la Santa Cruzada* . . . Madrid. (Imprenta Real.)

PIERNAS Y HURTADO, José M.:
1907   *La Casa de la Contratación de las Indias.* Madrid.

PIZARRO, Francisco Pizarro, Marquis:
1900   *Carta á los señores Justicias é regimiento de la ciudad de Panamá
        . . . In Libro Primero de Cabildos, III, pp. 39–48. Lima.
        (Dated at Jauja, 25 May, 1534.)*

PIZARRO, Hernando:
1872   *Letter to the Royal Audience of Santo Domingo, November,
        1533. Translated and edited by Clements R. Markham in Re-
        ports on the Discovery of Peru, pp. 111–127. London. (Hak-
        luyt Society.)*

PIZARRO, Pedro: (In Peru 1530 to after 1572.)
1917   *Relación del descubrimiento y conquista de los Reynos del Perú.
        . . . Edited by Drs. H. H. Urteaga and Carlos A. Romero.
        CLDHP, VI, pp. 1–185. Lima.*

1921   *Relation of the Discovery and Conquest of the Kingdoms of
        Peru. Translated and edited by Philip Ainsworth Means.
        New York. (Cortes Society.) 2 vols.*

PIZARRO Y ORELLANA, Fernando:
1639   *Varones ilvstres del Nvevo Mvndo. Madrid. (Diego Diaz de la
        Carrera.) (The Discurso Legal y Político should be bound in
        with the main work, but separately paged.)*

POLO DE ONDEGARDO, Lic. Juan:
1571   *Relación de los fundamentos acerca del notable daño que re-
        sulta de no guardar a los Indios sus fueros. MS. in Bib. Nac.,
        Madrid, signature T.9. (Signed at Cuzco, June 26th, 1571.)*

1571b   *Relación del linaje de los Incas . . . MS. in Bib. Nac., Madrid,
        signature B.31. (Addressed to the Viceroy Toledo in 1571.)*

1585   *Tratado sobre los errores y supersticiones de los Indios. In Con-
        fessionarios para los curas de Indios, folios 7–16. Lima. (An-
        tonio Ricardo.)*

1872   *Relación de los fundamentos, etc. Edited by Marcos Jiménez
        de la Espada. CDI, XVII, pp. 1–177. Madrid.*

1873   *Of the Lineage of the Yncas, . . . Translated and edited by
        Clements R. Markham, in Rites and Laws of the Yncas, pp.
        151–170. London. (Hakluyt Society.)*

1916   *Los errores y supersticiones de los Indios . . . Edited by H. H.
        Urteaga and Carlos A. Romero. CLDHP, III, pp. 3–34. Lima.*

1916b   *Relación de los fundamentos, etc. Edited by H. H. Urteaga and
        Carlos A. Romero. CLDHP, III, pp. 45–188. Lima.*

1917   *Relación del linaje de los Incas . . . Edited by H. H. Urteaga and
        Carlos A. Romero. CLDHP, IV, pp. 45–94. Lima.*

PRADO Y UGARTECHE, Javier:
1894   *Estado social del Perú durante la dominación española. Lima.*

1918   *El genio de la Lengua y de la Literatura Castellana y sus Carac-
        teres en la historia intelectual del Perú.*

PRESCOTT, William Hickling:
1847   *History of the Conquest of Peru. New York. 2 vols.*

PURCHAS, Samuel:
1905–1907 *Hakluytus Posthumus or Purchas His Pilgrimes.* Glasgow. (James MacLehose & Sons. Also issued by the Hakluyt Society in London.)

QUESADA, Vicente G.:
1881 *Vireinato del Río de La Plata.* Buenos Aires.
1910 *La vida intelectual en la América Española durante los siglos XVI, XVII y XVIII.* Buenos Aires.

QUIROGA, Father Pedro de: (Writing ca. 1555–1566.)
1922 *Libro intitulado Coloquios de la Verdad.* Edited by Father Julián Zarco Cuevas. Seville.

RADA Y GAMIO, Pedro José:
1917 *El Arzobispo Goyeneche y Apuntes para la Historia del Perú.* Rome.
1917b *La Cristiada.* Madrid.

RAIMONDI, Antonio:
1874–1913 *El Perú.* Lima. 6 vols.

RALEIGH, Sir Walter:
1928 *The Discoverie of the large and bewtiful Empire of Guiana.* Edited by V. T. Harlow. London. (Argonaut Press.)

RALEIGH, Walter: (Modern.)
1905 *The English Voyages of the Sixteenth Century.* In Hakluyt, 1903–1905, XII, pp. 1–120, which see.

RAMIREZ, Balthasar:
1906 *Descripción del reyno del Perú.* In *Juicio de Límites,* I, pp. 281–363, which see. (Dedicated to Don Gaspar de Çúñiga y Acevedo, Count of Monterrey. Signed in Mexico in 1597.)

RAMOS GAVILÁN, Friar Alonso:
1621 *Historia del célebre Santuario de Nuestra Señora de Copacabana,* . . . Lima. (Gerónimo de Contreras.)

RAVENEAU DE LUSSAN, Le Sieur:
1930 *Journal of a Voyage into the South Seas in 1684 and the following years with the Filibusters.* Translated and edited by Marguerite Eyer Wilbur. Cleveland, Ohio. (First edition, in French, Paris, 1689.)

REAL DECRETO EN QUE S. M. HA RESUELTO AMPLIAR LA CONCESSION DEL COMERCIO LIBRE, CONTENIDA EN EL DECRETO DE 16 DE OCTUBRE DE 1765.
1778 Madrid. (Juan de San Martín.)

RECOPILACIÓN DE LEYES DE LOS REYNOS DE LAS INDIAS.
1681 Madrid. (J. de Paredes.) 4 vols.
1756 Madrid. (Antonio Balbas.) 4 vols.
1774 Madrid. (Antonio Ortega.) 4 vols.
1791 Madrid. (Viuda Ibarra.) 3 vols.
1841 Madrid. (Boix.) 4 vols. (Each edition after the first includes new laws without disturbing the order of those printed in earlier editions. I have generally used the 1791 edition.)

RELACIÓN DE LO ACAECIDO EN EL PERU DESDE QUE FRAN-
CISCO HERNANDEZ GIRON SE ALZÓ HASTA EL DÍA
QUE MURIÓ.
1879   Edited by Marcos Jiménez de la Espada. CLERC, XIII, pp.
199–235. Madrid.

RELACIONES DE LOS VIREYES Y AUDIENCIAS QUE HAN GO-
BERNADO EL PERÚ.
1867–1872   Edited by Sebastián Lorente. Lima (Vol. I, 1867) and Madrid.
(Vols. II and III.)

REZABAL Y UGARTE, Joseph de:
1792   *Tratado del real derecho de las medias anatas seculares y del
servicio de lanzas a que están obligados los títulos de Castilla.*
Madrid. (Cano.)

RIBEIRO TEIXERA DE MORAIS, Manuel:
Ca. 1635   *Sobre varias cosas pertenicientes al bien general de Indias.* MS.
in Br. Mus., Add. MSS. 13,977, folios 294–313. (Dedicated to
Gaspar de Guzmán, Count-Duke of San Lucar and of Olivares.)

RITES AND LAWS OF THE YNCAS.
1873   Translated and edited by Clements R. Markham. London.
(Hakluyt Society.)

RIVA–AGÜERO, José de la:
1905   *Carácter de la literatura del Perú independiente.* Lima.

1910   *La historia en el Perú.* Lima.

1915   *Un capítulo de la primitiva literatura colonial.* In *Cultura*, I, pp.
30–37, 41–53, 87–96. Lima.

1919   *Un cantor de Santa Rosa.* Lima.

1921   *El Perú histórico y artístico.* Santander, Spain.

1922   [*Prologue to Levillier*, 1922, which see.] Madrid. (Printed separately.)

RODRÍGUEZ DE FIGUEROA, Diego: (In Peru in 1565.)
1913   *Narrative* . . . Translated and edited by Sir Clements R. Markham in the same volume as Cieza, 1913, pp. 170–199, which see.
London. (Hakluyt Society.)

ROMERO, Carlos A.:
1905   *Negros y caballos.* Lima.

1906   *Un inédito sobre Bartolomé Ruiz.* RH, I, pp. 65–69. Lima.

1919   *Los de la isla del Gallo.* RH, VII, pp. 105–170. Lima.

RUIZ GUIÑAZÚ, Enrique:
1916   *La magistratura Indiana.* Buenos Aires.

RUIZ NAHARRO, Father Pedro:
1855   *Relación de los hechos de los españoles en el Perú desde su descubrimiento hasta la muerte del Marqués Francisco Pizarro.*
Madrid.

1917   *Relación*, etc. Edited by H. H. Urteaga and Carlos A. Romero.
CLDHP, VI, pp. 189–213. Lima.

SALINAS Y CÓRDOBA, Friar Buenaventura de:
1631   *Memorial de las Historias del Nvevo Mvndo Perv.* . . . *Lima.* (Gerónimo de Contreras.) (Excessively rare. The only copy in good condition known to me is that in the Bib. Nac., Madrid.)

SAMANOS, Juan: (In Peru soon after the Conquest.)
1844   *Relación de los primeros descubrimientos de Francisco Pizarro y Diego de Almagro.* CDIHE, V, pp. 193–201. Madrid.

SANCHEZ, Luis Alberto:
1921   *Los Poetas de la Colonia.* Lima.

1927   *Góngora en América y el Lunarejo y Góngora.* Lima.

SANCHEZ, Tristán: (Latter half of sixteenth century.)
1867   *Virey D. Francisco de Toledo.* CDI, VIII, pp. 212–293. Madrid.

SANCHO, Pedro: (Ca. 1505 to 1548.)
1917   *An Account of the Conquest of Peru.* Translated and edited by Philip Ainsworth Means. New York. (Cortes Society.)

SANTA CRUZ PACHACUTI-YAMQUI SALCAMAYHUA, Juan de: (Seventeenth Century.)
1873   *An Account of the Antiquities of Peru.* Translated and edited by Clements R. Markham in *Rites and Laws of the Yncas,* pp. 67–120, which see. London. (Hakluyt Society.)

1879   *Relación de antigüedades deste reyno del Pirú.* Edited by Marcos Jiménez de la Espada in *Tres Relaciones de Antigüedades Peruanas,* pp. 231–328, which see. Madrid.

SANTILLÁN, Lic. Fernando de:
1572   *Relación* . . . MS. in the library of the Escorial, signature L. J. 5.

1879   *Relación* . . . Edited by Marcos Jiménez de la Espada in *Tres Relaciones,* pp. 3–133, which see. Madrid.

SARMIENTO DE GAMBOA, Captain Pedro: (1532 to after 1586.)
1895   *Narratives of the Voyages . . . to the Straits of Magellan.* Translated and edited by Clements R. Markham. London. (Hakluyt Society.)

1906   *Geschichte des Inkareiches.* Edited by Richard Pietschmann. Berlin.

1907   *History of the Incas.* Translated and edited by Sir Clements R. Markham. London. (Hakluyt Society.)

SAVILLE, Marshall H.:
1929   *The Wooden Kero of the Incas.* In *Indian Notes,* VI, pp. 221–225. New York.

SCELLE, Georges:
1906   *La traite négrière aux Indes de Castille.* Paris. 2 vols.

SCHURIG, Arthur:
1922   *Francisco Pizarro, der Eroberer von Peru.* Dresden.

SEDGWICK, Henry Dwight:
1925   *Spain, a Short History.* Boston.

SHAY, Frank:
1932   *Incredible Pizarro.* New York.

SHIPPEE, Robert:
1932   *The "Great Wall of Peru" and other aerial photographic studies by the Shippee-Johnson Expedition.* In GR, XXII, pp. 1–29. New York.

SOLANO, Bishop Friar Juan:
1913   *Letter . . . to the King.* Translated and edited by Sir Clements R. Markham in the same volume as Cieza, 1913, pp. 132–143, which see. London. (Hakluyt Society.) (Dated at Lima, March 10th, 1545.)

SOLÓRZANO PANIAGUA Y TREXO, Lic. Gabriel de:
1639   *Traducción de la Dedicatoria Real i Epistolas Proemiales del segundo tomo del derecho i govierno de las Indias Occidentales* . . . Madrid. (Francisco Martinez.)

SOLÓRZANO PEREIRA, Lic. Juan de:
1629–1639 *Dispvtationem de Indiarvm Ivre.* Madrid. (Francisco Martinez.) 2 vols.

1647–1648 *Politica Indiana.* Madrid. (Diego Diaz de la Carrera.)

SOLÓRZANO Y VELASCO, Lic. Alonso de:
1652   *Carta al Excmo. Señor D. Gaspar de Haro y Guzman, Marqués de Liche* . . . Seville. (Printer unknown.) (Signed at Seville, August 24th, 1652. See Riva-Agüero, 1921, p. 100.)

SPEILBERGEN, Joris van: (Early seventeenth century.)
1906   *The East and West Indian Mirror.* Translated and edited by J. A. J. de Villiers. London. (Hakluyt Society.)

SUAREZ, Sofía:
1920   *El fenómeno sociológico del trabajo industrial en las misiones Jesuíticas.* Buenos Aires.

TERAN, Juan B.:
1930   *La naissance de l'Amérique Espagnole.* Paris.

TITU CUSI YUPANQUI, Diego de Castro:
1913   *Murder of the Inca Manco* . . . Translated and edited by Sir Clements R. Markham in the same volume as Cieza, 1913, pp. 164–168, which see. London. (Hakluyt Society.)

1916   *Relación de la Conquista del Perú y hechos del Inca Manco II.* Edited by H. H. Urteaga and Carlos A. Romero. CLDHP, II. Lima.

TOLEDO, Viceroy Don Francisco de: (In Peru, 1569–1581.)
1867   *Memorial que dió al Rey Nuestro Señor, del estado en que dejó las cosas del Perú.* . . . Edited by Sebastián Lorente in *Relaciones de los Vireyes,* I, pp. 3–33, which see. Lima.

1867b   *Ordenanzas que el Señor Viso Rey Don Francisco de Toledo hizo para el buen gobierno de estos Reynos del Perú* . . . Edited by Sebastián Lorente in *Relaciones de los Vireyes,* I, pp. 33–363, which see. Lima.

1882   *Relación sumaria de lo que se contiene en la información de la tiranía de los Ingas.* Edited by Marcos Jiménez de la Espada. CLERC, XVI, pp. 185–203. Madrid.

1889 *Relación sumaria de lo que el Virey Don Francisco de Toledo escribió en lo tocante al gobierno espiritual, y temporal, y guerra y hacienda.* CDIHE, XCIV, pp. 255–298. Madrid.

1896 *Memoria . . . tocante á gobierno y pacificación del Perú.* NCDIHE, VI, pp. 295–306. Madrid.

1896b *Memorial espiritual.* NCDIHE, VI, pp. 306–323. Madrid.

1896c *Memorial de hacienda.* NCDIHE, VI, pp. 324–343. Madrid.

1896d *Memorial de gobierno temporal del Perú.* NCDIHE, VI, pp. 343–378. Madrid.
 These items are much the same as the materials in Toledo, 1889; but here they are quoted directly, not merely abstracted.

1921 *Memorial . . . del estado en que dejó*, etc. Edited by Ricardo Beltrán y Rózpide in *Colección de Memorias o Relaciones que escribieron los Virreyes del Peru*, I, pp. 71–107. Madrid.

1924 *Libro de la visita general del Virrey Don Francisco de Toledo, 1570–1575.* Edited by Carlos A. Romero. RH, VII, pp. 115–216. Lima.

TORRES SALDAMANDO, Enrique:
1879 *Reparto y composición de tierras en el Perú.* RP, III, pp. 28–34. Lima.

1879–1880 *Apuntes históricos sobre las encomiendas del Perú.* RP, III, pp. 99–111, 177–191, 241–256, 329–339, 428–441, IV, 199–204. Lima.

1880 *El marquesado de Pizarro.* RP, IV, pp. 41–46.

TRAVERSARI, Pedro P.:
1919 *Fundación-restablecimientos y escudo de armas de la ciudad muy noble y muy leal de San Pedro de Riobamba.* Quito.

TRES RELACIONES DE ANTIGÜEDADES PERUANAS:
1879 Edited by Marcos Jiménez de la Espada. Madrid. (Contains Santa Cruz, Santillán, and Valera.)

TRESLADO DE UNA CARTA EMBIADA DE LA CIUDAD DE LOS
1554 (?) REYES A ESTA CIUDAD DE SEVILLA . . .
 Seville. (Printer unknown.) (I owe my knowledge of this very rare printed document to Messrs. Maggs Brothers, of London.)

ULLOA MOGOLLÓN, Juan de:
1586 *Relación de la provincia de los Collaguas.* MS. in the Academy of History, Madrid.

1885 *Relación*, etc. Edited by Marcos Jiménez de la Espada. RGI, II, pp. 38–50. Madrid.

UNANÚE, Hipólito:
1815 *Observaciones sobre el clima de Lima.* Madrid. (This is the second edition, used by me. The first was brought out in Lima in 1806.)

VALCÁRCEL, Luis E.:
1932 *Vasos de madera del Cusco.* RMN, I, pp. 9–18. Lima.

VALDEZ DE LA TORRE, Carlos:
1921 *Evolución de las comunidades de indígenas.* Lima.

VALERA, Father Blas: (Born in Peru about 1550, died in Spain in 1597.)
1879   *Relación de las costumbres antiguas de los naturales del Pirú.*
            Edited by Marcos Jiménez de la Espada in *Tres Relaciones,*
            pp. 135–227, which see. Madrid. (For data on this writer and
            his work see Means, 1928, pp. 497–507.)

VALVERDE, Bishop Friar Vicente de:
1539   *Carta al Emperador Carlos Quinto.* MS. in Bib. Nac., Madrid,
            signature J. 130. (Dated Cuzco, April 2nd, 1539.)

1879   *Relación del sitio del Cuzco, 1535 á 1539.* Edited by the Marquis
            of la Fuensanta del Valle and Sancho Rayón. CLERC, XIII,
            pp. 1–195. Madrid. (Sir Arthur Helps identified these two as
            being the same thing, the modern edition not bearing a name
            of an author.)

VARGAS MACHUCA, Bernardo:
1599   *Milicia y descripcion de las Indias.* Madrid. (Pedro Madrigal.)

VARINAS, Gabriel Fernández de Villalobos, Marquis of: (Seventeenth
            Century.)
1873   *Proposiciones . . . sobre los abusos de Yndias, fraudes en su
            comercio y fortificacion de sus puertos.* CDI, 1st ser., XIX,
            pp. 239–304. Madrid.

1899   *Cartas, informes y memoriales.* CDI, 2nd ser., XII, Madrid.
            (With an Introduction by Cesáreo Fernández Duro.)

VAZ, López:
1904   *A discourse on the West Indies and South Sea.* In *Hakluyt,*
            1903–1905, XI, pp. 227–290, which see. Glasgow.

VEGA, Friar Bartolomé de: (Writing in 1562.)
1896   *Memorial al Real Consejo de Indias sobre los agravios que reciben
            los indios del Perú.* NCDIHE, VI, pp. 105–131. Madrid.

VEITIA LINAGE, Joseph de:
1672   *Norte de la Contratacion de las Indias Occidentales . . .* Seville.
            (Juan Francisco de Blas.) (Two Books or Volumes bound as
            one, but paged separately.)

1702   *The Spanish Rule of Trade to the West Indies.* Translated by
            Captain John Stevens. London. (Samuel Crouch.)

VELASCO, Father Juan de:
1841–1844   *Historia del Reino de Quito.* Quito. 3 vols.

VELASCO, Viceroy Don Luis de:
1871   *Relación . . . sobre el estado del Perú.* In *Relaciones de los
            Vireyes,* II, pp. 5–28, which see. Madrid.

VELEZ SARSFIELD, Dalmacio:
1871   *Relaciones del estado con la iglesia en la antigua América Espa-
            ñola.* Buenos Aires.

1919   *Relaciones del estado con la iglesia.* With a Preliminary Notice
            by Ricardo Rojas. Buenos Aires.

VERRILL, A. Hyatt:
1931   *The Inquisition.* New York and London.

VILLAGOMEZ, Archbishop Pedro de:
1649 *Carta pastoral de exortacion é instruccion contra las idolatrías de los Indios del Arzobispado de Lima.* Lima. (J. Lopez de Herrera.)

WIENER, Charles:
1880 *Pérou et Bolivie.* Paris.

WYCHERLEY, George:
1928 *Buccaneers of the Pacific.* Indianapolis.

XEREZ, Francisco de:
1534 *Verdadera relación de la conquista del Perú.* Seville. (Bartolomé Perez.)

1872 *Narrative of the Conquest of Peru.* Translated and edited by Clements R. Markham. London. (Hakluyt Society.) (This work, both editions, includes Estete, whom see.)

X. Y. Z.:
1879 *Títulos de Castilla en el Perú.* RP, I, pp. 205–211. Lima.

ZÁRATE, Agustín de:
1555 *Historia del descubrimiento y conquista del Peru* . . . Antwerp. (Martin Nucio.)

1577 *Historia, etc.* Seville. (Alonso Escrivano.)

ZERDA, Liborio:
1885 *El Dorado, estudio histórico, etnográfico, y arqueológico de los Chibchas* . . . Bogotá.

ZIMMERMAN, Arthur Franklin:
1929 *Francisco de Toledo; Fifth Viceroy of Peru, 1569–1581.* Urbana, Illinois.

ZURKALOWSKI, Erich:
1919 *El establecimiento de las encomiendas en el Perú y sus antecedentes.* RH, VI, pp. 254–269.

COMBINED INDEX AND GLOSSARY

COMBINED INDEX AND GLOSSARY

NOTE: Although every Quechua and every Spanish term used in this book has been defined at the place of its first appearance, it has been thought well to define anew all those terms in an alphabetical list. In order to save space, therefore, I have worked the definitions into my Index. The abbreviations Que. and Sp. indicate, respectively, Quechua and Spanish.

ACA (Que.): Maize-beer, or CHICHA, which see.

ACOSTA, Father José de: Writings of, foster foreign envy, 229; scientific work of, 271.

ADELANTADO (Sp.): A title given to a man sent forth to seek and conquer new lands.

AGRICULTURE: In the Colca Valley, 158–159; decay of, under Toledo, 163; in the Trujillo region, 194–196 and 204–208; the Indian peasantry and agriculture, 211–213.

AGÜERO, Diego de: One of the original citizens of Trujillo, 55.

AGUILAR Y CÓRDOBA, Diego de: Poetry of, 273.

ALCABALA (Sp.): Tax on sales, 188.

ALCÁNTARA, Francisco Martín de: Half-brother of Francisco Pizarro, with whom he joins up, 26; dies defending Pizarro, 71.

ALCEDO Y HERRERA, Dionisio de: Evidence of, concerning the importance of Guayaquil, 241.

ALDANA, Lorenzo de: Governor of Quito for Gonzalo Pizarro, 78; serves with Governor Vaca, 82; deserts Gonzalo Pizarro, 94.

ALEXANDER VI, Pope: 32; his Bull of Donation, 54 and 139.

ALGUACIL MAYOR (Sp.): High Constable.

ALMAGRO, Diego de: Birth and early career of, 17; expedition of, in 1524, 18; expedition of, in 1526–1527, 19–22; stays at Panama in 1531–1532 to get recruits, 27; arrival of, at Cajamarca, 35; quarrels with Hernando Pizarro, 36–37; hostile attitude of, towards Atahualpa, 43; plots with Inca Manco, 46–47; goes to San Miguel and Quito, 49–51; negotiations of, with Alvarado, 51–52; quarrels with Pizarro regarding Cuzco, 52–64; receives grant of New Toledo and governorship thereof, 54; founds Trujillo, 55; made Governor of Cuzco by Pizarro, 56; makes a contract with Pizarro at Cuzco, 57–58; decides to inspect New Toledo (now parts of Bolivia, Argentina, and Chile) and makes journey thither and back, 57–60; wars with Pizarro about Cuzco, 62–64; defeated at battle of las Salinas, 64; wrongfully executed, 64; character of, 64–65; anonymous poem about, 272.

ALMAGRO, Diego de, called The Lad: Natural son of Governor Almagro, 64; befriended at Court by Diego de Alvarado and others, 68–69; sojourn and doings of, in Lima, 69–70; wars with Governor Vaca, 78–80; defeated at Chupas, captured, and killed, 80; note on, 103.

ATIENZA, Father Lope de: His criticism of the clergy, 168–169 and 198.

AUDIENCE: Same as AUDIENCIA, which see.

AUDIENCIA (Sp.): High Court, presided over by a viceroy or by a president; also territory controlled by such a High Court. Number, powers, and functions of Audiencias, 84 and 144; unfortunate aspects of Audiencias, 178–179; criticisms levelled at Audiencias, 245–248.

AUGUSTINIANS: 166.

AUTO DE FÉ (Sp.): Act of Faith, public punishment for religious reasons under the auspices of the Inquisition. Examples of Autos de Fé, 131; 169.

ÁVALOS Y FIGUEROA, Diego de: Literary work of, 273.

AVERÍA (Sp.): Convoy tax on shipping, 188.

AYLLÓN, Friar Juan de: Literary work of, 278.

AYLLU (Que.): A tribe or kinship group in which the kinship may be either real or feigned. Survival of the, 154 and 161–162. This term also means BOLA, which see.

BACHICAO, Hernando: Acts for Gonzalo Pizarro at Panama, 91.

BALBOA, Vasco Nuñez de: See NUÑEZ DE BALBOA.

BALSA (Coast language, also Que. and Sp.): A raft-like boat, with or without sails. A richly laden balsa out of Tumbez met by Ruiz, at sea, 20 and 23.

BARLOW, Roger: Nearly invades Peru from the East with S. Cabot, 254.

BATH: Atahualpa's, with plumbing, near Cajamarca, 30.

BEATRIZ, Princess: Wife of Mancio Sierra de Leguízamo, negotiates with Inca Sayri Tupac, 110; note on, 134.

BEATRIZ, Princess: Wife, successively, of Martín de Mustincia and of Diego Hernández; note on, 134.

BEATRIZ CLARA, Princess: Wife, successively, of Prince Felipe Quispi Titu and of Don Martín García Oñaz de Lóyola; note on her career and descendants, 134.

BELLES LETTRES: Colonial, outline of, 272–282.

BENALCAZAR, Captain Sebastián de: Left in command at San Miguel, 28; sent to Quito by Pizarro, 49; doubts concerning his good faith, 49–50; part taken by, in negotiations with Alvarado, 51–52.

BISHOPRICS: Foundation of, 166–168; notes on, 174.

BOLA (Sp.): A weapon made of two or three stones lashed to long cords; called ayllu in Quechua; thrown from the hand and used for entangling men, horses, etc.; employed at siege of Cuzco, by the Indians, 61.

BORLA (Sp.): See LLAUTU.

BOURBONS: Coming of the, to the throne of Spain, 190–192; commercial policy of, 225–226; political conditions under, 294–295.

BUCCANEERS: See PIRATES.

BUENO, Cosme: Scientific work of, 272.

BUENOS AIRES: Commerce of, 221–222.

BULL OF DONATION: Given by Pope Alexander VI, 54 and 139.

BULLET: New type of, brought from Flanders and used at battle of las Salinas, 64.

CHIPPENDALE, Thomas: Influence of, on Peruvian furniture, 268; note on, 284.

CHIRIGUANOS: Make mock of Toledo, 127–128; notes on, 137–138; under Alejo García invade Peru from the East, 253–254.

CHRISTIANITY: Scorn of Atahualpa for, 32–33; established in Cuzco, 45; produces turmoil and bloodshed in Peru, 78; studied and accepted by various Incas, 114–116; course of, in Vilcapampa, 121; Tupac Amaru I accepts just before his execution, 123; triumph of, 125–126; made mock of, by the Chiriguanos, 127–128; vicissitudes of, in Peru, 289–292. See also CHURCH.

CHUPAS: Battle of, 80; note on, 103.

CHUQUISACA: See LA PLATA.

CHURCH, the: Advent of, in Peru, 27–28; at Cuzco, 45; condition of, in Toledo's time, 130–131; omnipresence of, 150 and 166; theoretical aspect of, 165–170; supremacy of the Crown in affairs of, 165–166; bishops and archbishops, 167; ideals of, 167; missionary labors of, 167–168; real conditions in, 197–202; intellectual aspects of, 268–270 and 271–272; part taken by, in Spanish colonization, 289–290; career of, in colonial period, 290–295. See also CHRISTIANITY, INQUISITION, JESUITS, and ORDERS, Religious.

CIEZA DE LEÓN, Captain Pedro de: Writings of, foster foreign envy, 229–230.

CIUDAD DE LOS REYES: See LIMA.

"CLARINDA": Discussion of literary work and identity of, 274.

COBO, Father Bernabé: Scientific work of, 271–272.

COLBERT, Minister: With Louis XIV founds commercial companies, 234–237.

COLCA VALLEY: Sociological structure in, 158–160.

COLI and CHIPI: Chiefs whose territory was included in Pizarro's New Castile, 53; note on, 74.

COLLAGUAS, Province of: Sociological structure in, 158–160.

COLLAS: Expected to aid Huáscar, but fail, 10.

COLUMBUS, Christopher: 15.

COMMERCE: Monopolistic character of, 218–220; carried on by system of fleets, 219–221; contraband commerce of Buenos Aires, 221–222; nature of merchandise carried by, 222–223 and 264–266; causes of failure of commercial system, 223–225; free commerce, rise of, under Bourbons, 225–226; how commerce was carried on by land, 226–228; French efforts to share in Peru's commerce, 234–237; England's efforts, 237–240; proposed formation of a Royal Commercial Company to superintend commerce, 248–250; remarks of a British writer on, 250; notes on liberalization of commerce, 251; commerce and industry in Spain and Peru, important notes on, 251–252.

COMMUNES: Of the Indians, 154; importance of, 161–163.

COMPAGNIE DES INDES ORIENTALES: 235.

COMPAGNIE ROYALE DE LA MER PACIFIQUE: 235–236.

CONSULADO: 140; 218.

CONTRABAND: See COMMERCE.

CORICANCHA: Temple of the Sun in Cuzco, image of the Sun from, 122 and 125–126; note on, 137.

CORREGIDOR (Sp.): Magistrate in charge of a city or town and its dependent district. Office of CORREGIDOR: origin, function and powers of, 147–150; note on patronage aspect of, 171; adverse criticisms of, 179–181 and 182–193; criticized by Viceroy Amat, 196–197; remarks on, 294–295.

CORREGIMIENTO (Sp.): The jurisdiction of a CORREGIDOR.

CORREO MAYOR (Sp.): Postmaster General. Office of hereditary in the CARVAJAL FAMILY, which see.

CORSAIRS: 132–133. See also PIRATES.

CORTES, Hernando: Aids Pizarro in recruiting, 26.

COYA (Que.): The Empress, wife of the Inca, 7–8.

CREOLES: Condition of the, 208–213.

CRIOLLO (Sp.): A creole, a person of Spanish blood but born in the Indies.

CROWN OF CASTILE, the: Emissaries of, and the discovery of New World regions, 15–16; empowers Pizarro to explore and conquer Peru, 24–27; Atahualpa invited to become vassal to, 32–33; Inca Manco becomes vassal to, 46–47; absolute right of to be supreme in America because of Alexander VI's Bull of Donation, 83; supremacy of, 84; threatened overthrow of by G. Pizarro, 81–96, and by Hernández Girón, 100; Inca Sayri Tupac a vassal of, 101 and 110; Toledo seeks to strengthen absolutism of, 128–130; sole owner of Spanish America, 139; interests of served by the royal officials, 144–147; supreme overlord of encomenderos and itself holder of many encomiendas, 150–153; official attitude of towards the Indians, 154–156; as a landowner, 159–160; supremacy of in Church affairs, 165–167; factual general impotence of, 177–179 and 288–298. See also CHARLES I, CHARLES II, CHARLES III, CHURCH, PHILIP II, PHILIP III, PHILIP IV, and PHILIP V.

CULTURANISM: See GONGORISM.

CURA (Sp.): A parish priest.

CURACA (Que.): A chief in power over the Indians. Tyranny of the curacas, 128–130; powers and functions of, 153–163; their abusive conduct, 183–187.

CUSI HUARCAY, Doña Coya María: Wife of Inca Sayri Tupac, 110.

CUZCO: Under the Incas, 9–10; march of the Spaniards to, and their taking possession of, 45; Pizarro departs from, leaving Juan Pizarro in charge, 51–52; Pizarro abandons as capital city, 55; he makes Almagro governor of, 56; Juan and Gonzalo Pizarro bidden to retake, 57; Pizarro and Almagro make contract at, 57–58; Almagro departs from, to go into New Toledo and other expeditions set out from, 57–59; Almagro returns to, 59; H. Pizarro in charge of, 60; siege of by Inca Manco, 60–62; war between Almagro and Pizarro about, 62–64; King Charles I's final award gives Cuzco to Pizarro, 63–65; held by Almagro the Lad, 79; Toledo at, 115–116, 120–130; bishopric of, 166; suggested removal of the capital to, 178; architecture in, 260–262 and 267; notes on architecture and earthquakes in, 282–283.

DAMPIER, William: His piratical invasion of Peru, 236–237.

the battle of Huarina, 94–95; goes to Lima to strengthen his cause, 95; letter from Gasca to Gonzalo Pizarro, 95; letter to Gasca from F. de Carvajal, 95; wins battle of Xaquixahuana against G. Pizarro and F. de Carvajal, 96; consults with Archbishop Loaysa in apportioning rewards among enemies of G. Pizarro, 97; rule of, in Peru, 97–98; departure of, from Peru and his last years, 98–99.

GEOGRAPHIC FACTOR: See SPACE-TIME COMPLEX.

"GOLDEN HIND": Drake's ship, 132.

GÓNGORA, Luís de Argote y: Literary influence of, 277–282.

GONGORISM: Effect of on Peruvian literature, 277–282.

GORGONA, Island of: Pizarro and his men at, 22–23.

GOVERNMENT: Of the Incas, 10–12 and note on, 14; further remarks on, 288–289 and 293–295. Of the Spaniards, under Toledo, 116–133; further remarks on, 139–153, 177–197, and 288–295. See also MINOR GOVERN-MENT.

GRANJA, Count of La: See LA GRANJA.

GREGORY XIII, Pope: Approves appointment of Toledo, 117; calendrical reform by, 271–272.

GROGNIET: French pirate, 234.

GUADALQUIVIR RIVER: Silting up of gives Cadiz supremacy over Seville, 218–219.

GUAYAQUIL: Chief port for Quito, 220; Dutch pirates raid, 234; French pirates at, 234; English pirates at, 236–237; commercial importance of, 241; recommendations of Varinas regarding, 243.

GUIANA: Raleigh's ideas concerning, 230–231; important note on, 254.

GUIDO, Angel: Ideas of on "Hispano-Indigenous" architecture, 262–263.

HACIENDA (Sp.): A landed estate.

HANKE, Lewis: Important remarks by, about Casas, 253.

HATUN-RUNA (Que.): Under the Incas, a head of a household and a tribute-payer; under the Spaniards, an Indian subject to TRIBUTE and to the MITA, both which see. Condition of Hatun-runa class under the Incas, 162; under the Spaniards, 163–164.

HAWKINS, Sir Richard: Piratical invasion of Peru by, 233; note on, 254.

HENRY VIII, King of England: His attitude towards Spain, 228; Barlow and Cabot nearly invade Peru from the East on behalf of, 254.

HEREMITE, Admiral Jacob l': Piratical attack of, on Peru, raids of, on Guayaquil, and death of, near Callao, 233–234.

HERNÁNDEZ GIRÓN, Francisco: Rebellion of, 100–101.

HERRADA, Juan de: Befriends Atahualpa, 44; ringleader in the murder of Marquis Pizarro, 71; note on, 72; chief man among the Almagrists, 78–80.

"HISPANO-INDIGENOUS" architecture: Sr. Angel Guido's ideas on, 262–263.

HOJEDA: See OJEDA.

HORSES: In the conquest of Peru, 19 and 27; display of before Atahualpa at Cajamarca, 30–31.

HUACA (Que.): An artificial mound, or pyramid; any holy place or thing.

HUACO (Que.): A pot or any vessel of native manufacture in ancient times.

HUAMANGA: Modern Ayacucho, battle of Chupas near, 80; town of founded, 109; bishopric of, 167.

HUANCAVÉLICA: Mercury mines at, 126–127; labor conditions at, 185 and 189.

HUARINA: Battle of, in which G. Pizarro and F. de Carvajal defeat Centeno to Gasca's chagrin, 94.

HUÁSCAR, Inca: His career, 7–10; capture of, 10; death of, 34–35.

HUAYNA CAPAC. Inca: Reign of, 3–8; divides his empire between Huáscar and Atahualpa, 7–8; death of, 8.

HURTADO DE ARBIETO, General Martín: Activity of, against Inca Tupac Amaru I, 122–123; corregidor of the Indian town of San Francisco de la Victoria de Vilcapampa, 123.

INCA (Que.): Any member of the imperial caste of Ttahua-ntin-suyu. The Inca, the Emperor. INCAS: The members of the family of the, in Spanish times, 108–116; important note on the careers and marriages of some of them, 134; their rule contrasted with Spanish rule, 293–295; paternalism of their rule beneficial to the Indian peasantry, 295–298.

INCA EMPIRE: Condition of, before the Spaniards came, 3–12; contrasted with Spanish rule, 142, 288, 293–295; paternalism of, 295–298. See also MINOR GOVERNMENT.

INDIES, Compendium of the Laws of the Kingdoms of the: See RE-COPILACION.

INDIES, Royal Council of the: Functions of the, 84 and 139–149; opposes Philip V with respect to French participation in commerce, 235–236; ignores complaints addressed to it, 276.

INGA: A mythical monarch, supposed by Raleigh to be descended from the Incas and to rule in Manoa and Guiana, whom Raleigh wishes to make a vassal to Queen Elizabeth, 230–231; important note on, 254. See also GUIANA, INCA, INCA EMPIRE, MANOA, and RALEIGH.

INQUISITION, Holy Tribunal of the: Established in Lima by Toledo, 119; activities of the, 131 and 168–169; intellectual effects of, 268–269; note on, 284–285.

INSTITUTIONS OF NATIVE ORIGIN: Significance and character of, 153–163. See also MINOR GOVERNMENT.

INSTITUTIONS OF SPANISH ORIGIN: Significance and character of, 138–153. See also GOVERNMENT.

JAUJA: Founded by Pizarro, but not chosen as capital city, 55.

JESUITS: The arrival of in Peru, 119–120; labors of, 166–169; note on, 175; expulsion of, 201–202 and 272; career and architectural achievements of in Quito, 263–264; intellectual work of, 269–271.

JEWS: In colonial Peru, 269.

JIMÉNEZ, Gonzalo: Malevolent interpreter who falsifies evidence against Tupac Amaru I, 123–125 and 129.

JOURDAN DE GROUÉE: French merchant, 235.

JUAN FERNÁNDEZ, Island of: Alexander Selkirk ("Robinson Crusoe") at, 236.

NEGROES AND SLAVERY: Note on Philip III's attitude towards, 174; relations of Negroes to Indians, 155, 181, and 183; condition of the Negroes in Peru, 202–208; note on slave-trade, 216; asiento treaty concerning Negro slaves, 239; Negroes in Lima, 241; Negroes forbidden to attend University of San Marcos but still do so, 270.

NETHERLANDS, the: Envious attitude of, 233; pirates from, attack Peru, 233–234.

NEW CASTILE: See PIZARRO, Francisco.

NEW LAWS: Radical legislation promulgated by Charles I under the influence of Casas, 82–85; tidings of, reach Peru, 85–86; provisions of, 83–85; Gonzalo Pizarro called upon to combat, 87; Viceroy Nuñez Vela's course regarding, 86–89; revocation of, by Gasca, 93–94 and 97; Casas brings about a modified revival of, 99; notes on, 103–104.

NEW TOLEDO: see ALMAGRO.

NIEVA, Viceroy Count of: His bad rule and evil courses, 101–102; reference to, 246.

NOBILITY: Notes on Peruvian colonial, 171; general account of, 208–211; note on, 217; nobility of England dabbles in South Sea stock, 238; wealth becomes chief criterion of Peruvian colonial nobility, 246–247.

NOORT, Olivier van: Pirate from the Netherlands, his ineffectual attack on Chile and Peru, 233.

NOUVELLE COMPAGNIE: See COMPAGNIE ROYALE DE LA MER PACIFIQUE.

NUÑEZ DE BALBOA, Vasco: Explorations made by, 15–16; death of, 16.

NUÑEZ VELA, Viceroy Don Blasco: Appointed by Charles I, 85–86; journey of, to Peru, 86–87; insensate course of, regarding the New Laws, 86–89; murders the Factor Illán Suárez de Carvajal, and is taken prisoner by the Oidores, 90; defeated at Añaquito by G. Pizarro and killed by Benito Suárez de Carvajal, 91; note on, 105; reference to, 246.

ÑUSTA (Que.): A princess of the blood imperial of the Incas.

OBRAJE (Sp.): A cloth factory. Conditions of work in obrajes, 212–213; productions of, 264–266.

OFICIOS REALES (Sp.): ROYAL OFFICIALS, which see.

OIDOR (Sp.): A judge who forms part of the High Court called AUDIENCIA, which see. Appointment of the first Oidores for Peru, 85–86; they are left at Panama by Viceroy Nuñez Vela, 86–87; they arrive at Paita and proceed to Lima, 89–90; they take Nuñez Vela prisoner and try to send him to Spain, 90; rule of the Oidores after Gasca's departure, 98–99; and after Viceroy Mendoza's death, 100; left in charge of Lima by Toledo, 120; shortcomings of Oidores, 178–179; criticism of Oidores, 245–248.

OJEDA, Friar Diego de: Literary work of, 277.

OLAVIDE Y JÁUREGUI, Pablo de: Career and literary work of, 281–282.

OÑAZ DE LÓYOLA: See GARCÍA OÑAZ DE LÓYOLA.

ORDENANZA (Sp.): Ordinance; Law.

ORDERS, Religious: Present in Peru, 166; part taken by, in education, 269–270.

ORELLANA, Francisco de: Traitor to Gonzalo Pizarro, crosses South America by way of the Amazon, 81.

make G. Pizarro independent King of Peru, 91–93; Gasca's procedure against him, 93–94; with Carvajal defeats Centeno at Huarina, 94; campaign of Gasca against him, 95–96; defeated by Gasca at Xaquixahuana and afterwards slain, 96; note on, 103; note on his death, 106.

PIZARRO, Hernando: Joins up with F. Pizarro and journeys to Peru, 26–27; interviews Atahualpa, 30; journeys to Pachacamac and back to Cajamarca, 35; quarrels with Almagro and is sent to Spain, 36–37; in Spain, 52–54; departs for Peru and meets F. Pizarro in Lima, 54 and 60; defends Cuzco against Inca Manco, 60–62; fights against Almagro, 63–64; at battle of las Salinas and afterwards, 64 and 67; is sent to Spain a second time, 68; imprisoned by King Charles I's orders, marries, dies, 69.

PIZARRO, Juan: Joins up with F. Pizarro, 26; made a regidor of Cuzco, 46; in command at Cuzco, 52; in Cuzco, 56–57; at siege of Cuzco by Inca Manco, 60; his gallant death, 62.

PIZARRO, Pedro: Joins up with F. Pizarro, 26; references to, 30 and 50.

PLATE, River: Commerce on the, 221–222.

POLO DE ONDEGARDO, Lic. Juan de: Aids in legislation of Toledo, 128.

PORTO BELLO, Fair of: 146; importance of, 220–221; piratical attacks on, 234.

PORTS: Open to trade with Spanish America, 218–219, 221–222, 225–226; note on, 250–251.

POSTMASTER GENERAL OF THE INDIES: Post of given to Dr. Lorenzo Galíndez de Carvajal and his descendants, 227–228; note on, 252.

POST OFFICE: In colonial times, 226–228; important notes on the functioning of the, 252–253.

POTOSÍ: Silver mines at, 126–127; 129; importance of, 146; "accurséd hill of Potosí," 163; labor conditions at, 185–189; proletariat at, 213; share of in River Plate commerce, 221–222; time consumed in going to, from Lima, 228.

PRADO Y UGARTECHE, Javier: Note on his magnificent collection of antiquities, 284. (For works of his see Bibliography.)

PRIMERA PERSONA (Sp.): Term for an Indian chief in charge of 500 families or of a village, 154.

PROLETARIAT: Formation and functions of the, 211–213.

PUNÁ, Island of: Pizarro at, 23–24; appointed as Pizarro's northern boundary, being called also Santiago and other names, 25–26; Tumpala or Tumbala, chief of, 27; fight between natives and Spaniards at, 27–28; notes on, 38–40; Alvarado invades country north of, 48–49; location of boundaries calculated from, 53–54 and 63; Raleigh's ideas concerning, 230.

QUERO (Que.): A wooden cup. Use of, in Inca and Spanish times, 266.

QUIPU (Que.): Mnemonic record made with knotted strings. New kind of, used by Inca Huayna Capac for his will, 8.

QUISPI TITU, Prince Felipe: Son of Inca Sayri Tupac, notes on his marriage to Princess Beatriz Clara, 134; and on his baptism, 135.

QUITO: Spanish for QUITU, which see. Aldana left in charge of, by G. Pizarro, 82; G. Pizarro defeats Viceroy Nuñez Vela near, 91; Audiencia of, 144; bishopric of, 166; life in, 194; nobility in, 210; commerce of, 220 and 241; architecture in, 263–264; literature in, 275.